Exploring Premium Media Site

Improve your grade with hands-on tools and resources!

- Master *Key Terms* to expand your vocabulary.
- Prepare for exams by taking practice quizzes in the *Online Chapter Review*.
- Download *Student Data Files* for the applications projects in each chapter.

And for even more tools, you can access the following Premium Resources using your Access Code. Register now to get the most out of *Exploring!*

- *Hands-On Exercise Videos* accompany each Hands-On Exercise in the chapter. These videos demonstrate both how to accomplish individual skills as well as why they are important.*
- *Soft Skills Videos* are necessary to complete the Soft Skills Beyond the Classroom Exercise, and introduce students to important professional skills.*

*Access code required for these premium resources

Your Access Code is:

Note: If there is no silver foil covering the access code, it may already have been redeemed, and therefore may no longer be valid. In that case, you can purchase online access using a major credit card or PayPal account. To do so, go to **www.pearsonhighered.com/exploring**, select your book cover, click on "Buy Access" and follow the on-screen instructions.

To Register:

- To start you will need a valid email address and this access code.
- Go to **www.pearsonhighered.com/exploring** and scroll to find your text book.
- Once you've selected your text, on the Home Page, click the link to access the Student Premium Content.
- Click the Register button and follow the on-screen instructions.
- After you register, you can sign in any time via the log-in area on the same screen.

System Requirements

Windows 7 Ultimate Edition; IE 8
Windows Vista Ultimate Edition SP1; IE 8
Windows XP Professional SP3; IE 7
Windows XP Professional SP3; Firefox 3.6.4
Mac OS 10.5.7; Firefox 3.6.4
Mac OS 10.6; Safari 5

Technical Support

http://247pearsoned.custhelp.com

Photo credits: Goodluz/wrangler/Elena Elisseeva/Shutterstock

(ex·ploring)

SERIES

1. Investigating in a systematic way: examining. 2. Searching into or ranging over for the purpose of discovery.

Microsoft®

Access 2013

INTRODUCTORY

Series Editor **Mary Anne Poatsy**

Krebs | Cameron

Series Created by Dr. Robert T. Grauer

Boston   Columbus   Indianapolis   New York   San Francisco   Upper Saddle River
Amsterdam   Cape Town   Dubai   London   Madrid   Milan   Munich   Paris   Montréal   Toronto
Delhi   Mexico City   São Paulo   Sydney   Hong Kong   Seoul   Singapore   Taipei   Tokyo

Editor in Chief: Michael Payne
Senior Editor: Samantha McAfee Lewis
Editorial Project Manager: Keri Rand
Product Development Manager: Laura Burgess
Development Editor: Jennifer Lynn
Editorial Assistant: Laura Karahalis
Director of Marketing: Maggie Moylan Leen
Marketing Manager: Brad Forrester
Marketing Coordinator: Susan Osterlitz
Managing Editor: Camille Trentacoste
Production Project Manager: Ilene Kahn
Senior Operations Specialist: Maura Zaldivar
Senior Art Director: Jonathan Boylan
Interior Design: Studio Montage
Cover Design: Studio Montage
Cover Photos: Supri Suharjoto/Shutterstock, wavebreakmedia/Shutterstock, Terry Chan/Shutterstock, Csaba Peterdi/Shutterstock
Associate Director of Design: Blair Brown
Digital Media Editor: Eric Hakanson
Director of Media Development: Taylor Ragan
Media Project Manager, Production: Renata Butera
Full Service Project Management: Andrea Stefanowicz/PreMediaGlobal
Composition: PreMediaGlobal

Credits and acknowledgments borrowed from other sources and reproduced, with permission, in this textbook appear on the appropriate page within text.

---

10 9 8 7 6 5 4 3 2

ISBN 10: 0-13-341219-9
ISBN 13: 978-0-13-341219-2

Dedications

For my husband, Ted, who unselfishly continues to take on more than his share to support me throughout the process; and for my children, Laura, Carolyn, and Teddy, whose encouragement and love have been inspiring.

Mary Anne Poatsy

To my students—you continue to inspire me. Thank you for all you have taught me and shared with me.

Cynthia Krebs

I dedicate this book to my fiancée, Anny, for encouraging me throughout the writing process and for being the person she is, to Sonny, to Drs. Hubey, Boyno, Bredlau, and Deremer at Montclair State University for educating and inspiring me, and to my students, who I hope will inspire others someday.

Eric Cameron

About the Authors

Mary Anne Poatsy, Series Editor

Mary Anne is a senior faculty member at Montgomery County Community College, teaching various computer application and concepts courses in face-to-face and online environments. She holds a B.A. in Psychology and Education from Mount Holyoke College and an M.B.A. in Finance from Northwestern University's Kellogg Graduate School of Management.

Mary Anne has more than 12 years of educational experience. She is currently adjunct faculty at Gwynedd-Mercy College and Montgomery County Community College. She has also taught at Bucks County Community College and Muhlenberg College, as well as conducted personal training. Before teaching, she was Vice President at Shearson Lehman in the Municipal Bond Investment Banking Department.

Cynthia Krebs, Access Author

Cynthia Krebs is the Director of Business and Marketing Education at Utah Valley University. She is a professor in the Information Systems and Technology Department at Utah Valley University (UVU). In 2008, she received the UVU College of Technology and Computing Scholar Award. She has also received the School of Business Faculty Excellence Award twice during her tenure at UVU. Cynthia teaches the Methods of Teaching Digital Media class to future teachers, as well as classes in basic computer proficiency, business proficiency applications, and business graphics.

Cynthia is active in the Utah Business and Computer Education Association, the Western Business Education Association, the National Business Education Association, and the Utah Association of Career and Technical Educators. She was awarded the WBEA Outstanding Educator at the University Level in 2009. Cynthia has written multiple texts on Microsoft Office software, consulted with government and business, and has presented extensively at the local, regional, and national levels to professional and business organizations.

Cynthia lives by a peaceful creek in Springville, Utah. When she isn't teaching or writing, she enjoys spending time with her children, spoiling her grandchildren Ava, Bode, Solee, and Morgan. She loves traveling and reading.

Eric Cameron, Access Author

Eric holds a M.S. in computer science and a B.S. degree in Computer Science with minors in Mathematics and Physics, both from Montclair State University. He is a tenured Assistant Professor at Passaic County Community College, where he has taught in the Computer and Information Sciences department since 2001. Eric is also the author of the *Your Office: Getting Started with Web 2.0* and *Your Office: Getting Started with Windows 8* textbooks. Eric maintains a professional blog at profcameron.blogspot.com.

Rebecca Lawson, Office Fundamentals Author

Rebecca Lawson is a professor in the Computer Information Technologies program at Lansing Community College. She coordinates the curriculum, develops the instructional materials, and teaches for the E-Business curriculum. She also serves as the Online Faculty Coordinator at the Center for Teaching Excellence at LCC. In that role, she develops and facilitates online workshops for faculty learning to teach online. Her major areas of interest include online curriculum quality assurance, the review and development of printed and online instructional materials, the assessment of computer and Internet literacy skill levels to facilitate student retention, and the use of social networking tools to support learning in blended and online learning environments.

Dr. Robert T. Grauer, Creator of the Exploring Series

Bob Grauer is an Associate Professor in the Department of Computer Information Systems at the University of Miami, where he is a multiple winner of the Outstanding Teaching Award in the School of Business, most recently in 2009. He has written numerous COBOL texts and is the vision behind the Exploring Office series, with more than three million books in print. His work has been translated into three foreign languages and is used in all aspects of higher education at both national and international levels. Bob Grauer has consulted for several major corporations including IBM and American Express. He received his Ph.D. in Operations Research in 1972 from the Polytechnic Institute of Brooklyn.

Brief Contents

Contents

Acknowledgments

The Exploring team would like to acknowledge and thank all the reviewers who helped us throughout the years by providing us with their invaluable comments, suggestions, and constructive criticism.

We'd like to especially thank our Focus Group attendees and User Diary Reviewers for this edition:

Stephen Z. Jourdan
Auburn University at Montgomery

Ann Rovetto
Horry-Georgetown Technical
College

Jacqueline D. Lawson
Henry Ford Community College

Diane L. Smith
Henry Ford Community College

Sven Aelterman
Troy University

Suzanne M. Jeska
County College of Morris

Susan N. Dozier
Tidewater Community College

Robert G. Phipps Jr.
West Virginia University

Mike Michaelson
Palomar College

Mary Beth Tarver
Northwestern State University

Alexandre C. Probst
Colorado Christian University

Phil Nielson
Salt Lake Community College

Carolyn Barren
Macomb Community College

Sue A. McCrory
Missouri State University

Lucy Parakhovnik
California State University, Northridge

Jakie Brown Jr.
Stevenson University

Craig J. Peterson
American InterContinental University

Terry Ray Rigsby
Hill College

Biswadip Ghosh
Metropolitan State University of Denver

Cheryl Sypniewski
Macomb Community College

Lynn Keane
University of South Carolina

Sheila Gionfriddo
Luzerne College

Dick Hewer
Ferris State College

Carolyn Borne
Louisiana State University

Sumathy Chandrashekar
Salisbury University

Laura Marcoulides
Fullerton College

Don Riggs
SUNY Schenectady County Community
College

Gary McFall
Purdue University

James Powers
University of Southern Indiana

James Brown
Central Washington University

Brian Powell
West Virginia University

Sherry Lenhart
Terra Community College

Chen Zhang
Bryant University

Nikia Robinson
Indian River State University

Jill Young
Southeast Missouri State University

Debra Hoffman
Southeast Missouri State University

Tommy Lu
Delaware Technical Community College

Mimi Spain
Southern Maine Community College

We'd like to thank everyone who has been involved in reviewing and providing their feedback, including for our previous editions:

Adriana Lumpkin
Midland College

Alan S. Abrahams
Virginia Tech

Ali Berrached
University of Houston–Downtown

Allen Alexander
Delaware Technical & Community College

Andrea Marchese
Maritime College, State University of New York

Andrew Blitz
Broward College; Edison State College

Angel Norman
University of Tennessee, Knoxville

Angela Clark
University of South Alabama

Ann Rovetto
Horry-Georgetown Technical College

Astrid Todd
Guilford Technical Community College

Audrey Gillant
Maritime College, State University of New York

Barbara Stover
Marion Technical College

Barbara Tollinger
Sinclair Community College

Ben Brahim Taha
Auburn University

Beverly Amer
Northern Arizona University

Beverly Fite
Amarillo College

Bonita Volker
Tidewater Community College

Bonnie Homan
San Francisco State University

Brad West
Sinclair Community College

Brian Powell
West Virginia University

Carol Buser
Owens Community College

Carol Roberts
University of Maine

Carolyn Barren
Macomb Community College

Cathy Poyner
Truman State University

Charles Hodgson
Delgado Community College

Cheri Higgins
Illinois State University

Cheryl Hinds
Norfolk State University

Chris Robinson
Northwest State Community College

Cindy Herbert
Metropolitan Community College–Longview

Dana Hooper
University of Alabama

Dana Johnson
North Dakota State University

Daniela Marghitu
Auburn University

David Noel
University of Central Oklahoma

David Pulis
Maritime College, State University of New York

David Thornton
Jacksonville State University

Dawn Medlin
Appalachian State University

Debby Keen
University of Kentucky

Debra Chapman
University of South Alabama

Derrick Huang
Florida Atlantic University

Diana Baran
Henry Ford Community College

Diane Cassidy
The University of North Carolina at Charlotte

Diane Smith
Henry Ford Community College

Don Danner
San Francisco State University

Don Hoggan
Solano College

Doncho Petkov
Eastern Connecticut State University

Donna Ehrhart
State University of New York at Brockport

Elaine Crable
Xavier University

Elizabeth Duett
Delgado Community College

Erhan Uskup
Houston Community College–Northwest

Eric Martin
University of Tennessee

Erika Nadas
Wilbur Wright College

Floyd Winters
Manatee Community College

Frank Lucente
Westmoreland County Community College

G. Jan Wilms
Union University

Gail Cope
Sinclair Community College

Gary DeLorenzo
California University of Pennsylvania

Gary Garrison
Belmont University

George Cassidy
Sussex County Community College

Gerald Braun
Xavier University

Gerald Burgess
Western New Mexico University

Gladys Swindler
Fort Hays State University

Heith Hennel
Valencia Community College

Henry Rudzinski
Central Connecticut State University

Irene Joos
La Roche College

Iwona Rusin
Baker College; Davenport University

J. Roberto Guzman
San Diego Mesa College

Jan Wilms
Union University

Jane Stam
Onondaga Community College

Janet Bringhurst
Utah State University

Jeanette Dix
Ivy Tech Community College

Jennifer Day
Sinclair Community College

Jill Canine
Ivy Tech Community College

Jim Chaffee
The University of Iowa Tippie College of Business

Joanne Lazirko
University of Wisconsin–Milwaukee

Jodi Milliner
Kansas State University

John Hollenbeck
Blue Ridge Community College

John Seydel
Arkansas State University

Judith A. Scheeren
Westmoreland County Community College

Judith Brown
The University of Memphis

Juliana Cypert
Tarrant County College

Kamaljeet Sanghera
George Mason University

Karen Priestly
Northern Virginia Community College

Karen Ravan
Spartanburg Community College

Kathleen Brenan
Ashland University

Ken Busbee
Houston Community College

Kent Foster
Winthrop University

Kevin Anderson
Solano Community College

Kim Wright
The University of Alabama

Kristen Hockman
University of Missouri–Columbia

Kristi Smith
Allegany College of Maryland

Laura McManamon
University of Dayton

Leanne Chun
Leeward Community College

Lee McClain
Western Washington University

Linda D. Collins
Mesa Community College

Linda Johnsonius
Murray State University

Linda Lau
Longwood University

Linda Theus
Jackson State Community College

Linda Williams
Marion Technical College

Lisa Miller
University of Central Oklahoma

Lister Horn
Pensacola Junior College

Lixin Tao
Pace University

Loraine Miller
Cayuga Community College

Lori Kielty
Central Florida Community College

Lorna Wells
Salt Lake Community College

Lorraine Sauchin
Duquesne University

Lucy Parakhovnik (Parker)
California State University, Northridge

Lynn Mancini
Delaware Technical Community College

Mackinzee Escamilla
South Plains College

Marcia Welch
Highline Community College

Margaret McManus
Northwest Florida State College

Margaret Warrick
Allan Hancock College

Marilyn Hibbert
Salt Lake Community College

Mark Choman
Luzerne County Community College

Mary Duncan
University of Missouri–St. Louis

Melissa Nemeth
Indiana University-Purdue University
Indianapolis

Melody Alexander
Ball State University

Michael Douglas
University of Arkansas at Little Rock

Michael Dunklebarger
Alamance Community College

Michael G. Skaff
College of the Sequoias

Michele Budnovitch
Pennsylvania College of Technology

Mike Jochen
East Stroudsburg University

Mike Scroggins
Missouri State University

Muhammed Badamas
Morgan State University

NaLisa Brown
University of the Ozarks

Nancy Grant
Community College of Allegheny
County–South Campus

Nanette Lareau
University of Arkansas Community
College–Morrilton

Pam Brune
Chattanooga State Community College

Pam Uhlenkamp
Iowa Central Community College

Patrick Smith
Marshall Community and Technical College

Paul Addison
Ivy Tech Community College

Paula Ruby
Arkansas State University

Peggy Burrus
Red Rocks Community College

Peter Ross
SUNY Albany

Philip H. Nielson
Salt Lake Community College

Ralph Hooper
University of Alabama

Ranette Halverson
Midwestern State University

Richard Blamer
John Carroll University

Richard Cacace
Pensacola Junior College

Richard Hewer
Ferris State University

Rob Murray
Ivy Tech Community College

Robert Dušek
Northern Virginia Community College

Robert Sindt
Johnson County Community College

Robert Warren
Delgado Community College

Rocky Belcher
Sinclair Community College

Roger Pick
University of Missouri at Kansas City

Ronnie Creel
Troy University

Rosalie Westerberg
Clover Park Technical College

Ruth Neal
Navarro College

Sandra Thomas
Troy University

Sheila Gionfriddo
Luzerne County Community College

Sherrie Geitgey
Northwest State Community College

Sophia Wilberscheid
Indian River State College

Sophie Lee
California State University,
Long Beach

Stacy Johnson
Iowa Central Community College

Stephanie Kramer
Northwest State Community College

Stephen Jourdan
Auburn University Montgomery

Steven Schwarz
Raritan Valley Community College

Sue McCrory
Missouri State University

Susan Fuschetto
Cerritos College

Susan Medlin
UNC Charlotte

Suzan Spitzberg
Oakton Community College

Sven Aelterman
Troy University

Sylvia Brown
Midland College

Tanya Patrick
Clackamas Community College

Terri Holly
Indian River State College

Thomas Rienzo
Western Michigan University

Tina Johnson
Midwestern State University

Tommy Lu
Delaware Technical and Community College

Troy S. Cash
NorthWest Arkansas Community College

Vicki Robertson
Southwest Tennessee Community

Weifeng Chen
California University of Pennsylvania

Wes Anthony
Houston Community College

William Ayen
University of Colorado at Colorado Springs

Wilma Andrews
Virginia Commonwealth University

Yvonne Galusha
University of Iowa

Special thanks to our development and technical team:

Barbara Stover

Cheryl Slavick

Elizabeth Lockley

Heather Hetzler

Jennifer Lynn

Joyce Nielsen

Linda Pogue

Lisa Bucki

Lori Damanti

Mara Zebest

Susan Fry

Preface

The Exploring Series and You

Exploring is Pearson's Office Application series that requires students like you to think "beyond the point and click." In this edition, we have worked to restructure the Exploring experience around the way you, today's modern student, actually use your resources.

The goal of Exploring is, as it has always been, to go further than teaching just the steps to accomplish a task—the series provides the theoretical foundation for you to understand when and why to apply a skill.

As a result, you achieve a deeper understanding of each application and can apply this critical thinking beyond Office and the classroom.

You are practical students, focused on what you need to do to be successful in this course and beyond, and want to be as efficient as possible. Exploring has evolved to meet you where you are and help you achieve success efficiently. Pearson has paid attention to the habits of students today, how you get information, how you are motivated to do well in class, and what your future goals look like. We asked you and your peers for acceptance of new tools we designed to address these points, and you responded with a resounding "YES!"

Here Is What We Learned About You

You are goal-oriented. You want a good grade in this course—so we rethought how Exploring works so that you can learn the how and why behind the skills in this course to be successful now. You also want to be successful in your future career—so we used motivating case studies to show relevance of these skills to your future careers and incorporated Soft Skills, Collaboration, and Analysis Cases in this edition to set you up for success in the future.

You read, prepare, and study differently than students used to. You use textbooks like a tool—you want to easily identify what you need to know and learn it efficiently. We have added key features such as Step Icons, Hands-On Exercise Videos, and tracked everything via page numbers that allow you to navigate the content efficiently, making the concepts accessible and creating a map to success for you to follow.

You go to college now with a different set of skills than students did five years ago. The new edition of Exploring moves you beyond the basics of the software at a faster pace, without sacrificing coverage of the fundamental skills that you need to know. This ensures that you will be engaged from page 1 to the end of the book.

You and your peers have diverse learning styles. With this in mind, we broadened our definition of "student resources" to include Compass, an online skill database; movable Student Reference cards; Hands-On Exercise videos to provide a secondary lecture-like option of review; Soft Skills video exercises to illustrate important non-technical skills; and the most powerful online homework and assessment tool around with a direct 1:1 content match with the Exploring Series, MyITLab. Exploring will be accessible to all students, regardless of learning style.

Providing You with a Map to Success to Move Beyond the Point and Click

All of these changes and additions will provide you with an easy and efficient path to follow to be successful in this course, regardless of your learning style or any existing knowledge you have at the outset. Our goal is to keep you more engaged in both the hands-on and conceptual sides, helping you to achieve a higher level of understanding that will guarantee you success in this course and in your future career. In addition to the vision and experience of the series creator, Robert T. Grauer, we have assembled a tremendously talented team of Office Applications authors who have devoted themselves to teaching you the ins and outs of Microsoft Word, Excel, Access, and PowerPoint. Led in this edition by series editor Mary Anne Poatsy, the whole team is equally dedicated to providing you with a **map to success** to support the Exploring mission of **moving you beyond the point and click**.

Key Features

- **White Pages/Yellow Pages** clearly distinguish the theory (white pages) from the skills covered in the Hands-On Exercises (yellow pages) so students always know what they are supposed to be doing.

- **Enhanced Objective Mapping** enables students to follow a directed path through each chapter, from the objectives list at the chapter opener through the exercises in the end of chapter.
  - **Objectives List:** This provides a simple list of key objectives covered in the chapter. This includes page numbers so students can skip between objectives where they feel they need the most help.
  - **Step Icons:** These icons appear in the white pages and reference the step numbers in the Hands-On Exercises, providing a correlation between the two so students can easily find conceptual help when they are working hands-on and need a refresher.
  - **Quick Concepts Check:** A series of questions that appear briefly at the end of each white page section. These questions cover the most essential concepts in the white pages required for students to be successful in working the Hands-On Exercises. Page numbers are included for easy reference to help students locate the answers.
  - **Chapter Objectives Review:** Appears toward the end of the chapter and reviews all important concepts throughout the chapter. Newly designed in an easy-to-read bulleted format.

- **Key Terms Matching:** A new exercise that requires students to match key terms to their definitions. This requires students to work actively with this important vocabulary and prove conceptual understanding.

- **Case Study** presents a scenario for the chapter, creating a story that ties the Hands-On Exercises together.

- **Hands-On Exercise Videos** are tied to each Hands-On Exercise and walk students through the steps of the exercise while weaving in conceptual information related to the Case Study and the objectives as a whole.

- **End-of-Chapter Exercises** offer instructors several options for assessment. Each chapter has approximately 12–15 exercises ranging from multiple choice questions to open-ended projects. Newly included in this is a Key Terms Matching exercise of approximately 20 questions, as well as a Collaboration Case and Soft Skills Case for every chapter.

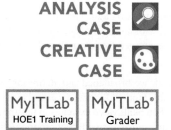

- **Enhanced Mid-Level Exercises** include a **Creative Case** (for PowerPoint and Word), which allows students some flexibility and creativity, not being bound by a definitive solution, and an **Analysis Case** (for Excel and Access), which requires students to interpret the data they are using to answer an analytic question, as well as **Discover Steps**, which encourage students to use Help or to problem-solve to accomplish a task.

- **MyITLab** provides an auto-graded homework, tutorial, and assessment solution that is built to match the book content exactly. Every Hands-On Exercise is available as a simulation training. Every Capstone Exercise and most Mid-Level Exercises are available as live-in-the-application Grader projects. Icons are included throughout the text to denote which exercises are included.

Instructor Resources

The Instructor's Resource Center, available at **www.pearsonhighered.com**, includes the following:

- **Instructor Manual** provides an overview of all available resources as well as student data and solution files for every exercise.

- **Solution Files with Scorecards** assist with grading the Hands-On Exercises and end-of-chapter exercises.

- **Prepared Exams** allow instructors to assess all skills covered in a chapter with a single project.

- **Rubrics** for Mid-Level Creative Cases and Beyond the Classroom Cases in Microsoft® Word format enable instructors to customize the assignments for their classes.

- **PowerPoint® Presentations** with notes for each chapter are included for out-of-class study or review.

- **Lesson Plans** provide a detailed blueprint to achieve chapter learning objectives and outcomes.

- **Objectives Lists** map chapter objectives to Hands-On Exercises and end-of-chapter exercises.

- **Multiple Choice and Key Terms Matching Answer Keys**

- **Test Bank** provides objective-based questions for every chapter.

- **Grader Projects** textual versions of auto-graded assignments for Grader.

- **Additional Projects** provide more assignment options for instructors.

- **Syllabus Templates**

- **Scripted Lectures** offer an in-class lecture guide for instructors to mirror the Hands-On Exercises.

- **Assignment Sheet**

- **File Guide**

Student Resources

Companion Web Site

www.pearsonhighered.com/exploring offers expanded IT resources and self-student tools for students to use for each chapter, including:

- Online Chapter Review
- Web Resources
- Glossary
- Student Data Files
- Chapter Objectives Review

In addition, the Companion Web Site is now the site for Premium Media, including the videos for the Exploring Series:

- Hands-On Exercise Videos*
- Audio PPTs*
- Soft Skills Exercise Videos*

*Access code required for these premium resources.

Student Reference Cards

A two-sided card for each application provides students with a visual summary of information and tips specific to each application.

Office Fundamentals and File Management

Taking the First Step

Andresr/Shutterstock

OBJECTIVES AFTER YOU READ THIS CHAPTER, YOU WILL BE ABLE TO:

1. Log in with your Microsoft account p. 2
2. Identify the Start screen components p. 3
3. Interact with the Start screen p. 4
4. Access the desktop p. 4
5. Use File Explorer p. 10
6. Work with folders and files p. 13
7. Select, copy, and move multiple files and folders p. 15
8. Identify common interface components p. 22
9. Get Office Help p. 28
10. Open a file p. 36
11. Print a file p. 38
12. Close a file and application p. 39
13. Select and edit text p. 45
14. Use the Clipboard group commands p. 49
15. Use the Editing group commands p. 52
16. Insert objects p. 60
17. Review a file p. 62
18. Use the Page Setup dialog box p. 66

CASE STUDY | Spotted Begonia Art Gallery

You are an administrative assistant for Spotted Begonia, a local art gallery. The gallery deals in local artists' work, including fiber art, oil paintings, watercolors, prints, pottery, and metal sculptures. The gallery holds four seasonal showings throughout the year. Much of the art is on consignment, but there are a few permanent collections. Occasionally, the gallery exchanges these collections with other galleries across the country. The gallery does a lot of community outreach and tries to help local artists develop a network of clients and supporters. Local schools are invited to bring students to the gallery for enrichment programs. Considered a major contributor to the local economy, the gallery has received both public and private funding through federal and private grants.

As the administrative assistant for Spotted Begonia, you are responsible for overseeing the production of documents, spreadsheets, newspaper articles, and presentations that will be used to increase public awareness of the gallery. Other clerical assistants who are familiar with Microsoft Office will prepare the promotional materials, and you will proofread, make necessary corrections, adjust page layouts, save and print documents, and identify appropriate templates to simplify tasks. Your experience with Microsoft Office 2013 is limited, but you know that certain fundamental tasks that are common to Word, Excel, and PowerPoint will help you accomplish your oversight task. You are excited to get started with your work!

Windows 8.1.1 Startup

You use computers for many activities for work, school, or pleasure. You probably have never thought too much about what makes a computer function and allows you to do so many things with it. But all of those activities would not be possible without an operating system running on the computer. An *operating system* is software that directs computer activities such as checking all components, managing system resources, and communicating with application software. *Windows 8.1.1* is a Microsoft operating system released in April 2014 and is available on laptops, desktops, and tablet computers.

The *Start screen* is what you see after starting your computer and entering your username and password. It is where you start all of your computing activities. See Figure 1.1 to see a typical Start screen.

FIGURE 1.1 Typical Start Screen Components and Charms

In this section, you will explore the Start screen and its components in more detail. You will also learn how to log in with your Microsoft account and access the desktop.

Logging In with Your Microsoft Account

Although you can log in to Windows 8.1.1 as a local network user, you can also log in using a Microsoft account. When you have a Microsoft account, you can sign in to any Windows 8.1.1 computer and you will be able to access the saved settings associated with your Microsoft account. That means the computer will have the same familiar look that you are used to seeing. Your Microsoft account will allow you to be automatically signed in to all of the apps and services that use a Microsoft account as the authentication. You can also save your sign-in credentials for other Web sites that you frequently visit.

Logging in with your Microsoft account not only provides all of the benefits just listed, but also provides additional benefits such as being connected to all of Microsoft's resources on the Internet. These resources include a free Outlook account and access to cloud storage at OneDrive. *Cloud storage* is a technology used to store files and to work with programs that are stored in a central location on the Internet. *OneDrive* is an app used to store, access, and share files and folders. It is accessible using an installed desktop app or as cloud storage using a Web address. Files and folders in either location can be synced. For Office 2013 applications, OneDrive is the default location for saving files. Documents saved in OneDrive are accessible from any computer that has an Internet connection. As long as the document has been saved in OneDrive, the most recent version of the document will be accessible from any computer connected to the Internet. OneDrive allows you to collaborate with others. You can easily share your documents with others or add Reply Comments next to the text that you are discussing together. You can work with others on the same document simultaneously.

STEP 1 › You can create a Microsoft account at any time by going to live.com. You simply work through the Sign-up form to set up your account by creating a username from your e-mail address and creating a password. After filling in the form, you will be automatically signed in to Outlook and sent to your Outlook Inbox. If you already have a Microsoft account, you can just go ahead and log in to Outlook. See Figure 1.2 to see the Sign-up page at live.com.

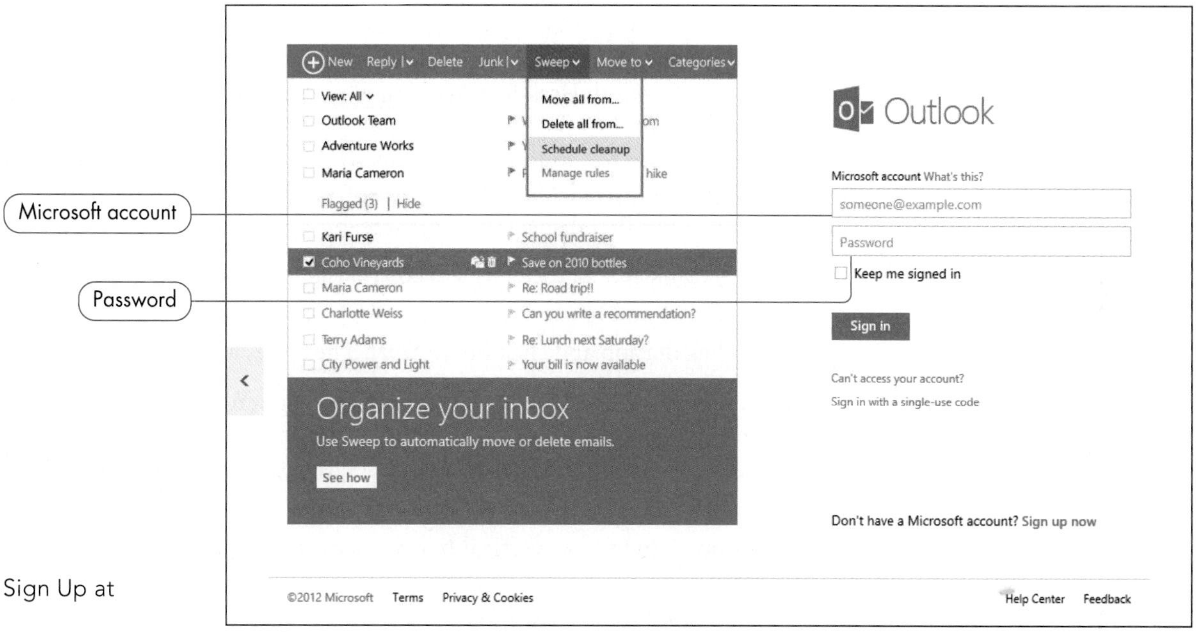

FIGURE 1.2 Sign Up at live.com

Identifying the Start Screen Components

The first thing you will notice when you turn on a computer running Windows 8.1.1 is that the Start screen has a new sleek, clean look and large readable type (refer to Figure 1.1). The user is identified in the top-right corner of the screen. You can click the user's name to access settings such as locking or signing out of the account. You can also change the picture associated with the account here.

You will notice that the Start screen is made up of several colorful block images called *tiles*. When you click a tile, you will be taken to a program, file, folder, or other *Windows 8.1.1 app*. Windows 8.1.1 apps are applications specifically designed to run in the Start screen interface of Windows 8.1.1. Some Windows 8.1.1 apps, such as desktop, Mail, and OneDrive, are already installed and ready to use. Others can be downloaded from the Windows Store. The default apps are brightly colored. Tiles for programs that run on the traditional Windows desktop are smaller and more transparent. The look of the tiles is customizable, but all tiles include the name of the app or program. Depending on the number of apps that you have installed, as you move your mouse to the bottom of the screen, you will see a horizontal scroll bar display. This can be used to access any app that does not display within the initial view of the Start screen.

STEP 2 › The traditional Start button is not present in Windows 8.1.1. Instead, the *Charms* are available (refer to Figure 1.1). The Charms are made up of five icons that provide similar functionality to the Start button found in previous versions of Windows. The icons are Search, Share, Start, Devices, and Settings. Using the Charms, you can search for files and applications, share information with others within an application that is running, or return to the Start screen. You can also control devices that are connected to your computer or modify various settings depending on which application is running when accessing the Setting icon. To display the Charms, point to the top-right or bottom-right corners of the screen. Refer to Figure 1.1 to view the Start screen components and the Charms.

Interacting with the Start Screen

To interact with any tile on the Start screen (refer to Figure 1.1), simply click it. If you have signed in with your Microsoft account, you will automatically be able to access any of the Internet-enabled programs. For example, if you click Mail, you will go straight to your Outlook Inbox. If you right-click a tile, you will see several contextual options displayed. For example, the option to unpin the tile from the Start screen displays. To return to the Start screen from the desktop, point your mouse in the bottom-left corner of the screen. Pointing your mouse to the top-left corner reveals the open applications or programs that you have been accessing during this session. You can also use Charms to navigate back to the Start screen.

You may want to set up the Start screen so that programs and apps that you use most frequently are readily available. It is very easy to add tiles to or remove tiles from the Start screen. To add a tile, first display the Start screen.

1. Locate a blank area of the Start screen and right-click to display the *All apps* icon.
2. Click *All apps* and locate the desired new app that you want to add.
3. Right-click the app and click *Pin to Start*. The app is added to the Start screen.

The new app's tile is added at the end of your apps. You can move tiles by dragging the tile to the desired location. You can remove a tile from the Start screen by right-clicking the tile and clicking *Unpin from Start*. You can also group the tiles and name the groups:

1. To create a new group of tiles, drag a tile to the space to the left or right of an existing tile group. A light gray vertical bar displays to indicate where the new group will be located.
2. Add more tiles to this new group as needed.
3. To name the group, right-click any blank area of the Start screen and click Name groups. Type in the space provided to name a group. If a name is not entered for a group, the horizontal Name group bar disappears.

Accessing the Desktop

Although the Start screen is easy to use, you may want to access the more familiar desktop that you used in previous versions of Windows. The Desktop tile is available on the Start screen. Click the tile to bring up the desktop. Alternatively, you can be pushed to the desktop when you click other tiles such as Word. In Windows 8.1.1, the desktop is simplified to accommodate use on mobile devices where screen space is limited. However, on a laptop or desktop computer, you may want to have more features readily available. The familiar Notification area is displayed in the bottom-right corner. You will see the Windows Start screen, File Explorer, and Internet Explorer icons. See Figure 1.3 to locate these desktop components.

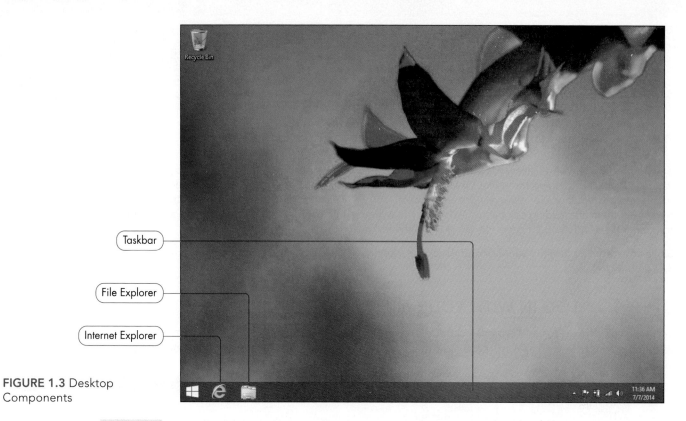

FIGURE 1.3 Desktop Components

STEP 3» You can add more toolbars, such as the Address bar, to the taskbar by right-clicking the taskbar, pointing to Toolbars, and then selecting Address. The Address bar can be used to locate Web sites using the URL or to perform a keyword search to locate Web sites about a specific topic. You can also add programs such as the *Snipping Tool*. The Snipping Tool is a Windows 8.1.1 accessory program that allows you to capture, or *snip*, a screen display so that you can save, annotate, or share it. You can remove all of the icons displayed on the taskbar by right-clicking the icon you want to remove and selecting *Unpin this program from taskbar*.

TIP | Using the Snipping Tool

The Snipping Tool can be used to take all sizes and shapes of snips of the displayed screen. Options include Free-form Snip, Rectangle Snip, Window Snip, and Full-screen Snip. You can save your snip in several formats, such as PNG, GIF, JPEG, or Single file HTML. In addition, you can use a pen or highlighter to mark up your snips. This option is available after taking a snip and is located under the Tools menu in the Snipping Tool dialog box.

You can return to the Start screen by clicking the Start screen icon on the taskbar.

Quick Concepts

1. Logging in to Windows 8.1.1 with your Microsoft account provides access to Internet resources. What are some benefits of logging in this way? *p. 2*

2. OneDrive allows you to collaborate with others. How might you use this service? *p. 3*

3. What is the Start screen, and how is it different from the desktop? *p. 3*

4. The desktop has been a feature of previous Windows operating systems. How is the Windows 8.1.1 desktop different from previous versions? *p. 4*

Hands-On Exercises

Watch the Video
for this Hands-
On Exercise!

MyITLab®
HOE1 Training

1 Windows 8.1.1 Startup

The Spotted Begonia Art Gallery has just hired several new clerical assistants to help you develop promotional materials for the various activities coming up throughout the year. It will be necessary to have a central storage space where you can save the documents and presentations for retrieval from any location. You will also need to be able to collaborate with others on the documents by sharing them and adding comments. To begin, you will get a Microsoft account. Then you will access the desktop and pin a toolbar and a Windows 8.1.1 accessory program to the taskbar.

Skills covered: Log In with Your Microsoft Account • Identify the Start Screen Components and Interact with the Start Screen • Access the Desktop

---

STEP 1 ≫ LOG IN WITH YOUR MICROSOFT ACCOUNT

You want to sign up for a Microsoft account so you can store documents and share them with others using the resources available with a Microsoft account, such as OneDrive. Refer to Figure 1.4 as you complete Step 1.

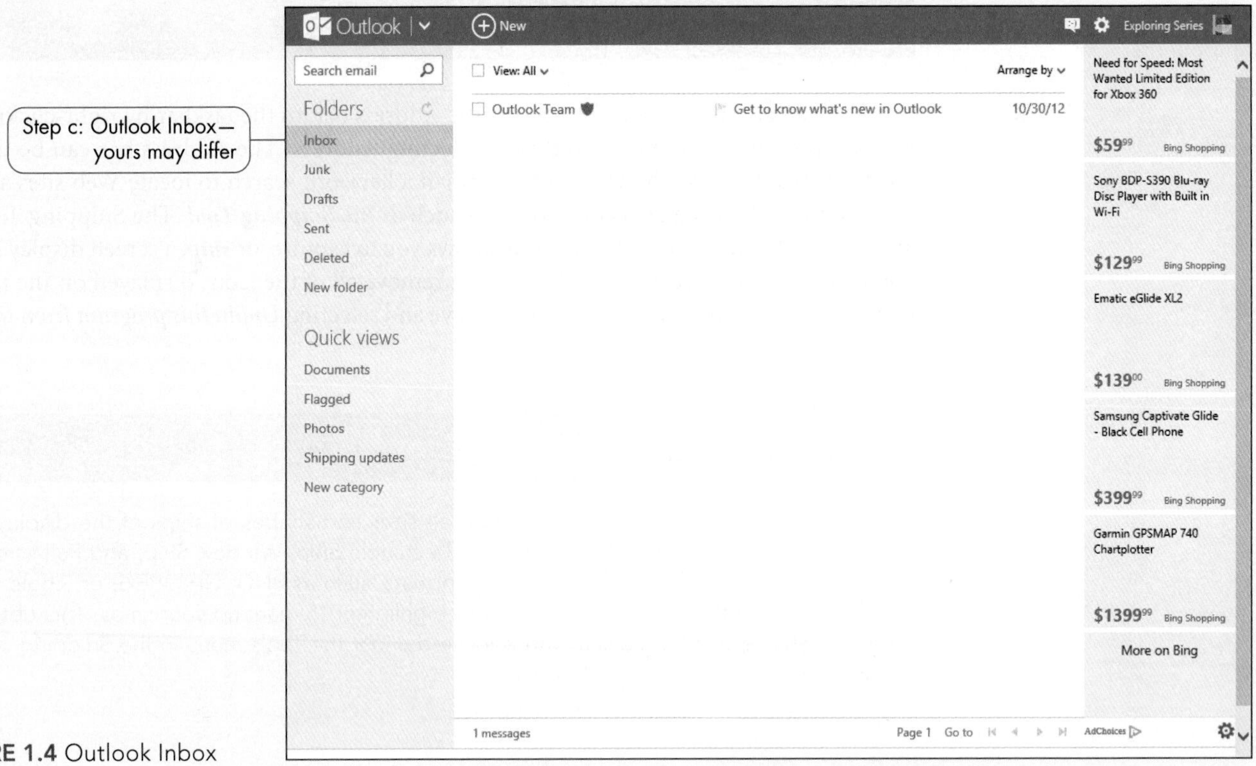

Step c: Outlook Inbox—
yours may differ

FIGURE 1.4 Outlook Inbox

a. Start your computer and enter your local username and password. On the Start screen, click the **Internet Explorer tile**. Click in the **Address bar** at the bottom of the screen. Type **live.com** and press **Enter**.

Internet Explorer displays, and you are taken to the Sign-up page for Outlook. This is where you can create a username and password for your Microsoft account.

> **TROUBLESHOOTING:** If you already have a Microsoft account, you can skip Step 1 and continue with Step 2. If someone else was already signed in at your computer, you can locate your username and click it to begin to log in.

b. Click the **Sign up now** link at the bottom of the screen. Fill in all text boxes and make all menu selections on the screen. Scroll down as needed. Type the **CAPTCHA code** carefully.

CAPTCHA is a scrambled code used with online forms to prevent mass sign-ups. It helps to ensure that a real person is requesting the account. You can choose not to accept e-mail with promotional offers by clicking the check box near the bottom of the screen to remove the check.

> **TROUBLESHOOTING:** You may want to write down your username and password so that you do not forget it the next time you want to log in with your Microsoft account. Keep this information in a safe and confidential location.

c. Click **I accept**. Your screen should display similarly to Figure 1.4.

Your Microsoft account is created, and you are taken to your Outlook Inbox.

d. Keep Internet Explorer open if you plan to continue using Outlook. Otherwise, sign out of Outlook and close Internet Explorer.

STEP 2 ≫ IDENTIFY THE START SCREEN COMPONENTS AND INTERACT WITH THE START SCREEN

You decide to explore the Start screen components. Then you use the Desktop tile on the Start screen to access the desktop. Refer to Figure 1.5 as you complete Step 2.

Step d: Display the Windows 8.1.1 desktop

FIGURE 1.5 Desktop

a. Point to the top-right corner to display the Charms. Click the **Start screen charm**.

Because you finished on the desktop after completing Step 1, clicking the Start screen charm takes you to the Start screen.

> **TROUBLESHOOTING:** If you skipped Step 1, log in to Windows with your username and password to display the Start screen.

b. Point to the bottom of the Start screen to display the horizontal scroll bar. Drag the scroll bar to the right to view all of the tiles available. Then drag the scrollbar back to the left to its original position.

Many components of the Start screen do not display until they are needed. This saves screen space on mobile devices. In this case, the horizontal scroll bar is hidden until needed.

c. Point to the bottom-right corner of the screen to display the Charms.

The Charms will display whenever you point to the top-right or bottom-right corners of the screen, regardless of the application you are using.

d. Locate and click the **Desktop tile**. See Figure 1.5.

STEP 3 ➤➤ ACCESS THE DESKTOP

You would like to add some components to make the desktop easier to use. You customize the desktop by adding the Address toolbar and the Snipping Tool to the taskbar. Refer to Figure 1.6 as you complete Step 3.

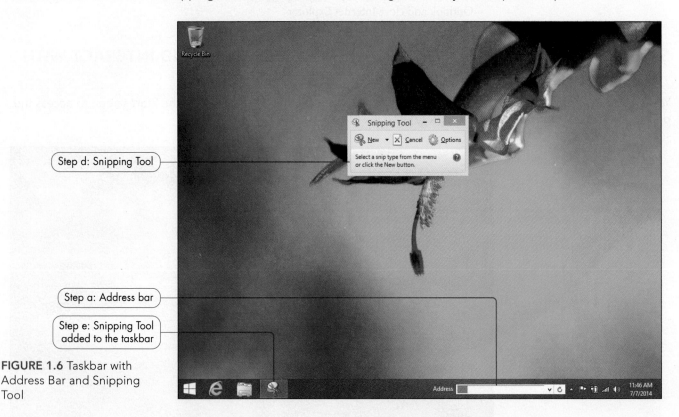

Step d: Snipping Tool

Step a: Address bar

Step e: Snipping Tool added to the taskbar

FIGURE 1.6 Taskbar with Address Bar and Snipping Tool

a. Locate and right-click the taskbar. Point to *Toolbars* and select **Address**.

The Address bar now displays on the right side of the taskbar.

b. Point to the top-right corner of the screen to display the Charms. Click the **Search charm**.

The Search pane displays on the right. The Search pane is organized into categories that you may want to search. For whatever category is selected, the relevant content is displayed.

In Windows 8.1.1, many dialog boxes have been changed to panes. This is in keeping with the sleek, clean look of Windows 8.1.1. Even though the look is different, the functionality remains the same.

c.   Type **Sn** in the **Search box**. Below the search box, the results listed display everything that begins with Sn.

d.   Click the **Snipping Tool app** in the results list.

The Snipping Tool app displays on the desktop and the Snipping Tool icon displays on the taskbar.

e.   Right-click the **Snipping Tool icon** on the taskbar. Click **Pin this program to taskbar**. See Figure 1.6.

The Snipping Tool and the Address bar will now be part of your taskbar.

> **TROUBLESHOOTING:** If you are in a lab and cannot keep these changes, you can remove the Snipping Tool icon from the taskbar. Right-click the icon and click *Unpin this program from taskbar*. You can remove the Address bar by right-clicking the taskbar, pointing to Toolbars, and then clicking Address to remove the check mark.

f.   Click the **Snipping Tool icon**. Click the **New arrow** in the Snipping Tool on the desktop. Click **Full-screen Snip**.

A snip of your desktop displays in the Snipping Tool program.

g.   Click **File** and click **Save As**. Navigate to the location where you are saving your student files. Name your file **f01h1Desktop_LastFirst** using your own last name and first name. Check to see that *Portable Network Graphic file (PNG)* displays in the *Save as type* box. Click **Save**.

You have created your first snip. Snips can be used to show what is on your screen. Notice the Snipping Tool app does not display in your snip. When you save files, use your last and first names. For example, as the Office Fundamentals author, I would name my document *f01h1Desktop_LawsonRebecca*.

> **TROUBLESHOOTING:** If PNG does not display in the *Save as type* box, click the arrow on the right side of the box and select *Portable Network Graphic file (PNG)*.

h.   Close the Snipping Tool. Submit the file based on your instructor's directions.

i.   Shut down your computer if you are ready to stop working. Point to the top-right corner to display the Charms. Click the **Settings charm**, click the **Power icon**, and then click **Shut down**. Otherwise, leave your computer turned on for the next Hands-On Exercise.

Files and Folders

Most activities that you perform using a computer produce some type of output. That output could be games, music, or the display of digital photographs. Perhaps you use a computer at work to produce reports, financial worksheets, or schedules. All of those items are considered computer *files*. Files include electronic data such as documents, databases, slide shows, and worksheets. Even digital photographs, music, videos, and Web pages are saved as files.

You use software to create and save files. For example, when you type a document on a computer, you first open a word processor such as Microsoft Word. In order to access files later, you must save them to a computer storage medium such as a hard drive or flash drive, or in the cloud at OneDrive. And just as you would probably organize a filing cabinet into a system of folders, you can organize storage media by *folders* that you name and into which you place data files. That way, you can easily retrieve the files later. Windows 8.1.1 provides tools that enable you to create folders and to save files in ways that make locating them simple.

In this section, you will learn to use File Explorer to manage folders and files.

Using File Explorer

File Explorer is an app that you can use to create and manage folders and files. The sole purpose of a computer folder is to provide a labeled storage location for related files so that you can easily organize and retrieve items. A folder structure can occur across several levels, so you can create folders within other folders—called *subfolders*—arranged according to purpose. Windows 8.1.1 uses the concept of libraries, which are folders that gather files from different locations and display the files as if they were all saved in a single folder, regardless of where they are physically stored. Using File Explorer, you can manage folders, work with libraries, and view favorites (areas or folders that are frequently accessed).

Understand and Customize the Interface

You can access File Explorer in any of the following ways:

- Click the File Explorer icon from the taskbar on the desktop.
- Click File Explorer from the Start screen.
- Display the Charms (refer to Figure 1.1) and click the Search charm. Type F in the Search box and in the results list on the left, click File Explorer.

Figure 1.7 shows the File Explorer interface containing several areas. Some of those areas are described in Table 1.1.

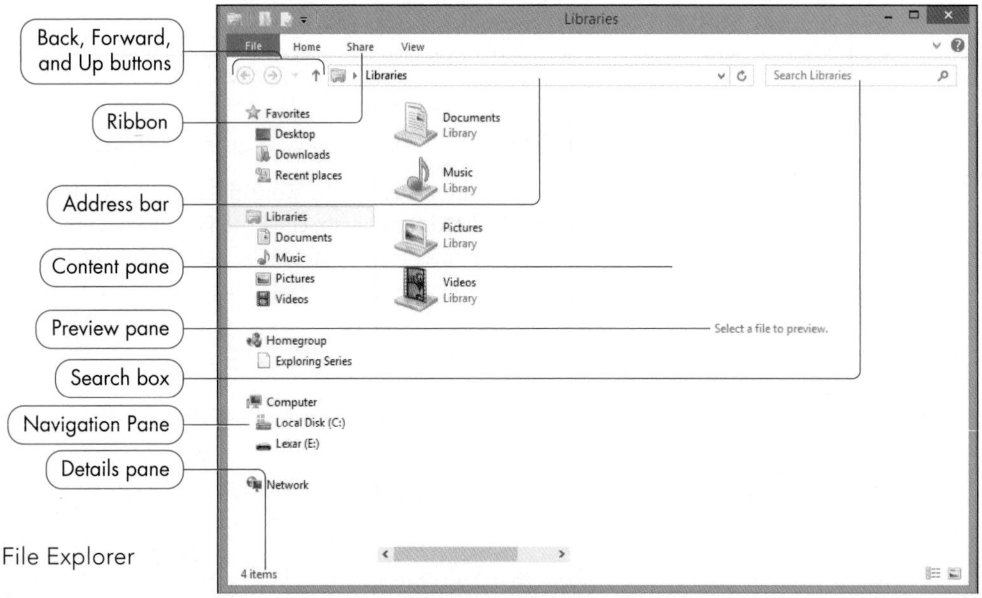

FIGURE 1.7 File Explorer Interface

TABLE 1.1 File Explorer Interface

Navigation Pane	The Navigation Pane contains five areas: Favorites, Libraries, Homegroup, Computer, and Network. Click an item in the Navigation Pane to display contents and to manage files that are housed within a selected folder.
Back, Forward, and Up Buttons	Use these buttons to visit previously opened folders or libraries. Use the Up button to open the parent folder for the current location.
Ribbon	The Ribbon includes tabs and commands that are relevant to the currently selected item. If you are working with a music file, the Ribbon commands might include one for burning to a CD, whereas if you have selected a document, the Ribbon would enable you to open or share the file.
Address bar	The Address bar enables you to navigate to other folders or libraries.
Content pane	The Content pane shows the contents of the currently selected folder or library.
Search box	Find files and folders by typing descriptive text in the Search box. Windows immediately begins a search after you type the first character, further narrowing results as you type.
Details pane	The Details pane shows properties that are associated with a selected file. Common properties include information such as the author name and the date the file was last modified. This pane does not display by default but can display after clicking the View tab.
Preview pane	The Preview pane provides a snapshot of a selected file's contents. You can see file contents before actually opening the file. The Preview pane does not show the contents of a selected folder. This pane does not display by default but can display after clicking the View tab.

File Explorer has a Ribbon like all the Office applications. As you work with File Explorer, you might want to customize the view. The file and folder icons might be too small for ease of identification, or you might want additional details about displayed files and folders. Modifying the view is easy. To make icons larger or to provide additional detail, click the View tab (refer to Figure 1.7) and select from the views provided in the Layout group. If you want additional detail, such as file type and size, click Details. You can also change the size of icons by selecting Small, Medium, Large, or Extra Large icons. The List view shows the file names without added detail, whereas Tiles and Content views are useful to show file thumbnails (small pictures describing file contents) and varying levels of detail regarding file locations. To show or hide File Explorer panes, click the View tab and select the pane to hide or show in the Panes group. You can widen or narrow panes by dragging a border when the mouse changes to a double-headed arrow.

Work with Groups on the Navigation Pane

The **Navigation Pane** provides ready access to computer resources, folders, files, and networked peripherals such as printers. It is divided into five areas: Favorites, Libraries, Homegroup, Computer, and Network. Each of those components provides a unique way to organize contents. In Figure 1.8, the currently selected area is Computer.

Earlier, we used the analogy of computer folders to folders in a filing cabinet. Just as you would title folders in a filing cabinet according to their contents, computer folders are also titled according to content. Folders are physically located on storage media such as a hard drive or flash drive. You can also organize folders into **libraries**, which are collections of files from different locations that are displayed as a single virtual folder. For example, the Pictures library includes files from the My Pictures folder and from the Public Pictures folder, both of which are physically housed on the hard drive. Although the library content comes from two separate folders, the contents are displayed as a single virtual folder.

Windows 8.1.1 includes several libraries that contain default folders or devices. For example, the Documents library includes the My Documents and Public Documents folders, but you can add subfolders if you wish so that they are also housed within the Documents library. To add a folder to a library, right-click the library, point to New, and then select Folder. You can name the folder at this point by typing the folder name. To remove a folder from the Documents library, open File Explorer, right-click the folder, and then select Delete.

The Computer area provides access to specific storage locations, such as a hard drive, CD/DVD drives, and removable media drives, including a flash drive. Files and folders housed on those storage media are accessible when you click Computer. For example, click drive C, shown under Computer in the Navigation Pane, to view its contents in the Content pane on the right. If you simply want to see the subfolders of the hard drive, click the arrow to the left of drive C to expand the view, showing all subfolders. The arrow is filled in and pointing down. Click the arrow again to collapse the view, removing subfolder detail. The arrow is open and pointing right. It is important to understand that clicking the arrow—as opposed to clicking the folder or area name—does not actually select an area or folder. It merely displays additional levels contained within the area. Clicking the folder or area, however, does select the item. Figure 1.8 illustrates the difference between clicking the folder or area name in the Navigation Pane and clicking the arrow to the left.

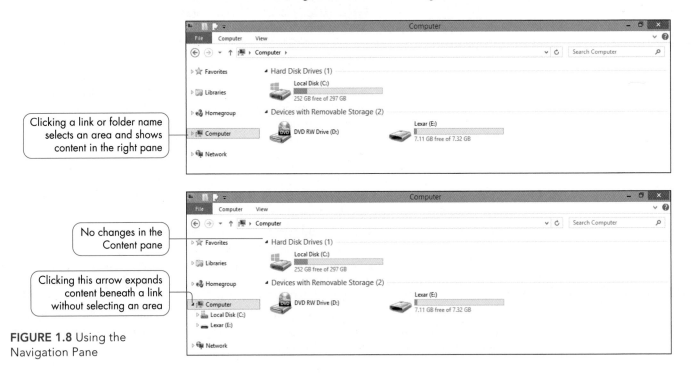

Clicking a link or folder name selects an area and shows content in the right pane

No changes in the Content pane

Clicking this arrow expands content beneath a link without selecting an area

FIGURE 1.8 Using the Navigation Pane

To locate a folder using File Explorer:

1. Click the correct drive in the Navigation Pane (or double-click the drive in the Content pane).
2. Continue navigating through the folder structure until you find the folder that you want.
3. Click the folder in the Navigation Pane (or double-click the folder in the Content pane) to view its contents.

The Favorites area contains frequently accessed folders and recent searches. You can drag a folder, saved search, library, or disk drive to the Favorites area. To remove a favorite, simply right-click the favorite and select Remove. You cannot add files or Web sites as favorites.

Homegroup is a Windows 8.1.1 feature that enables you to share resources on a home network. You can easily share music, pictures, videos, and libraries with other people in your home through a homegroup. It is password protected, so you do not have to worry about privacy.

Windows 8.1.1 makes creating a home network easy, sharing access to the Internet and peripheral devices such as printers and scanners. The Network area provides quick access to those devices, enabling you to see the contents of network computers.

Working with Folders and Files

As you work with software to create a file, such as when you type a report using Microsoft Word, your primary concern will be saving the file so that you can retrieve it later if necessary. If you have created an appropriate and well-named folder structure, you can save the file in a location that is easy to find later.

Create a Folder

You can create a folder a couple of different ways. You can use File Explorer to create a folder structure, providing appropriate names and placing the folders in a well-organized hierarchy. You can also create a folder from within a software application at the time that you need it. Although it would be wonderful to always plan ahead, most often you will find the need for a folder at the same time that you have created a file. The two methods of creating a folder are described next.

STEP 1 »   Suppose you are beginning a new college semester and are taking four classes. To organize your assignments, you plan to create four folders on a flash drive, one for each class. After connecting the flash drive and closing any subsequent dialog box (unless the dialog box is warning of a problem with the drive), open File Explorer. Click Computer in the Navigation Pane. Click the removable (flash) drive in the Navigation Pane or double-click it in the Content pane. You can also create a folder on the hard drive in the same manner, by clicking drive C instead of the removable drive. Click the Home tab on the Ribbon. Click *New folder* in the New group. Type the new folder name, such as Biology, and press Enter. Repeat the process to create additional folders.

Undoubtedly, you will occasionally find that you have just created a file but have no appropriate folder in which to save the file. You might have just finished the slide show for your speech class but have forgotten first to create a speech folder for your assignments. Now what do you do? As you save the file, a process that is discussed later in this chapter, you can click Browse to bring up the Save As dialog box. Navigate to the drive where you want to store your file. Click *New folder* (see Figure 1.9), type the new folder name, and then double-click to save the name and open the new folder. After indicating the file name, click Save.

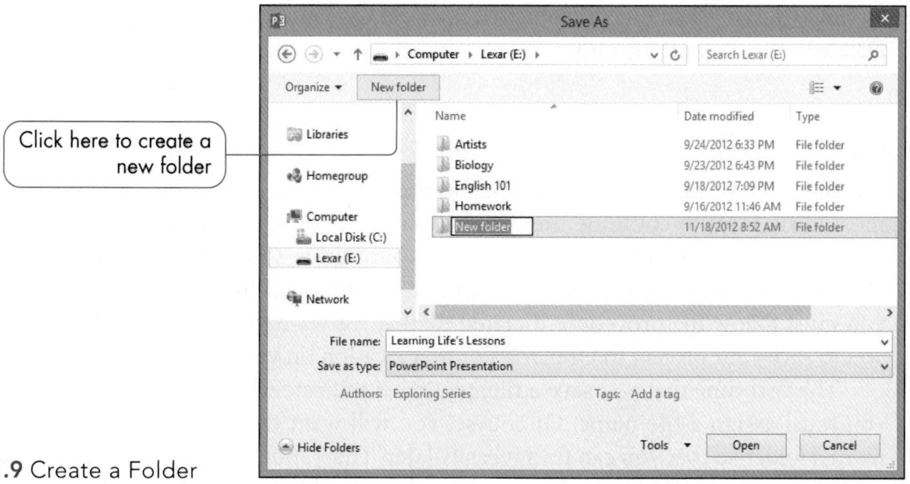

FIGURE 1.9 Create a Folder

OneDrive makes it easy to access your folders and files from any Internet-connected computer or mobile device. You can create new folders and organize existing folders just as you would when you use File Explorer. Other tasks that can be performed at OneDrive include opening, renaming, and deleting folders and files. To create a new folder at OneDrive, you can simply click the OneDrive tile on the Start screen. By default, you will see three items: Documents, Pictures, and Public Shared. You can right-click any of these three items to access icons for creating a new folder or to upload files. Once files and folders are added or created here, you can access them from any computer with Internet access at onedrive.live. com. Similarly, you can create folders or upload files and folders at OneDrive and then access them using the OneDrive tile on your Start screen.

Open, Rename, and Delete Folders and Files

You have learned that folders can be created in File Explorer but files are more commonly created in other ways, such as within a software package. File Explorer can create a new file, and you can use it to open, rename, and delete files just as you use it for folders.

Using the Navigation Pane, you can locate and select a folder containing a file that you want to open. For example, you might want to open the speech slide show so that you can practice before giving a presentation to the class. Open File Explorer and navigate to the speech folder. In your storage location, the file will display in the Content pane. Double-click the file. The program that is associated with the file will open the file. For example, if you have the PowerPoint program associated with that file type on your computer, then PowerPoint will open the file. To open a folder and display the contents, just click the folder in the Navigation Pane or double-click it in the Content pane.

STEP 3 ≫ At times, you may want to give a different name to a file or folder than the one that you originally gave it. Or perhaps you made a typographical mistake when you entered the name. In these situations, you should rename the file or folder. In File Explorer, move through the folder structure to find the folder or file. Right-click the name and select Rename. Type the new name and press Enter. You can also rename an item when you click the name twice— but much more slowly than a double-click. Type the new name and press Enter. Finally, you can click a file or folder once to select it, click the Home tab, and then select Rename in the Organize group. Type the new name and press Enter.

It is much easier to delete a folder or file than it is to recover it if you remove it by mistake. Therefore, be very careful when deleting items so that you are sure of your intentions before proceeding. When you delete a folder, all subfolders and all files within the folder are also removed. If you are certain you want to remove a folder or file, the process is simple. Right-click the item, click Delete, and then click Yes if asked to confirm removal to the Recycle Bin. Items are placed in the Recycle Bin only if you are deleting them from a hard drive. Files and folders deleted from a removable storage medium, such as a flash drive, are immediately and permanently deleted, with no easy method of retrieval. You can also delete an item (file or folder) when you click to select the item, click the Home tab, and then click Delete in the Organize group.

Save a File

STEP 2 ≫ As you create or modify a project such as a document, presentation, or worksheet, you will most likely want to continue the project at another time or keep it for later reference. You need to save it to a storage medium such as a hard drive, CD, flash drive, or in the cloud with OneDrive. When you save a file, you will be working within a software package. Therefore, you must follow the procedure dictated by that software to save the file. Office 2013 allows you to save your project to OneDrive or to a location on your computer.

The first time that you save a file, you must indicate where the file should be saved, and you must assign a file name. Of course, you will want to save the file in an appropriately named folder so that you can find it easily later. Thereafter, you can quickly save the file with the same settings, or you can change one or more of those settings, perhaps saving the file to a different storage device as a backup copy. Figure 1.10 shows a typical Save As pane for Office 2013 that enables you to select a location before saving the file.

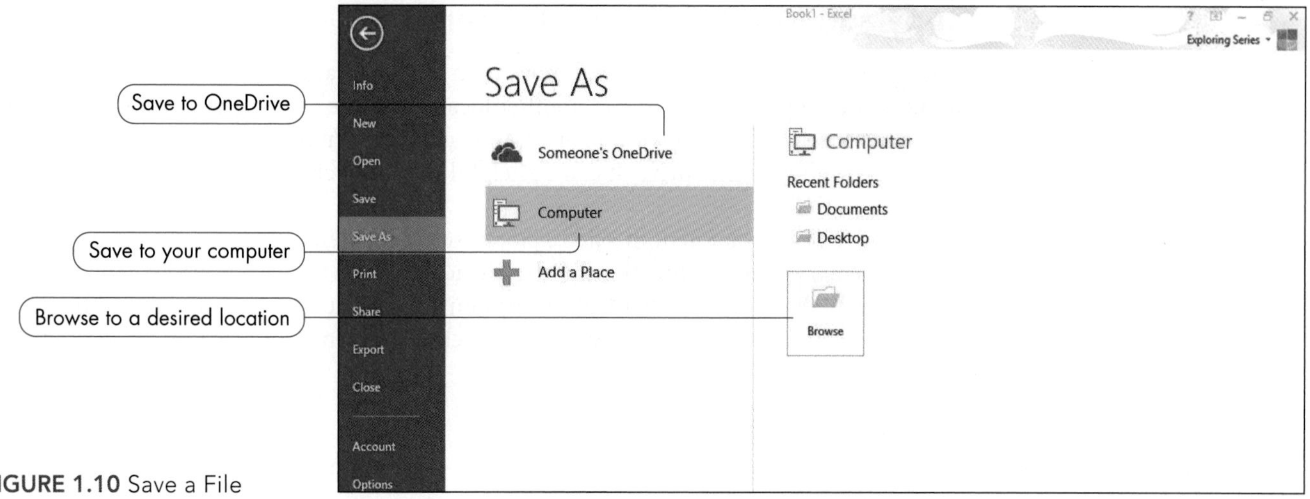

Save to OneDrive

Save to your computer

Browse to a desired location

FIGURE 1.10 Save a File

Selecting, Copying, and Moving Multiple Files and Folders

You will want to select folders and files when you need to rename, delete, copy, or paste them, or open files and folders so that you can view the contents. Click a file or folder to *select* it; double-click a file or folder (in the Content pane) to *open* it. To apply an operation to several files at once, such as deleting or moving them, you will want to select all of them.

Select Multiple Files and Folders

You can select several files and folders, regardless of whether they are adjacent to each other in the file list. Suppose that your digital pictures are contained in the Pictures folder. You might want to delete some of the pictures because you want to clear up some hard drive space. To select pictures in the Pictures folder, open File Explorer and click the Pictures library. Locate the desired pictures in the Content pane. To select the adjacent pictures, select the first picture, press and hold Shift, and then click the last picture. All consecutive picture files will be highlighted, indicating that they are selected. At that point, you can delete, copy, or move the selected pictures at the same time.

If the files or folders to be selected are not adjacent, click the first item. Press and hold Ctrl while you click all desired files or folders, releasing Ctrl only when you have finished selecting the files or folders.

To select all items in a folder or disk drive, use File Explorer to navigate to the desired folder. Open the folder, press and hold Ctrl, and then press A on the keyboard. You can also click the Home tab, and in the Select group, click *Select all* to select all items.

> **TIP | Using a Check Box to Select Items**
>
> In Windows 8.1.1, it is easy to make multiple selections, even if the items are not adjacent. Open File Explorer and select your drive or folder. Click the View tab and select Item check boxes in the Show/Hide group. As you move the mouse pointer along the left side of files and folders, a check box displays. Click in the check box to select the file. If you want to quickly select all items in the folder, click the check box that displays in the Name column heading.

Copy and Move Files and Folders

When you copy or move a folder, you move both the folder and any files that it contains. You can move or copy a folder or file to another location on the same drive or to another drive. If your purpose is to make a *backup*, or copy, of an important file or folder, you will probably want to copy it to another drive. It can be helpful to have backup copies saved in the cloud at OneDrive as well.

STEP 4 ▶▶   To move or copy an item in File Explorer, select the item. If you want to copy or move multiple items, follow the directions in the previous section to select them all at once. Right-click the item(s) and select either Cut or Copy on the shortcut menu. In the Navigation Pane, locate the destination drive or folder, right-click the destination drive or folder, and then click Paste.

Quick
Concepts ✓

1. The File Explorer interface has several panes. Name them and identify their characteristics. *p. 11*

2. After creating a file, such as a PowerPoint presentation, you want to save it. However, as you begin to save the file, you realize that you have not yet created a folder in which to place the file. Is it possible to create a folder as you are saving the file? If so, how? *p. 13*

3. What should you consider when deleting files or folders from a removable storage medium such as a flash drive? *p. 14*

4. Office 2013 enables you to save files to OneDrive or your computer. Why might it be helpful to save a file in both locations? *p. 14*

5. You want to delete several files, but the files are not consecutively listed in File Explorer. How would you select and delete them? *p. 15*

Hands-On Exercises

Watch the Video for this Hands-On Exercise!

MyITLab® HOE2 Training

2 Files and Folders

You will soon begin to collect files from volunteers who are preparing promotional and record-keeping material for the Spotted Begonia Art Gallery. It is important that you save the files in appropriately named folders so that you can easily access them later. You can create folders on a hard drive, flash drive, or at OneDrive. You will select the drive on which you plan to save the various files. As you create a short document, you will save it in one of the folders. You will then make a backup copy of the folder structure, including all files, so that you do not run the risk of losing the material if the drive is damaged or misplaced.

Skills covered: Create Folders and Subfolders • Create and Save a File • Rename and Delete a Folder • Open and Copy a File

STEP 1 » CREATE FOLDERS AND SUBFOLDERS

You decide to create a folder titled *Artists* and then subdivide it into subfolders that will help categorize the artists' artwork promotional files as well as for general record keeping for the art gallery. Refer to Figure 1.11 as you complete Step 1.

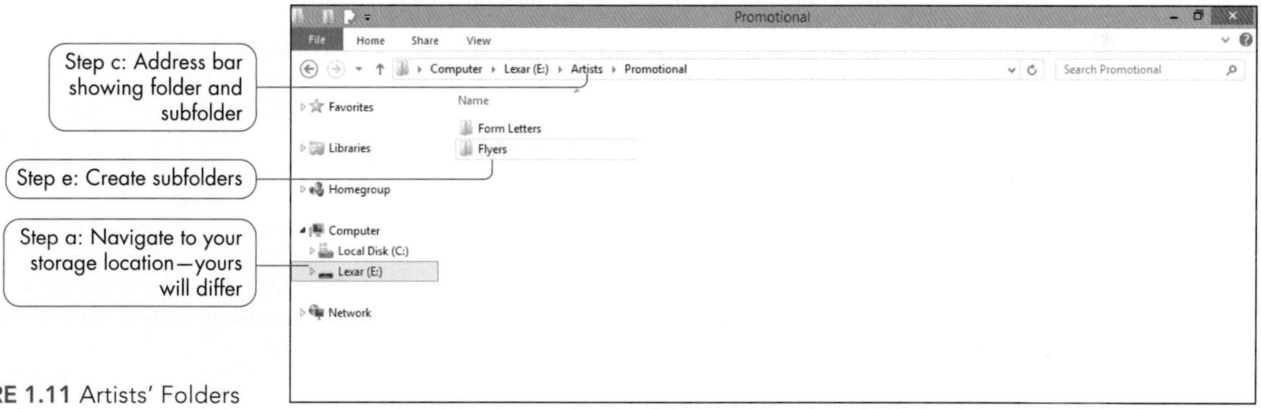

FIGURE 1.11 Artists' Folders

a. Navigate to the location where you are storing your files. If storing on your computer or a flash drive, navigate to the desktop. Click **File Explorer** on the taskbar and maximize the window. Click the **VIEW tab** and click to display the **Preview pane**, if necessary.

A removable drive is shown in Figure 1.11 and is titled *Lexar (E:)*, describing the drive manufacturer and the drive letter. Your storage area will be designated in a different manner, perhaps also identified by manufacturer (or perhaps you are saving your files on OneDrive). The storage area identification is likely to be different because the configuration of disk drives on your computer is unique.

TROUBLESHOOTING: If you do not have a flash drive, you can use the hard drive. In the next step, simply click drive C in the Navigation Pane instead of the removable drive. You can also create and save folders and files at OneDrive.

b. Click the removable drive in the Navigation Pane (or click **drive C** if you are using the hard drive). Click the **HOME tab**, click **New folder** in the New group, type **Artists**, and then press **Enter**.

You create a folder where you can organize subfolders and files for the artists and their promotional materials and general record-keeping files.

> **TROUBLESHOOTING:** If the folder you create is called *New folder* instead of *Artists*, you probably clicked away from the folder before typing the name, so that it received the default name. To rename it, right-click the folder, click Rename, type the correct name, and then press Enter.

c. Double-click the **Artists folder** in the Content pane. The Address bar at the top of the File Explorer window should show that it is the currently selected folder. Click the **HOME tab**, click **New folder** in the New group, type **Promotional**, and then press **Enter**.

You decide to create subfolders of the *Artists* folder to contain promotional material, presentations, and office records.

d. Check the Address bar to make sure *Artists* is still the current folder. Using the same technique, create a new folder named **Presentations** and create a new folder named **Office Records**.

You create two more subfolders, appropriately named.

e. Double-click the **Promotional folder** in the Navigation Pane. Right-click in a blank area, point to *New*, and then click **Folder**. Type **Form Letters** and press **Enter**. Using the same technique, create a new folder named **Flyers** and press **Enter**.

To subdivide the promotional material further, you create two subfolders, one to hold form letters and one to contain flyers (see Figure 1.11).

f. Take a full-screen snip of your screen and name it **f01h2Folders_LastFirst**. Close the Snipping Tool.

g. Close File Explorer.

STEP 2 ≫ CREATE AND SAVE A FILE

To keep everything organized, you assign volunteers to take care of certain tasks. After creating an Excel worksheet listing those responsibilities, you will save it in the Office Records folder. Refer to Figure 1.12 as you complete Step 2.

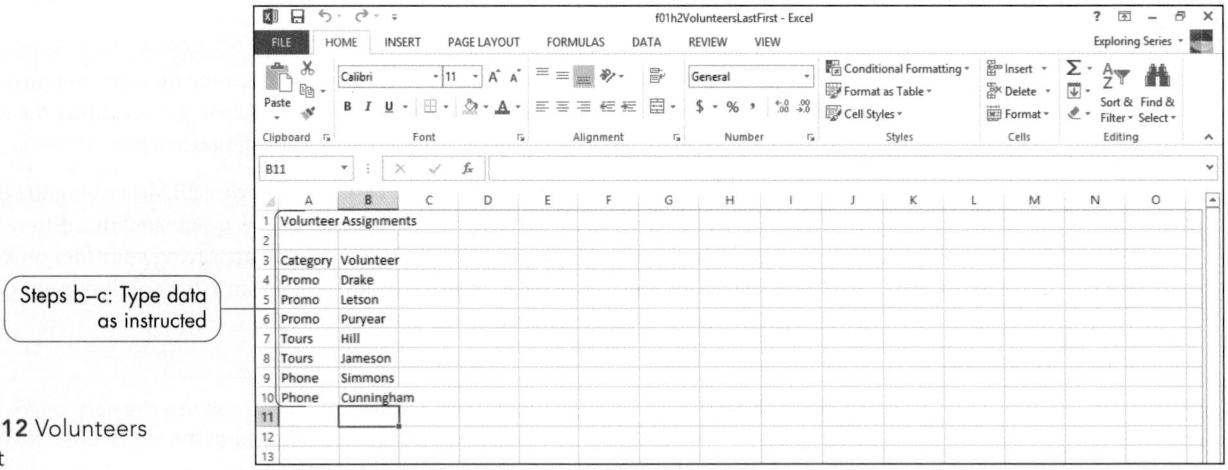

FIGURE 1.12 Volunteers Worksheet

a. Navigate to the Start screen. Scroll across the tiles and click **Excel 2013**. If necessary, use the Search charm to locate Excel.

You use Excel 2013 to create the Volunteers worksheet.

b. Click **Blank workbook** in the Excel 2013 window that displays. Type **Volunteer Assignments** in **cell A1**. Press **Enter** twice.

Cell A3 is the active cell, as indicated by a green box that surrounds the cell.

c. Type **Category**. Press **Tab** to make the next cell to the right the active cell and type **Volunteer**. Press **Enter**. Complete the remaining cells of the worksheet as shown in Figure 1.12.

> **TROUBLESHOOTING:** If you make a mistake, click in the cell and retype the entry.

d. Click the **FILE tab** and click **Save**.

The Save As pane displays. The Save As pane is where you determine the location where your file will be saved, either your Computer or OneDrive.

e. Click **Browse** to display the Save As dialog box. Scroll down if necessary and click **Computer** or the location where you are saving your files in the Navigation Pane. In the Content pane, locate the Artists folder that you created in Step 1 and double-click to open the folder. Double-click **Office Records**. Click in the **File name box** and type **f01h2Volunteers_LastFirst**. Click **Save**. Refer to Figure 1.12.

The file is now saved as *f01h2Volunteers_LastFirst*. The workbook is saved in the Office Records subfolder of the Artists folder. You can check the title bar of the workbook to confirm the file has been saved with the correct name.

f. Click the **Close (X) button** in the top-right corner of the Excel window to close Excel.

STEP 3 ≫ RENAME AND DELETE A FOLDER

As often happens, you find that the folder structure you created is not exactly what you need. You will remove the Flyers folder and the Form Letters folder and will rename the Promotional folder to better describe the contents. Refer to Figure 1.13 as you complete Step 3.

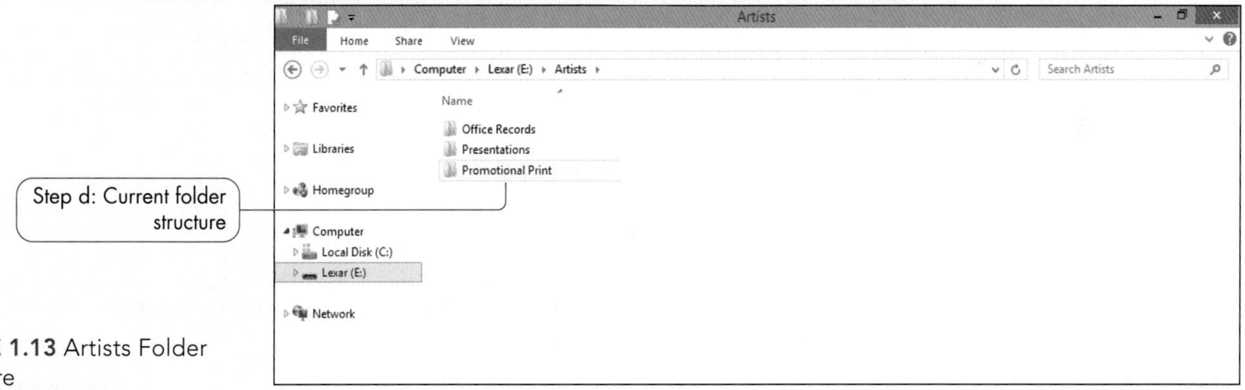

Step d: Current folder structure

FIGURE 1.13 Artists Folder Structure

a. Navigate to the desktop, if necessary. Click **File Explorer** on the taskbar. Click the location where you are saving your files. Double-click the **Artists folder** in the Content pane.

b. Click the **Promotional folder** to select it.

> **TROUBLESHOOTING:** If you double-click the folder instead of using a single-click, the folder will open and you will see its title in the Address bar. To return to the correct view, click Artists in the Address bar.

c. Click the **HOME tab**. In the Organize group, click **Rename**, type **Promotional Print**, and then press **Enter**.

Because the folder will be used to organize all of the printed promotional material, you decide to rename the folder to better reflect the contents.

d. Double-click the **Promotional Print folder**. Click **Flyers**. Press and hold **Shift** and click **Form Letters**. Both folders should be selected (highlighted). Right-click either folder and click **Delete**. If asked to confirm the deletion, click **Yes**. Click **Artists** in the Address bar.

Your screen should appear as shown in Figure 1.13. You decide that dividing the promotional material into flyers and form letters is not necessary, so you deleted both folders.

e. Take a full-screen snip of your screen and name it **f01h2Artists_LastFirst**. Close the Snipping Tool.

f. Leave File Explorer open for the next step.

STEP 4 ≫ OPEN AND COPY A FILE

You hope to recruit more volunteers to work with the Spotted Begonia Art Gallery. The Volunteers worksheet will be a handy way to keep up with people and assignments, and as the list grows, knowing exactly where the file is saved will be important for easy access. You will modify the Volunteers worksheet and make a backup copy of the folder hierarchy. Refer to Figure 1.14 as you complete Step 4.

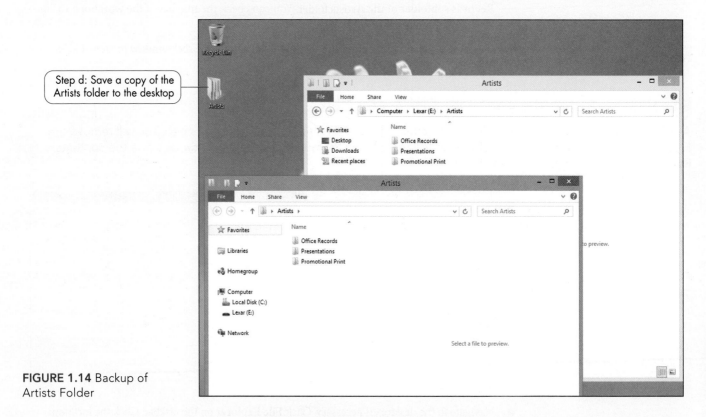

Step d: Save a copy of the Artists folder to the desktop

FIGURE 1.14 Backup of Artists Folder

a. Double-click the **Office Records folder**. Double-click *f01h2Volunteers_LastFirst*. Save the file with the new name **f01h2Stp4Volunteers_LastFirst** in the same location.

Because the file was created with Excel, that program opens, and the Volunteers worksheet is displayed.

b. Click **cell A11**, if necessary, and type **Office**. Press **Tab**, type **Adams**, and then press **Enter**. Click the **FILE tab** and click **Save**. The file is automatically saved in the same location with the same file name as before. Close Excel.

A neighbor, Sarah Adams, has volunteered to help in the office. You record that information on the worksheet and save the updated file in the Office Records folder.

c. Click the location where you save files in the Navigation pane in File Explorer so that the Artists folder displays in the Content pane. Right-click the **Artists folder** and click **Copy**.

d. Right-click **Desktop** in the Favorites group on the Navigation Pane and click **Paste**. Close File Explorer. If any other windows are open, close them also.

You made a copy of the Artists folder on the desktop.

e. Double-click the **Artists folder** on the desktop. Double-click the **Office Records folder**. Verify that the *f01h2Stp4Volunteers_LastFirst* worksheet displays in the folder. Take a full-screen snip of your screen and name it **f01h2Backup_LastFirst**. Close the Snipping Tool and close File Explorer.

f. Right-click the **Artists folder** on the desktop, select **Delete**, and then click **Yes** if asked to confirm the deletion.

You deleted the Artists folder from the desktop of the computer because you may be working in a computer lab and want to leave the computer as you found it. You may also want to empty the Recycle Bin.

g. Submit your files based on your instructor's directions.

Microsoft Office Software

Organizations around the world rely heavily on *Microsoft Office* software to produce documents, spreadsheets, presentations, and databases. Microsoft Office is a productivity software suite including a set of software applications, each one specializing in a particular type of output. You can use *Word* to produce all sorts of documents, including memos, newsletters, forms, tables, and brochures. *Excel* makes it easy to organize records, financial transactions, and business information in the form of worksheets. With *PowerPoint*, you can create dynamic presentations to inform groups and persuade audiences. *Access* is relational database software that enables you to record and link data, query databases, and create forms and reports.

You will sometimes find that you need to use two or more Office applications to produce your intended output. You might, for example, find that a Word document you are preparing for your investment club should also include a summary of stock performance. You can use Excel to prepare the summary and then incorporate the worksheet in the Word document. Similarly, you can integrate Word tables and Excel charts into a PowerPoint presentation. The choice of which software applications to use really depends on what type of output you are producing. Table 1.2 describes the major tasks of these four primary applications in Microsoft Office.

TABLE 1.2 Microsoft Office Software	
Office 2013 Product	**Application Characteristics**
Word 2013	Word processing software used with text to create, edit, and format documents such as letters, memos, reports, brochures, resumes, and flyers.
Excel 2013	Spreadsheet software used to store quantitative data and to perform accurate and rapid calculations with results ranging from simple budgets to financial analyses and statistical analyses.
PowerPoint 2013	Presentation graphics software used to create slide shows for presentation by a speaker, to be published as part of a Web site, or to run as a stand-alone application on a computer kiosk.
Access 2013	Relational database software used to store data and convert it into information. Database software is used primarily for decision making by businesses that compile data from multiple records stored in tables to produce informative reports.

As you become familiar with Microsoft Office, you will find that although each software application produces a specific type of output, all applications share common features. Such commonality gives a similar feel to each software application so that learning and working with Microsoft Office software products is easy. In this section, you will identify features common to Microsoft Office software, including such interface components as the Ribbon, the Backstage view, and the Quick Access Toolbar. You will also learn how to get help with an application.

Identifying Common Interface Components

As you work with Microsoft Office, you will find that each application shares a similar *user interface*. The user interface is the screen display through which you communicate with the software. Word, Excel, PowerPoint, and Access share common interface elements, as shown in Figure 1.15. One of the feature options includes the availability of templates as well as new and improved themes when each application is opened. A **template** is a predesigned file that incorporates formatting elements, such as a theme and layouts, and may include content that can be modified. A **theme** is a collection of design choices that includes colors, fonts, and special effects used to give a consistent look to a document, workbook, or presentation. As you can imagine, becoming familiar with one application's interface makes it that much easier to work with other Office software.

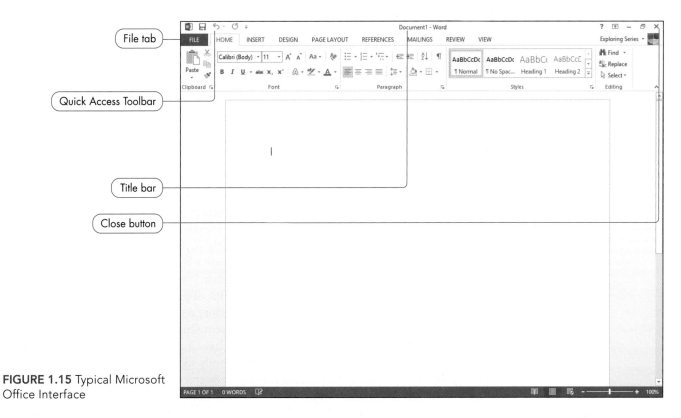

FIGURE 1.15 Typical Microsoft Office Interface

Use the Backstage View and the Quick Access Toolbar

The **Backstage view** is a component of Office 2013 that provides a concise collection of commands related to an open file. Using the Backstage view, you can find out information such as protection, permissions, versions, and properties. A file's properties include the author, file size, permissions, and date modified. You can create a new document or open, save, print, share, export, or close. The **Quick Access Toolbar**, located at the top-left corner of any Office application window, provides fast access to commonly executed tasks such as saving a file and undoing recent actions. The **title bar** identifies the current file name and the application in which you are working. It also includes control buttons that enable you to minimize, maximize, restore down, or close the application window (see Figure 1.15).

You access the Backstage view by clicking the File tab. When you click the File tab, you will see the Backstage view (see Figure 1.16). Primarily focusing on file activities such as opening, closing, saving, printing, and beginning new files, the Backstage view also includes options for customizing program settings, signing in to your Office account, and exiting the program. It displays a file's properties, providing important information on file permission and sharing options. When you click the File tab, the Backstage view will occupy the entire application window, hiding the file with which you might be working. For example, suppose that as you are typing a report you need to check the document's properties. Click the File tab to display a Backstage view similar to that shown in Figure 1.16. You can return to the application—in this case, Word—in a couple of ways. Either click the Back arrow in the top-left corner or press Esc on the keyboard.

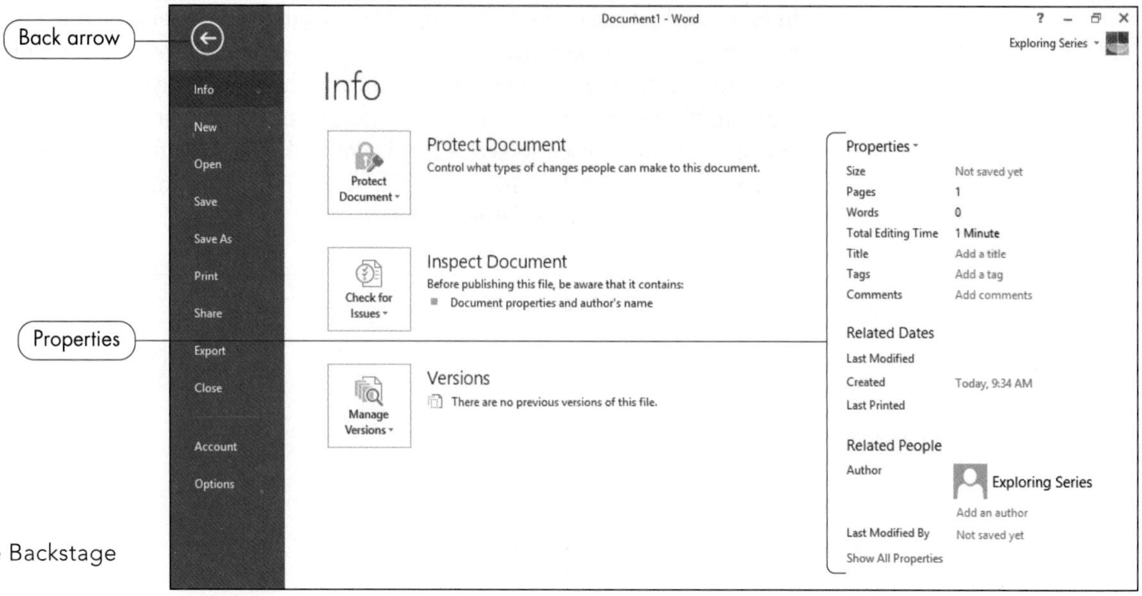

Back arrow

Properties

FIGURE 1.16 The Backstage View

STEP 4 ▶▶

The Quick Access Toolbar provides one-click access to common activities, as shown in Figure 1.17. By default, the Quick Access Toolbar includes buttons for saving a file and for undoing or redoing recent actions. You will probably perform an action countless times in an Office application and then realize that you made a mistake. You can recover from the mistake by clicking Undo on the Quick Access Toolbar. If you click the arrow beside Undo—known as the Undo arrow—you can select from a list of previous actions in order of occurrence. The Undo list is not maintained when you close a file or exit the application, so you can erase an action that took place during the current Office session only. Similar to Undo, you can also Redo (or Replace) an action that you have just undone. You can customize the Quick Access Toolbar to include buttons for frequently used commands such as printing or opening files. Because the Quick Access Toolbar is onscreen at all times, the most commonly accessed tasks are just a click away.

To customize the Quick Access Toolbar, click Customize Quick Access Toolbar (see Figure 1.17) and select from a list of commands. You can also click More Commands near the bottom of the menu options. If a command that you want to include on the toolbar is not on the list, you can right-click the command on the Ribbon and click *Add* to *Quick Access Toolbar*. Similarly, remove a command from the Quick Access Toolbar by right-clicking the icon on the Quick Access Toolbar and clicking *Remove from Quick Access Toolbar*. If you want to display the Quick Access Toolbar beneath the Ribbon, click Customize Quick Access Toolbar (see Figure 1.17) and click *Show Below the Ribbon*.

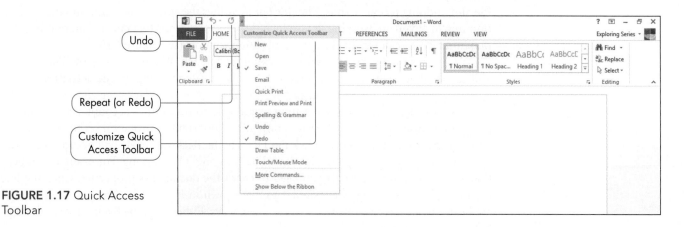

Undo

Repeat (or Redo)

Customize Quick Access Toolbar

FIGURE 1.17 Quick Access Toolbar

Familiarize Yourself with the Ribbon

The **Ribbon** is the command center of Office applications. It is the long bar located just beneath the title bar, containing tabs, groups, and commands. Each **tab** is designed to appear much like a tab on a file folder, with the active tab highlighted. The File tab is always a darker shade than the other tabs and a different color depending on the application. Remember that clicking the File tab opens the Backstage view. Other tabs on the Ribbon enable you to modify a file. The active tab in Figure 1.18 is the Home tab.

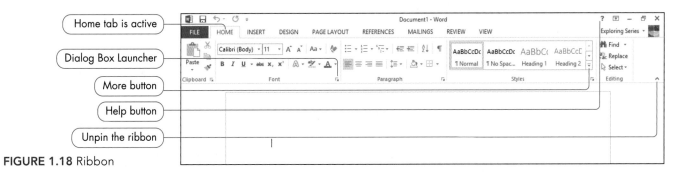

FIGURE 1.18 Ribbon

When you click a tab, the Ribbon displays several task-oriented **groups**, with each group containing related **commands**. A group is a subset of a tab that organizes similar tasks together. A command is a button or area within a group that you click to perform tasks. Microsoft Office is designed to provide the most functionality possible with the fewest clicks. For that reason, the Home tab, displayed when you first open an Office software application, contains groups and commands that are most commonly used. For example, because you will often want to change the way text is displayed, the Home tab in each Office application includes a Font group with activities related to modifying text. Similarly, other tabs contain groups of related actions, or commands, many of which are unique to the particular Office application.

Because Word, PowerPoint, Excel, and Access all share a similar Ribbon structure, you will be able to move at ease among those applications. Although the specific tabs, groups, and commands vary among the Office programs, the way in which you use the Ribbon and the descriptive nature of tab titles is the same regardless of which program you are working with. For example, if you want to insert a chart in Excel, a header in Word, or a shape in PowerPoint, you will click the Insert tab in any of those programs. The first thing that you should do as you begin to work with an Office application is to study the Ribbon. Take a look at all tabs and their contents. That way, you will have a good idea of where to find specific commands and how the Ribbon with which you are currently working differs from one that you might have used previously in another application.

If you are working with a large project, you might want to maximize your workspace by temporarily hiding the Ribbon. You can hide the Ribbon in several ways. Double-click the active tab to hide the Ribbon and double-click any tab to redisplay it. You can click *Unpin the ribbon* (see Figure 1.18), located at the right side of the Ribbon, and click any tab to redisplay the Ribbon.

The Ribbon provides quick access to common activities such as changing number or text formats or aligning data or text. Some actions, however, do not display on the Ribbon because they are not so common but are related to commands displayed on the Ribbon. For example, you might want to change the background of a PowerPoint slide to include a picture. In that case, you will need to work with a **dialog box** that provides access to more precise, but less frequently used, commands. Figure 1.19 shows the Font dialog box in Word, for example. Some commands display a dialog box when they are clicked. Other Ribbon groups include a **Dialog Box Launcher** that, when clicked, opens a corresponding dialog box (refer to Figure 1.18).

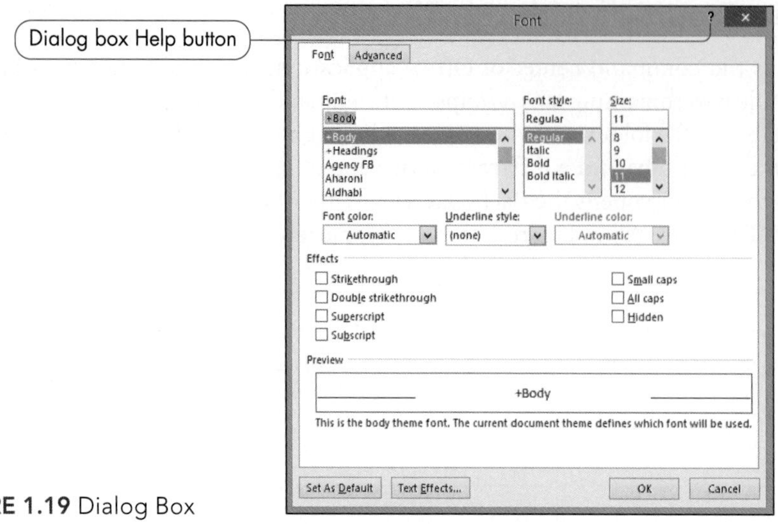

FIGURE 1.19 Dialog Box

The Ribbon contains many selections and commands, but some selections are too numerous to include in the Ribbon's limited space. For example, Word provides far more text styles than it can easily display at once, so additional styles are available in a *gallery*. A gallery also provides a choice of Excel chart styles and PowerPoint transitions. Figure 1.20 shows an example of a PowerPoint Themes gallery. Most often, you can display a gallery of additional choices by clicking the More button (refer to Figure 1.18) that is found in some Ribbon selections.

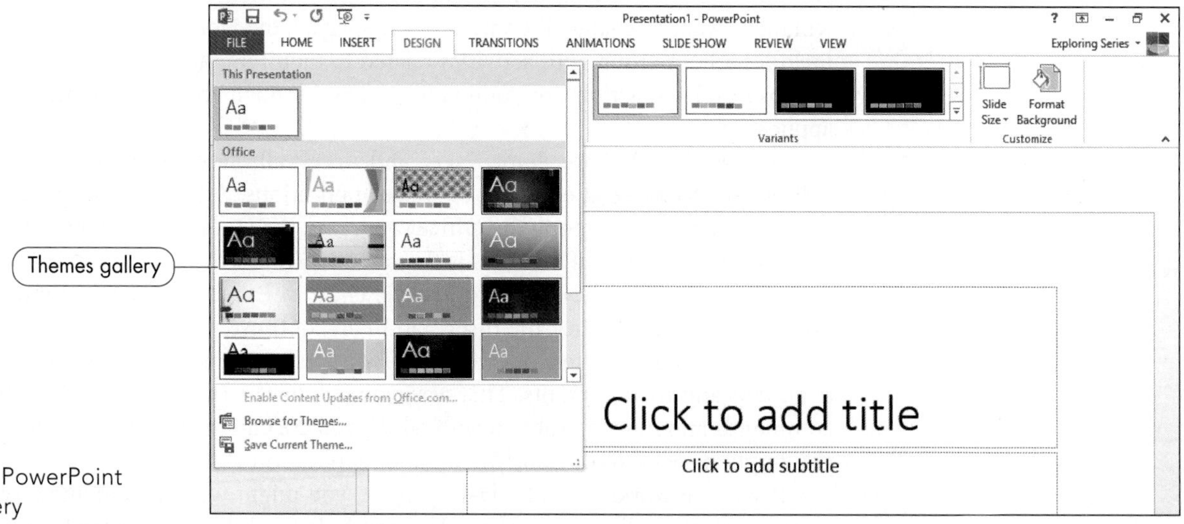

Themes gallery

FIGURE 1.20 PowerPoint Themes Gallery

STEP 3 ▸▸

When editing a document, worksheet, or presentation, it is helpful to see the results of formatting changes before you make final selections. The feature that displays a preview of the results of a selection is called *Live Preview*. You might, for example, be considering changing the font color of a selection in a document or worksheet. As you place the mouse pointer over a color selection in a Ribbon gallery or group, the selected text will temporarily display the color to which you are pointing. Similarly, you can get a preview of how color designs would display on PowerPoint slides by pointing to specific themes in the PowerPoint Themes group and noting the effect on a displayed slide. When you click the item, such as the font color, the selection is applied. Live Preview is available in various Ribbon selections among the Office applications.

Office applications also make it easy for you to work with objects such as pictures, *clip art*, shapes, charts, and tables. Clip art is an electronic illustration that can be inserted into an Office project. When you include such objects in a project, they are considered separate components that you can manage independently. To work with an object, you must click to select it. When you select an object, the Ribbon is modified to include one or more *contextual tabs* that contain groups of commands related to the selected object. Figure 1.21 shows a contextual tab related to a selected SmartArt object in a Word document. When you click outside the selected object, the contextual tab disappears.

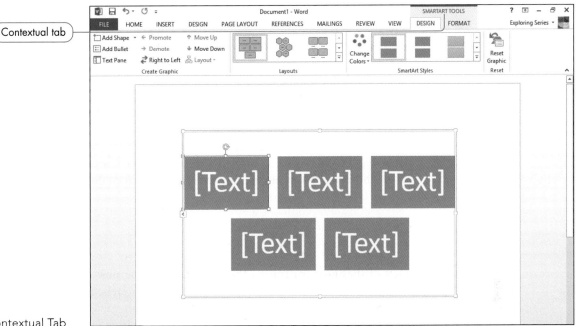

FIGURE 1.21 Contextual Tab

TIP   Using Keyboard Shortcuts

You might find that you prefer to use keyboard shortcuts, which are keyboard equivalents for software commands, when they are available. Universal keyboard shortcuts include Ctrl+C (copy), Ctrl+X (cut), Ctrl+V (paste), and Ctrl+Z (undo). To move to the beginning of a Word document, to cell A1 in Excel, or to the first PowerPoint slide, press Ctrl+Home. To move to the end of those items, press Ctrl+End. Press Alt to display keyboard shortcuts, called a *Key Tip*, for items on the Ribbon and Quick Access Toolbar. You can press the letter or number corresponding to Ribbon items to invoke the action from the keyboard. Press Alt again to remove the Key Tips.

Use the Status Bar

The *status bar* is located at the bottom of the program window and contains information relative to the open file. It also includes tools for changing the view of the file and for changing the zoom size of onscreen file contents. Contents of the status bar are unique to each specific application. When you work with Word, the status bar informs you of the number of pages and words in an open document. The Excel status bar displays summary information, such as average and sum, of selected cells. The PowerPoint status bar shows the slide number, total slides in the presentation, and the applied theme. It also provides access to notes and comments.

STEP 3» Regardless of the application in which you are working, the status bar includes view buttons and a Zoom slider. You can also use the View tab on the Ribbon to change the current view or zoom level of an open file. The status bar's view buttons (see Figure 1.22) enable you to change the *view* of the open file. When creating a document, you might find it helpful to change the view. You might, for example, view a PowerPoint slide presentation with multiple slides displayed (Slide Sorter view) or with only one slide in large size (Normal view). In Word, you could view a document in Print Layout view (showing margins, headers, and footers), Web Layout view, or Read Mode.

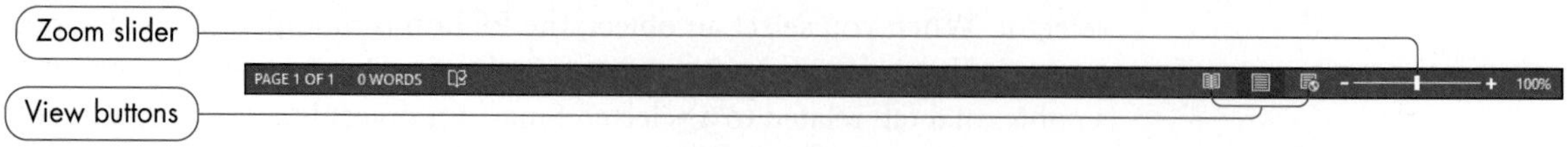

FIGURE 1.22 Word Status Bar

Additional views are available in the View tab. Word's Print Layout view is useful when you want to see both the document text and such features as margins and page breaks. Web Layout view is useful to see what the page would look like on the Internet. The Read Mode view provides a clean look that displays just the content without the Ribbon or margins. It is ideal for use on a tablet where the screen may be smaller than on a laptop or computer. PowerPoint, Excel, and Access also provide view options, although they are unique to the application. The most common view options are accessible from *View shortcuts* on the status bar of each application. As you learn more about Office applications, you will become aware of the views that are specific to each application.

STEP 1 ≫   The *Zoom slider* always displays at the far right side of the status bar. You can drag the tab along the slider in either direction to increase or decrease the magnification of the file. Be aware, however, that changing the size of text onscreen does not change the font size when the file is printed or saved.

Getting Office Help

One of the most frustrating things about learning new software is determining how to complete a task. Thankfully, Microsoft includes comprehensive help in Office so that you are less likely to feel such frustration. As you work with any Office application, you can access help online as well as within the current software installation. Help is available through a short description that displays when you rest the mouse pointer on a command. Additionally, you can get help related to a currently open dialog box by clicking the question mark in the top-right corner of the dialog box, or when you click Help in the top-right corner of the application.

Use Office Help

STEP 2 ≫   To access the comprehensive library of Office Help, click the Help button, displayed as a question mark on the far right side of the Ribbon (refer to Figure 1.18). The Help window provides assistance with the current application as well as a direct link to online resources and technical support. Figure 1.23 shows the Help window that displays when you click the Help button while in Excel. For general information on broad topics, click a link in the window. However, if you are having difficulty with a specific task, it might be easier to simply type the request in the Search online help box. Suppose you are seeking help with using the Goal Seek feature in Excel. Simply type *Goal Seek* or a phrase such as *find specific result by changing variables* in the Search box and press Enter (or click the magnifying glass on the right). Then select from displayed results for more information on the topic.

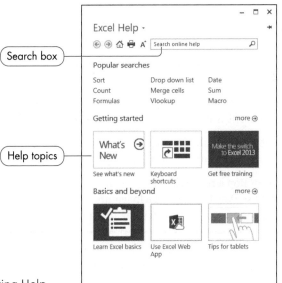

FIGURE 1.23 Getting Help

Labels: Search box, Help topics

Use Enhanced ScreenTips

For quick summary information on the purpose of a command button, place the mouse pointer over the button. An *Enhanced ScreenTip* displays, giving the purpose of the command, short descriptive text, and a keyboard shortcut if applicable. Some ScreenTips include a suggestion for pressing F1 for additional help. The Enhanced ScreenTip in Figure 1.24 provides context-sensitive assistance.

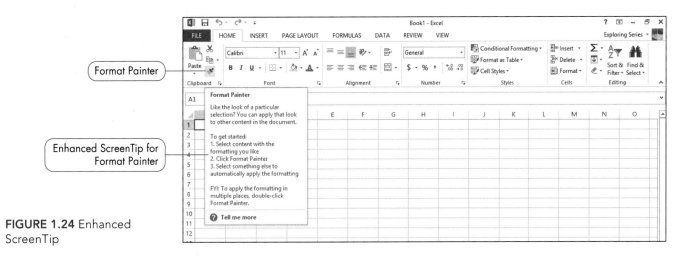

FIGURE 1.24 Enhanced ScreenTip

Labels: Format Painter, Enhanced ScreenTip for Format Painter

Get Help with Dialog Boxes

Getting help while you are working with a dialog box is easy. Simply click the Help button that displays as a question mark in the top-right corner of the dialog box (refer to Figure 1.19). The subsequent Help window will offer suggestions relevant to your task.

Quick Concepts ✓

1. How do you access the Backstage view, and what can you do there? *p. 23*

2. What is the purpose of the Quick Access Toolbar? Suppose you often engage in an activity such as printing. What steps would you take to add that command to the Quick Access Toolbar? *pp. 23–24*

3. The Ribbon is an important interface component of Office applications. What can you do with it? How is it organized? Is it always visible? *pp. 25–27*

4. Occasionally, the Ribbon is modified to include a contextual tab. Define a contextual tab and give an example of when a contextual tab is displayed. *p. 27*

5. After using Word to develop a research paper, you learn that the margins you used are incorrect. You plan to use Word's built-in Help feature to obtain information on how to change margins. Explain the process of obtaining help on the topic. *pp. 28–29*

Hands-On Exercises

Watch the Video for this Hands-On Exercise!

MyITLab®
HOE3 Training

3 Microsoft Office Software

As the administrative assistant for the Spotted Begonia Art Gallery, you need to get the staff started on a proposed schedule of gallery showings worksheet. Although you do not have access to information on all of the artists and their preferred media, you want to provide a suggested format for a worksheet to keep up with showings as they get booked. You will use Excel to begin design of the worksheet.

Skills covered: Open an Office Application, Get Enhanced ScreenTip Help, and Use the Zoom Slider • Get Help and Use the Backstage View • Change the View and Use Live Preview • Use the Quick Access Toolbar and Explore PowerPoint Views

STEP 1 ≫ OPEN AN OFFICE APPLICATION, GET ENHANCED SCREENTIP HELP, AND USE THE ZOOM SLIDER

Because you will use Excel to create the gallery showings worksheet, you will open the application. You will familiarize yourself with items on the Ribbon by getting Enhanced ScreenTip Help. For a better view of worksheet data, you will use the Zoom slider to magnify cell contents. Refer to Figure 1.25 as you complete Step 1.

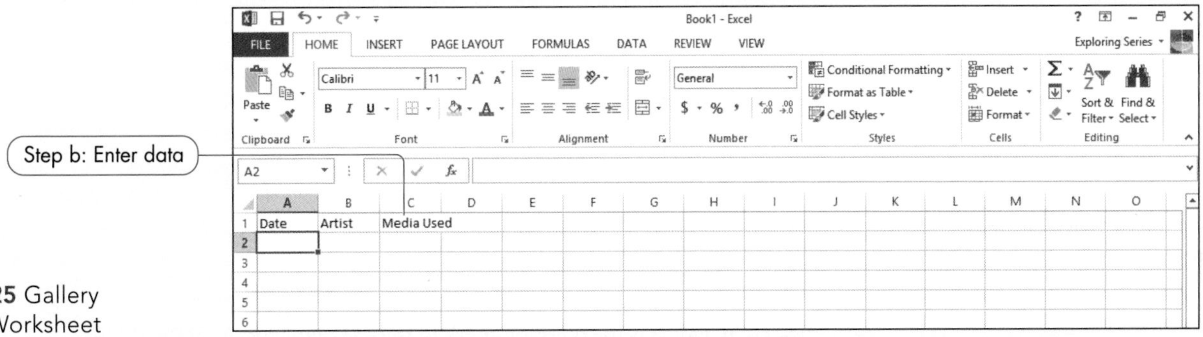

FIGURE 1.25 Gallery Showings Worksheet

a. Navigate to the Start screen. Scroll across the tiles, if necessary, and click **Excel 2013**. Click **Blank workbook** in the Excel 2013 window that displays.

You have opened Microsoft Excel because it is the program in which the gallery showings worksheet will be created.

b. Type **Date** in **cell A1**. As you type, the text appears in the current worksheet cell. Press **Tab** and type **Artist**. Press **Tab** and type **Media Used**. Press **Enter**. See Figure 1.25.

The worksheet that you create is only a beginning. Your staff will later suggest additional columns of data that can better summarize the upcoming gallery showings.

c. Hover the mouse pointer over any command on the Ribbon and note the Enhanced ScreenTip that displays, informing you of the purpose of the command. Explore other commands and identify their purpose.

d. Click the **PAGE LAYOUT tab**, click **Orientation** in the Page Setup group, and then select **Landscape**.

The PAGE LAYOUT tab is also found in Word, enabling you to change margins, orientation, and other page settings. Although you will not see much difference in the Excel screen display after you change the orientation to landscape, the worksheet will be oriented so that it is wider than it is tall when printed.

e. Drag the tab on the Zoom slider, located at the far right side of the status bar, to 190% to temporarily magnify the text. Take a full-screen snip of your screen and name it **f01h3Showings_LastFirst**.

f. Click the **VIEW tab** and click **100%** in the Zoom group to return the view to its original size.

When you change the zoom, you do not change the text size that will be printed or saved. The change merely magnifies or decreases the view while you work with the file.

g. Keep the workbook open for the next step in this exercise. Submit the file based on your instructor's directions.

STEP 2 ≫ GET HELP AND USE THE BACKSTAGE VIEW

Because you are not an Excel expert, you occasionally rely on the Help feature to provide information on tasks. You need assistance with saving a worksheet, previewing it before printing, and printing the worksheet. From what you learn, you will find that the Backstage view enables you to accomplish all of those tasks. Refer to Figure 1.26 as you complete Step 2.

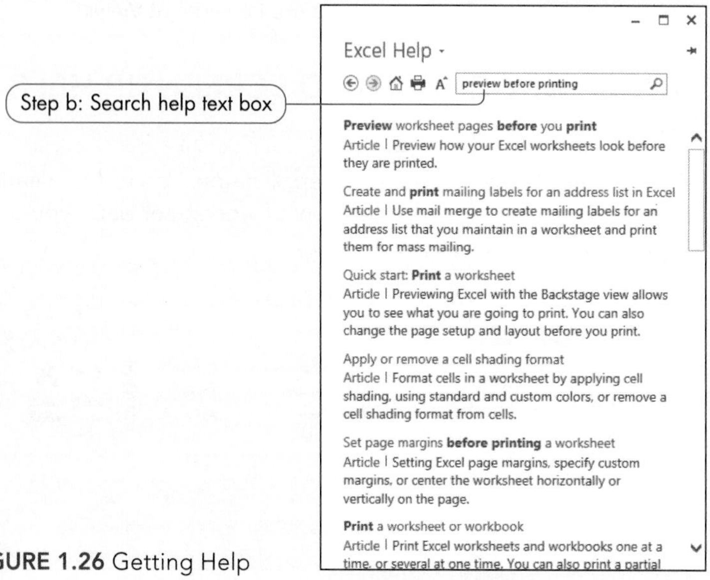

Step b: Search help text box

Excel Help ·

preview before printing

Preview worksheet pages **before** you **print**
Article | Preview how your Excel worksheets look before they are printed.

Create and **print** mailing labels for an address list in Excel
Article | Use mail merge to create mailing labels for an address list that you maintain in a worksheet and print them for mass mailing.

Quick start: **Print** a worksheet
Article | Previewing Excel with the Backstage view allows you to see what you are going to print. You can also change the page setup and layout before you print.

Apply or remove a cell shading format
Article | Format cells in a worksheet by applying cell shading, using standard and custom colors, or remove a cell shading format from cells.

Set page margins **before printing** a worksheet
Article | Setting Excel page margins, specify custom margins, or center the worksheet horizontally or vertically on the page.

Print a worksheet or workbook
Article | Print Excel worksheets and workbooks one at a time, or several at one time. You can also print a partial

FIGURE 1.26 Getting Help

a. Click **Help**, which is the question mark in the top-right corner of the Ribbon.

The Help dialog box displays.

> **TIP** Using Shortcuts to Access Help
>
> You can discover alternative ways to access Help. For example, the ScreenTip that displays as you point to the Help button suggests that you could press the F1 key.

b. Click in the **Search online help text box** at the top of the Help dialog box. Type **preview before printing** and press **Enter** (see Figure 1.26). In the Excel Help window, click **Preview worksheet pages before you print**. Read about how to preview a worksheet before printing. From what you read, can you identify a keyboard shortcut for previewing worksheets? Click the **Close (X) button**.

Before you print the worksheet, you would like to see how it will look when printed. You used Help to find information on previewing before printing.

c. Click the **FILE tab** and click **Print**.

Having used Office Help to learn how to preview before printing, you follow the directions to view the worksheet as it will look when printed. The preview of the worksheet displays on the right. To print the worksheet, you would click Print. However, you can first select any print options, such as the number of copies, from the Backstage view.

d. Click the **Back arrow** on the top left of the screen. Click **Help**. Excel Help presents several links related to the worksheet. Explore any that look interesting. Return to previous Help windows by clicking **Back** at the top-left side of the Help window. Close the Help dialog box.

e. Click the **HOME tab**. Point to *Bold* in the Font group.

You will find that, along with Excel, Word and PowerPoint also include formatting features in the Font group, such as Bold and Italic. When the Enhanced ScreenTip appears, identify the shortcut key combination that could be used to bold a selected text item. It is indicated as Ctrl plus the letter B.

f. Click the **Close (X) button** in the top-right corner of the Excel window to close both the workbook and the Excel program. When asked whether you want to save changes, click **Don't Save**.

You decide not to print or save the worksheet right now because you did not change anything during this step.

STEP 3 ≫ CHANGE THE VIEW AND USE LIVE PREVIEW

It is important that the documents you prepare or approve are error free and as attractive as possible. Before printing, you will change the view to get a better idea of how the document will look when printed. In addition, you will use Live Preview to experiment with font settings before actually applying them. Refer to Figure 1.27 as you complete Step 3.

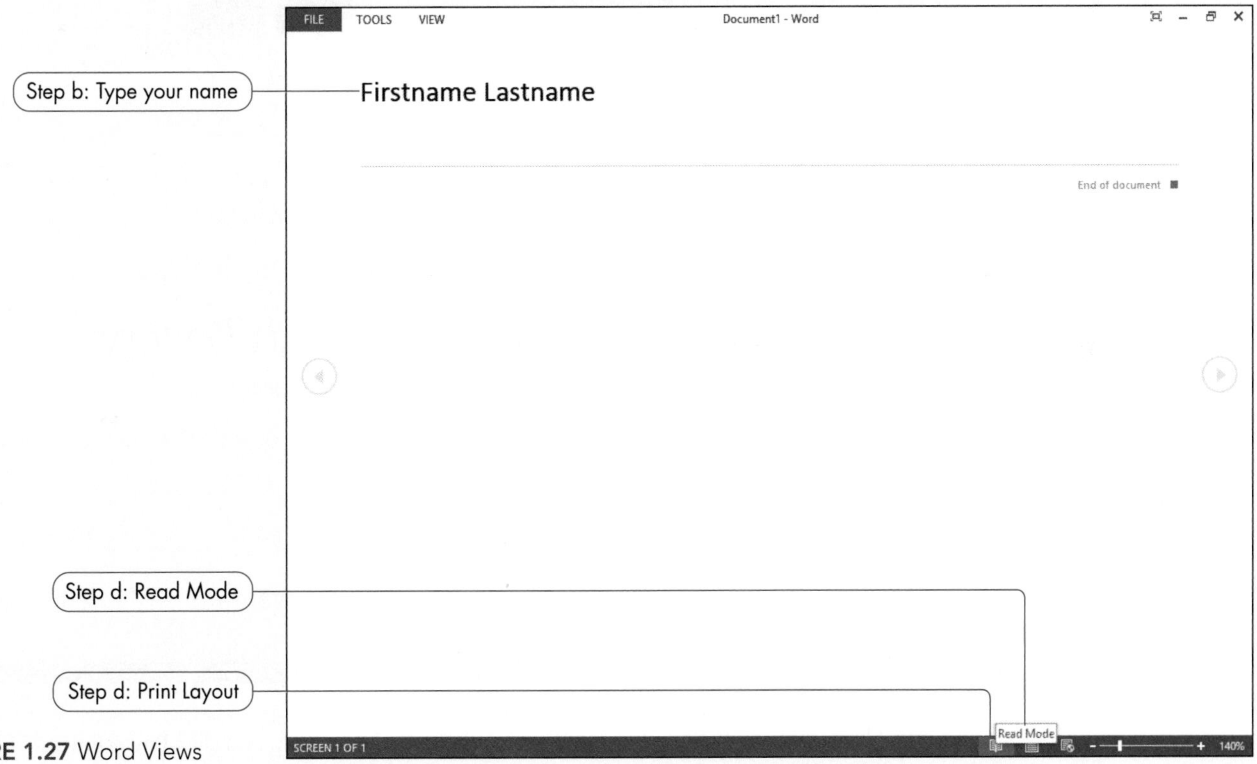

FIGURE 1.27 Word Views

a. Navigate to the Start screen. Scroll across the tiles, if necessary, and click **Word 2013**. Click **Blank document**.

You have opened a blank Word document. You plan to familiarize yourself with the program for later reference.

b. Type your first and last names and press **Enter**. Drag to select your name.

Your name should be highlighted, indicating that it is selected. You have selected your name because you want to experiment with using Word to change the way text looks.

c. Click the **Font Size arrow** in the Font group. If you need help locating Font Size, check for an Enhanced ScreenTip. Place the mouse pointer over any number in the list, but do not click. As you move to different font sizes, notice the size of your name changes. The feature you are using is called Live Preview. Click **16** in the list to change the font size of your name.

d. Click any white space to deselect your name. Click **Read Mode** in the *View shortcuts* group on the status bar to change the view (see Figure 1.27). Click **Print Layout** to return to the original view.

e. Save the file as **f01h3Read_LastFirst** and click the **Close (X) button** to close the Word program. Submit the file based on your instructor's directions.

STEP 4 ≫ USE THE QUICK ACCESS TOOLBAR AND EXPLORE POWERPOINT VIEWS

In your position as administrative assistant, you will be asked to review documents, presentations, and worksheets. It is important that you explore each application to familiarize yourself with operations and commonalities. Specifically, you know that the Quick Access Toolbar is common to all applications and that you can place commonly used commands there to streamline processes. Also, learning to change views will enable you to see the project in different ways for various purposes. Refer to Figure 1.28 as you complete Step 4.

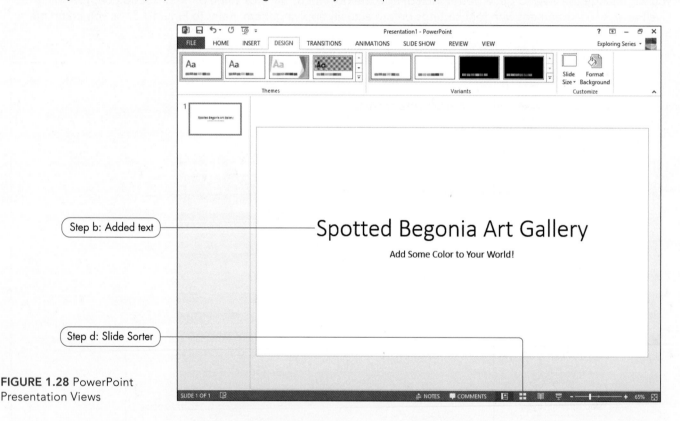

FIGURE 1.28 PowerPoint Presentation Views

a. Navigate to the Start screen. Scroll across the tiles, if necessary, and click **PowerPoint 2013**. Click **Blank Presentation**.

You have opened PowerPoint. A blank presentation displays.

b. Click **Click to add title** and type **Spotted Begonia Art Gallery**. Click in the bottom, subtitle box and type **Add Some Color to Your World!** Click the bottom-right corner of the slide to deselect the subtitle. Your PowerPoint presentation should look like that shown in Figure 1.28.

c. Click **Undo** two times on the Quick Access Toolbar.

The subtitle on the current slide is selected and removed because those are the most recent actions.

> **TROUBLESHOOTING:** If all of the subtitle text is not removed after two clicks, you should continue clicking until it is removed.

d. Click **Slide Sorter** in the *View shortcuts* group on the status bar.

The Slide Sorter view shows thumbnails of all slides in a presentation. Because this presentation has only one slide, you see a small version of one slide.

e. Move the mouse pointer to any button on the Quick Access Toolbar and hold it steady. See the tip giving the button name and the shortcut key combination, if any. Move to another button and see the description.

The Quick Access Toolbar has at least three buttons: Save, Undo, and Redo. In addition, a small arrow is included at the far-right side. If you hold the mouse pointer steady on the arrow, you will see the ScreenTip Customize Quick Access Toolbar.

f. Click **Customize Quick Access Toolbar** and select **New**. The New button is added to the toolbar. The New button enables you to quickly create a new presentation (also called a document).

g. Right-click **New** and click **Remove from Quick Access Toolbar**. The button is removed from the Quick Access Toolbar.

You can customize the Quick Access Toolbar by adding and removing items.

h. Click **Normal** in the *View shortcuts* group on the status bar.

The presentation returns to the original view in which the slide displays full size.

i. Click **Slide Show** in the *View shortcuts* group on the status bar.

The presentation is shown in Slide Show view, which is the way it will be presented to audiences.

j. Press **Esc** to end the presentation.

k. Save the presentation as **f01h3Views_LastFirst** and click the **Close (X) button** to close the PowerPoint program. Submit the presentation based on your instructor's directions.

The Backstage View Tasks

When you work with Microsoft Office files, you will often want to open previously saved files, create new ones, print items, and save and close files. You will also find it necessary to indicate options, or preferences, for settings. For example, you might want a spelling check to occur automatically, or you might prefer to initiate a spelling check only occasionally. Because those tasks are applicable to each software application within the Office 2013 suite, they are accomplished through a common area in the Office interface—the Backstage view. Open the Backstage view by clicking the File tab. Figure 1.29 shows the area that displays when you click the File tab in PowerPoint. The Backstage view also enables you to exit the application and to identify file information, such as the author or date created.

In this section, you will explore the Backstage view, learning to create, open, close, and print files.

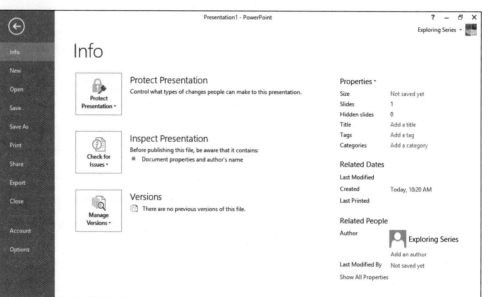

FIGURE 1.29 The Backstage View

Opening a File

When working with an Office application, you can begin by opening an existing file that has already been saved to a storage medium, or you can begin work on a new file. Both actions are available when you click the File tab. When you first open an application within the Office 2013 suite, you will need to decide which template you want to work with before you can begin working on a new file. You can also open a project that you previously saved to a disk.

Create a New File

After opening an Office application, such as Word, Excel, or PowerPoint, you will be presented with template choices. Click *Blank document* to start a new blank document. The word *document* is sometimes used generically to refer to any Office file, including a Word document, an Excel worksheet, or a PowerPoint presentation. Perhaps you are already working with a document in an Office application but want to create a new file. Simply click the File tab and click New. Click *Blank document* (or *Blank presentation* or *Blank workbook*, depending on the specific application).

Open a File Using the Open Dialog Box

STEP 1 ≫   You may choose to open a previously saved file, such as when you work with the data files for this book or when you want to access any previously created file. You will work with the Open dialog box, as shown in Figure 1.30. The Open dialog box displays after you click Open from the File tab. You will click Computer and the folder or drive where your document is stored.

If it is not listed under Recent Folders, you can browse for it. Using the Navigation Pane, you will make your way to the file to be opened. Double-click the file or click the file name once and click Open. Most likely, the file will be located within a folder that is appropriately named to make it easy to find related files. Obviously, if you are not well acquainted with the file's location and file name, the process of opening a file could become quite cumbersome. However, if you have created a well-designed system of folders, as you learned to do in the "Files and Folders" section of this chapter, you will know exactly where to find the file.

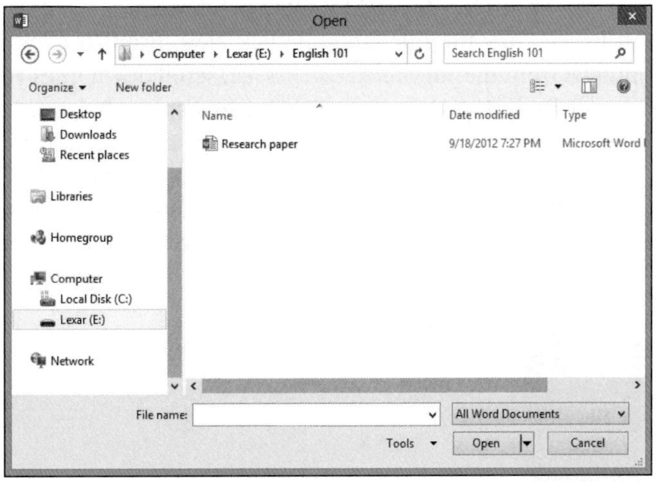

FIGURE 1.30 Open Dialog Box

Open a File Using the Recent Documents List

STEP 3 »
You will often work with a file, save it, and then continue the project at a later time. Office simplifies the task of reopening the file by providing a Recent Documents list with links to your most recently opened files (see Figure 1.31). To access the list, click the File tab, click Open, and then select Recent Documents. Click any file listed in the Recent Documents list to open that document. The list constantly changes to reflect only the most recently opened files, so if it has been quite some time since you worked with a particular file, you might have to work with the Open dialog box instead of the Recent Documents list.

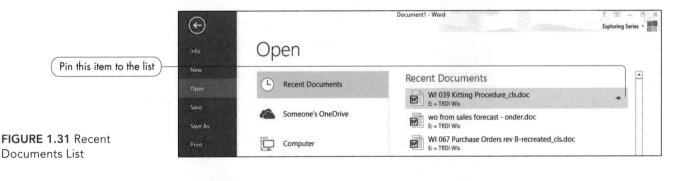

FIGURE 1.31 Recent Documents List

Pin this item to the list

TIP Keeping Files on the Recent Documents List

The Recent Documents list displays a limited list of only the most recently opened files. You might, however, want to keep a particular file in the list regardless of how recently it was opened. In Figure 1.31, note the *Pin this item to the list* icon displays to the right of each file. Click the icon to pin the file to the list. At that point, you will always have access to the file by clicking the File tab and selecting the file from the Recent Documents list. The pushpin of the "permanent" file will change direction so that it appears to be inserted, indicating that it is a pinned item. If later you want to remove the file from the list, click the inserted pushpin, changing its direction and allowing the file to be bumped off the list when other, more recently opened, files take its place.

Open a File from the Templates List

You do not need to create a new file if you can access a predesigned file that meets your needs or one that you can modify fairly quickly to complete your project. Office provides templates, making them available when you click the File tab and New (see Figure 1.32). The Templates list is comprised of template groups available within the current Office installation on your computer. The Search box can be used to locate other templates that are available from Office.com. When you click one of the Suggested searches, you are presented with additional choices.

For example, you might want to prepare a home budget. After opening a blank worksheet in Excel, click the File tab and click New. From the template categories, you could click Budget from the *Suggested searches* list, scroll down until you find the right template, such as Family Budget, and then click Create to display the associated worksheet (or simply double-click Family Budget). If a Help window displays along with the worksheet template, click to close it or explore Help to learn more about the template. If you know only a little bit about Excel, you could then make a few changes so that the worksheet would accurately represent your family's financial situation. The budget would be prepared much more quickly than if you began the project with a blank workbook, designing it yourself.

Templates available from Office.com

Templates available in a typical Office installation

FIGURE 1.32 Working with Templates

Printing a File

There will be occasions when you will want to print an Office project. Before printing, you should preview the file to get an idea of how it will look when printed. That way, if there are obvious problems with the page setup, you can correct them before wasting paper on something that is not correct. When you are ready to print, you can select from various print options, including the number of copies and the specific pages to print. If you know that the page setup is correct and that there are no unique print settings to select, you can simply print the project without adjusting any print settings.

STEP 2 It is a good idea to take a look at how your document will appear before you print it. The Print Preview feature of Office enables you to do just that. In the Print pane, you will see all items, including any headers, footers, graphics, and special formatting. To view a project before printing, click the File tab and click Print. The subsequent Backstage view shows the file preview on the right, with print settings located in the center of the Backstage screen. Figure 1.33 shows a typical Backstage Print view.

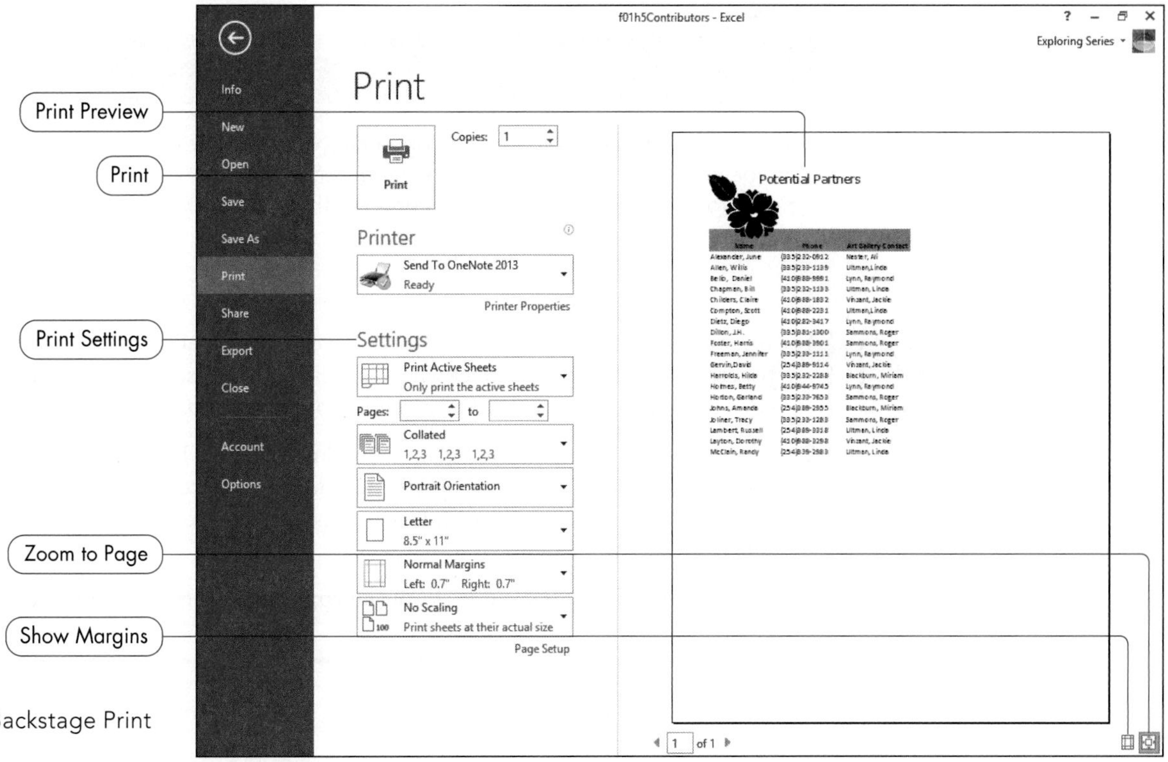

FIGURE 1.33 Backstage Print View

To show the margins of the document, click Show Margins (see Figure 1.33). To increase the size of the file preview, click *Zoom to Page* (see Figure 1.33). Both are found on the bottom-right corner of the preview. Remember that increasing the font size by adjusting the zoom applies to the current display only; it does not actually increase the font size when the document is printed or saved. To return the preview to its original view, click *Zoom to Page* once more.

Other options in the Backstage Print view vary depending on the application in which you are working. Regardless of the Office application, you will be able to access Settings options from the Backstage view, including page orientation (landscape or portrait), margins, and paper size. You will find a more detailed explanation of those settings in the "Page Layout Tab Tasks" section later in this chapter. To print a file, click Print (see Figure 1.33).

The Backstage Print view shown in Figure 1.33 is very similar across all Office applications. However, you will find slight variations specific to each application. For example, PowerPoint's Backstage Print view includes options for printing slides and handouts in various configurations and colors, whereas Excel's focuses on worksheet selections and Word's includes document options. Regardless of software, the manner of working with the Backstage view print options remains consistent.

Closing a File and Application

Although you can have several documents open at one time, limiting the number of open files is a good idea. Office applications have no problem keeping up with multiple open files, but you can easily become overwhelmed with them. When you are done with an open project, you will need to close it.

You can easily close any files that you no longer need. With the desired file on the screen, click the FILE tab and click the Close (X) button. Respond to any prompt that might display suggesting that you save the file. The application remains open, but the selected file is closed. To close the application, click the Close (X) button in the top-right corner.

TIP | Closing an Application

When you close an application, all open files within the application are also closed. You will be prompted to save any files before they are closed. A quick way to close an application is to click the X in the top-right corner of the application window.

Quick
Concepts ✓

1. You want to continue to work with a PowerPoint presentation that you worked with yesterday, but cannot remember where you saved the presentation on your hard drive. How can you open a file that you recently worked with? *p. 37*

2. As part of your job search, you plan to develop a resume. However, you find it difficult to determine the right style for your resume, and wish you could begin with a predesigned document that you could modify. Is that possible with Word? If so, what steps would you take to locate a predesigned resume? *p. 38*

3. Closing a file is not the same as closing an application, such as closing Excel. What is the difference? *p. 39*

4 The Backstage View Tasks

Projects related to the Spotted Begonia Art Gallery's functions have begun to come in for your review and approval. You have received an informational flyer to be distributed to schools and supporting organizations around the city. It contains a new logo along with descriptive text. Another task on your agenda is to keep the project moving according to schedule. You will identify a calendar template to print and distribute. You will explore printing options, and you will save the flyer and the calendar as directed by your instructor.

Skills covered: Open and Save a File • Preview and Print a File • Open a File from the Recent Documents List and Open a Template

STEP 1 ≫ OPEN AND SAVE A FILE

You have asked your staff to develop a flyer that can be used to promote the Spotted Begonia Art Gallery. You will open a Word document that may be used for the flyer, and you will save the document to a disk drive. Refer to Figure 1.34 as you complete Step 1.

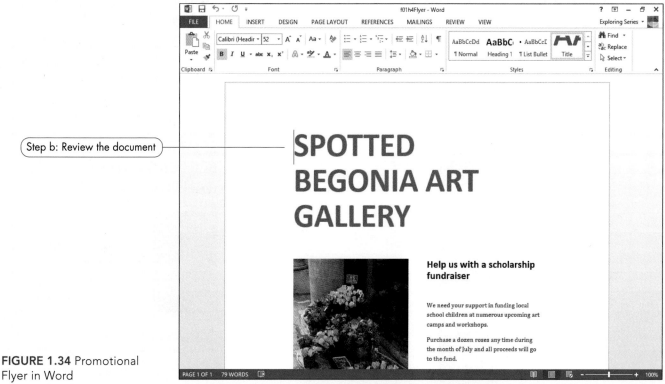

FIGURE 1.34 Promotional Flyer in Word

a. Navigate to the Start screen. Scroll across the tiles, if necessary, and click **Word 2013**. Click **Open Other Documents** at the bottom-left corner of the Word 2013 window.

You have opened Microsoft Word because it is the program in which the promotional flyer is saved.

b. Click **Computer** and click **Browse**. Navigate to the location of your student files. Double-click *f01h4Flyer* to open the file shown in Figure 1.34. Familiarize yourself with the document. Then, if necessary, click **Read Mode** in the *View shortcuts* group on the Status bar to change to that view. Read through the document.

The graphic and the flyer are submitted for your approval. A paragraph next to the graphic will serve as the launching point for an information blitz and the beginning of the fundraising drive.

Read Mode displays the document. If the document is large enough, multiple screens may display. You can use the arrows found on the middle edges of the document to navigate and view the entire document.

c. Click **Print Layout** on the Status bar to change to that view. Click the **FILE tab** and click **Save As**.

You choose the Save As command because you know that it enables you to indicate the location to which the file should be saved, as well as the file name.

d. Click **Browse**, navigate to the drive where you save your files, and then double-click the **Artists folder** you created earlier. Double-click **Office Records**, click in the **File name box**, type **f01h4Flyer_LastFirst**, and then click **Save**.

STEP 2 ➤➤ PREVIEW AND PRINT A FILE

You approve of the flyer, so you will print the document for future reference. You will first preview the document as it will appear when printed. Then you will print the document. Refer to Figure 1.35 as you complete Step 2.

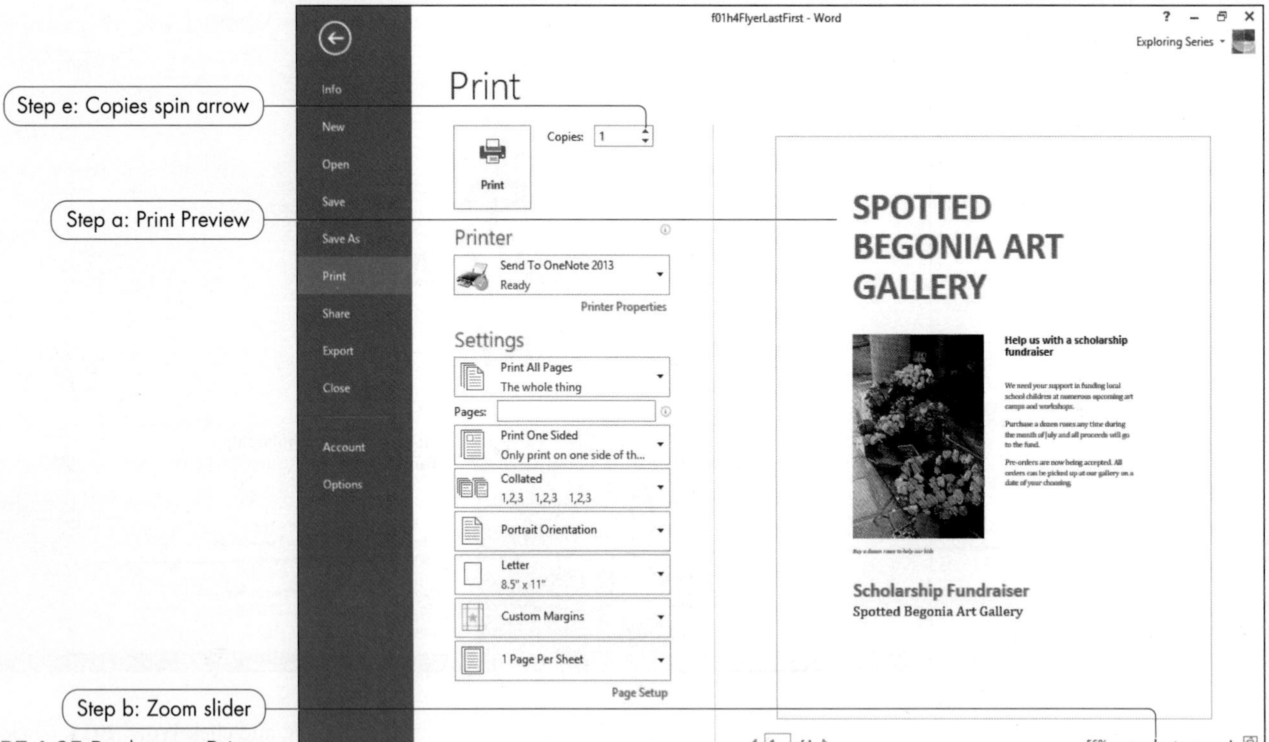

Step e: Copies spin arrow

Step a: Print Preview

Step b: Zoom slider

FIGURE 1.35 Backstage Print

a. Click the **FILE tab** and click **Print**.

Figure 1.35 shows the flyer preview. It is always a good idea to check the way a file will look when printed before actually printing it.

b. Drag the **Zoom slider** to increase the document view. Click **Zoom to Page** to return to the original size.

c. Click **Portrait Orientation** in the Print settings area in the center of the screen. Click **Landscape Orientation** to show the flyer in a wider and shorter view.

d. Click **Landscape Orientation** and click **Portrait Orientation** to return to the original view.

You decide that the flyer is more attractive in portrait orientation, so you return to that setting.

e. Click the **Copies spin arrow** repeatedly to increase the copies to **5**.

You will need to print five copies of the flyer to distribute to the office assistants for their review.

f. Click **Close** on the left side of the screen. When asked, click **Don't Save** so that changes to the file are not saved. Keep Word open for the next step.

STEP 3 ≫ OPEN A FILE FROM THE RECENT DOCUMENTS LIST AND OPEN A TEMPLATE

A large part of your responsibility is proofreading Spotted Begonia Art Gallery material. You will correct an error by adding a phone number in the promotional flyer. You must also keep the staff on task, so you will identify a calendar template on which to list tasks and deadlines. Refer to Figure 1.36 as you complete Step 3.

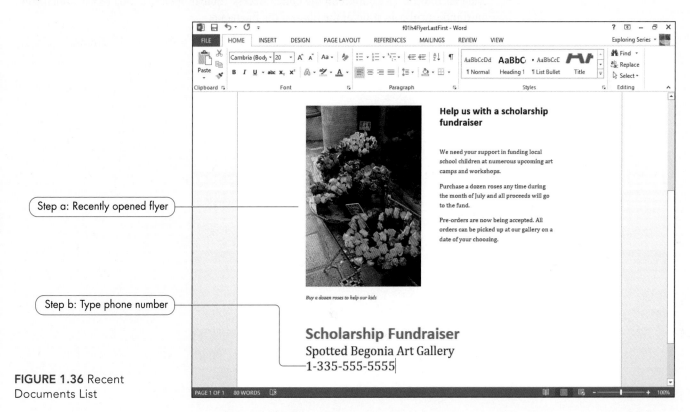

Step a: Recently opened flyer

Step b: Type phone number

FIGURE 1.36 Recent Documents List

a. Click the **FILE tab**, click **Recent Documents** if necessary, and then click **f01h4Flyer_LastFirst** in the **Recent Documents list**.

> **TROUBLESHOOTING:** If the file opens in Read Mode, use the status bar to change to the Print Layout view.

b. Press **Ctrl+End** to move the insertion point to the end of the document and press **Enter**. Type **1-335-555-5555**.

Figure 1.36 shows the phone number correction.

c. Click **Save** on the Quick Access Toolbar, click the **FILE tab**, and then click **Close**.

When you click Save on the Quick Access Toolbar, the document is saved in the same location with the same file name as was indicated in the previous save.

d. Click the **FILE tab** and click **New**. Click **Calendar** from the list of the *Suggested searches* category just beneath the *Search online templates* box.

Office.com provides a wide range of calendar choices. You will select one that is appealing and that will help you keep projects on track.

e. Click a calendar of your choice from the gallery and click **Create**. Respond to and close any windows that may open.

The calendar that you selected opens in Word.

TROUBLESHOOTING: It is possible to select a template that is not certified by Microsoft. In that case, you might have to confirm your acceptance of settings before you click Download.

---

f. Click **Save** on the Quick Access Toolbar. If necessary, navigate to your Office Records subfolder (a subfolder of Artists) on the drive where you are saving your student files. Save the document as **f01h4Calendar_LastFirst**. Because this is the first time to save the calendar file, the Save button on the Quick Access Toolbar opens a dialog box in which you must indicate the location of the file and the file name.

g. Click **Save** and exit Word. Submit your files based on your instructor's directions.

Home Tab Tasks

You will find that you will repeat some tasks often, whether in Word, Excel, or PowerPoint. You will frequently want to change the format of numbers or words, selecting a different *font* or changing font size or color. A font is a complete set of characters, both upper- and lowercase letters, numbers, punctuation marks, and special symbols, with the same design including size, spacing, and shape. You might also need to change the alignment of text or worksheet cells. Undoubtedly, you will find a reason to copy or cut items and paste them elsewhere in the document, presentation, or worksheet. And you might want to modify file contents by finding and replacing text. All of those tasks, and more, are found on the Home tab of the Ribbon in Word, Excel, and PowerPoint. The Access interface is unique, sharing little with other Office applications, so this section will not address Access.

In this section, you will explore the Home tab, learning to format text, copy and paste items, and find and replace words or phrases. Figure 1.37 shows Home tab groups and tasks in the various applications. Note the differences and similarities between the groups.

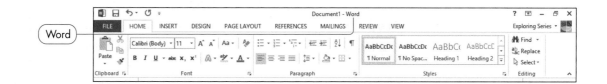

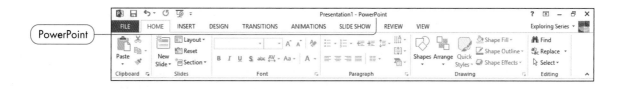

FIGURE 1.37 Home Tab in Word, PowerPoint, and Excel

Selecting and Editing Text

After creating a document, worksheet, or presentation, you will probably want to make some changes. You might prefer to center a title, or maybe you think that certain budget worksheet totals should be formatted as currency. You can change the font so that typed characters are larger or in a different style. You might even want to underline text to add emphasis. In all Office applications, the Home tab provides tools for selecting and editing text. You can also use the Mini toolbar for making quick changes to selected text.

Select Text to Edit

Before making any changes to existing text or numbers, you must first select the characters. A general rule that you should commit to memory is "Select, then do." A foolproof way to select text or numbers is to place the mouse pointer before the first character of the text you want to select, and then drag to highlight the intended selection. Before you drag, be sure that the mouse pointer takes on the shape of the letter *I*, called the *I-bar*. Although other methods for selecting exist, if you remember only one way, it should be the click-and-drag method. If your attempted selection falls short of highlighting the intended area, or perhaps highlights too much, simply click outside the selection and try again.

Sometimes it can be difficult to precisely select a small amount of text, such as a single character or a single word. Other times, the task can be overwhelming, such as when selecting an entire 550-page document. Shortcut methods for making selections in Word and PowerPoint are shown in Table 1.3. When working with Excel, you will more often need to select multiple cells. Simply drag the intended selection, usually when the mouse pointer displays as a large white plus sign. The shortcuts shown in Table 1.3 are primarily applicable to Word and PowerPoint.

TABLE 1.3 Shortcut Selection in Word and PowerPoint

Item Selected	Action
One word	Double-click the word.
One line of text	Place the mouse pointer at the left of the line, in the margin area. When the mouse changes to a right-pointing arrow, click to select the line.
One sentence	Press and hold Ctrl while you click in the sentence to select.
One paragraph	Triple-click in the paragraph.
One character to the left of the insertion point	Press and hold Shift while you press the left arrow on the keyboard.
One character to the right of the insertion point	Press and hold Shift while you press the right arrow on the keyboard.
Entire document	Press and hold Ctrl while you press A on the keyboard.

After having selected a string of characters, such as a number, word, sentence, or document, you can do more than simply format the selection. Suppose you have selected a word. If you begin to type another word, the newly typed word will immediately replace the selected word. With an item selected, you can press Delete to remove the selection. You will learn later in this chapter that you can also find, replace, copy, move, and paste selected text.

Use the Mini Toolbar

STEP 3 ❯❯

You have learned that you can always use commands on the Ribbon to change selected text within a document, worksheet, or presentation. All it takes is locating the desired command on the Home tab and clicking to select it. Although using the Home tab to perform commands is simple enough, an item called the *Mini toolbar* provides an even faster way to accomplish some of the same formatting changes. When you select any amount of text within a worksheet, document, or presentation, you can move the mouse pointer only slightly within the selection to display the Mini toolbar (see Figure 1.38). The Mini toolbar provides access to the most common formatting selections, such as adding bold or italic, or changing font type or color. Unlike the Quick Access Toolbar, the Mini toolbar is not customizable, which means that you cannot add or remove options from the toolbar.

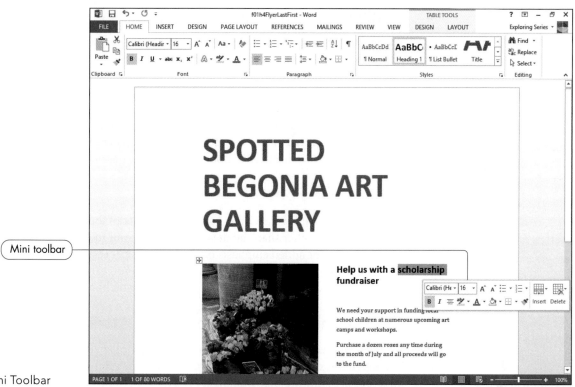

FIGURE 1.38 Mini Toolbar

The Mini toolbar will display only when text is selected. The closer the mouse pointer is to the Mini toolbar, the darker the toolbar becomes. As you move the mouse pointer away from the Mini toolbar, it becomes almost transparent. Make any selections from the Mini toolbar by clicking the corresponding button. To temporarily remove the Mini toolbar from view, press Esc.

If you want to permanently disable the Mini toolbar so that it does not display in any open file when text is selected, click the FILE tab and click Options. As shown in Figure 1.39, click General, if necessary. Deselect the *Show Mini Toolbar on selection* setting by clicking the check box to the left of the setting and clicking OK.

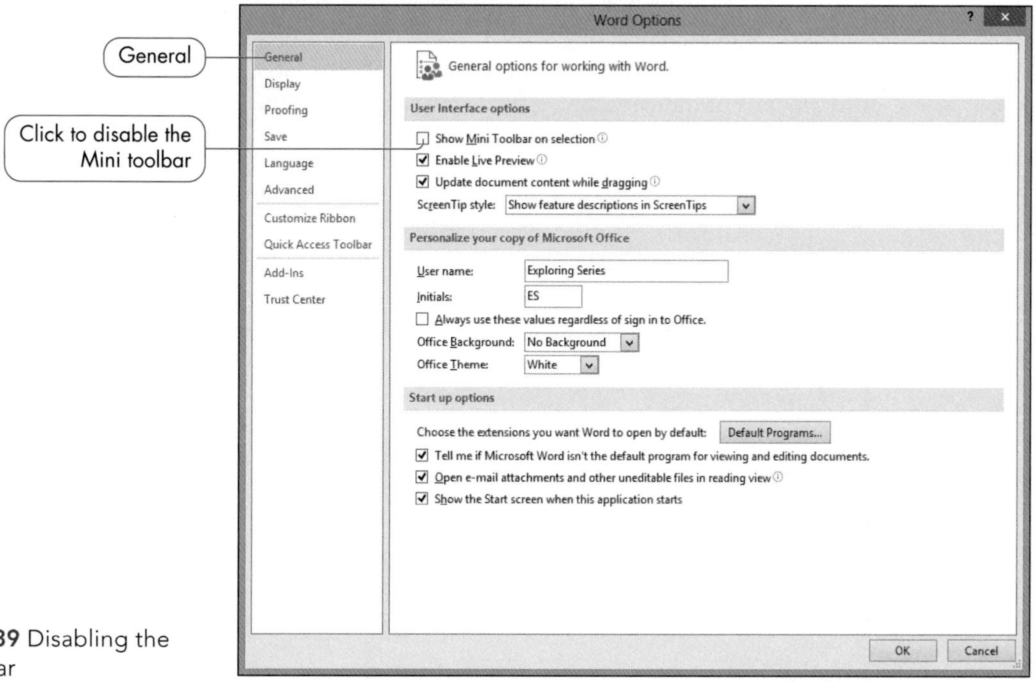

FIGURE 1.39 Disabling the Mini Toolbar

Apply Font Attributes

The way characters appear onscreen, including qualities such as size, spacing, and shape, is determined by the font. Each Office application has a default font, which is the font that will be in effect unless you change it. Other font attributes include boldfacing, italicizing, and font color, all of which can be applied to selected text. Some formatting changes, such as Bold and Italic, are called *toggle* commands. They act somewhat like light switches that you can turn on and off. For example, after having selected a word that you want to add bold to, click Bold in the Font group of the Home tab to turn the setting "on." If, at a later time, you want to remove bold from the word, select it again and click Bold. This time, the button turns "off" the bold formatting.

Change the Font

All applications within the Office suite provide a set of fonts from which you can choose. If you prefer a font other than the default, or if you want to apply a different font to a section of your project for added emphasis or interest, you can easily make the change by selecting a font from within the Font group on the Home tab. You can also change the font by selecting from the Mini toolbar, although that works only if you have first selected text.

Change the Font Size, Color, and Attributes

STEP 2》 At times, you will want to make the font size larger or smaller, change the font color, underline selected text, or apply other font attributes. For example, if you are creating a handout for a special event, you may want to apply a different font to emphasize key information such as dates and times. Because such changes are commonplace, Office places those formatting commands in many convenient places within each Office application.

You can find the most common formatting commands in the Font group on the Home tab. As noted earlier, Word, Excel, and PowerPoint all share very similar Font groups that provide access to tasks related to changing the character font (refer to Figure 1.37). Remember that you can place the mouse pointer over any command icon to view a summary of the icon's purpose, so although the icons might at first appear cryptic, you can use the mouse pointer to quickly determine the purpose and applicability to your desired text change. You can also find a subset of those commands plus a few additional choices on the Mini toolbar.

If the font change that you plan to make is not included as a choice on either the Home tab or the Mini toolbar, you can probably find what you are looking for in the Font dialog box. Click the Dialog Box Launcher in the bottom-right corner of the Font group. Figure 1.40 shows a sample Font dialog box. Because the Font dialog box provides many formatting choices in one window, you can make several changes at once. Depending on the application, the contents of the Font dialog box vary slightly, but the purpose is consistent—providing access to choices related to modifying characters.

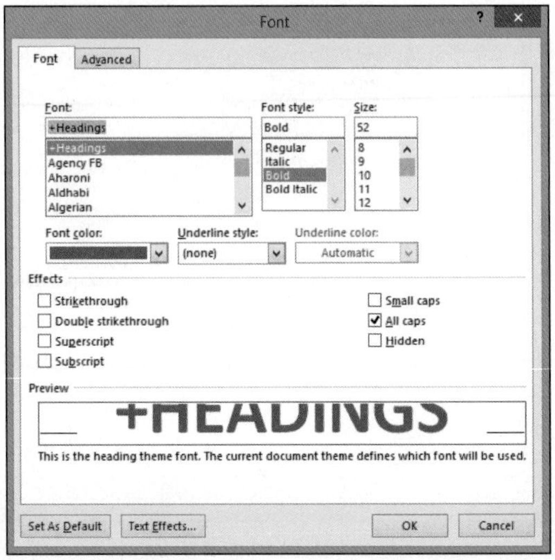

FIGURE 1.40 Font Dialog Box

Using the Clipboard Group Commands

On occasion, you will want to move or copy a selection from one area to another. Suppose that you have included text on a PowerPoint slide that you believe would be more appropriate on a different slide. Or perhaps an Excel formula should be copied from one cell to another because both cells should be totaled in the same manner. You can easily move the slide text or copy the Excel formula by using options found in the Clipboard group on the Home tab. The Office *Clipboard* is an area of memory reserved to temporarily hold selections that have been *cut* or *copied* and allows you to paste the selections. To cut means to remove a selection from the original location and place it in the Office Clipboard. To copy means to duplicate a selection from the original location and place a copy in the Office Clipboard. Although the Clipboard can hold up to 24 items at one time, the usual procedure is to *paste* the cut or copied selection to its final destination fairly quickly. To paste means to place a cut or copied selection into another location. When the computer is shut down or loses power, the contents of the Clipboard are erased, so it is important to finalize the paste procedure during the current session.

The Clipboard group enables you not only to copy and cut text and objects but also to copy formatting. Perhaps you have applied a font style to a major heading of a report and you realize that the same formatting should be applied to other headings. Especially if the heading includes multiple formatting features, you will save a great deal of time by copying the entire set of formatting options to the other headings. In so doing, you will ensure the consistency of formatting for all headings because they will appear exactly alike. Using the Clipboard group's *Format Painter*, you can quickly and easily copy all formatting from one area to another in Word, PowerPoint, and Excel.

In Office, you can usually accomplish the same task in several ways. Although the Ribbon provides ample access to formatting and Clipboard commands (such as Format Painter, Cut, Copy, and Paste), you might find it convenient to access the same commands on a *shortcut menu*. Right-click a selected item or text to open a shortcut menu such as the one shown in Figure 1.41. A shortcut menu is also called a *context menu* because the contents of the menu vary depending on the location at which you right-clicked.

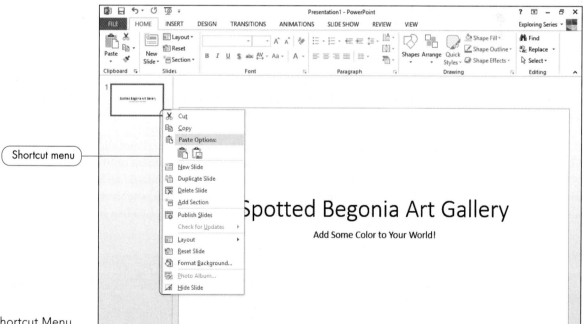

FIGURE 1.41 Shortcut Menu

Copy Formats with the Format Painter

STEP 3 ›› As described earlier, the Format Painter makes it easy to copy formatting features from one selection to another. You will find the Format Painter command conveniently located in the Clipboard group of the Home tab (see Figure 1.42). To copy a format, you must first select the text containing the desired format. If you want to copy the format to only one other selection, *single-click* Format Painter. If, however, you plan to copy the same format to multiple areas, *double-click* Format Painter. As you move the mouse pointer, you will find that it has the appearance of a paintbrush with an attached I-bar. Select the area to which the copied format should be applied. If you single-clicked Format Painter to copy the format to one other selection, Format Painter turns off once the formatting has been applied. If you double-clicked Format Painter to copy the format to multiple locations, continue selecting text in various locations to apply the format. Then, to turn off Format Painter, click Format Painter again or press Esc.

FIGURE 1.42 Clipboard Group Commands

Move and Copy Text

Undoubtedly, there will be times when you want to revise a project by moving or copying items such as Word text, PowerPoint slides, or Excel cell contents, either within the current application or among others. For example, a section of a Word document might be appropriate as PowerPoint slide content. To keep from retyping the Word text in the PowerPoint slide, you can copy the text and paste it in a blank PowerPoint slide. At other times, it might be necessary to move a paragraph within a Word document or to copy selected cells from one Excel worksheet to another. The Clipboard group contains a Cut command with which you can select text to move (see Figure 1.42). You can also use the Copy command to duplicate items and the Paste command to place cut or copied items in a final location (see Figure 1.42).

TIP | Using Ribbon Commands with Arrows

Some commands, such as Paste in the Clipboard group, contain two parts: the main command and an arrow. The arrow may be below or to the right of the command, depending on the command, window size, or screen resolution. Instructions in the *Exploring* series use the command name to instruct you to click the main command to perform the default action (e.g., Click Paste). Instructions include the word *arrow* when you need to select the arrow to access an additional option (e.g., Click the Paste arrow).

The first step in moving or copying text is to select the text. Then do the following:

1. Click the appropriate icon in the Clipboard group either to cut or copy the selection. Remember that cut or copied text is actually placed in the Clipboard, remaining there even after you paste it to another location. It is important to note that you can paste the same item multiple times, because it will remain in the Clipboard until you power down your computer or until the Clipboard exceeds 24 items.

2. Click the location where you want the cut or copied text to be placed. The location can be in the current file or in another open file within any Office application.

3. Click Paste in the Clipboard group on the HOME tab.

In addition to using the Clipboard group icons, you can also cut, copy, and paste in any of the ways listed in Table 1.4.

TABLE 1.4	Cut, Copy, and Paste Options
Command	**Actions**
Cut	• Click Cut in Clipboard group. • Right-click selection and select Cut. • Press Ctrl+X.
Copy	• Click Copy in Clipboard group. • Right-click selection and select Copy. • Press Ctrl+C.
Paste	• Click in destination location and select Paste in Clipboard group. • Right-click in destination location and select Paste. • Click in destination location and press Ctrl+V. • Click the Clipboard Dialog Box Launcher to open the Clipboard task pane. Click in destination location. With the Clipboard task pane open, click the arrow beside the intended selection and select Paste.

Use the Office Clipboard

When you cut or copy selections, they are placed in the Office Clipboard. Regardless of which Office application you are using, you can view the Clipboard by clicking the Clipboard Dialog Box Launcher, as shown in Figure 1.43.

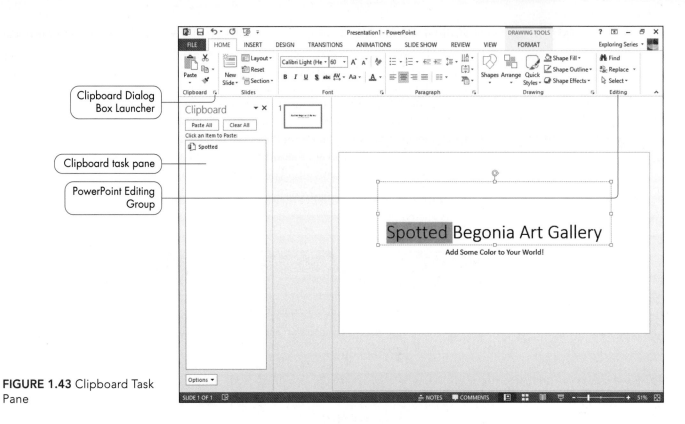

FIGURE 1.43 Clipboard Task Pane

Labels pointing to the figure:
- Clipboard Dialog Box Launcher
- Clipboard task pane
- PowerPoint Editing Group

Unless you specify otherwise when beginning a paste operation, the most recently added Clipboard item is pasted. You can, however, select an item from the Clipboard task pane to paste. Similarly, you can delete items from the Clipboard by making a selection in the Clipboard task pane. You can remove all items from the Clipboard by clicking Clear All. The Options button in the Clipboard task pane enables you to control when and where the Clipboard is displayed. Close the Clipboard task pane by clicking the Close (X) button in the top-right corner of the task pane or by clicking the arrow in the title bar of the Clipboard task pane and selecting Close.

Using the Editing Group Commands

The process of finding and replacing text is easily accomplished through options in the Editing group of the Home tab. The Editing group also enables you to select all contents of a project document, all text with similar formatting, or specific objects, such as pictures or charts. The Editing group is found at the far-right side of the Home tab in Excel, Word, and PowerPoint.

The Excel Editing group is unique in that it also includes options for sorting, filtering, and clearing cell contents; filling cells; and summarizing numeric data. Because those commands are relevant only to Excel, this chapter will not address them specifically.

Find and Replace Text

STEP 4 ▶▶ Especially if you are working with a lengthy project, manually seeking a specific word or phrase can be time-consuming. Office enables you not only to *find* each occurrence of a series of characters, but also to *replace* what it finds with another series. You will at times find it necessary to locate each occurrence of a text item so that you can replace it with another or so that you can delete, move, or copy it. If you have consistently misspelled a person's name throughout a document, you can find the misspelling and replace it with the correct spelling in a matter of a few seconds, no matter how many times the misspelling occurs in the document. To begin the process of finding and replacing a specific item:

1. Click Replace in the Editing group on the HOME tab of Word or PowerPoint.
2. Or click Find & Select in the Editing group on the HOME tab of Excel. Then click Replace. The dialog box that displays enables you to indicate the word or phrase to find and replace.

The Advanced Find feature is one that you will use often as you work with documents in Word. It is beneficial to find each occurrence of a word you are searching for. But it is also very helpful to see all the occurrences of the word at once. Click Reading Highlight in the *Find and Replace* dialog box and select Highlight All to display each word highlighted, as shown in Figure 1.44. Click Reading Highlight again and select Clear Highlighting to remove the illumination.

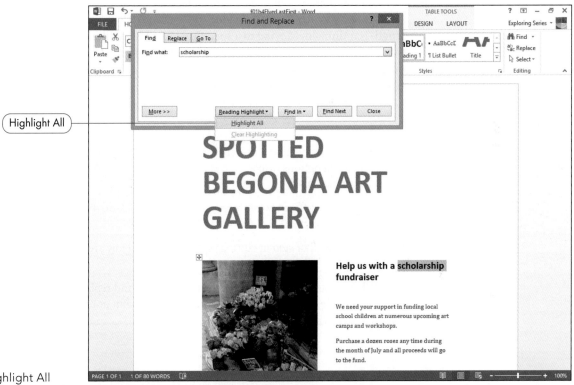

FIGURE 1.44 Highlight All

> ## TIP Using a Shortcut to Find Items
>
> Ctrl+F is a shortcut used to find items in a Word, Excel, or PowerPoint file. When you press Ctrl+F, the *Find and Replace* dialog box displays in Excel and PowerPoint. Pressing Ctrl+F in Word displays a feature—the Navigation Pane—at the left side of a Word document. When you type a search term in the Search Document area, Word finds and highlights all occurrences of the search term. The Navigation Pane also makes it easy to move to sections of a document based on levels of headings.

To find and replace selected text, type the text to locate in the *Find what* box and the replacement text in the *Replace with* box. You can narrow the search to require matching case or find whole words only. If you want to replace all occurrences of the text, click Replace All. If you want to replace only some occurrences, click Find Next repeatedly until you reach the occurrence that you want to replace. At that point, click Replace. When you are finished, click the Close button (or click Cancel).

Use Advanced Find and Replace Features

The *Find and Replace* feature enables you not only to find and replace text, but also to restrict and alter the format of the text at the same time. To establish the format criteria associated with either the *Find or Replace* portion of the operation:

1. Click the More button to expand the dialog box options. Click Format in the bottom-left corner of the dialog box.
2. Add formatting characteristics from the Font dialog box or Paragraph dialog box (as well as many other formatting features).

In addition to applying special formatting parameters on a *Find and Replace* operation, you can specify that you want to find or replace special characters. Click Special at the bottom of the *Find and Replace* dialog box to view the punctuation characters from which you can choose. For example, you might want to look for all instances in a document where an exclamation point is being used and replace it with a period.

An Excel worksheet can include more than 1,000,000 rows of data. A Word document's length is unlimited. Moving to a specific point in large files created in either of those applications can be a challenge. That task is simplified by the Go To option, found in the Editing group as an option of the Find command in Word (or under Find & Select in Excel). Click Go To and enter the page number (or other item, such as section, comment, bookmark, or footnote) in Word or the specific Excel cell. Click Go To in Word (or OK in Excel).

Quick
Concepts ✓

1. After selecting text in a presentation or document, you see a small transparent bar with formatting options displayed just above the selection. What is the bar called and what is its purpose? *p. 46*

2. What is the difference between using a single-click on the Format Painter and using a double-click? *p. 50*

3. What is the first step in cutting or copying text? How are cutting and copying related to the concept of the Clipboard? *p. 51*

4. What feature can you use to very quickly locate and replace text in a document? Provide an example of when you might want to find text but not replace it. *p. 52*

Hands-On Exercises

5 Home Tab Tasks

You have created a list of potential contributors to the Spotted Begonia Art Gallery. You have used Excel to record that list in worksheet format. Now you will review the worksheet and format its appearance to make it more attractive. You will also modify a promotional flyer. In working with those projects, you will put into practice the formatting, copying, moving, and editing information from the preceding section.

Skills covered: Move, Copy, and Paste Text • Select Text, Apply Font Attributes, and Use the Mini Toolbar • Use Format Painter and Work with the Mini Toolbar • Use the Font Dialog Box and Find and Replace Text

---

STEP 1 ≫ MOVE, COPY, AND PASTE TEXT

Each contributor to the Spotted Begonia Art Gallery is assigned a contact person. You manage the worksheet that keeps track of those assignments, but the assignments sometimes change. You will copy and paste some worksheet selections to keep from having to retype data. You will also reposition a clip art image to improve the worksheet's appearance. Refer to Figure 1.45 as you complete Step 1.

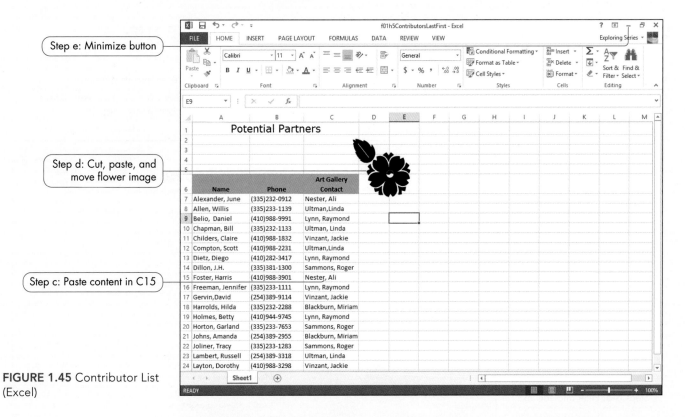

FIGURE 1.45 Contributor List (Excel)

a. Navigate to the Start screen. Scroll across the tiles, if necessary, and click **Excel 2013**. Click **Open Other Workbooks**.

You have opened Microsoft Excel because it is the program in which the contributors list is saved.

b. Open the student data file *f01h5Contributors*. Save the file as **f01h5Contributors_LastFirst** in the Office Records folder (a subfolder of Artists) you created.

The potential contributors list shown in Figure 1.45 is displayed.

c. Click **cell C7** to select the cell that contains *Nester, Ali*, and click **Copy** in the Clipboard group on the HOME tab. Click **cell C15** to select the cell that contains *Sammons, Roger*, click **Paste** in the Clipboard group, and then press **Esc** to remove the selection from *Nester, Ali*.

Ali Nester has been assigned as the Spotted Begonia Art Gallery contact for Harris Foster, replacing Roger Sammons. You make that replacement on the worksheet by copying and pasting Ali Nester's name in the appropriate worksheet cell.

d. Click the picture of the begonia. A box displays around the image, indicating that it is selected. Click **Cut** in the Clipboard group, click **cell D2**, and then click **Paste**. Drag the picture to resize and position it as needed (see Figure 1.45) so that it does not block any information in the list. Click anywhere outside the begonia picture to deselect it.

You decide that the picture of the begonia will look better if it is placed on the right side of the worksheet instead of the left. You move the picture by cutting and pasting the object.

> **TROUBLESHOOTING:** A Paste Options icon might display in the worksheet after you have moved the begonia picture. It offers additional options related to the paste procedure. You do not need to change any options, so ignore the button.

e. Click **Save** on the Quick Access Toolbar. Click **Minimize** to minimize the worksheet without closing it.

STEP 2 ≫ SELECT TEXT, APPLY FONT ATTRIBUTES, AND USE THE MINI TOOLBAR

As the opening of a new showing at the Spotted Begonia Art Gallery draws near, you are active in preparing promotional materials. You are currently working on an informational flyer that is almost set to go. You will make a few improvements before approving the flyer for release. Refer to Figure 1.46 as you complete Step 2.

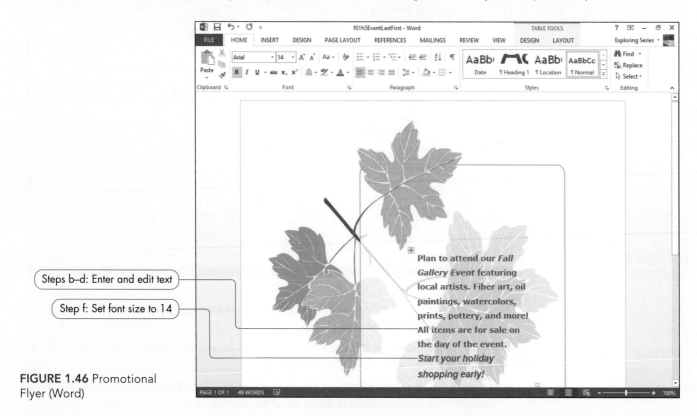

Steps b–d: Enter and edit text

Step f: Set font size to 14

FIGURE 1.46 Promotional Flyer (Word)

a. Navigate to the Start screen. Scroll across the tiles, if necessary, and click **Word 2013**. Click **Open Other Documents**. Open *f01h5Event* and save the document as **f01h5Event_LastFirst** in the Promotional Print folder (a subfolder of Artists) you created.

You plan to modify the promotional flyer slightly to include additional information about the Spotted Begonia Art Gallery.

> **TROUBLESHOOTING:** If you make any major mistakes in this exercise, you can close the file without saving it, open *f01h5Event* again, and then start this exercise over.

b. Click after the exclamation mark after the word *more* at the end of the first paragraph. Press **Enter** and type the following text. As you type, do not press Enter at the end of each line. Word will automatically wrap the lines of text.

All items are for sale on the day of the event. Start your holiday shopping early! You'll find gifts for everyone on your list.

> **TROUBLESHOOTING:** If you make any mistakes while typing, press Backspace and correct them.

c. Select the sentence beginning with *You'll find gifts*. Press **Delete**.

When you press Delete, selected text (or characters to the right of the insertion point) is removed. Deleted text is not placed in the Clipboard.

d. Select the words *Start your holiday shopping early!* Click **Italic** in the Font group on the HOME tab and click anywhere outside the selection to see the result.

e. Select both paragraphs but not the final italicized line. While still within the selection, move the mouse pointer slightly to display the Mini toolbar, click the **Font arrow** on the Mini toolbar, and then scroll to select **Verdana**.

> **TROUBLESHOOTING:** If you do not see the Mini toolbar, you might have moved too far away from the selection. In that case, click outside the selection and drag to select it once more. Without leaving the selection, move the mouse pointer slightly to display the Mini toolbar.

You have changed the font of the two paragraphs.

f. Click after the period following the word *event* before the last sentence in the second paragraph. Press **Enter** and press **Delete** to remove the extra space before the first letter, if necessary. Drag to select the new line, click **Font Size arrow** in the Font group, and then select **14**. Click anywhere outside the selected area. Your document should appear as shown in Figure 1.46.

You have increased font size to draw attention to the text.

g. Save the document and keep open for Step 3.

STEP 3 ≫ USE FORMAT PAINTER AND WORK WITH THE MINI TOOLBAR

You are on a short timeline for finalizing the promotional flyer, so you will use a few shortcuts to avoid retyping and reformatting more than is necessary. You know that you can easily copy formatting from one area to another using Format Painter. The Mini toolbar can also help you make changes quickly. Refer to Figure 1.47 as you complete Step 3.

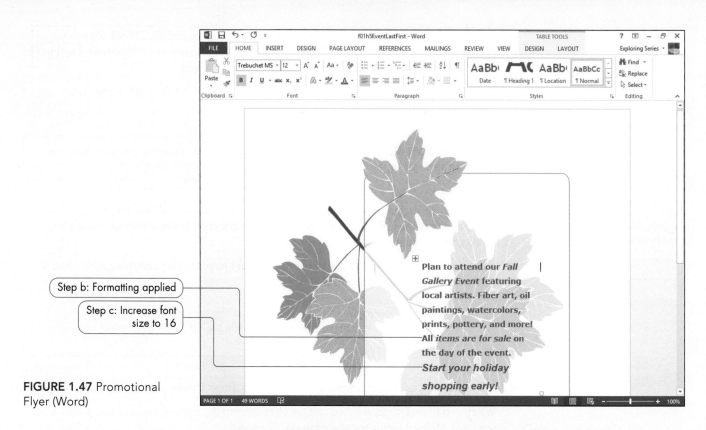

Step b: Formatting applied

Step c: Increase font size to 16

FIGURE 1.47 Promotional Flyer (Word)

a. Select the words *Fall Gallery Event* in the first paragraph and click **Format Painter** in the Clipboard group.

b. Select the words *items are for sale* in the sixth line. Click anywhere outside the selection to deselect the phrase.

The format of the area that you first selected (*Fall Gallery Event*) is applied to the line containing the phrase.

c. Select the text *Start your holiday shopping early!* in the Mini toolbar, click in the **Font Size box**, and then select **16** to increase the font size slightly. Click outside the selected area.

Figure 1.47 shows the final document as it should now appear.

d. Save the document as **f01h5Stp3Event_LastFirst** in the Promotional Print folder you created and close Word. Submit your file based on your instructor's directions.

The flyer will be saved with the same file name and in the same location as it was when you last saved the document in Step 2. As you close Word, the open document will also be closed.

STEP 4 ›› USE THE FONT DIALOG BOX AND FIND AND REPLACE TEXT

The contributors worksheet is almost complete. However, you first want to make a few more formatting changes to improve the worksheet's appearance. You will also quickly change an incorrect area code by using Excel's *Find and Replace* feature. Refer to Figure 1.48 as you complete Step 4.

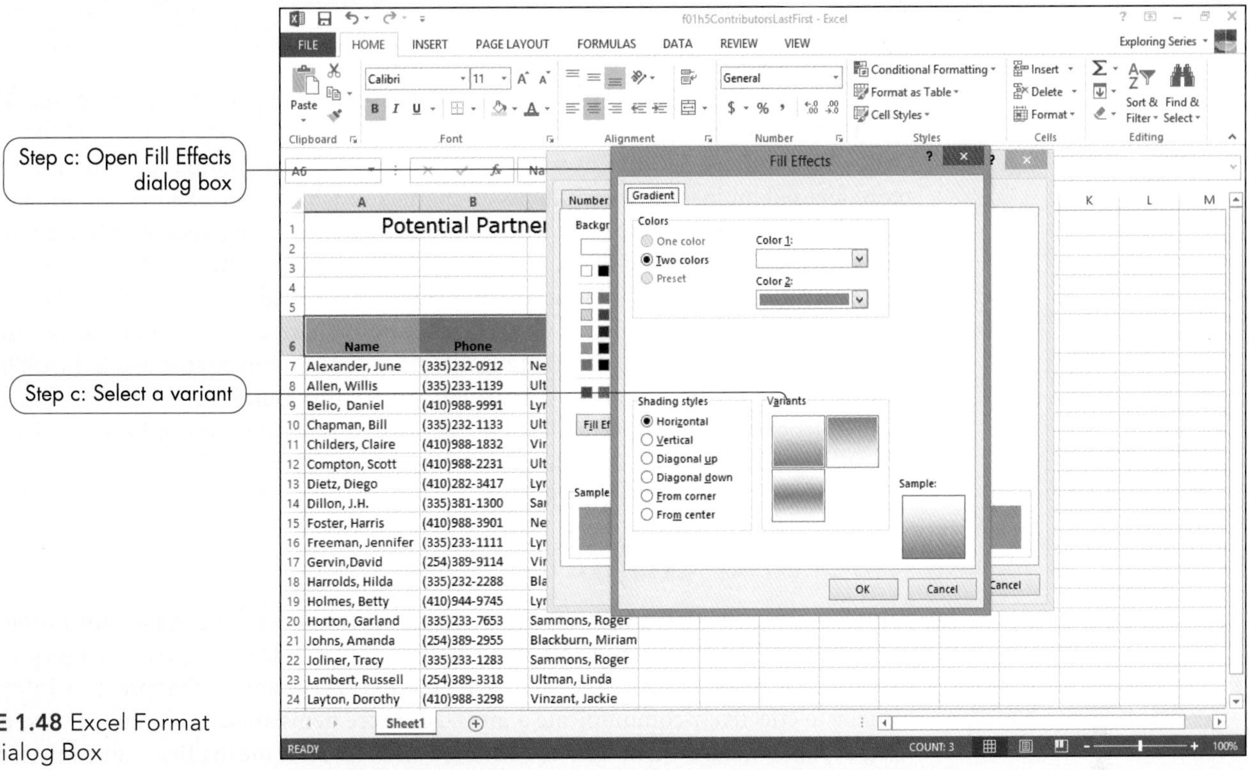

Step c: Open Fill Effects dialog box

Step c: Select a variant

FIGURE 1.48 Excel Format Cells Dialog Box

a. Click the **Excel icon** on the taskbar to redisplay the contributors worksheet that you minimized in Step 1.

The Excel potential contributors list displays.

> **TROUBLESHOOTING:** If you closed Excel, you can find the correct worksheet in your Recent Documents list.

b. Drag to select **cells A6** through **C6**.

> **TROUBLESHOOTING:** Make sure the mouse pointer looks like a large white plus sign before dragging. It is normal for the first cell in the selected area to be a different shade. If you click and drag when the mouse pointer does not resemble a white plus sign, text may be moved or duplicated. In that case, click Undo on the Quick Access Toolbar.

c. Click the **Dialog Box Launcher** in the Font group to display the Format Cells dialog box. Click the **Fill tab** and click **Fill Effects**, as shown in Figure 1.48. Click any style in the *Variants* section, click **OK**, and then click **OK** once more to close the Format Cells dialog box. Click outside the selected area to see the final result.

The headings of the worksheet are shaded more attractively.

d. Click **Find & Select** in the Editing group and click **Replace**. Type **410** in the **Find what box**. Type **411** in the **Replace with box**, click **Replace All**, and then click **OK** when notified that Excel has made seven replacements. Click **Close** in the *Find and Replace* dialog box.

You discovered that you consistently typed an incorrect area code. You used Find and Replace to make the corrections quickly.

e. Save the workbook as **f01h5Stp4Contributors_LastFirst** in the Office Records folder you created. Exit Excel, if necessary. Submit your files based on your instructor's directions.

Insert Tab Tasks

As its title implies, the Insert tab enables you to insert, or add, items into a file. Much of the Insert tab is specific to the particular application, with some commonalities to other Office applications. Word's Insert tab includes text-related commands, whereas Excel's is more focused on inserting such items as charts and tables. Word allows you to insert apps from the Microsoft app store, so you could add an application such as Merriam-Webster Dictionary. Both Word and Excel allow you to insert Apps for Office to build powerful Web-backed solutions. PowerPoint's Insert tab includes multimedia items and links. Despite their obvious differences in focus, all Office applications share a common group on the Insert tab—the Illustrations group. In addition, all Office applications enable you to insert headers, footers, text boxes, and symbols. Those options are also found on the Insert tab in various groups, depending on the particular application. In this section, you will work with common activities on the Insert tab, including inserting online pictures.

Inserting Objects

With few exceptions, all Office applications share common options in the Illustrations group of the Insert tab. PowerPoint places some of those common features in the Images group. You can insert pictures, shapes, and *SmartArt*. SmartArt is a diagram that presents information visually to effectively communicate a message. These items are considered objects, retaining their separate nature when they are inserted in files. That means that you can select them and manage them independently of the underlying document, worksheet, or presentation.

After an object has been inserted, you can click the object to select it or click anywhere outside the object to deselect it. When an object is selected, a border surrounds it with handles, or small dots, appearing at each corner and in the middle of each side. Figure 1.49 shows a selected object, surrounded by handles. Unless an object is selected, you cannot change or modify it. When an object is selected, the Ribbon expands to include one or more contextual tabs. Items on the contextual tabs relate to the selected object, enabling you to modify and manage it.

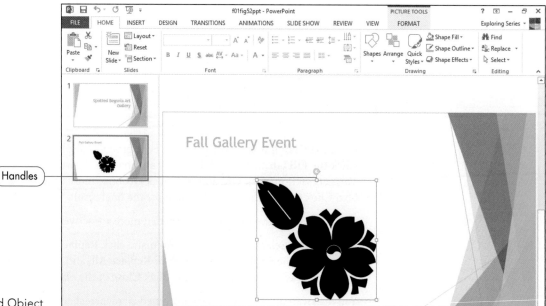

FIGURE 1.49 Selected Object

You can resize and move a selected object. Place the mouse pointer on any handle and drag (when the mouse pointer looks like a two-headed arrow) to resize the object. Be careful! If you drag a side handle, the object is likely to be skewed, possibly resulting in a poor image. Instead, drag a corner handle to proportionally resize the image. To move an object, drag the object when the mouse pointer looks like a four-headed arrow.

Insert Pictures

STEP 2 › Documents, worksheets, and presentations can include much more than just words and numbers. You can easily add energy and additional description to the project by including pictures and other graphic elements. Although a *picture* is usually just that—a digital photo—it is actually defined as a graphic element retrieved from storage media such as a hard drive or a CD. A picture could actually be a clip art item that you saved from the Internet onto your hard drive.

The process of inserting a picture is simple.

1. Click in the project where you want the picture to be placed. Make sure you know where the picture that you plan to use is stored.
2. Click the INSERT tab.
3. Click Pictures in the Illustrations group (or Images group in PowerPoint). The Insert Picture dialog box is shown in Figure 1.50. You can also use Online Pictures to search for and insert pictures.
4. Navigate to where your picture is saved and click Insert (or simply double-click the picture).

Insert Picture dialog box

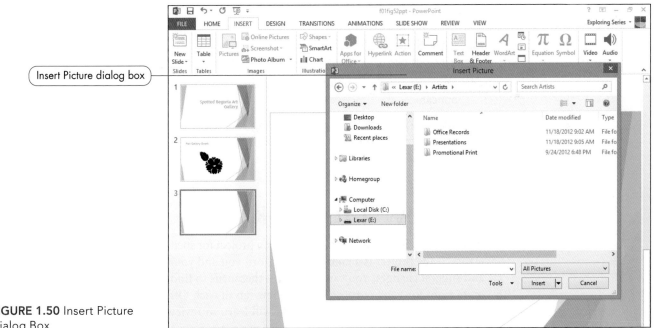

FIGURE 1.50 Insert Picture Dialog Box

In addition, on some slide layouts, PowerPoint displays Pictures and Online Pictures buttons that you can click to search for and select a picture for the slide.

Insert and Modify SmartArt

The SmartArt feature enables you to create a diagram and to enter text to provide a visual representation of data. To create a SmartArt diagram, choose a diagram type that fits the purpose: List, Process, Cycle, Hierarchy, Relationships, Matrix, Pyramid, and Picture. You can get additional SmartArt diagrams at Office.com. To insert a SmartArt object, do the following:

1. Click the INSERT tab.
2. Click SmartArt in the Illustrations group to display the Choose a SmartArt Graphic dialog box.
3. Click the type of SmartArt diagram you want in the left pane of the dialog box.
4. Click the SmartArt subtype from the center pane.
5. Preview the selected SmartArt and subtype in the right pane and click OK.

Once you select the SmartArt diagram type and the subtype, a Text pane opens in which you can enter text. The text you enter displays within the selected object. If the SmartArt diagram contains more objects than you need, click the object and press Delete.

The SmartArt Tools Design tab enables you to customize the design of a SmartArt diagram. You can modify the diagram by changing its layout, colors, and style. The layout controls the construction of the diagram. The style controls the visual effects, such as embossing and rounded corners of the diagram. The SmartArt Tools Format tab controls the shape fill color, border, and size options.

Insert and Format Shapes

You can insert a shape to add a visual effect to a worksheet. You can insert various types of lines, rectangles, basic shapes (such as an oval, a pie shape, or a smiley face), block arrows, equation shapes, flowchart shapes, stars and banners, and callouts. You can insert shapes, such as a callout, to draw attention to particular worksheet data. To insert a shape, do the following:

1. Click the INSERT tab.
2. Click Shapes in the Illustrations group.
3. Select the shape you want to insert from the Shapes gallery.
4. Drag the cross-hair pointer to create the shape in the worksheet where you want it to appear.

After you insert the shape, the Drawing Tools Format tab displays so that you can change the shape, apply a shape style with fill color, and adjust the size.

Review Tab Tasks

As a final touch, you should always check a project for spelling, grammatical, and word usage errors. If the project is a collaborative effort, you and your colleagues might add comments and suggest changes. You can even use a thesaurus to find synonyms for words that are not quite right for your purpose. The Review tab in each Office application provides all these options and more. In this section, you will learn to review a file, checking for spelling and grammatical errors. You will also learn to use a thesaurus to identify synonyms.

Reviewing a File

As you create or edit a file, you will want to make sure no spelling or grammatical errors exist. You will also be concerned with wording, being sure to select words and phrases that best represent the purpose of the document, worksheet, or presentation. On occasion, you might even find yourself at a loss for an appropriate word. Not to worry. Word, Excel, and PowerPoint all provide standard tools for proofreading, including a spelling and grammar checker and a thesaurus.

Check Spelling and Grammar

STEP 1 ≫ In general, all Office applications check your spelling and grammar as you type. If a word is unrecognized, it is flagged as misspelled or grammatically incorrect. Misspellings are identified with a red wavy underline, grammatical problems are underlined in green, and word usage errors (such as using *bear* instead of *bare*) have a blue underline. If the word or phrase is truly in error—that is, it is not a person's name or an unusual term that is not in the application's dictionary—you can correct it manually, or you can let the software correct it for you. If you right-click a word or phrase that is identified as a mistake, you will see a shortcut menu similar to that shown in Figure 1.51. If the application's dictionary can make a suggestion as to the correct spelling, you can click to accept the suggestion and make the change. If a grammatical rule is violated, you will have an opportunity to select a correction. However, if the text is actually correct, you can click Ignore or Ignore All (to bypass all occurrences of the flagged error in the current document). Click *Add to Dictionary* if you want the word to be considered correct whenever it appears in all documents. Similar selections on a shortcut menu enable you to ignore grammatical mistakes if they are not errors.

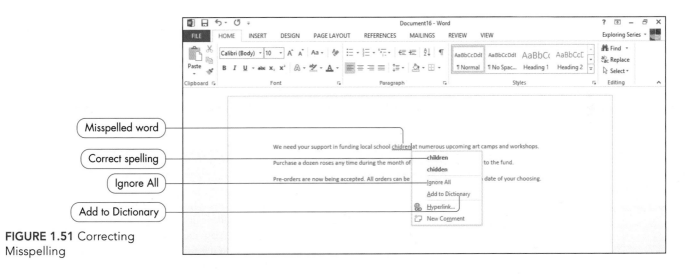

FIGURE 1.51 Correcting Misspelling

You might prefer the convenience of addressing possible misspellings and grammatical errors without having to examine each underlined word or phrase. To do so, click Spelling & Grammar in the Proofing group on the Review tab. Beginning at the top of the document, each identified error is highlighted in a pane similar to Figure 1.52. You can then choose how to address the problem by making a selection from the options in the pane.

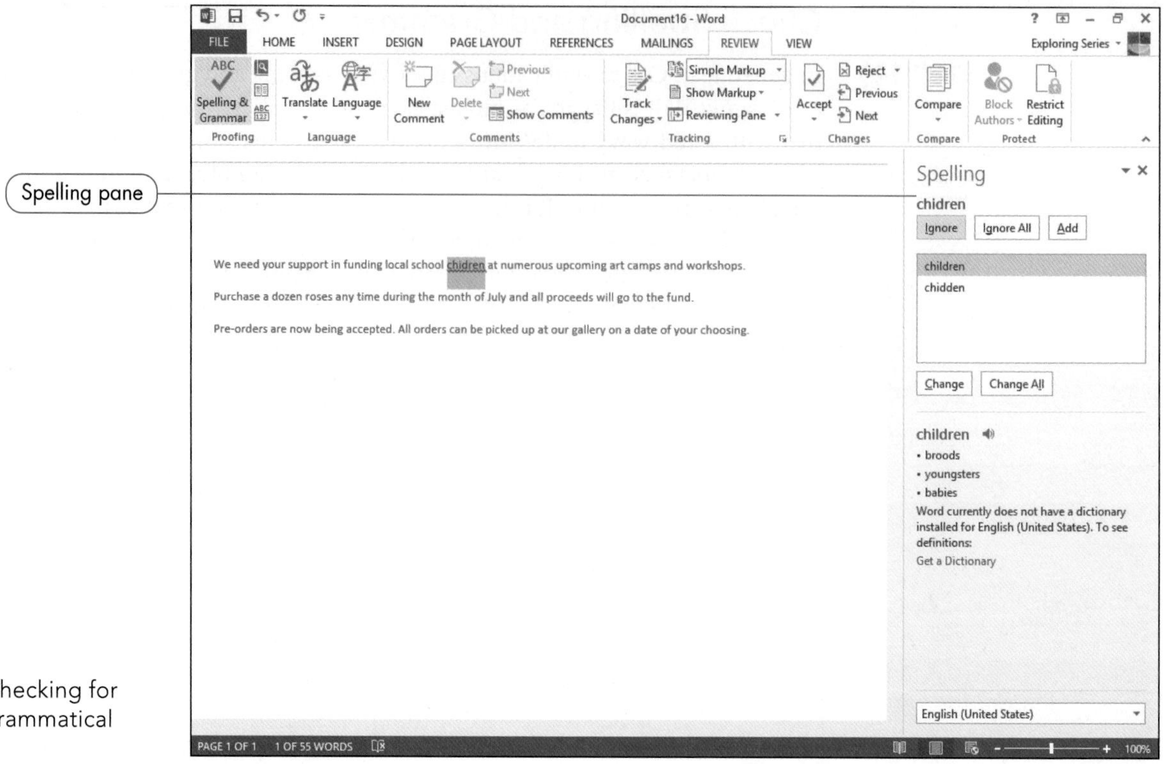

Spelling pane

FIGURE 1.52 Checking for Spelling and Grammatical Errors

TIP **Understanding Software Options**

Many Office settings are considered *default* options. Thus, unless you specify otherwise, the default options are in effect. One such default option is the automatic spelling and grammar checker. If you prefer to enable and disable certain options or change default settings in an Office application, you can click the FILE tab and select Options. From that point, you can work through a series of categories, selecting or deselecting options at will. For example, if you want to change how the application corrects and formats text, you can select or deselect settings in the Proofing group.

Use the Thesaurus

As you write, there will be times when you are at a loss for an appropriate word. Perhaps you feel that you are overusing a word and want to find a suitable substitute. The Thesaurus is the Office tool to use in such a situation. Located in the Proofing group on the Review tab, Thesaurus enables you to search for synonyms, or words with similar meanings. Select a word and click Thesaurus in the Proofing group on the Review tab. A task pane displays on the right side of the screen, and synonyms are listed similar to those shown in Figure 1.53. You can also use the Thesaurus before typing a word to find substitutes. Simply click Thesaurus and type the word for which you are seeking a synonym in the Search box. Press Enter or click the magnifying glass to the right of the Search box for some suggestions. Finally, you can also identify synonyms when you right-click a word and point to Synonyms (if any are available). Click any word from the options offered to place it in the document.

Thesaurus pane

FIGURE 1.53 Thesaurus

Page Layout Tab Tasks

When you prepare a document or worksheet, you are concerned with the way the project appears onscreen and possibly in print. Unlike Word and Excel, a PowerPoint presentation is usually designed as a slide show, so it is not nearly as critical to concern yourself with page layout settings. The Page Layout tab in Word and Excel provides access to a full range of options such as margin settings and page orientation. In this section, you will identify page layout settings that are common to Office applications.

Because a document is most often designed to be printed, you will want to make sure it looks its best in printed form. That means that you will need to know how to adjust margins and how to change the page orientation. Perhaps the document or spreadsheet should be centered on the page vertically or the text should be aligned in columns. By adjusting page settings, you can do all these things and more. You will find the most common page settings, such as margins and page orientation, in the Page Setup group on the Page Layout tab. For less common settings, such as determining whether headers should print on odd or even pages, you can use the Page Setup dialog box.

Changing Margins

A *margin* is the area of blank space that displays to the left, right, top, and bottom of a document or worksheet. Margins are evident only if you are in Print Layout or Page Layout view or if you are in the Backstage view, previewing a document to print. To set or change margins, click the Page Layout tab. As shown in Figure 1.54, the Page Setup group enables you to change such items as margins and orientation. To change margins:

1. Click Margins in the Page Setup group on the PAGE LAYOUT tab.
2. If the margins that you intend to use are included in any of the preset margin options, click a selection. Otherwise, click Custom Margins to display the Page Setup dialog box in which you can create custom margin settings.
3. Click OK to accept the settings and close the dialog box.

You can also change margins when you click Print on the File tab.

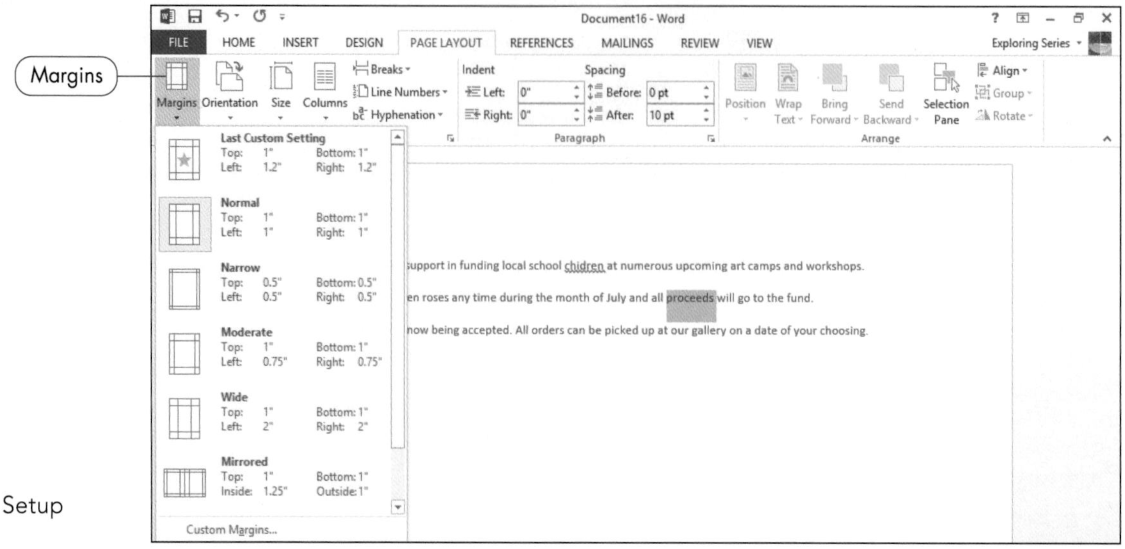

FIGURE 1.54 Page Setup Group

Changing Page Orientation

STEP 3 ▶▶ Documents and worksheets can be displayed in *portrait* orientation or in *landscape*. A page displayed or printed in portrait orientation is taller than it is wide. A page in landscape orientation is wider than it is tall. Word documents are usually more attractive displayed in portrait orientation, whereas Excel worksheets are often more suitable in landscape. To select page orientation, click Orientation in the Page Setup group on the Page Layout tab (see Figure 1.55). Orientation is also an option in the Print area of the Backstage view.

Using the Page Setup Dialog Box

The Page Setup group contains the most commonly used page options in the particular Office application. Some are unique to Excel, and others are more applicable to Word. Other less common settings are available in the Page Setup dialog box only, displayed when you click the Page Setup Dialog Box Launcher. The subsequent dialog box includes options for customizing margins, selecting page orientation, centering vertically, printing gridlines, and creating headers and footers, although some of those options are available only when working with Word; others are unique to Excel. Figure 1.55 shows both the Excel and Word Page Setup dialog boxes.

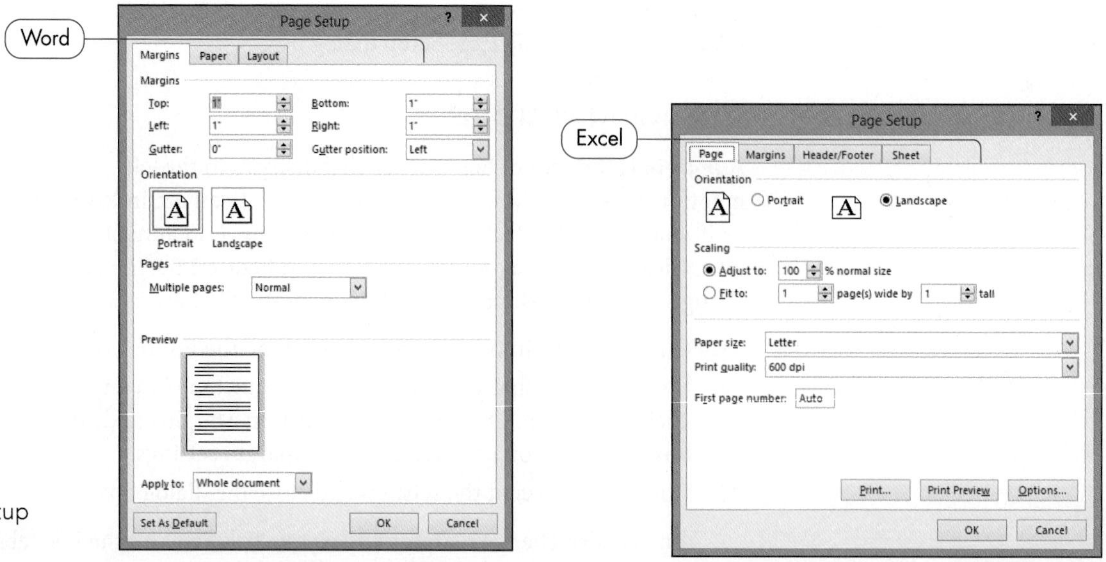

FIGURE 1.55 Page Setup Dialog Boxes

1. Give two ways to resize an object, such as a picture, that has been inserted in a document. *p. 61*

2. Often, an Office application will identify a word as misspelled that is not actually misspelled. How can that happen? If a word is flagged as misspelled, how can you correct it (or ignore it if it is not actually an error)? *p. 63*

3. Give two ways to change a document from a portrait orientation to landscape. Identify at least one document type that you think would be better suited for landscape orientation rather than portrait. *p. 66*

4. What dialog box includes options for selecting margins, centering vertically, and changing page orientation? *p. 66*

Hands-On Exercises

Watch the Video
for this Hands-
On Exercise!

MyITLab®
HOE6 Training

6 Insert Tab Tasks, Page Layout Tab Tasks, and Review Tab Tasks

A series of enrichment programs at the Spotted Begonia Art Gallery is nearing kickoff. You are helping plan a ceremony to commemorate the occasion. To encourage interest and participation, you will edit a PowerPoint presentation that is to be shown to civic groups, the local retiree association, and to city and county leaders to solicit additional funding. You know that pictures add energy to a presentation when used appropriately, so you will check for those elements, adding whatever is necessary. A major concern is making sure the presentation is error free and that it is available in print so that meeting participants can review it later. As a reminder, you also plan to have available a handout giving the time and date of the dedication ceremony. You will use the Insert tab to work with illustrations and the Review tab to check for errors, and you will use Word to generate an attractive handout as a reminder of the date.

Skills covered: Check Spelling and Use the Thesaurus • Insert Pictures • Change Margins and Page Orientation

---

STEP 1 ≫ CHECK SPELLING AND USE THE THESAURUS

As you check the PowerPoint presentation that will be shown to local groups, you make sure no misspellings or grammatical mistakes exist. You also use the Thesaurus to find a suitable substitution for a word you feel should be replaced. Refer to Figure 1.56 as you complete Step 1.

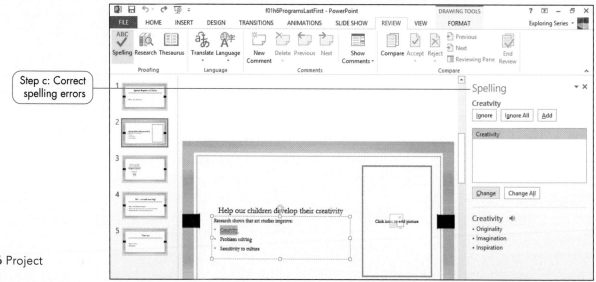

FIGURE 1.56 Project Presentation

a. Navigate to the Start screen. Scroll across the tiles, if necessary, and click **PowerPoint 2013**. Click **Open Other Presentations**. Open *f01h6Programs* and save the document as **f01h6Programs_LastFirst** in the Promotional Print folder (a subfolder of Artists) you created.

The PowerPoint presentation opens, with Slide 1 shown in Normal view.

b. Click the **SLIDE SHOW tab** and click **From Beginning** in the Start Slide Show group to view the presentation. Click to advance from one slide to another. After the last slide, click to return to Normal view.

c. Click the **REVIEW tab** and click **Spelling** in the Proofing group. Correct any words that are misspelled by clicking the correction and clicking Change or Ignore in the Spelling pane. Click **Change** to accept *Creativity* on Slide 2, click **workshops** and click **Change** on Slide 3, and click **Change** to accept *Thank* for Slide 5. Refer to Figure 1.56. Click **OK** when the spell check is complete and close the pane.

d. Click **Slide 2** in the Slides pane on the left. Double-click the bulleted word *Creativity*, click **Thesaurus** in the Proofing group, point to *Imagination* in the Thesaurus pane, click the arrow to the right of the word, and then select **Insert**.

The word *Creativity* is replaced with the word *Imagination*.

e. Click the **Close (X) button** in the top-right corner of the Thesaurus pane.

f. Save the presentation.

STEP 2 ›› INSERT PICTURES

Although the presentation provides the necessary information and encourages viewers to become active participants in the enrichment programs, you believe that pictures might make it a little more exciting. Where appropriate, you will include a picture. Refer to Figure 1.57 as you complete Step 2.

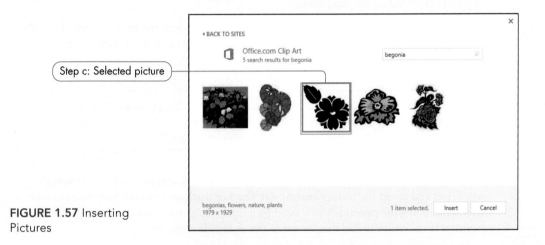

FIGURE 1.57 Inserting Pictures

a. Click **Slide 2** in the Slides pane on the left, if necessary. Click the **INSERT tab** and click **Online Pictures** in the Images group.

The Insert Pictures pane displays on the screen.

> **TROUBLESHOOTING:** You can add your own pictures to slides using the Pictures command. Or you can copy and paste images directly from a Web page.

b. Type **begonia** in the **Office.com Clip Art search box** and press **Enter**.

You will identify pictures that may be displayed on Slide 2.

c. Click to select the black flower shown in Figure 1.57 or use a similar image. Click **Insert**.

The picture may not be placed as you would like, but you will move and resize it in the next substep as necessary. Also, notice that the picture is selected, as indicated by the box and handles surrounding it.

> **TROUBLESHOOTING:** It is very easy to make the mistake of inserting duplicate pictures on a slide, perhaps because you clicked the image more than once in the task pane. If that should happen, you can remove any unwanted picture by clicking to select it and pressing Delete.

d. Click a corner handle—the small square on the border of the picture. Make sure the mouse pointer appears as a double-headed arrow. Drag to resize the image so that it fits well on the slide. Click in the center of the picture. The mouse pointer should appear as a four-headed arrow. Drag the picture slightly to the right corner of the slide. Make sure the picture is still selected (it should be surrounded by a box and handles). If it is not selected, click to select it.

> **TROUBLESHOOTING:** You may not need to perform this substep if the picture came in as desired. Proceed to the next substep if this occurs.

e. Click **Slide 5** in the Slides pane on the left. Click the **INSERT tab** and select **Online Pictures**. Type **happy art** in the **Office.com Clip Art search box** and press **Enter**. Click the **Three handprints picture** and click **Insert**.

A picture is placed on the final slide.

f. Click to select the picture, if necessary. Drag a corner handle to resize the picture. Click the center of the picture and drag the picture to reposition it in the bottom-right corner of the slide, as shown in Figure 1.57.

> **TROUBLESHOOTING:** You can only move the picture when the mouse pointer looks like a four-headed arrow. If instead you drag a handle, the picture will be resized instead of moved. Click Undo on the Quick Access Toolbar and begin again.

g. Click **Slide 3**. Click the **INSERT tab**, click **Online Pictures**, and then search for **school art**. Select and insert the picture named **Art Teacher working with student on a project in school**. Using the previously practiced technique, resize the image height to **3.9"** and position as necessary to add the picture to the right side of the slide.

h. Save the presentation and exit PowerPoint. Submit your file based on your instructor's directions.

STEP 3 ⟫ CHANGE MARGINS AND PAGE ORIENTATION

You are ready to finalize the flyer promoting the workshops, but before printing it you want to see how it will look. You wonder if it would be better in landscape or portrait orientation, so you will try both. After adjusting the margins, you are ready to save the flyer for later printing and distribution. Refer to Figure 1.58 as you complete Step 3.

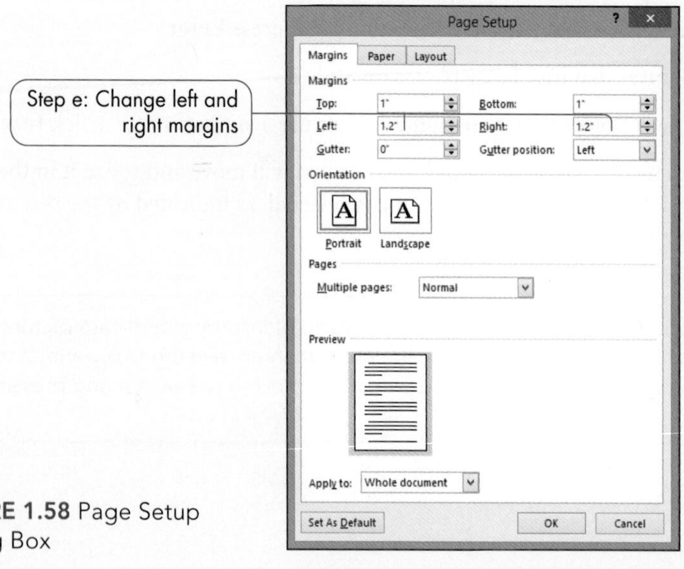

FIGURE 1.58 Page Setup Dialog Box

a. Navigate to the Start screen. Scroll across the tiles, if necessary, and click **Word 2013**. Click **Open Other Documents**. Open *f01h6Handout* and save the document as **f01h6Handout_LastFirst** in the Promotional Print folder (a subfolder of Artists) you created.

b. Click the **PAGE LAYOUT tab**, click **Orientation** in the Page Setup group, and then select **Landscape** to view the flyer in landscape orientation.

   You want to see how the handout will look in landscape orientation.

c. Click the **FILE tab**, click **Print**, and then click **Next Page** and click **Previous Page** (right- and left-pointing arrows at the bottom center of the preview page).

   The second page of the handout shows only the last two bullets and the contact information. You can see that the two-page layout is not an attractive option.

d. Click the **Back arrow** in the top-left corner. Click **Undo** on the Quick Access Toolbar. Click the **FILE tab** and click **Print**.

   The document fits on one page. Portrait orientation is a much better choice for the handout.

e. Click the **Back arrow** in the top-left corner. Click the **PAGE LAYOUT tab** if necessary, click **Margins** in the Page Setup group, and then select **Custom Margins**. Click the **spin arrow** beside the left margin box to increase the margin to **1.2**. Similarly, change the right margin to **1.2**. Refer to Figure 1.58. Click **OK**.

f. Save the document and exit Word. Submit your file based on your instructor's directions.

Chapter Objectives Review

After reading this chapter, you have accomplished the following objectives:

1. **Log in with your Microsoft account.**
   - Your Microsoft account connects you to all of Microsoft's Internet-based resources.

2. **Identify the Start screen components.**
   - The Start screen has a sleek, clean interface that is made up of tiles and Charms.

3. **Interact with the Start screen.**
   - Customize the Start screen to access programs and apps.

4. **Access the desktop.**
   - Simplified to accommodate mobile devices, laptops, and desktops.

5. **Use File Explorer.**
   - Understand and customize the interface: Change the view to provide as little or as much detail as you need.
   - Work with groups on the Navigation Pane: Provides access to all resources, folders, and files.

6. **Work with folders and files.**
   - Create a folder: A well-named folder structure can be created in File Explorer or within a program as you save a file.
   - Open, rename, and delete folders and files: File Explorer can be used to perform these tasks.
   - Save a file: When saving a file for the first time, you need to indicate the location and the name of the file.

7. **Select, copy, and move multiple files and folders.**
   - Select multiple files and folders: Folders and files can be selected as a group.
   - Copy and move files and folders: Folders and the files within them can be easily moved to the same or a different drive.

8. **Identify common interface components.**
   - Use the Backstage view and the Quick Access Toolbar: The Backstage view can perform several commands.
   - Familiarize yourself with the Ribbon: Provides access to common tasks.
   - Use the status bar: The status bar provides information relative to the open file and quick access to View and Zoom level options.

9. **Get Office Help.**
   - Use Office Help: The Help button links to online resources and technical support.
   - Use Enhanced ScreenTips: Provides the purpose of a command button as you point to it.
   - Get help with dialog boxes: Use the Help button in the top-right corner of a dialog box to get help relevant to the task.

10. **Open a file.**
    - Create a new file: A document can be created as a blank document or with a template.
    - Open a file using the Open dialog box: Previously saved files can be located and opened using a dialog box.
    - Open a file using the Recent Documents list: Documents that you have worked with recently display here.
    - Open a file from the Templates list: Templates are a convenient way to save time when designing a document.

11. **Print a file.**
    - Check and change orientation or perform other commands related to the look of your file before printing.

12. **Close a file and application.**
    - Close files you are not working on to avoid becoming overwhelmed.

13. **Select and edit text.**
    - Select text to edit: Commit to memory: "Select, then do."
    - Use the Mini toolbar: Provides instant access to common formatting commands after text is selected.
    - Apply font attributes: These can be applied to selected text with toggle commands.
    - Change the font: Choose from a set of fonts found within all Office applications.
    - Change the font size, color, and attributes: These commands are located in the Font group on the Ribbon.

14. **Use the Clipboard group commands.**
    - Copy formats with the Format Painter: Copy formatting features from one section of text to another.
    - Move and copy text: Text can be selected, copied, and moved between applications or within the same application.
    - Use the Office Clipboard: This pane stores up to 24 cut or copied selections for use later on in your computing session.

15. **Use the Editing group commands.**
    - Find and replace text: Finds each occurrence of a series of characters and replaces them with another series.
    - Use advanced find and replace feature: Change the format of every occurrence of a series of characters.

16. **Insert objects.**
    - Insert pictures: You can insert pictures from a CD or other media, or from an online resource such as Office.com.
    - Insert and modify SmartArt: Create a diagram and to enter text to provide a visual of data.
    - Insert and format shapes: You can insert various types of lines and basic shapes.

17. **Review a file.**
    - Check spelling and grammar: All Office applications check and mark these error types as you type for later correction.
    - Use the Thesaurus: Enables you to search for synonyms.

18. **Use the Page Setup dialog box.**
    - Change margins: You can control the amount of blank space that surrounds the text in your document.
    - Change margins and page orientations, and create headers and footers.

Key Terms Matching

Match the key terms with their definitions. Write the key term letter by the appropriate numbered definition.

a. Backstage view
b. Charms
c. Cloud storage
d. Find
e. Font
f. Format Painter
g. Group
h. Mini toolbar
i. Navigation Pane
j. Operating system

k. Quick Access Toolbar
l. Ribbon
m. OneDrive
n. Snip
o. Snipping Tool
p. Start screen
q. Subfolder
r. Tile
s. Windows 8.1.1
t. Windows 8.1.1 app

1. _____ A tool that copies all formatting from one area to another. **p. 49**

2. _____ Software that directs computer activities such as checking all components, managing system resources, and communicating with application software. **p. 2**

3. _____ A task-oriented section of the Ribbon that contains related commands. **p. 25**

4. _____ An app used to store, access, and share files and folders. **p. 2**

5. _____ Any of the several colorful block images found on the Start screen that when clicked takes you to a program, file, folder, or other Windows 8.1.1 app. **p. 3**

6. _____ A component of Office 2013 that provides a concise collection of commands related to an open file. **p. 23**

7. _____ A tool that displays near selected text that contains formatting commands. **p. 46**

8. _____ A level of folder structure indicated as a folder within another folder. **p. 10**

9. _____ An application specifically designed to run in the Start screen interface of Windows 8.1.1. **p. 3**

10. _____ A command used to locate each occurrence of a series of characters. **p. 52**

11. _____ A Windows 8.1.1 accessory program that allows you to capture a screen display so that you can save, annotate, or share it. **p. 5**

12. _____ What you see after starting your Windows 8.1.1 computer and entering your username and password. **p. 2**

13. _____ Provides handy access to commonly executed tasks such as saving a file and undoing recent actions. **p. 23**

14. _____ A Microsoft operating system released in 2012 that is available on laptops, desktops, and tablet computers. **p. 2**

15. _____ A component made up of five icons that provide similar functionality to the Start button found in previous versions of Windows. **p. 3**

16. _____ The captured screen display created by the Snipping Tool. **p. 5**

17. _____ The long bar located just beneath the title bar containing tabs, groups, and commands. **p. 25**

18. _____ Provides access to computer resources, folders, files, and networked peripherals. **p. 11**

19. _____ A technology used to store files and to work with programs that are stored in a central location on the Internet. **p. 2**

20. _____ A character design or the way characters display onscreen. **p. 45**

Multiple Choice

1. The Recent Documents list shows documents that have been previously:

   (a) Printed.

   (b) Opened.

   (c) Saved in an earlier software version.

   (d) Deleted.

2. Which of the following File Explorer features collects related data from folders and gives them a single name?

   (a) Network

   (b) Favorites

   (c) Libraries

   (d) Computer

3. When you want to copy the format of a selection but not the content, you should:

   (a) Double-click Copy in the Clipboard group.

   (b) Right-click the selection and click Copy.

   (c) Click Copy Format in the Clipboard group.

   (d) Click Format Painter in the Clipboard group.

4. Which of the following is *not* a benefit of using OneDrive?

   (a) Save your folders and files in the cloud.

   (b) Share your files and folders with others.

   (c) Hold video conferences with others.

   (d) Simultaneously work on the same document with others.

5. What does a red wavy underline in a document, spreadsheet, or presentation mean?

   (a) A word is misspelled or not recognized by the Office dictionary

   (b) A grammatical mistake exists

   (c) An apparent word usage mistake exists

   (d) A word has been replaced with a synonym

6. When you close a file:

   (a) You are prompted to save the file (unless you have made no changes since last saving it).

   (b) The application (Word, Excel, or PowerPoint) is also closed.

   (c) You must first save the file.

   (d) You must change the file name.

7. Live Preview:

   (a) Opens a predesigned document or spreadsheet that is relevant to your task.

   (b) Provides a preview of the results of a choice you are considering before you make a final selection.

   (c) Provides a preview of an upcoming Office version.

   (d) Enlarges the font onscreen.

8. You can get help when working with an Office application in which one of the following areas?

   (a) Help button

   (b) Status bar

   (c) The Backstage view

   (d) Quick Access Toolbar

9. The *Find and Replace* feature enables you to do which of the following?

   (a) Find all instances of misspelling and automatically correct (or replace) them

   (b) Find any grammatical errors and automatically correct (or replace) them

   (c) Find any specified font settings and replace them with another selection

   (d) Find any character string and replace it with another

10. A document or worksheet printed in landscape orientation is:

    (a) Taller than it is wide.

    (b) Wider than it is tall.

    (c) A document with 2" left and right margins.

    (d) A document with 2" top and bottom margins.

Practice Exercises

1 Designing Web Pages

You have been asked to make a presentation to the local business association. With the mayor's renewed emphasis on growing the local economy, many businesses are interested in establishing a Web presence. The business owners would like to know a little bit more about how Web pages are designed. In preparation for the presentation, you need to proofread and edit your PowerPoint file. This exercise follows the same set of skills as used in Hands-On Exercises 1–6 in the chapter. Refer to Figure 1.59 as you complete this exercise.

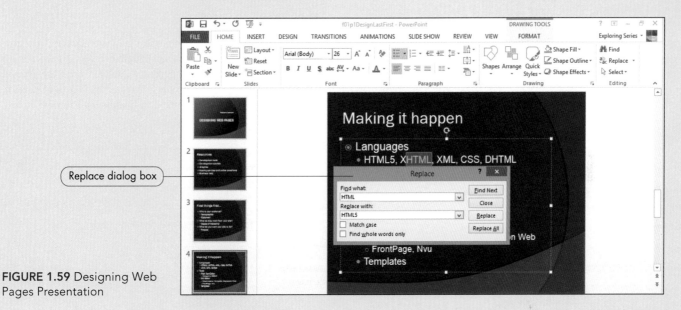

FIGURE 1.59 Designing Web Pages Presentation

a. Click **File Explorer** on the taskbar and select the location where you save your files. Click the **HOME tab** and click **New folder** in the New group. Type **Designing Web Pages** and press **Enter**.

  Take a snip, name it **f01p1DesignSnip_LastFirst**, and then save it in the Designing Web Pages folder. Close File Explorer.

b. Point to the bottom-right corner of your screen to display the Charms and click the **Start charm**. Scroll if necessary and click **PowerPoint 2013** to start PowerPoint. Open *f01p1Design* and save it as **f01p1Design_LastFirst** in the Designing Web Pages folder. In Slide 1, drag to select the text *Firstname Lastname* and type your own first and last names. Click an empty area of the slide to cancel the selection.

c. Click the **REVIEW tab** and click **Spelling** in the Proofing group. In the Spelling pane, click **Change** or **Ignore** to make or not make a change as needed. Most identified misspellings should be changed. The words *KompoZer* and *Nvu* are not misspelled, so you should ignore them when they are flagged. Click **OK** to end the spell check.

d. Click the **SLIDE SHOW tab**. Click **From Beginning** in the Start Slide Show group. Click each slide to view the show and press **Esc** on the last slide.

e. Click **Slide 2** in the Slides pane on the left. Drag to select the *Other tools* text and press **Backspace** on the keyboard to delete the text.

f. Click **Slide 4** in the Slides pane. Click the **HOME tab** and click **Replace** in the Editing group. Type **HTML** in the **Find what box** and **HTML5** in the **Replace with box**. Click **Find Next**. Read the slide and click **Replace** to change the first instance of *HTML*. Refer to Figure 1.59. Click **Close**.

g. Click **Replace** in the Editing group. Type **CSS** in the **Find what box** and **CSS5** in the **Replace with box**. Click **Replace All** and click **OK**. Click **Close**.

h. Drag to select the *FrontPage, Nvu* text and press **Backspace** on the keyboard to delete the text.

i. Press **Ctrl+End** to place the insertion point at the end of *Templates* and press **Enter**. Type **Database Connectivity** to create a new bulleted item.

j. Click the **FILE tab** and click **Print**. Click the **Full Page Slides arrow** and click **6 Slides Horizontal** to see a preview of all of the slides as a handout. Click the **Back arrow** and click the **HOME tab**.

k. Click **Slide 1** in the Slides pane to move to the beginning of the presentation.

l. Drag the **Zoom slider** on the status bar to the right to **130%** to magnify the text. Then use the **Zoom Slider** to return to **60%**.

m. Save and close the file. Submit your files based on your instructor's directions.

2 · Upscale Bakery

You have always been interested in baking and have worked in the field for several years. You now have an opportunity to devote yourself full time to your career as the CEO of a company dedicated to baking cupcakes, pastries, and catering. One of the first steps in getting the business off the ground is developing a business plan so that you can request financial support. You will use Word to develop your business plan. This exercise follows the same set of skills as used in Hands-On Exercises 1, 3, 4, and 5 in the chapter. Refer to Figure 1.60 as you complete this exercise.

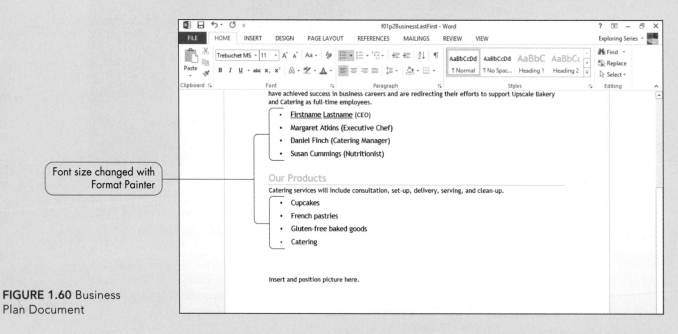

FIGURE 1.60 Business Plan Document

a. Click **File Explorer** on the taskbar and select the location where you save your files. Click the **HOME tab** and click **New folder** in the New group. Type **Business Plan** and press **Enter**.

Take a snip, name it **f01p2BusinessSnip_LastFirst**, and save it in the Business Plan folder. Close File Explorer.

b. Point to the bottom-right corner of your screen to display the Charms and click the **Start charm**. Scroll if necessary and click **Word 2013** to start Word. Open *f01p2Business* and save it as **f01p2Business_LastFirst** in the Business Plan folder.

c. Click the **REVIEW tab** and click **Spelling & Grammar** in the Proofing group. Click **Change** for all suggestions.

d. Drag the paragraphs beginning with *Our Staff* and ending with *(Nutritionist)*. Click the **HOME tab** and click **Cut** in the Clipboard group. Click to the left of *Our Products* and click **Paste**.

e. Select the text *Your name* in the first bullet and replace it with your first and last names. Select that entire bullet and use the Mini toolbar to use Live Preview to see some other Font sizes. Then click **11** to increase the size.

f. Double-click the **Format Painter** in the Clipboard group on the HOME tab. Drag the Format Painter to change the other *Our Staff* bullets to **11**. Drag all four *Our Products* bullets. Click the **Format Painter button** to toggle it off and click outside of the text to deselect it. Refer to Figure 1.60.

g. Select the last line in the document, which says *Insert and position picture here.*, and press **Delete**. Click the **INSERT tab** and click **Online Pictures** in the Illustrations group.

- Click in the **Office.com Clip Art search box**, type **Cupcakes**, and then press **Enter**.
- Select **Cupcake with a single birthday candle** or select any image and click **Insert**. Do not deselect the image.
- Click the **PICTURE TOOLS FORMAT tab**, if necessary, click the **More button** in the Picture Styles group, and then click the **Soft Edge Rectangle** (sixth from the left on the top row).
- Click outside the picture.

h. Click the **FILE tab** and click **Print**. Change *Normal Margins* to **Moderate Margins**. Click the **Back arrow**.

i. Click the picture and click **Center** in the Paragraph group on the HOME tab.

j. Save and close the file. Submit your files based on your instructor's directions.

3 Best Friends Pet Care

You and a friend are starting a pet sitting service and have a few clients already. Billing will be a large part of your record keeping, so you are planning ahead by developing a series of folders to maintain those records. This exercise follows the same set of skills as used in Hands-On Exercises 1, 2, and 5 in the chapter. Refer to Figure 1.61 as you complete this exercise.

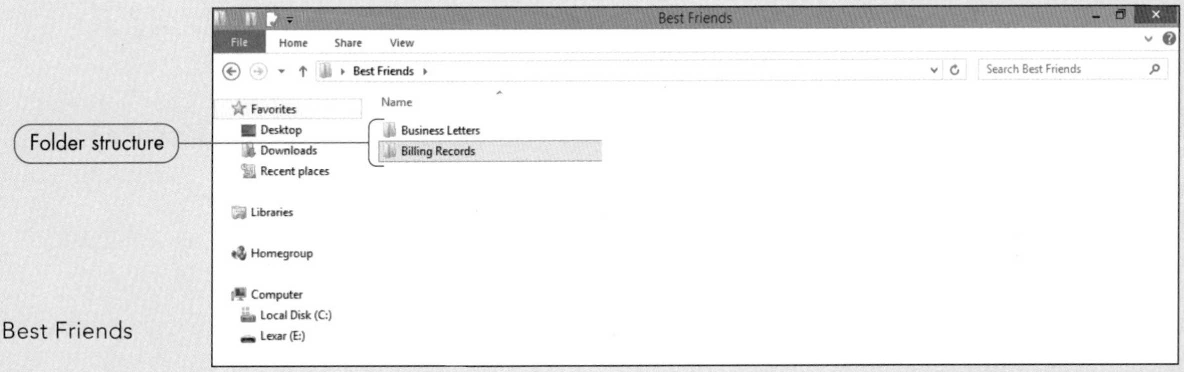

FIGURE 1.61 Best Friends Pet Care

a. Click **File Explorer** on the taskbar and select the location where you save your files. Click the **Home tab** and click **New folder** in the New group. Type **Best Friends** and press **Enter**.

b. Double-click **Best Friends** in the Content pane to open the folder. Create new subfolders as follows:

- Click the **Home tab** and click **New folder** in the New group. Type **Business Letters** and press **Enter**.
- Click the **Home tab** and click **New folder** in the New group. Type **Billing Records** and press **Enter**. Compare your results to Figure 1.61. Take a snip and name it **f01p3FriendsSnip_LastFirst**. Save it in the Billing Records subfolder of the Best Friends folder. Close File Explorer.

c. Navigate to the Start screen and click on **Word 2013**. Click **Open Other Documents** and open *f01p3Friends*. Save it as **f01p3Friends_LastFirst** in the Business Letters subfolder of the Best Friends folder.

d. Use *Find and Replace* to replace the text *Your Name* with your name by doing the following:

- Click **Replace** in the Editing group on the HOME tab.
- Type **Your name** in the **Find what box**. Type your first and last names in the **Replace with box**.
- Click **Replace** and click **OK**. Close the *Find and Replace* dialog box. Close, save changes to the document, and exit Word.

e. Click **File Explorer** on the taskbar so that you can rename one of your folders:

- Click **Computer** in the Navigation Pane.
- In the Content pane, navigate to the drive where you earlier created the Best Friends folder. Double-click the **Best Friends folder**.
- Right-click **Billing Records**, click **Rename**, type **Accounting Records**, and then press **Enter**.

f. Take a snip and name it **f01p3FolderSnip_LastFirst**. Save it in the Business Letters subfolder of the Best Friends folder. Submit your files based on your instructor's directions.

Mid-Level Exercises

1 Reference Letter

You are an instructor at a local community college. A student has asked you to provide her with a letter of reference for a job application. You have used Word to prepare the letter, but now you need to make a few changes before it is finalized.

a. Open File Explorer. Create a new folder named **References** in the location where you are saving your student files. Take a snip, name it **f01m1ReferencesSnip_LastFirst**, and save it in the References folder. Close File Explorer.

b. Start Word. Open *f01m1Letter* and save it in the References folder as **f01m1Letter_LastFirst**.

c. Select the date and point to several font sizes in the Mini toolbar. Use the Live Preview to compare them. Click **11**.

d. Double-click the date and use the **Format Painter** to change the rest of the letter to font size 11.

e. Apply bold to the student's name, *Stacy VanPatten*, in the first sentence.

f. Correct all errors using Spelling & Grammar. Her last name is spelled correctly. Use the Thesaurus to find a synonym for *intelligent* and replace wih **gifted**. Change the *an* to *a* just before the new word. Replace each occurrence of *Stacy* with **Stacey**.

g. Move the last paragraph—beginning with *In my opinion*—to position it before the second paragraph—beginning with *Stacey is a gifted*.

h. Move the insertion point to the beginning of the document.

i. Change the margins to **Narrow**.

j. Preview the document as it will appear when printed.

k. Save and close the file. Submit your files based on your instructor's directions.

2 Medical Monitoring

You are enrolled in a Health Informatics program of study in which you learn to manage databases related to health fields. For a class project, your instructor requires that you monitor your blood pressure, recording your findings in an Excel worksheet. You have recorded the week's data and will now make a few changes before printing the worksheet for submission.

a. Open File Explorer. Create a new folder named **Medical** in the location where you are saving your student files. Take a snip, name it **f01m2MedicalSnip_LastFirst**, and save it in the Medical folder. Close File Explorer.

b. Start Excel. Open *f01m2Tracker* and save it as **f01m2Tracker_LastFirst** in the Medical folder.

c. Preview the worksheet as it will appear when printed. Change the orientation of the worksheet to **Landscape**. Preview the worksheet again.

d. Click in the cell to the right of *Name* and type your first and last names. Press **Enter**.

e. Change the font of the text in **cell C1** to **Verdana**. Use Live Preview to try some font sizes. Change the font size to **20**.

f. Check the spelling for the worksheet.

DISCOVER 🅷 **g.** Get help on showing decimal places. You want to increase the decimal places for the values in **cells E22, F22, and G22** so that each value shows two places to the right of the decimal. Use Excel Help to learn how to do that. You might use *Increase Decimals* as a Search term. When you find the answer, select the three cells and increase the decimal places to **2**.

h. Click **cell A1** and insert a picture of your choice related to blood pressure. Be sure the image includes content from Office.com. Resize and position the picture so that it displays in an attractive manner. Format the picture with **Soft Edges** set to **4 pt**. Change the margins to **Wide**.

i. Open the Backstage view and adjust print settings to print two copies. You will not actually print two copies unless directed by your instructor.

j. Save and close the file. Submit your files based on your instructor's directions.

3 Today's Musical Artists

COLLABORATION CASE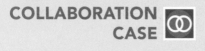

CREATIVE CASE ★

With a few of your classmates, you will use PowerPoint to create a single presentation on your favorite musical artists. Each student must create at least one slide and then all of the slides will be added to the presentation. Because everyone's schedule is varied, you should use either your Outlook account or OneDrive to pass the presentation file among the group.

a. Open File Explorer. Create a new folder named **Musical** in the location where you are saving your student files. Take a snip, name it **f01m3MusicalSnip_LastFirst**, and then save it in the Musical folder. Close File Explorer.

b. Start PowerPoint. Create a new presentation and save it as **f01m3Music_GroupName** in the Musical folder.

c. Add one slide that contains the name of the artist, the genre, and two or three interesting facts about the artist.

d. Insert a picture of the artist or clip art that represents the artist.

e. Put your name on the slide that you created. Save the presentation.

f. Pass the presentation to the next student so that he or she can perform the same tasks and save the presentation before passing it on to the next student. Continue until all group members have created a slide in the presentation.

g. Save and close the file. Submit your file based on your instructor's directions.

Beyond the Classroom

Fitness Planner

RESEARCH CASE

You will use Microsoft Excel to develop a fitness planner. Open *f01b2Exercise* and save it as **f01b2Exercise_LastFirst**. Because the fitness planner is a template, the exercise categories are listed, but without actual data. You will personalize the planner. Change the orientation to **Landscape**. Move the contents of **cell A2** (*Exercise Planner*) to **cell A1**. Click **cell A8** and use the Format Painter to copy the format of that selection to **cells A5** and **A6**. Increase the font size of **cell A1** to **26**. Use Excel Help to learn how to insert a header and put your name in the header. Begin the fitness planner, entering at least one activity in each category (warm-up, aerobics, strength, and cool-down). Submit as directed by your instructor.

Household Records

DISASTER RECOVERY

FROM SCRATCH

Use Microsoft Excel to create a detailed record of your household appliances and other items of value that are in your home. In case of burglary or disaster, an insurance claim is expedited if you are able to itemize what was lost along with identifying information such as serial numbers. You will then make a copy of the record on another storage device for safekeeping outside your home (in case your home is destroyed by a fire or weather-related catastrophe). Connect a flash drive to your computer and then use File Explorer to create a folder on the hard drive titled **Home Records**. Design a worksheet listing at least five fictional appliances and electronic equipment along with the serial number of each. Save the workbook as **f01b3Household_LastFirst** in the Home Records folder. Close the workbook and exit Excel. Use File Explorer to copy the Home Records folder from the hard drive to your flash drive. Use the Snipping Tool to create a full-screen snip of the screen display. Save it as **f01b3Disaster_LastFirst** in the Home Records folder. Close all open windows and submit as directed by your instructor.

Meetings

SOFT SKILLS CASE

FROM SCRATCH

After watching the Meetings video, you will use File Explorer to create a series of folders and subfolders to organize meetings by date. Each folder should be named by month, day, and year. Three subfolders should be created for each meeting. The subfolders should be named **Agenda**, **Handouts**, and **Meeting Notes**. Use the Snipping Tool to create a full-screen snip of the screen display. Save it as **f01b4Meetings_LastFirst**. Submit as directed by your instructor.

Capstone Exercise

MyITLab®
Grader

You are a member of the Student Government Association (SGA) at your college. As a community project, the SGA is sponsoring a Stop Smoking drive designed to provide information on the health risks posed by smoking cigarettes and to offer solutions to those who want to quit. The SGA has partnered with the local branch of the American Cancer Society as well as the outreach program of the local hospital to sponsor free educational awareness seminars. As the secretary for the SGA, you will help prepare a PowerPoint presentation that will be displayed on plasma screens around campus and used in student seminars. You will use Microsoft Office to help with those tasks.

Manage Files and Folders

You will open, review, and save an Excel worksheet providing data on the personal monetary cost of smoking cigarettes over a period of years.

a. Create a folder called **SGA Drive**.

b. Start Excel. Open *f01c1Cost* from the student data files and save it in the SGA Drive folder as **f01c1Cost_LastFirst**.

c. Click **cell A10** and type your first and last names. Press **Enter**.

Modify the Font

To highlight some key figures on the worksheet, you will format those cells with additional font attributes.

a. Draw attention to the high cost of smoking for 10, 20, and 30 years by changing the font color in **cells G3 through I4** to **Red**.

b. Italicize the Annual Cost cells (**F3** and **F4**).

c. Click **Undo** on the Quick Access Toolbar to remove the italics. Click **Redo** to return the text to italics.

Insert a Picture

You will add a picture to the worksheet and then resize it and position it.

a. Click **cell G7** and insert an online picture appropriate for the topic of smoking.

b. Resize the picture and reposition it near cell B7.

c. Click outside the picture to deselect it.

Preview Print, Change Page Layout, and Print

To get an idea of how the worksheet will look when printed, you will preview the worksheet. Then you will change the orientation and margins before printing it.

a. Preview the document as it will appear when printed.

b. Change the page orientation to **Landscape**. Click the **PAGE LAYOUT tab** and change the margins to **Narrow**.

c. Preview the document as it will appear when printed.

d. Adjust the print settings to print two copies. You will not actually print two copies unless directed by your instructor.

e. Save and close the file.

Find and Replace

You have developed a PowerPoint presentation that you will use to present to student groups and for display on plasma screens across campus. The presentation is designed to increase awareness of the health problems associated with smoking. The PowerPoint presentation has come back from the reviewers with only one comment: A reviewer suggested that you spell out Centers for Disease Control and Prevention, instead of abbreviating it. You do not remember exactly which slide or slides the abbreviation might have been on, so you use *Find and Replace* to make the change quickly.

a. Start PowerPoint. Open *f01c1Quit* and save it in the SGA Drive folder as **f01c1Quit_LastFirst**.

b. Replace all occurrences of *CDC* with **Centers for Disease Control and Prevention**.

Cut and Paste and Insert a Text Box

The Mark Twain quote on Slide 1 might be more effective on the last slide in the presentation, so you will cut and paste it there in a text box.

a. On Slide 1, select the entire Mark Twain quote by clicking on the placeholder border. When the border is solid, the entire placeholder and its contents are selected.

b. On Slide 22, paste the quote, reposition it more attractively, and then format it in a larger font size.

Check Spelling and Change View

Before you call the presentation complete, you will spell check it and view it as a slide show.

a. Check spelling. The word *hairlike* is not misspelled, so it should not be corrected.

b. View the slide show and take the smoking quiz. Click after the last slide to return to the presentation.

c. Save and close the presentation. Exit PowerPoint. Submit both files included in this project as directed by your instructor.

Introduction to Access

Finding Your Way Through an Access Database

OBJECTIVES | AFTER YOU READ THIS CHAPTER, YOU WILL BE ABLE TO:

1. Understand database fundamentals p. 84
2. Use an existing database p. 91
3. Sort table data on one or multiple fields p. 102
4. Create, modify, and remove filters p. 103
5. Know when to use Access or Excel to manage data p. 111
6. Understand relational power p. 112
7. Create a database p. 119

CASE STUDY | Managing a Business in the Global Economy

Northwind Traders* is an international gourmet food distributor that imports and exports specialty foods from around the world. Northwind's products include meats, seafood, dairy products, beverages, and produce. Keeping track of customers, vendors, orders, and inventory is a critical task. The owners of Northwind have just purchased an order-processing database created with Microsoft Office Access 2013 to help manage their customers, suppliers, products, and orders.

You have been hired to learn, use, and manage the database. Northwind's owners are willing to provide training about their business and Access. They expect the learning process to take about three months. After three months, your job will be to support the order-processing team as well as to provide detail and summary reports to the sales force as needed. Your new job at Northwind Traders will be a challenge, but it is also a good opportunity to make a great contribution to a global company. Are you up to the task?

*Northwind Traders was created by the Microsoft Access Team as a sample database for Access 2003. Access 2013 does not include a sample database, so you will use a modified version of Northwind Traders. The names of companies, products, people, characters, and/or data are fictitious.

Databases Are Everywhere!

A *database* is a collection of data organized as meaningful information that can be accessed, managed, stored, queried, sorted, and reported. You probably participate in data collection and are exposed to databases on a regular basis. For example, your community college or university uses a database to store registration data. When you enrolled at your institution, you created a profile that was saved in a database. When you registered for this course, your data was entered into a database. If you have a bank account, have a Social Security card, have a medical history, or have booked a flight with an airline, your information is stored in a record in a database.

If you use the Internet, you probably use databases often because the Internet can provide you with easy access to databases. For example, when you shop online or check your bank statement online, you connect to a database. Even when you type a search phrase into Google and click Search, you are using Google's massive database with all of its stored Web page references and keywords. Look for something on Amazon, and you are searching Amazon's database to find a product that you might want to buy. Need a new driver for golfing? Log on to Amazon, search for "golf clubs driver" (see Figure 1.1), and find the right driver with your preferred loft, hand orientation, flex, shaft material, and price range. All of this information is stored in Amazon's products database.

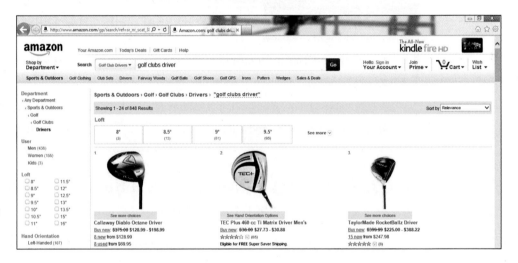

FIGURE 1.1 Amazon Web Site

Photo: Copyright © 2013 Amazon .com, Inc.

Organizations rely on data to conduct daily operations, regardless of whether the organization exists as a profit or not-for-profit environment. Organizations maintain data about their customers, employees, orders, volunteers, activities, and facilities. Organizations maintain data about their customers, employees, orders, volunteers, activities, and facilities, and this data needs to be stored, organized, and made available for analysis. *Data* and *information* are two terms that are often used interchangeably. However, when it comes to databases, the two terms mean different things. *Data* is what is entered into a database. *Information* is the finished product that is produced by the database. Data is converted to information by selecting, calculating, sorting, or summarizing records. Decisions in an organization are usually based on information produced by a database, rather than raw data.

In this section, you will learn the fundamentals of organizing data in a database, explore what Access database objects are and what their purpose is, and examine the Access interface.

Understanding Database Fundamentals

People use databases to store collections of data. A *database management system (DBMS)* is a software system that provides the tools needed to create, maintain, and use a database. Database management systems make it possible to access and control data and display the information in a variety of formats such as lists, forms, and reports. *Access* is the database management system included in the Office 2013 Professional suite and the Office 2013 Professional Academic suite. Access is a valuable decision-making tool that many organizations are using. Advanced Access users and software developers can even use Microsoft Access to develop software applications for specific solutions to the needs of organizations. For example, a health organization uses Access to track and understand disease reports.

Organize Information in a Database and Recognize Access Objects

STEP 2 ⟩⟩ An Access database is a structured collection of *objects*, the main components that are created and used to make the database function. The main object types in an Access database are listed below and discussed in the following paragraphs.

- Tables
- Forms
- Queries
- Reports
- Macros
- Modules

The objects that make up an Access database are available from the *Navigation Pane*. The Navigation Pane is an Access interface element that organizes and lists the database objects in an Access database. You will learn about the object types and their benefits in the remainder of this section. Later you will learn to create and use these objects.

The foundation of every database is a *table*, the object in which data, such as a person's name or a product number, is stored. The other objects in a database are based on one or more underlying tables. To understand how an Access database works and how to use Access effectively, you should learn the structure of a table. Tables organize data into columns and rows. Columns display a *field*, the smallest data element of a table. For example, in the Northwind database, a table containing information about customers would include a Customer ID field. Another field would contain the Company Name. Fields may be required or optional—a contact name may be required, for example, but a contact title may be optional.

Each row in a table contains a *record*, a complete set of all the fields (data elements) about one person, place, event, or concept. A customer record, for example, would contain all of the fields about a single customer, including the Customer ID, the Company Name, Contact Name, Contact Title, Address, City, etc. Figure 1.2 shows the Northwind database with the Customers table selected in the Navigation Pane. The Customers table is open and shows the records of Northwind customers in the table rows. Each record contains multiple fields, with the field name displaying at the top of each column.

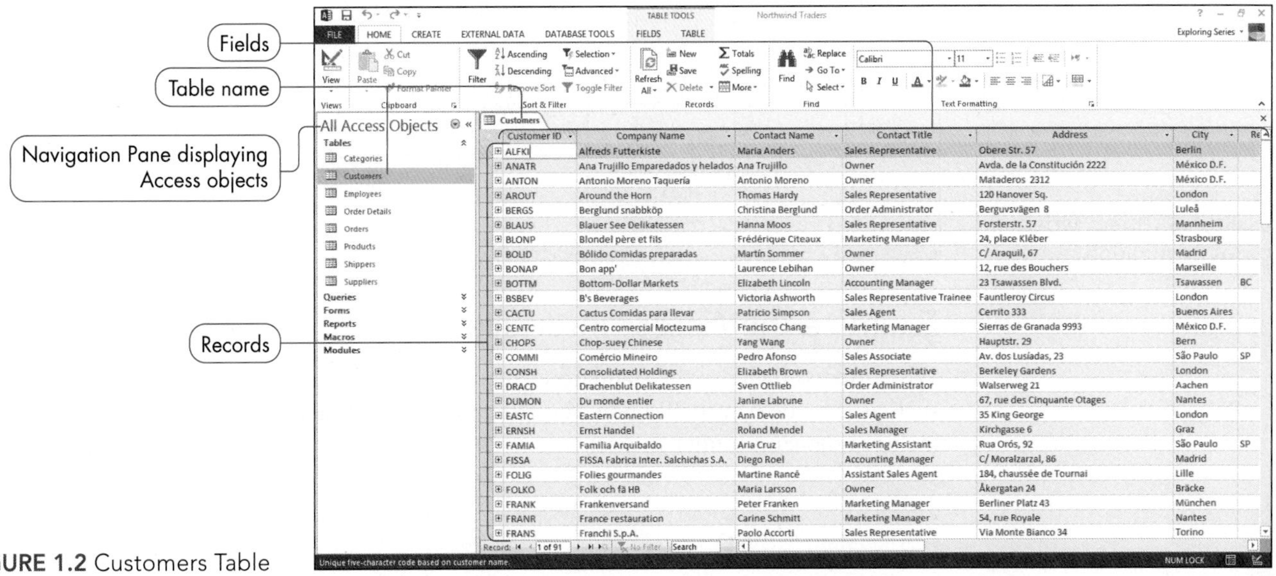

FIGURE 1.2 Customers Table

A *form* is an object that gives a user a way of entering and modifying data in databases. Forms enable you to enter, modify, or delete table data. They enable you to manipulate data in the same manner that you would in a table. The difference is that you can create a form that will limit the user to viewing only one record at a time. This helps the user to focus on the data being entered or modified and also provides for more reliable data entry. As an Access user, you will add, delete, and edit records in Form view. As the Access designer, you will create and edit the form structure.

A *query* is a question that you ask about the data in your database. For example, how many of our customers live in Boston? The answer is shown in the query results. A query can be used to display only records that meet certain conditions and only the fields that you require. In addition to helping you find and retrieve data that meets the conditions that you specify, you can use a query to update or delete records and to perform predefined or custom calculations with your data.

A *report* contains professional-looking formatted information from underlying tables or queries. Reports enable you to print the information in your database and are an effective way to present database information. You have control over the size and appearance of everything in a report. Access provides different views for designing, modifying, and running reports.

Two other object types, macros and modules, are used less frequently unless you are a power Access user. A *macro* object is a stored series of commands that carry out an action. You can create a macro to automate simple tasks by selecting an action from a list of macro actions. A *module* is similar to a macro, as it is an object that adds functionality to a database, but modules are written using the VBA (Visual Basic for Applications) programming language.

Figure 1.3 displays the different object types in Access with the foundation object—the table—in the center of the illustration. The purpose each object serves is explained underneath the object name. The flow of information between objects is indicated by single arrowhead arrows if the flow is one direction only. Two arrowhead arrows indicate that the flow goes both directions. For example, you can use forms to view, add, delete, or modify data from tables.

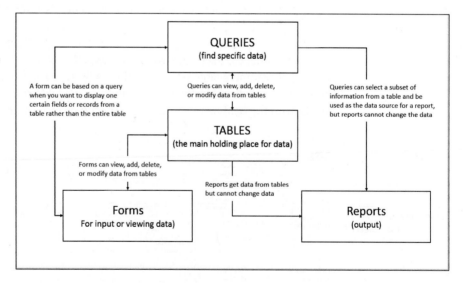

FIGURE 1.3 Object Types and Flow of Information

Examine the Access Interface

While Access includes the standard elements of the Microsoft Office applications interface such as the title bar, the Ribbon, the Home tab, the Backstage view, and scroll bars, it also includes elements unique to Access.

The Access Ribbon has five tabs that will always display, as well as contextual tabs that appear only when particular objects are open. The File tab leads to the Backstage view, which gives you access to a variety of database tools such as Save, Save As, Compact and Repair, Backup Database, and Print. The Home tab, the default Access tab, contains basic editing functions, such as cut and paste, filtering, find and replace, and most formatting actions. This tab also contains the features that enable you to work with record creation and deletion, totals, and spelling.

The Create tab contains all the tools used to create new objects in a database whereas the External Data tab contains all of the operations used to facilitate data import and export. Finally, the Database Tools tab contains the feature that enables users to create relationships between tables and enables use of the more advanced features of Access, such as setting relationships between tables, analyzing a table or query, and migrating data to SharePoint.

On the left side of the screen, you will see the Navigation Pane. The Navigation Pane organizes and lists all of the objects that are needed to make the current database function. You can open any object by double-clicking the object's name in the list. You can also open an object by right-clicking the object name and selecting Open from the shortcut menu. Right-clicking provides other options, such as renaming the object, cutting the object, and copying the object.

Most databases contain multiple tables, queries, forms, and reports. By default, the objects display in groups by object type in the Navigation Pane. If you wish, you can collapse the contents of an object group by clicking the group heading or the double arrows to the right of the group heading. To expand the contents of an object group that has been hidden, click the heading again or click the double arrows to the right of the group heading again. If you wish to change the way objects are grouped in the Navigation Pane, click the list arrow on the Navigation Pane title bar and select your preferred configuration of the available options.

TIP Navigation Pane Display

By default, Access uses a Tabbed Documents interface. That means that each object that is open has its own tab beneath the Ribbon and to the right of the Navigation Pane. You can switch between open objects by clicking a tab to make that object active. Figure 1.4 shows the Access interface for the Northwind Traders database, which was introduced in the Case Study at the beginning of the chapter. The Navigation Pane is grouped by object type. The Tables and Reports groups in the Navigation Pane are expanded. The Table Tools contextual tab displays because the Employees table is open. The Employees table shows the records for nine employees. The employee records contain multiple fields about each employee, including the employee's Last Name, First Name, Hire Date, Region, and so on. Occasionally a field does not contain a value for a particular record. For example, one of the employees, Nancy Davolio, has not been assigned a title yet. The value of that field is missing. Access shows a blank cell when data is missing.

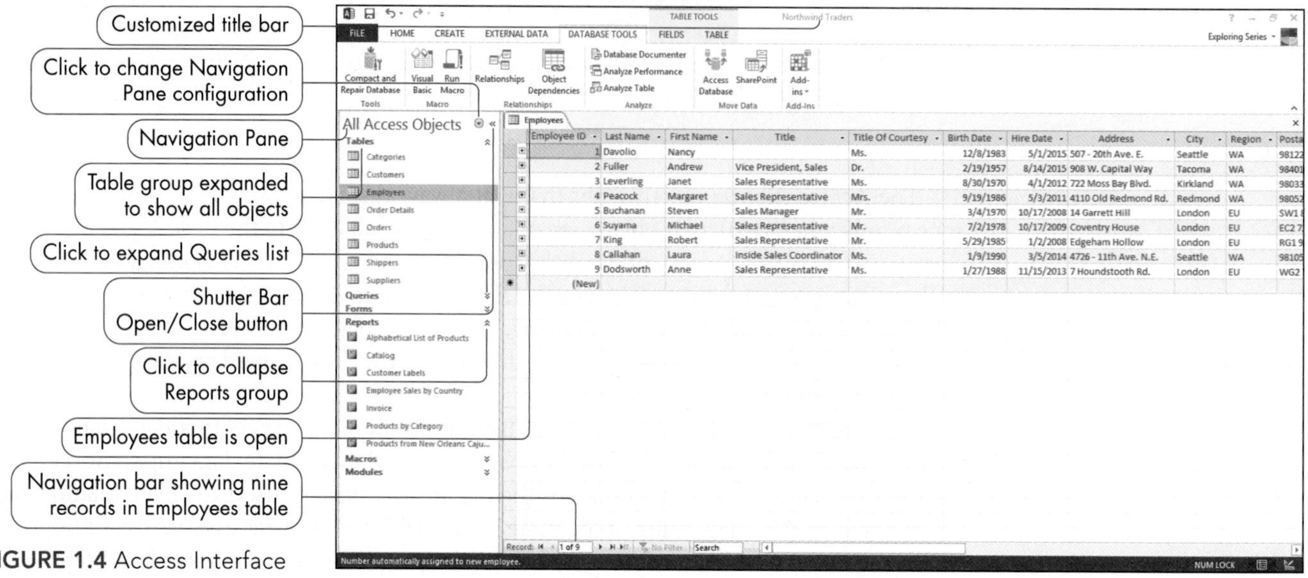

FIGURE 1.4 Access Interface

Explore Access Views

Access provides two different ways to view a table: the Datasheet view and the Design view. To switch between views:

- Click the HOME tab and click View in the Views group to toggle between the current view and the previous view.
- Click the HOME tab, click the View arrow in the Views group, and then select the view you want to use.
- Right-click the object tab and select the view you want to use.
- Right-click the object in the Navigation Pane and select the view you want to use.
- Click one of the view shortcuts in the lower-right corner of the Access window.

The *Datasheet view* is a grid containing fields (columns) and records (rows), similar to an Excel spreadsheet. You can view, add, edit, and delete records in the Datasheet view. Figure 1.5 shows the Datasheet view for the Northwind Customers table. Each row contains a record for a specific customer. Click the *record selector* at the beginning of a row to select the record. Each column represents a field or one attribute about a customer. Click the *field selector*, or column heading, to select a column.

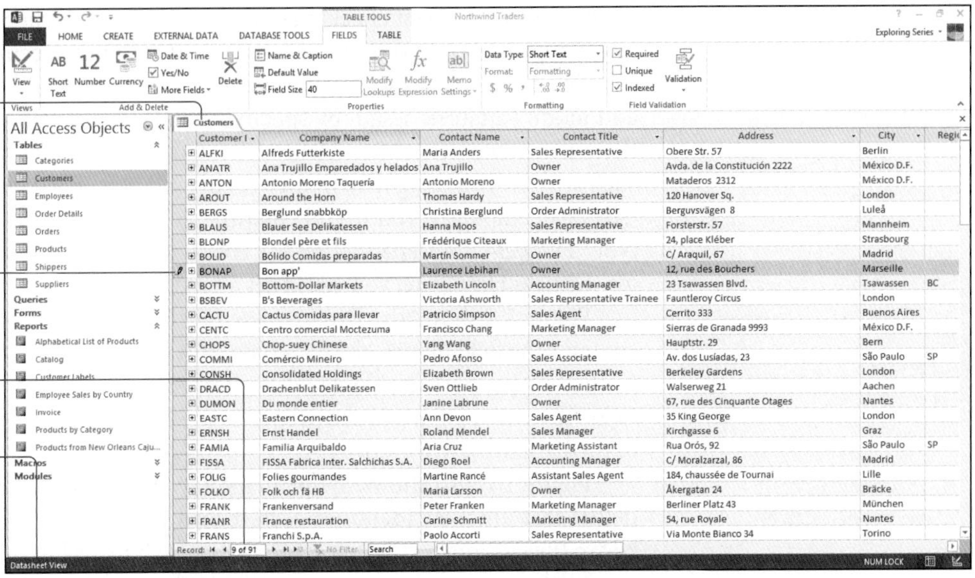

Customers table is open

Pencil in record selector indicates the record is being edited

Navigation bar indicates record 9 of 91 customers in the table is selected

Datasheet view

FIGURE 1.5 Customers Table in Datasheet View

The navigation bar at the bottom of Figure 1.5 shows that the Customers table has 91 records and that record number 9 is the current record. The vertical scroll bar on the right side of the window displays only when the table contains more records than can appear in the window at one time. Similarly, the horizontal scroll bar at the bottom of the window displays only when the table contains more fields than can appear in the window at one time.

The pencil symbol to the left of Record 9 indicates that the data in that record is being edited and that changes have not yet been saved. The pencil symbol disappears when you move to another record. It is important to understand that Access saves data automatically as soon as you move from one record to another. This may seem counterintuitive at first because other Office applications, such as Word and Excel, do not save changes and additions automatically.

Figure 1.6 shows the navigation buttons on the *navigation bar* that you use to move through the records in a table, query, or form. The buttons enable you to go to the first record, the previous record, the next record, or the last record. The button with the yellow asterisk is used to add a new (blank) record. You can also type a number directly into the current record field, and Access will take you to that record. Finally, the navigation bar enables you to find a record based on a single word. Type the word in the search box, and Access will locate the first record that contains the word.

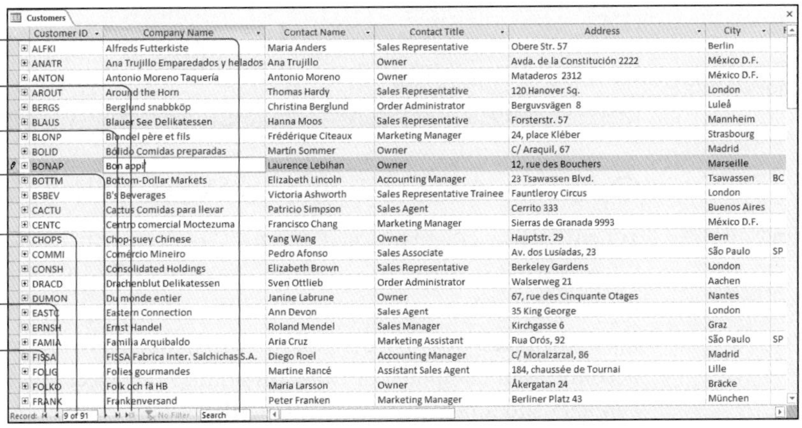

Type in a single search word

Create a new (blank) record

Go to the last record

Go to the next record

Type in the record you want to go to

Go to the previous record

Go to the first record

FIGURE 1.6 Navigation Buttons

You can also use the Find command in the Find group on the Home tab to locate specific records within a table, form, or query. You can search for a single field or the entire record, match all or part of the selected field(s), move forward or back in a table, or specify a case-sensitive search. The Replace command can be used to substitute one value for another. Select Replace All if you want Access to automatically search for and replace every instance of a value without first checking with you. Be careful when using the Replace All option for global replacement, however, because unintended replacements are possible.

The **Design view** gives you a detailed view of the table's structure and is used to create and modify a table's design by specifying the fields it will contain, the fields' data types, and their associated properties. Data types define the type of data that will be stored in a field, such as short text, long text, numeric, currency, etc. For example, if you need to store the hire date of an employee, you would enter the field name Hire Date and select the Date/Time data type. The **field properties** define the characteristics of the fields in more detail. For example, for the field Hire Date, you could set a field property that requires a Short Date format.

Figure 1.7 shows the Design view for the Customers table. In the top portion, each row contains the field names, the data type, and an optional description for each field in the table. In the bottom portion, the Field Properties pane contains the properties (details) for each field. Click on a field, and the properties for that field will be displayed in the bottom portion of the Design view window.

Figure 1.7 also shows the primary key. The **primary key** is the field (or combination of fields) that uniquely identifies each record in a table. The CustomerID field is the primary key in the Customers table; it ensures that each record in the table can be distinguished from every other record. It also helps prevent the occurrence of duplicate records. Primary key fields may be numbers, letters, or a combination of both. In Figure 1.7, the primary key has an **AutoNumber** data type (a number that is generated by Access and is automatically incremented each time a record is added). Another example of a primary key is an automatically generated Employee ID.

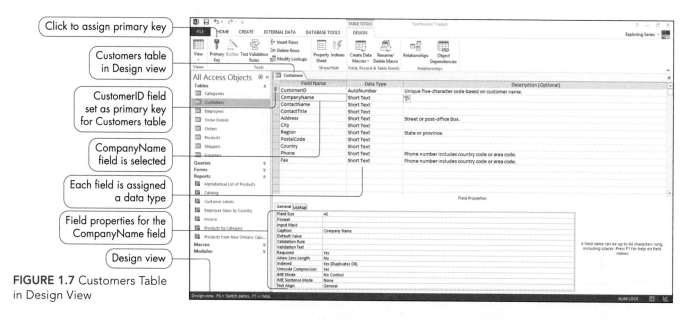

FIGURE 1.7 Customers Table in Design View

Open an Access File and Work with Content Security

STEP 1 ▶

When Access is first launched, the Backstage view displays. The left side of the view provides a list of databases you have recently used. Beneath the list of recently used databases is the Open Other Files option. Click Open Other Files to access the Open options. You will see a list of the places your account allows you to open a file from: a recent location, your SkyDrive account, your computer, or from any additional places you have added to your Places list. You can also add a new place by clicking the *Add a Place* option. If you select your SkyDrive or another place and the desired database is not in the recent list, you will need to click Browse to open the Open dialog box. Then you can locate and select the database and click Open.

If you are currently using Access and wish to open another database, do the following:

1. Click the FILE tab.
2. Click Open in Backstage view to access Open options.
3. Select the place where the database is stored.

4. Click Browse to open the Open dialog box.

5. Locate and select the database and click Open.

If you open a database from a location you have not designated as a trusted location or open a database that does not have a digital signature from a publisher you can trust, Access will display a message bar immediately below the Ribbon. The message bar displays a security warning designed to prevent you from opening a database that may contain harmful code that can be hidden in macros or VBA modules. Click the Enable Content button if you trust the database's source—it becomes a trusted location. After you click Enable Content, Access closes the database and reopens the file to enable the content. Access also adds the database to its list of trusted documents so you will not see the security message again. All content from this publisher and associated with this book can be trusted.

Using an Existing Database

Databases must be carefully managed to keep information accurate. Records need to be edited when changes occur and when new records are added, and records may need to be deleted on occasion. All of these processes are easily accomplished using Access. Managing a database also requires that you understand when data is saved and when you need to use the Save commands.

Understand the Difference Between Working in Storage and Memory

STEP 3 » The way Access performs its save function is different from the other Microsoft Office applications. Word, Excel, and PowerPoint all work primarily from memory. In those applications, your work is not automatically saved to your storage location. You must save your work. This could be catastrophic if you are working with a PowerPoint presentation and you forget to save it. If the power is lost, you may lose your presentation. Access, on the other hand, works primarily from storage. As you enter and update the data in an Access database, the changes are automatically saved to the storage location you specified when you saved the database. If a power failure occurs, you will lose only the changes to the record that you are currently editing.

When you make a change to a record's content in an Access table (for example, changing a customer's cell phone number), Access saves your changes as soon as you move the insertion point to a different record. However, you are required to save after you modify the design of a table, a query, a form, or a report. When you modify an object's design, such as widening a field display on the Customers form, and then close it, Access will prompt you with the message "Do you want to save changes to the design of form 'Customers'?" Click Yes to save your changes.

Also in Access, you can click Undo to reverse the most recent change (the phone number you just modified) to a single record immediately after making changes to that record. However, unlike other Office programs that enable multiple Undo steps, you cannot use Undo to reverse multiple edits in Access.

With an Access database file, several users can work in the same file at the same time. Databases are often located on company servers, making it easy to have multiple users working in the same database at the same time. As long as multiple users do not attempt to change the same record at the same time, Access will let these users access the database simultaneously. So one person can be adding records to the Customers table while another can be creating a query based on the Products table. Two users can even work on the same table as long as they are not working on the same record.

Add, Edit, and Delete Records

STEP 4 » To add a new record, click New in the Records group on the Home tab or click *New (blank) record* on the navigation bar. In a table, you can also click the first column of the blank row beneath the last record. As soon as you begin typing, the asterisk record indicator changes to a pencil icon to show that you are in editing mode. Press Tab to move to the next column so that you can enter the data for the next field. Pressing Tab in the last column in the record saves the record and moves the insertion point to the next record. You can also press Shift+Enter at any time in the record to save the record. The easiest way to save the record is to press the up or down arrow on your keyboard, which moves you to another record. As soon as you move to another record Access automatically saves the changes to the record you created or changed.

To edit a record, tab to the field you want to modify and type the new data. When you start typing, you erase all existing data in the field because the entire field is selected. You can switch to Edit mode by pressing F2. In Edit mode, you will not automatically delete all the data in the field. Instead, you can position your insertion point and make the changes you want.

REFERENCE Keyboard Shortcuts for Entering Data

Keystroke	Result
Up arrow (↑)	Moves insertion point up one row.
Down arrow (↓)	Moves insertion point down one row.
Left arrow (←)	Moves insertion point left one field in the same row.
Right arrow (→)	Moves insertion point right one field in the same row.
Tab or Enter	Moves insertion point right one field in the same row.
Shift+Tab	Moves insertion point left one field in the same row.
Home	Moves insertion point to the first field in the current row.
End	Moves insertion point to the last field in the current row.
Page Up	Moves insertion point up one screen.
Page Down	Moves insertion point down one screen.
Ctrl+Home	Moves insertion point to the first field in the first row.
Ctrl+End	Moves insertion point to the last field in the last row.
Esc	Cancels any changes made in the current field while in Edit mode.
Ctrl+Z	Reverses the last edit.
Ctrl+semicolon (;)	Enters the current date.
Ctrl+Alt+Spacebar	Enters the default value of a field.
Ctrl+single quote	Enters the value from the same field in the previous record.
Ctrl+plus sign (+)	Moves to a new record row.
Ctrl+minus sign (−)	Deletes the current record.

STEP 5 » To delete a record, click the row selector for the record you want to delete and click Delete in the Records group on the Home tab. You can also delete a selected record by pressing Delete on the keyboard, or by right-clicking the row selector and selecting Delete Record from the shortcut menu.

Save As, Compact and Repair, and Back Up Access Files

STEP 6 The Backstage view gives you access to the Save As command. When you click the Save As command, you can choose the file type you want to save: the database or the current object. Having the option of saving the entire database or just a component of it distinguishes Access from Word, Excel, and PowerPoint. Those applications have only one thing being saved—the primary document, workbook, or presentation. Save Database As enables you to select whether you want to save the database in the default database format (Access 2007–2013 file format), in one of the earlier Access formats, or as a template. Save Object As enables you to make a copy of the current Access object or publish a copy of the object as a PDF or XPS file. A PDF or XPS file looks the same on most computers because these file types preserve the object's formatting. PDF and XPS files also have a small file size. You can also click Save on the Quick Access Toolbar to save an active object—clicking Save on the Quick Access Toolbar does not save the database.

To help you manage your database so that it operates efficiently and securely, Access provides two utilities to help protect the data within a database: *Compact and Repair*, which reduces the size of the database, and *Back Up Database*, which creates a duplicate copy of the database.

Databases have a tendency to expand with everyday use and may become corrupt, so Access provides the *Compact and Repair Database* utility. Entering data, creating queries, running reports, and adding and deleting objects will all cause a database file to expand. This growth may increase storage requirements and may also impact database performance. When you run the Compact and Repair utility, it creates a new database file behind the scenes and copies all the objects from the original database into the new one. As it copies the objects into the new file, Access removes temporary objects and unclaimed space due to deleted objects, which results in a smaller database file. *Compact and Repair* will also defragment a fragmented database file if needed. When the utility is finished copying the data, it deletes the original file and renames the new one with the same name as the original. This utility can also be used to repair a corrupt database. In most cases, only a small amount of data—the last record modified—will be lost during the repair process. You should compact your database every day. To compact and repair an open database, do the following:

1. Close all open objects in the database.
2. Click the FILE tab.
3. Click *Compact and Repair Database* in the Info options.

As an alternative, you can click the Database Tools tab and click *Compact and Repair Database* in the Tools group.

The Back Up Database utility makes a copy of the entire database to protect your database from loss or damage. Imagine what would happen to a firm that loses the orders placed but not shipped, a charity that loses the list of donor contributions, or a hospital that loses the digital records of its patients. Making backups is especially important when you have multiple users working with the database. When you use the Back Up Database utility, Access provides a file name for the backup that uses the same file name as the database you are backing up, an underscore, and the current date. This makes it easy for you to keep track of databases by the date they were created. To back up a database, do the following:

1. Click the FILE tab and click Save As.
2. Click Save Database As under File Types, if necessary.
3. Click Back Up Database under the Advanced group.
4. Click Save As. Revise the location and file name if you want to change either and click Save.

In Hands-On Exercise 1, you will work with the Northwind Traders database discussed in the Case Study at the beginning of the chapter. You open the database and examine the interface and Access views, organize information, work with records, and save, compact, repair, and back up the database.

Quick
Concepts ✓

1. Name the six objects in an Access database and briefly describe the purpose of each. *p. 85*
2. What is the difference between Datasheet view and Design view in a table? *p. 88*
3. What is meant by the statement "Access works from storage"? *p. 91*
4. What is the purpose of the *Compact and Repair* utility? *p. 93*

Hands-On Exercises

1 Databases Are Everywhere!

Northwind purchases food items from suppliers around the world and sells them to restaurants and specialty food shops. Northwind depends on the data stored in its Access database to process orders and make daily decisions. In your new position with Northwind Traders, you need to spend time getting familiar with the Access database. You will open Northwind's database, examine the Access interface, review the existing objects in the database, and explore Access views. You will add, edit, and delete records using both tables and forms. Finally, you will compact and repair, and back up the database.

Skills covered: Open an Access File and Work with Content Security • Examine the Access Interface, Explore Access Views, Organize Information in a Database, and Recognize Access Objects and Edit a Record and Understand the Difference Between Working in Storage and Memory • Add a Record • Delete a Record • Save As, Compact and Repair, and Back Up the Database

STEP 1 » OPEN AN ACCESS FILE AND WORK WITH CONTENT SECURITY

This exercise introduces you to the Northwind Traders database. You will use this database to learn the fundamentals of working with database files. Refer to Figure 1.8 as you complete Step 1.

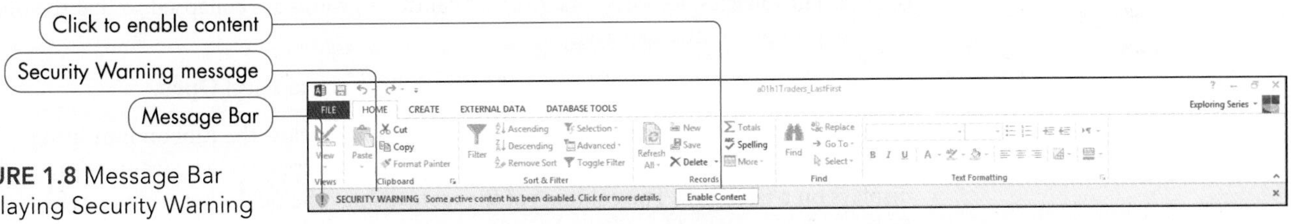

FIGURE 1.8 Message Bar Displaying Security Warning

- Click to enable content
- Security Warning message
- Message Bar

a. Open Access, click **Open Other Files**, click **Computer**, and then click **Browse**. Navigate to the folder location designated by your instructor. Click *a01h1Traders* and click **Open**.

b. Click the **FILE tab**, click **Save As**, click **Save Database As**, and then verify *Access Database* is selected under *Database File Types*. Click **Save As** and save the file as **a01h1Traders_LastFirst**.

When you save files, use your last and first names. For example, as the Access author, I would save my database as *a01h1traders_KrebsCynthia*. The Security Warning message bar appears below the Ribbon, indicating that some database content is disabled.

c. Click **Enable Content** on the Security Warning message bar.

When you open an Access file from the student files associated with this book, you will need to enable the content. You may be confident of the trustworthiness of the files for this book. Keep the database open for the rest of the exercise.

STEP 2 » EXAMINE THE ACCESS INTERFACE, EXPLORE ACCESS VIEWS, ORGANIZE INFORMATION IN A DATABASE, AND RECOGNIZE ACCESS OBJECTS

Now that you have opened Northwind Traders, you examine the Navigation Pane, objects, and views to become familiar with these fundamental Access features. Refer to Figure 1.9 as you complete Step 2.

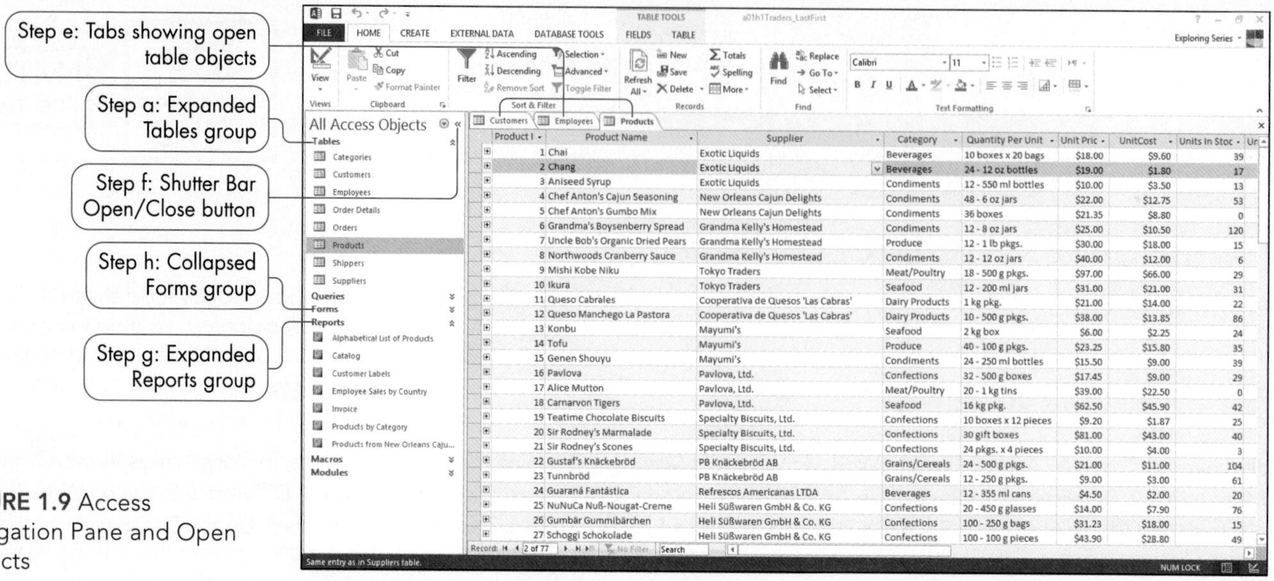

FIGURE 1.9 Access Navigation Pane and Open Objects

Callouts in figure:
- Step e: Tabs showing open table objects
- Step a: Expanded Tables group
- Step f: Shutter Bar Open/Close button
- Step h: Collapsed Forms group
- Step g: Expanded Reports group

a. Scroll through the Navigation Pane and note the Access objects listed under each expanded group.

The Tables group and the Forms group are expanded, displaying all of the tables and forms objects. The Queries, Reports, Macros, and Modules groups are collapsed so that the objects in those groups are not displayed.

b. Right-click the **Customers table** in the Navigation Pane and select **Open**.

The Customers table opens. The Customers tab displays below the Ribbon indicating the table object is open. The data contained in the table displays. Each customer's record displays on a table row. The columns of the table display the fields that comprise the records. You are viewing the table in Datasheet view.

c. Click **View** in the Views group on the HOME tab.

The view of the Customers table switches to Design view. The top portion of the view displays each field that comprises a customer record, the field's data type, and an optional description of what the field should contain. The bottom portion of the view displays the field properties (attributes) for the selected field.

d. Click **View** in the Views group on the HOME tab again.

Because View is a toggle button, your view returns to the Datasheet view, which resembles an Excel worksheet.

e. Double-click **Employees** in the Navigation Pane Tables group and double-click **Products** in the same location.

The tabs for three table objects display below the Ribbon: Customers, Employees, and Products.

f. Click the **Shutter Bar Open/Close button** on the title bar of the Navigation Pane to contract the Navigation Pane. Click the button again to expand the Navigation Pane.

The Shutter Bar Open/Close button toggles to allow you to view more in the open object window, or to enable you to view your database objects.

g. Scroll down in the Navigation Pane and click **Reports**.

The Reports group expands, and all report objects display.

h. Click the arrows to the right of Forms in the Navigation Pane.

The Forms group collapses and individual form objects no longer display.

STEP 3 >> EDIT A RECORD AND UNDERSTAND THE DIFFERENCE BETWEEN WORKING IN STORAGE AND MEMORY

You need to learn to edit the data in the Northwind database, because data can change. For example, employees will change their address and phone numbers when they move, and customers will change their order data from time to time. Refer to Figure 1.10 as you complete Step 3.

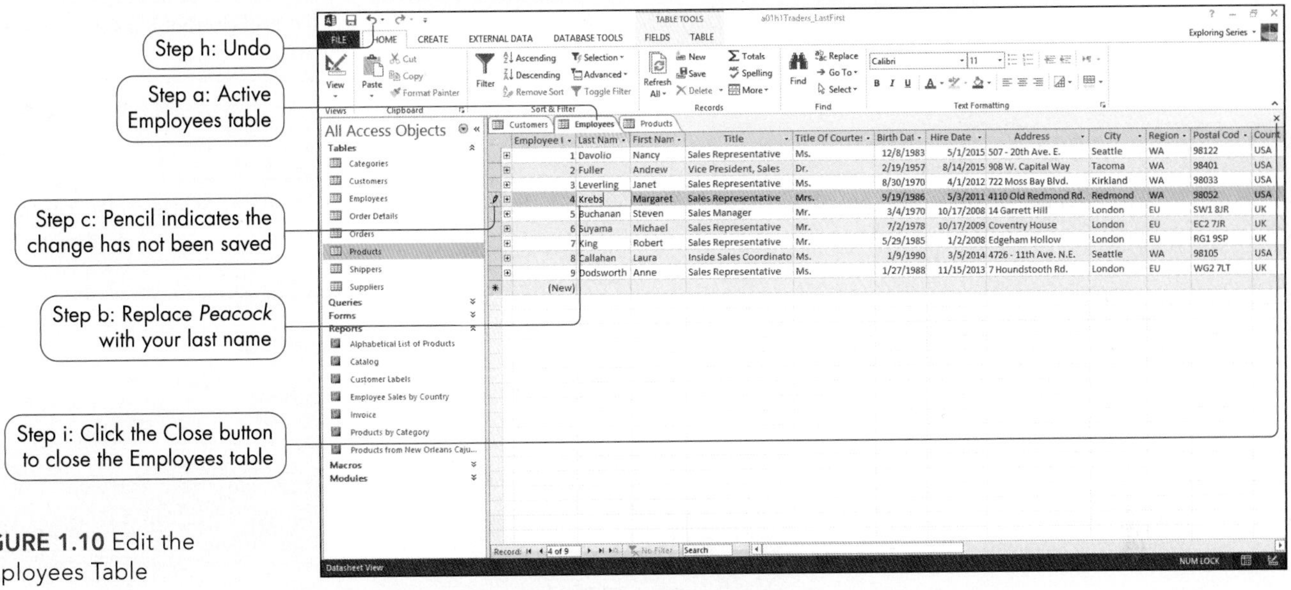

FIGURE 1.10 Edit the Employees Table

a. Click the **Employees tab** to activate the Employees table.

b. Click the **Last Name field** in the fourth row. Double-click **Peacock**; the entire name highlights. Type your last name to replace *Peacock*.

Your last name replaces Peacock. For example, as the Access author, my last name, Krebs, replaces Peacock.

c. Press **Tab** to move to the next field in the fourth row. Replace *Margaret* with your first name and press **Tab**.

Your first name replaces Margaret. For example, as the Access author, my first name, Cynthia, replaces Margaret. You have made changes to two fields in the same record. The pencil symbol in the row selector box indicates that the record has not yet been saved.

d. Click **Undo** on the Quick Access Toolbar.

Your first and last names revert back to *Margaret Peacock* because you have not yet left the record.

e. Type your first and last names again to replace *Margaret Peacock*. Press **Tab**.

You should now be in the title field and your title, *Sales Representative*, is selected. The record has not been saved, as indicated by the pencil symbol in the row selector box.

f. Click anywhere in the third row where Janet Leverling's data is stored.

The pencil symbol disappears, indicating your changes have been saved.

g. Click the **Address field** in the first record, Nancy Davolio's record. Select the entire address and then type **4004 East Morningside Dr**. Click anywhere on the second record, Andrew Fuller's record.

h. Click **Undo**.

Nancy Davolio's address reverts back to 507- 20th Ave. E. However, the Undo command is now faded. You can no longer undo the change that you made replacing Margaret Peacock's name with your own.

i. Click the **Close (X) button** at the top of the table to close the Employees table.

The Employees table closes. You are not prompted to save your changes; they have already been saved for you because Access works in storage, not memory. If you reopen the Employees table, you will see your name in place of Margaret Peacock's name.

> **TROUBLESHOOTING:** If you click the Close (X) button on the title bar at the top right of the window and accidentally close the database, locate the file and double-click it to reopen the file.

STEP 4 ›› ADD A RECORD

You need to add new products to the Northwind database because the company is adding a new line of products. Refer to Figure 1.11 as you complete Step 4.

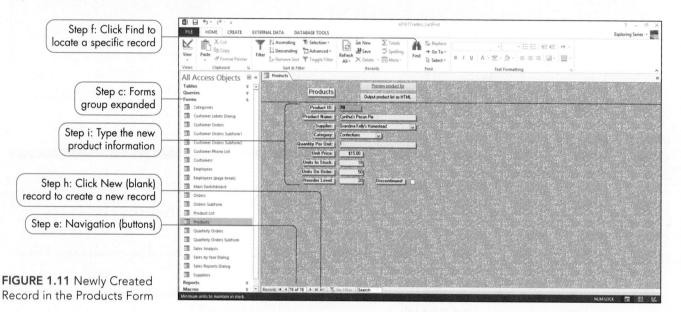

FIGURE 1.11 Newly Created Record in the Products Form

a. Right-click the **Customers tab** and click **Close All**.

b. Click the **Tables group** in the Navigation Pane to collapse it and collapse the **Reports group**.

c. Click the **Forms group** in the Navigation Pane to expand the list of available forms.

d. Double-click the **Products form** to open it.

e. Locate the navigation buttons at the bottom of the Access window. Practice moving from one record to the next. Click **Next record** and click **Last record**; click **Previous record** and click **First record**.

f. Click **Find** in the Find group on the HOME tab, type **Grandma** in the **Find What box**, click the **Match arrow**, and then select **Any Part of Field**. Click **Find Next**.

You should see the data for Grandma's Boysenberry Spread. Selecting the Any Part of the Field option will return a match even if it is contained in the middle of a word.

g. Close the Find dialog box.

h. Click **New (blank) record** on the navigation bar.

i. Enter the following information for a new product.

Field Name	Value to Type
Product Name	*Your name*'s Pecan Pie
Supplier	Grandma Kelly's Homestead (click the arrow to select from the list of Suppliers)
Category	Confections (click the arrow to select from the list of Categories)
Quantity Per Unit	1
Unit Price	15.00
Units in Stock	18
Units on Order	50
Reorder Level	20
Discontinued	No (leave the check box unchecked)

As soon as you begin typing in the product name box, Access assigns a Product ID, in this case 78, to the record. The Product ID is used as the primary key in the Products table.

j. Click anywhere on the Pecan Pie record you just entered. Click the **FILE tab**, click **Print**, and then click **Print Preview**.

The first four records display in the Print Preview.

k. Click **Last Page** in the navigation bar and click **Previous Page** to show the new record you entered.

The beginning of the Pecan Pie record is now visible. The record continues on the next page.

l. Click **Close Print Preview** in the Close Preview group.

m. Close the Products form.

STEP 5 ≫ DELETE A RECORD

To help you understand how Access stores data, you verify that the new product is in the Products table. You also attempt to delete a record. Refer to Figure 1.12 as you complete Step 5.

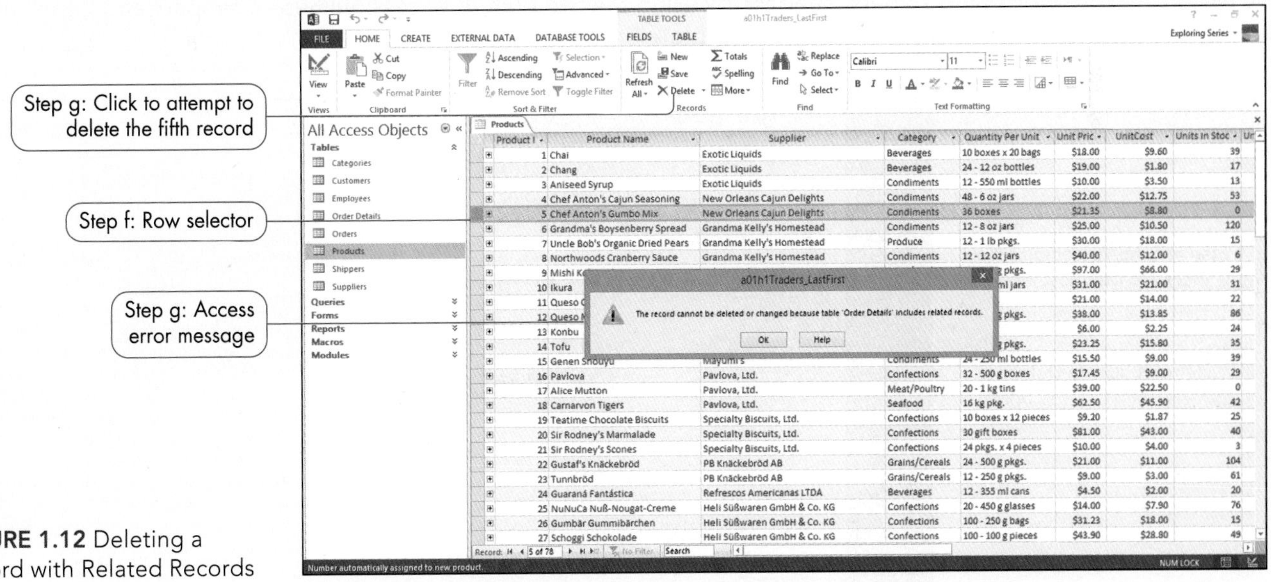

FIGURE 1.12 Deleting a Record with Related Records

a. Click the **Forms group** in the Navigation Pane to collapse it and expand the **Tables group**.

b. Double-click the **Products table** to open it.

c. Click **Last record** in the navigation bar.

The Pecan Pie record you entered in the Products form is listed as the last record in the Products table. The Products form was created from the Products table. Your newly created record, Pecan Pie, is stored in the Products table even though you added it using the form.

d. Navigate to the fifth record in the table, *Chef Anton's Gumbo Mix*.

e. Use the horizontal scroll bar to scroll right until you see the Discontinued field.

The check mark in the Discontinued check box tells you that this product has been discontinued.

f. Click the **row selector** to the left of the fifth record.

The row highlights with a red-colored border to show that it is selected.

g. Click **Delete** in the Records group and read the error message.

The error message that displays tells you that you cannot delete this record because the table 'Order Details' has related records. (Customers ordered this product in the past.) Even though the product is now discontinued and no stock remains, it cannot be deleted from the Products table because related records exist in the Order Detail table.

h. Click **OK**.

i. Navigate to the last record and click the **row selector** to highlight the entire row.

j. Click **Delete** in the Records group. Read the warning.

The warning box that appears tells you that this action cannot be undone. Although this product can be deleted because it was just entered and no orders were created for it, you do not want to delete the record.

k. Click **No**. You do not want to delete this record. Close the Products table.

> **TROUBLESHOOTING:** If you clicked Yes and deleted the record, return to Step i. Reenter the information for this record. You will need it later in the lesson.

STEP 6 ≫ SAVE AS, COMPACT AND REPAIR, AND BACK UP THE DATABASE

You will protect the Northwind Traders database by using the two built-in Access utilities—Compact and Repair and Back Up Database. Refer to Figure 1.13 as you complete Step 6.

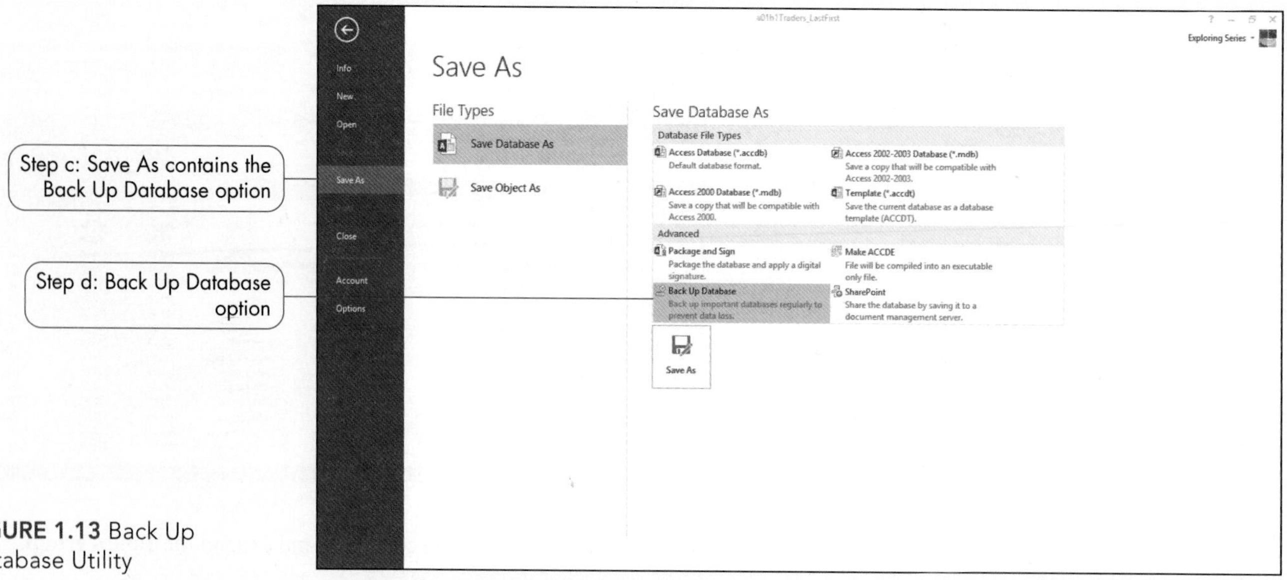

Step c: Save As contains the Back Up Database option

Step d: Back Up Database option

FIGURE 1.13 Back Up Database Utility

a. Click the **FILE tab** to open the Backstage view.

b. Click Compact & Repair Database.

Using the *Compact and Repair* utility helps improve the performance of your database.

c. Click the **FILE tab**, click **Save As**, and then click **Save Database As** under *File Types*, if necessary.

d. Double-click **Back Up Database** under the Advanced group to open the **Save As** dialog box.

The backup utility assigns the default name by adding a date to your file name.

e. Verify the *Save in* folder displays the location where you want your file saved and click **Save**.

You just created a backup of the database after completing Hands-On Exercise 1. The original database *a01h1traders_LastFirst* remains onscreen.

f. Keep the database open if you plan to continue with Hands-On Exercise 2. If not, close the database and exit Access.

Sorts and Filters

Access provides you with many tools that you can use to change the order of information and to identify and extract only the data needed at the moment. For example, you might need to display information by customer name in alphabetical order. Or you might need to know which suppliers are located in New Orleans or which customers have outstanding orders that were placed in the last seven days. You might use that information to identify possible disruptions to product deliveries or customers who may need a telephone call to let them know the status of their orders.

In this section, you will learn how to sort information and to isolate records in a table based on certain criteria.

Sorting Table Data on One or Multiple Fields

You can change the order of information by sorting one or more fields. A *sort* lists records in a specific sequence, such as alphabetically by last name or by ascending EmployeeID. To sort a table on one criteria, do the following:

STEP 4 ≫

1. Click in the field that you want to use to sort the records.
2. Click Ascending or Descending in the Sort & Filter group on the HOME tab.

Ascending sorts a list of text data in alphabetical order or a numeric list in lowest to highest order. *Descending* sorts a list of text data in reverse alphabetical order or a numeric list in highest to lowest order. Figure 1.14 shows the Customers table for a bank sorted in ascending order by state.

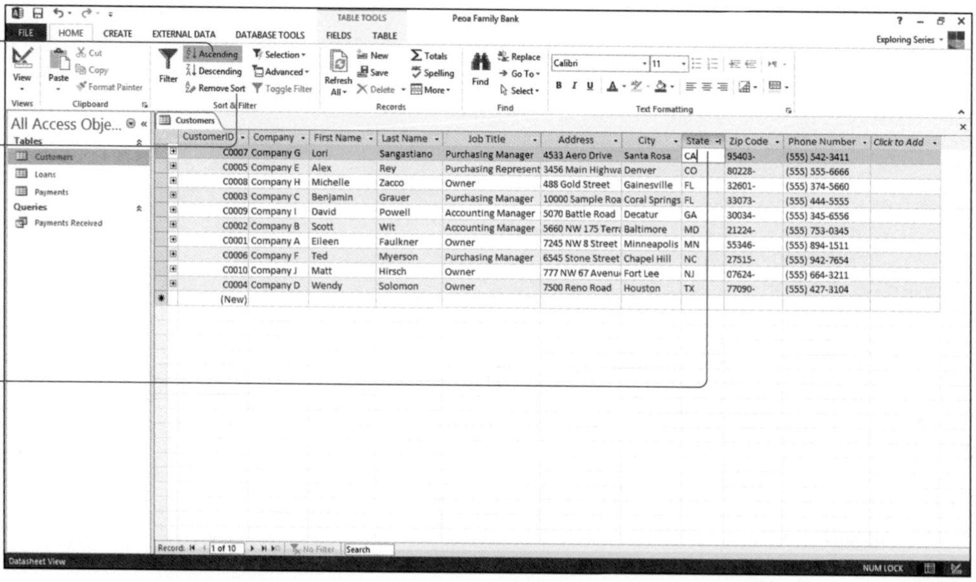

FIGURE 1.14 Customers Table Sorted by State

Access can sort records by more than one field. Access sorts multiple criteria by first sorting the column on the left. The column immediately to the right of that column is sorted next. Because of this, you must arrange your columns in this order. To move a column, select the column and hold down the left mouse button. A heavy black bar appears to the left of the column. Drag the column to the position where you want it for the multiple sort.

Creating, Modifying, and Removing Filters

In Hands-On Exercise 1, you added Pecan Pie to the Products table with a category of Confections, but you also saw many other products. Suppose you wanted to see a list of just the products in the Confections category. To obtain this list, you would open the Products table in Datasheet view and create a filter. A *filter* displays a subset of records based on specified criteria. A *criterion* (or criteria, plural) is a number, a text phrase, or an expression used to select records from a table. Therefore, to view a list of all Confections, you would need to filter the Category field of the Products table using Confections as the criterion.

You can use filters to analyze data quickly. Applying a filter does not delete any records; filters only *hide* records that do not match the criteria. Two types of filters are discussed in this section: *Filter by Selection* and *Filter by Form*.

Use, Modify, and Remove a Filter

Filter by Selection displays only the records that match a criterion you select. To use *Filter by Selection*, do the following:

STEP 1 ➤

1. Click in any field that contains the criterion on which you want to filter.
2. Click Selection in the Sort & Filter group on the HOME tab.
3. Select *Equals "criterion"* from the list of options.

Figure 1.15 displays a Customers table with 10 records. The records in the table are displayed in sequence according to the CustomerID, which is also the primary key (the field or combination of fields that uniquely identifies a record). The navigation bar at the bottom indicates that the active record is the first row in the table. *Owner* in the Job Title field is selected.

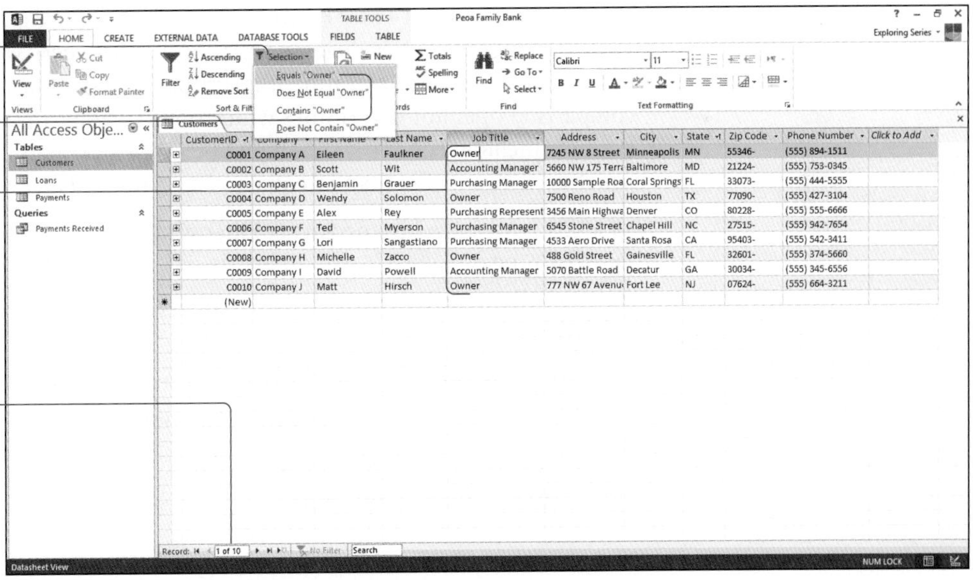

- Click Selection to use *Filter by Selection*
- Criterion set to Equals "Owner"
- All job titles are displayed
- 10 customers are showing

FIGURE 1.15 Unfiltered Customers Table

Figure 1.16 displays a filtered view of the Customers table, showing records with the job title *Owner*. The navigation bar shows that this is a filtered list containing 4 records matching the criteria. (The Customers table still contains the original 10 records, but only 4 records are visible with the filter applied.)

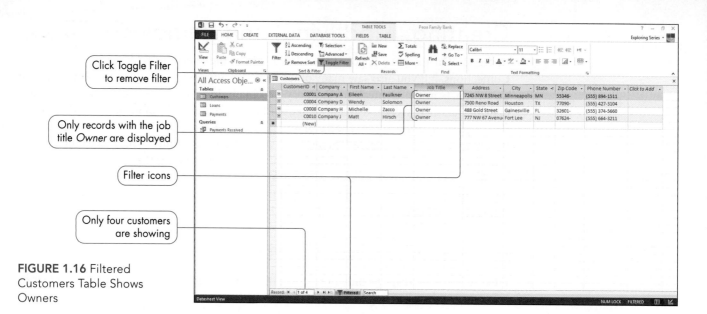

Click Toggle Filter to remove filter

Only records with the job title *Owner* are displayed

Filter icons

Only four customers are showing

FIGURE 1.16 Filtered Customers Table Shows Owners

Filter by Form is a more versatile method of selecting data because it enables you to display table records based on multiple criteria. When you use *Filter by Form*, all of the records are hidden and Access creates a blank form in a design grid. You see only field names with an arrow in the first field. Click on other fields and an arrow displays. Click an arrow and a list opens for you to use to specify your criterion. You can specify as many criteria as you need. When you apply the filter, Access displays the records that meet your criteria.

STEP 3

An advantage of using this filter method is that you can specify AND and OR logical operators. If you use the AND operator, a record is included in the results if all the criteria are true. If you use the OR operator, a record is included if at least one criterion is true. Another advantage of *Filter by Form* is that you can use a comparison operator. A ***comparison operator*** is used to evaluate the relationship between two quantities. For example, a comparison operator can determine if quantities are equal or not equal. If they are not equal, a comparison operator determines which one is greater than the other. Comparison operator symbols include: equal (=), not equal (<>), greater than (>), less than (<), greater than or equal to (>=), and less than or equal to (<=). To use *Filter by Form*, do the following:

1. Click Advanced in the Sort & Filter group on the HOME tab.
2. Click *Filter by Form*.
3. Click in the field you want to use as a criterion. Click the arrow to select the criterion from existing data.
4. Add additional criterion and comparison operators as needed.
5. Click Toggle Filter in the Sort & Filter group on the HOME tab to apply the filter.

In Figure 1.17, the Northwind Traders Products table is open. *Filter by Form* is set to select products with an inventory (Units in Stock) level greater than 30 (>30).

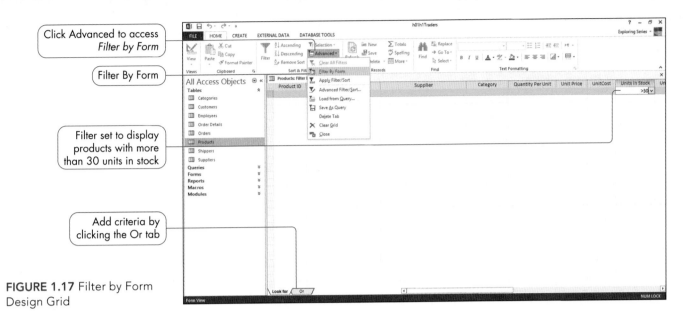

Click Advanced to access *Filter by Form*

Filter By Form

Filter set to display products with more than 30 units in stock

Add criteria by clicking the Or tab

FIGURE 1.17 Filter by Form Design Grid

The sort and filter operations can be done in any order; that is, you can sort a table first and apply a filter. Conversely, you can filter a table first to show only selected records and sort the filtered table to display the records in a certain order. It does not matter which operation is performed first.

STEP 2 You can also filter the table further by applying a second, third, or more criteria. For example, in the Products table shown in Figure 1.17, you can apply *Filter by Form* by clicking in the Supplier cell, selecting Exotic Liquids from the list, and then applying the filter. Then you could click Beverages and apply *Filter by Selection* to display all the beverages supplied by Exotic Liquids. You can also click Toggle Filter at any time to remove all filters and display all the records in the table. Filters are a temporary method for examining table data. If you close the filtered table and reopen it, the filter will be removed and all of the records will be restored.

TIP Use Undo After Applying a Filter by Selection

You can apply one *Filter by Selection* to a table, and then a second, and then a third to display certain records based on three criteria. If you click Toggle Filter, all three filters will be removed. What if you only want the last filter removed? Click Undo to remove only the last filter. Click Undo again and remove the second-to-last filter. This feature will help you apply and remove multiple filters, one at a time.

Quick Concepts ✓

1. What are the benefits of sorting the records in a table? *p. 102*

2. What is the purpose of creating a filter? *p. 103*

3. What is the difference between *Filter by Selection* and *Filter by Form*? *pp. 103–104*

4. What is a comparison operator and how is it used in a filter? *p. 104*

Hands-On Exercises

Watch the Video
for this Hands-
On Exercise!

MyITLab®
HOE2 Training

2 Sorts and Filters

The sales manager at Northwind Traders needs quick answers to her questions about customer orders. You use the Access database to filter tables to answer these questions, then sort the records based on the manager's needs.

Skills covered: Use Filter by Selection with an Equal Condition • Use Filter by Selection with a Contains Condition • Use Filter by Form with a Comparison Operator • Sort a Table

STEP 1 ▶ USE FILTER BY SELECTION WITH AN EQUAL CONDITION

The sales manager asks for a list of customers who live in London. You use *Filter by Selection* with an equal condition to locate these customers. Refer to Figure 1.18 as you complete Step 1.

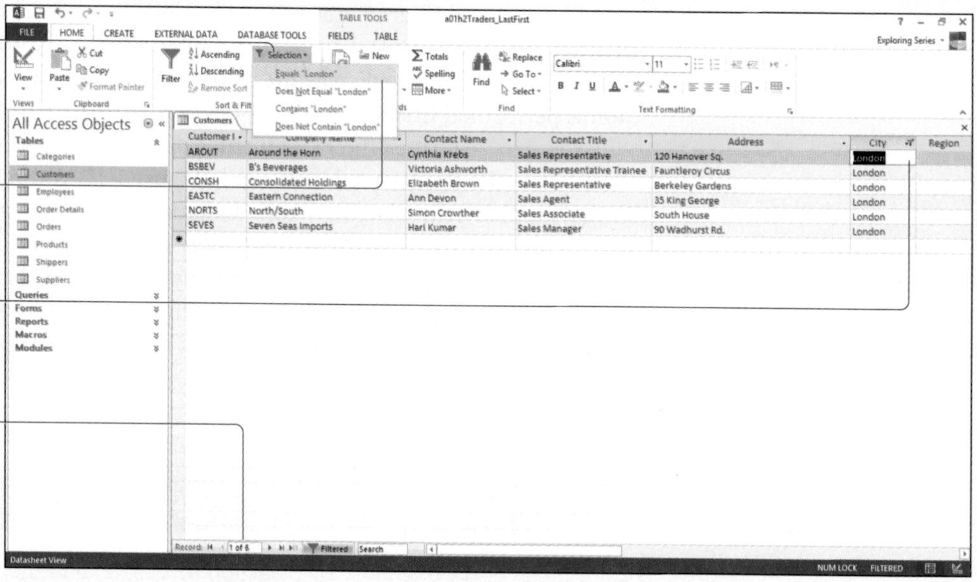

Step d: Click Selection

Step e: Select Equals "London"

Step c: Select London

Step e: Six customers match the criteria

FIGURE 1.18 Customers Table Filtered for London Records

a. Open the *a01h1traders_LastFirst* database if you closed it after the last Hands-On Exercise and save it as **a01h2Traders_LastFirst**, changing *h1* to *h2*.

> **TROUBLESHOOTING:** If you make any major mistakes in this exercise, you can close the file, open *a01h1Traders_LastFirst* again, and then start this exercise over.

b. Double-click the **Customers table** in the Navigation Pane under *Tables*, navigate to record 4, and then replace *Thomas Hardy* with your name in the Contact Name field.

c. Scroll right until the City field is visible. The fourth record has a value of *London* in the City field. Click the field to select it.

d. Click **Selection** in the Sort & Filter group on the HOME tab.

e. Select **Equals "London"** from the menu. Note that six customers were located.

   The navigation bar display shows that six records that meet the *London* criterion are available. The other records in the Customers table are hidden. The Filtered icon also displays on the navigation bar, indicating that the Customers table has been filtered.

f. Click **Toggle Filter** in the Sort & Filter group to remove the filter.

g. Click **Toggle Filter** again to reset the filter. Leave the Customers table open for the next step.

STEP 2 ≫ USE FILTER BY SELECTION WITH A CONTAINS CONDITION

The sales manager asks you to narrow the list of London customers so that it displays only Sales Representatives. To accomplish this task, you add a second layer of filtering using the *Filter by Selection* feature. Refer to Figure 1.19 as you complete Step 2.

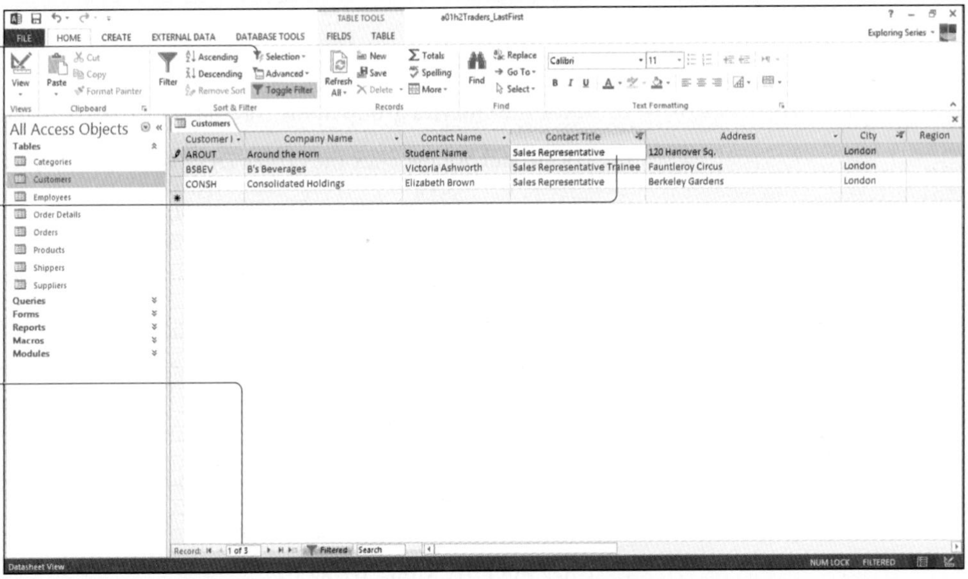

FIGURE 1.19 Customers in London with the Contact Title *Sales Representative*

a. Click in any field in the Contact Title column that contains the value *Sales Representative*.

b. Click **Selection** in the Sort & Filter group and click **Contains "Sales Representative"**. Locate your name in the filtered table. Compare your results to those shown in Figure 1.19.

Three records match the criteria you set. You have applied a second layer of filtering to the customers in London. The second layer further restricts the display to only those customers who have the words *Sales Representative* contained in their titles.

> **TROUBLESHOOTING:** If you do not see the record for Victoria Ashworth, you selected *Equals "Sales Representative"* instead of *Contains "Sales Representative"*. Repeat steps a and b, making sure you select *Contains "Sales Representative"*.

c. Close the Customers table. Click **Yes** if a dialog box asks if you want to save the design changes to the Customers table.

STEP 3 ≫ USE FILTER BY FORM WITH A COMPARISON OPERATOR

You are asked to provide a list of records that do not match just one set of criteria. You are asked to provide a list of all extended prices less than $50 for a specific sales representative. Use *Filter by Form* to provide the information when two or more criteria are needed. You also preview the results in Print Preview to see how the list would print. Refer to Figure 1.20 as you complete Step 3.

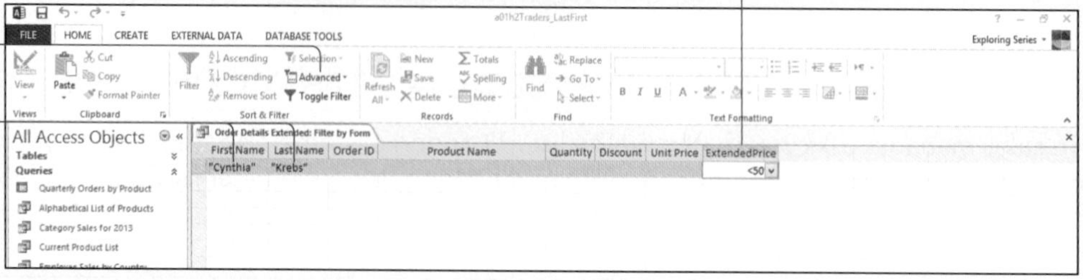

Step i: Enter <50 for the ExtendedPrice criteria

Step d: Click Advanced to select Filter by Form

Steps f–h: Select your first and last names

FIGURE 1.20 Filter by Form Selection Criteria

a. Click the **Tables group** in the Navigation Pane to collapse the listed tables.

b. Click the **Queries group** in the Navigation Pane to expand the list of available queries.

c. Locate and double-click the **Order Details Extended query** to open it.

This query contains information about orders. It has fields containing information about the sales person, the Order ID, the product name, the unit price, quantity ordered, the discount given, and an extended price. The extended price is a field used to total order information.

d. Click **Advanced** in the Sort & Filter group and select **Filter by Form** from the list.

All of the records are now hidden, and you see only field names and an arrow in the first field. Although you are applying *Filter by Form* to a query, you can use the same process as applying *Filter by Form* to a table. You are able to enter more than one criterion using *Filter by Form*.

e. Click in the first row under the First Name field, if necessary.

An arrow appears at the right of the box.

f. Click the **First Name arrow**.

A list of all available first names appears. Your name should be on the list. Figure 1.20 shows *Cynthia Krebs*, which replaced Margaret Peacock in Hands-On Exercise 1.

TROUBLESHOOTING: If you do not see your name and you do see Margaret on the list, you probably skipped steps in Hands-On Exercise 1. Close the query without saving changes, return to the first Hands-On Exercise, and then rework it, making sure not to omit any steps. Then you can return to this location and work the remainder of this Hands-On Exercise.

---

g. Select your first name from the list.

h. Click in the first row under the Last Name field to reveal the arrow. Locate and select your last name by clicking it.

i. Scroll right until you see the Extended Price field. Click in the first row under the Extended Price field and type **<50**.

This will select all of the items that you ordered where the total was under $50. You ignore the arrow and type the expression needed.

j. Click **Toggle Filter** in the Sort & Filter group.

You have specified which records to include and have executed the filtering by clicking Toggle Filter. You should have 31 records that match the criteria you specified.

k. Click the **FILE tab**, click **Print**, and then click **Print Preview**.

You instructed Access to preview the filtered query results. The preview displays the query title as a heading. The current filter is applied, as well as page numbers.

l. Click **Close Print Preview** in the Close Preview group.

m. Close the Order Details Extended query. Click **Yes** if a dialog box asks if you want to save your changes.

TIP **Deleting Filter by Form Criterion**

While working with *Filter by Selection* or *Filter by Form*, you may inadvertently save a filter. To view a saved filter, open the table or query that you suspect may have a saved filter. Click Advanced in the Sort & Filter group and click *Filter by Form*. If criteria appear in the form, then a filter has been saved. To delete a saved filter, toggle the filter, click Advanced, and then click Close All Filters. Close and save the table or query.

STEP 4 ≫ SORT A TABLE

The Sales Manager is pleased with your work; however, she would like some of the information to appear in a different order. You will now sort the records in the Customers table using the manager's new criteria. Refer to Figure 1.21 as you complete Step 4.

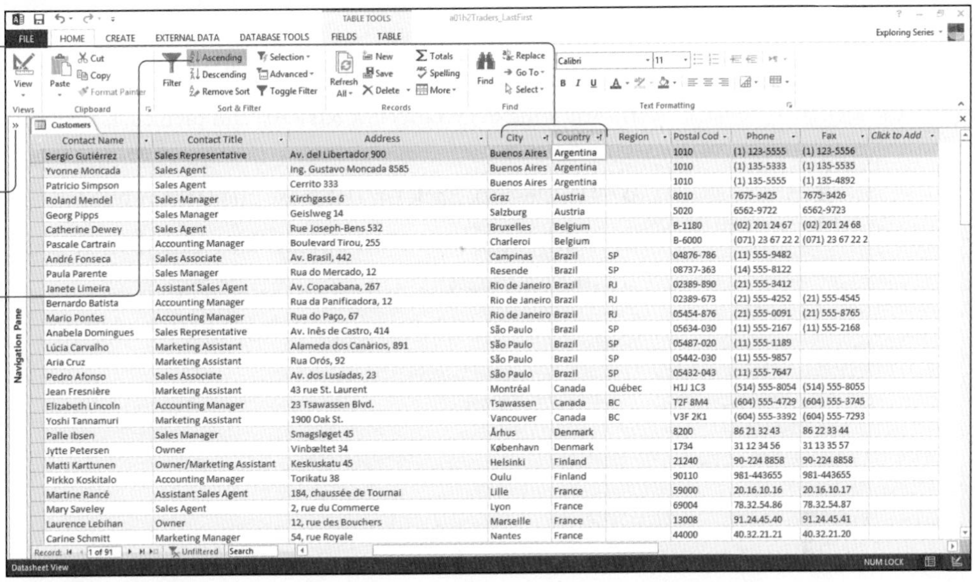

Step i and j: Records are sorted by Country, then City

Step c: Shutter Bar Open/Close button

Steps i and j: Click Ascending to sort by Country, then City

FIGURE 1.21 Customers Table Sorted by Country, Then City

a. Click the **Queries group** in the Navigation Pane to collapse the listed queries.

b. Click the **Tables group** in the Navigation Pane to expand the list of available tables and double-click the **Customers table** to open it.

   This table contains information about customers. The table is sorted in alphabetical order by Company Name.

c. Click the **Shutter Bar Open/Close button** in the Navigation Pane to close the Navigation Pane.

   It will be easier to locate fields in the Customer table if the Navigation Pane is closed.

d. Click any field in the Customer ID column, the first field in the table. Click **Descending** in the Sort & Filter group on the HOME tab.

   Sorting in descending order on a character field produces a reverse alphabetical order.

e. Scroll right until you can see both the Country and City fields.

f. Click the **Country column heading**.

   The entire column is selected.

g. Click the **Country column heading** again and hold down the **left mouse button**.

   A thick dark blue line displays on the left edge of the Country field.

h. Check to make sure that you see the thick blue line. Drag the **Country field** to the left until the thick black line moves between the City and Region fields. Release the mouse and the Country field position moves to the right of the City field.

You moved the Country field next to the City field so that you can easily sort the table based on both fields. In order to sort by two or more fields, they need to be placed adjacent to each other.

i. Click any city name in the City field and click **Ascending** in the Sort & Filter group.

The City field displays the cities in alphabetical order.

j. Click any country name in the Country field and click **Ascending**.

The countries are sorted in alphabetical order. The cities within each country also are sorted alphabetically. For example, the customer in Graz, Austria, is listed before the customer in Salzburg, Austria.

k. Close the Customers table. Click **Yes** to save the changes to the design of the table.

l. Click the **Shutter Bar Open/Close button** in the Navigation Pane to open the Navigation Pane.

m. Click the **FILE tab** to open the Backstage view and click **Compact & Repair Database**.

n. Click the **FILE tab**, click **Save As**, and then click **Save Database As** in File Types, if necessary.

o. Double-click **Back Up Database** under the Advanced group to open the Save As dialog box.

p. Verify the *Save in* folder displays the location where you want your file saved and click **Save**.

q. Close the database and submit based on your instructor's directions. Leave Access open if you plan to continue with Hands-On Exercise 3. If not, exit Access.

Access Versus Excel, and Relational Databases

Both Access and Excel contain powerful tools that enable you to extract the information you need and arrange it in a way that makes it easy to analyze. An important part of becoming a proficient Office user is learning which of these applications to use to accomplish a task.

In this section, you will learn how to decide whether to use Access or Excel by examining the distinct advantages of each application. Ideally, the type of data and the type of functionality you require should determine which program will work best.

Knowing When to Use Access or Excel to Manage Data

You are probably familiar with working in an Excel spreadsheet. You type the column headings, enter the data, perhaps add a formula or two, and then add totals to the bottom. Once the data has been entered, you can apply a filter, sort the data, or start all over—similar to what you learned to do in Access with filters. It is true that you can accomplish many of the same tasks using either Excel or Access. Although the two programs have much in common, they each have distinct advantages. How do you choose whether to use Access or Excel? The choice you make may ultimately depend on how well you know Access. Users who know Excel only are more likely to use a spreadsheet even if a database would be better. When database features are used in Excel, they are generally used on data that is in one table. When the data is better suited to be on two or more tables, then using Access is preferable. Learning how to use Access will be beneficial to you because it will enable you to work more efficiently with large groups of data.

Select the Software to Use

A contact list (for example, name, address, phone number) created in Excel may serve your needs just fine in the beginning. Each time you enter a new contact, you can add another row to the bottom of your worksheet. You can sort the list by last name for easier look-up of names. In Excel, you can easily move an entire column, insert a new column, or copy and paste data from one cell to another. This is the "ease of use" characteristic of Excel.

If you need to expand the information in Excel to keep track of each time you contacted someone on your contact list, you may need an additional worksheet. This additional sheet would only list the contacts whom you have contacted and some information about the nature of the contact. Which contact was it? When was the contact made? Was it a phone contact or a face-to-face meeting? As you track these entries, your worksheet will contain a reference to the first worksheet using the contact name.

If a contact is deleted on the first worksheet, that contact's information will still remain on the second worksheet, unless someone remembers to remove it. Similarly, information could be added about a contact on the second worksheet without the contact being officially entered into the first worksheet. As the quantity and complexity of the data increase, the need to organize your data logically also increases.

Access provides built-in tools to help organize data better than Excel. One tool that helps Access organize data is the ability to create relationships between tables. A *relationship* is a connection between two tables using a field that is common to the two tables. The benefit of a relationship is the ability to efficiently combine data from related tables for the purpose of creating queries, forms, and reports. Relationships are the reason Access is referred to as a relational database.

Use Access

STEP 1 >> Use Access to manage data when you:

- Require multiple related tables to store your data.
- Have a large amount of data.
- Need to connect to and retrieve data from external databases, such as Microsoft SQL Server.
- Need to group, sort, and total data based on various parameters.
- Have an application that requires multiple users to connect to one data source at the same time.

Use Excel

Use Excel to manage data when you:

- Need only one worksheet to handle all of your data.
- Have mostly numeric data—for example, you need to maintain an expense statement.
- Require subtotals and totals in your worksheet.
- Want to primarily run a series of "what if" scenarios on your data.
- Need to create complex charts and/or graphs.

Understanding Relational Power

In the previous section, we compared Excel worksheets to Access relational databases. Access has the ability to create relationships between two tables, whereas Excel does not. Access is known as a ***relational database management system*** (RDBMS); using an RDBMS, you can manage groups of data (tables) and set rules (relationships) between tables. When relational databases are designed properly, users can easily combine data from multiple tables to create queries, forms, and reports.

Good database design begins with grouping data into the correct tables. This practice, known as ***normalization***, will take time to learn, but over time you will begin to understand the fundamentals. The design of a relational database management system is illustrated in Figure 1.22, which shows the table design of the Northwind Traders database. The tables have been created, the field names have been added, and the data types have been set. The diagram shows the relationships that were created between tables using ***join lines***. Join lines enable you to create a relationship between two tables using a common field. Figure 1.22 also shows the join lines between related tables as a series of lines connecting common fields. For example, the Suppliers table is joined to the Products table using the common field SupplierID. If you examine some of the connections, you will see that the EmployeeID is linked to the Orders table by a join line. This means that you can produce a report displaying all orders for a customer and the employee who entered the order. The Orders table is joined to the Order Details table where the OrderID is the common field. The Products table is joined to the Order Details table where the ProductID is the common field. These table connections enable you to query the database for information stored in multiple tables. This feature gives the manager the ability to ask questions like "How many different beverages were shipped last week?" or "What was the total revenue generated from seafood orders last year?"

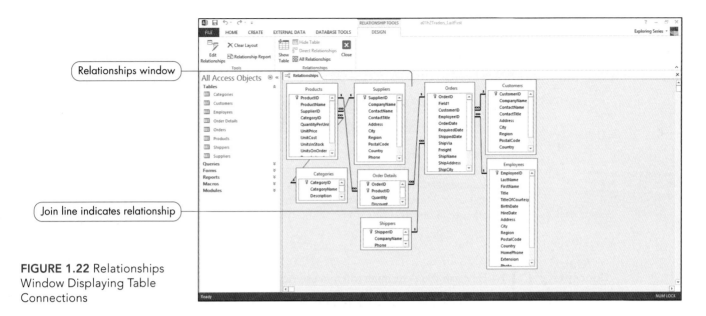

FIGURE 1.22 Relationships Window Displaying Table Connections

Use the Relationships Window

Relationships are set in the Relationships window by the database developer after the tables have been created but before any sample data is entered. The most common method of connecting two tables is to connect the primary key from one table to the foreign key of another. A *foreign key* is a field in one table that is also the primary key of another table. In the previous figure, Figure 1.22, the SupplierID (primary key) in the Suppliers table is joined to the SupplierID (foreign key) in the Products table. Remember, a primary key is a field that uniquely identifies each record in a table.

To create a relationship between two tables, follow these guidelines:

1. Click Relationships in the Relationships group on the DATABASE TOOLS tab.
2. Add the two tables that you want to join together to the Relationships window.
3. Drag the common field (e.g., SupplierID) from the primary table (e.g., Suppliers) onto the common field (e.g., SupplierID) of the related table (e.g., Products). The data types of the common fields must be the same.
4. Check the Enforce Referential Integrity check box.
5. Close the Relationships window.

STEP 2 >>

TIP View Join Lines

Databases with many tables with relationships may make it difficult to see the join lines between tables. Tables may be repositioned to make it easier to see the join lines. To reposition a table, drag the table by its table name to the new position.

Enforce Referential Integrity

STEP 3 >>

Enforce referential integrity is one of three options you can select when setting a table relationship. When *enforce referential integrity* is checked, Access ensures that data cannot be entered into a related table unless it first exists in the primary table. For example, in Figure 1.22 you cannot enter a product into the Products table using a SupplierID that does not exist in the Suppliers table. This rule ensures the integrity of the data in the database and improves overall data accuracy. Referential integrity also prohibits users from deleting a record in one table if it has records in related tables.

In Hands-on Exercise 3, you examine the strengths of Access and Excel in more detail so that you can better determine when to use which application to complete a given task. You will also explore relationships between tables and learn about the power of relational data.

TIP | Create Sample Data

When learning database skills, starting with a smaller set of sample data prior to entering all company records can be helpful. A small amount of data gives you the ability to check the tables and quickly see if your results are correct. Even though the data amounts are small, as you test the database tables and relationships, the results will prove useful as you work with larger data sets.

Quick
Concepts

1. How can you determine when to use Access or Excel to manage data? *p. 111*

2. Explain the term RDBMS. *p. 112*

3. What is the purpose of a join line? *p. 112*

Hands-On Exercises

Watch the Video
for this Hands-
On Exercise!

3 Access Versus Excel, and Relational Databases

In this exercise, you review the relationships set in the Northwind Traders database. This will help you learn more about the overall design of the database. Examining the relationships will also help you understand why Access rather than Excel is used by Northwind Traders for data management.

Skills covered: Know When to Use Access or Excel to Manage Data • Use the Relationships Window, Use Filter by Form with a Comparison Operator, and Reapply a Saved Filter • Enforce Referential Integrity

STEP 1 ≫ KNOW WHEN TO USE ACCESS OR EXCEL TO MANAGE DATA

In this exercise, you examine the connections between the tables in the Northwind Traders database and review the reasons that Access was selected as the application for this data. Refer to Figure 1.23 as you complete Step 1.

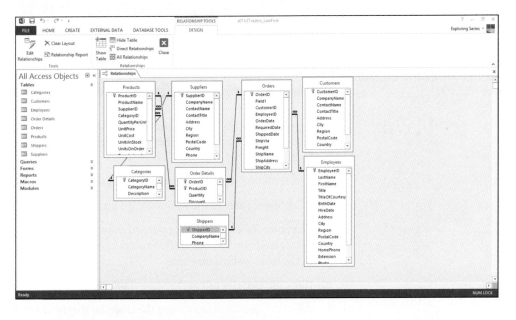

FIGURE 1.23 Relationships Window for the Northwind Database

a. Open the *a01h2Traders_LastFirst* database if you closed it after the last Hands-On Exercise and save it as **a01h3Traders_LastFirst**, changing *h2* to *h3*.

b. Click the **DATABASE TOOLS tab** and click **Relationships** in the Relationships group.

c. Examine the join lines showing the relationships that connect the various tables. For example, the Orders table is connected to the Order Details table.

Examining the number of tables in a database and their relationships is a good way to determine whether you need to use Excel or Access for your data. Because this data needs more than one table, involves a large amount of connected data, needs to group, sort, and total data based on various parameters, and needs to allow multiple users to connect to one data source at the same time, it is better to manipulate this data using Access rather than using Excel.

STEP 2 ›› USE THE RELATIONSHIPS WINDOW, USE FILTER BY FORM WITH A COMPARISON OPERATOR, AND REAPPLY A SAVED FILTER

Use the Relationships window to move tables to make the join lines easier to view. To reinforce your filter skills, use *Filter by Form* to solve more complex questions about the Northwind data. After you retrieve the records, save the *Filter by Form* specifications so that you can reapply the filter later. Refer to Figure 1.24 as you complete Step 2.

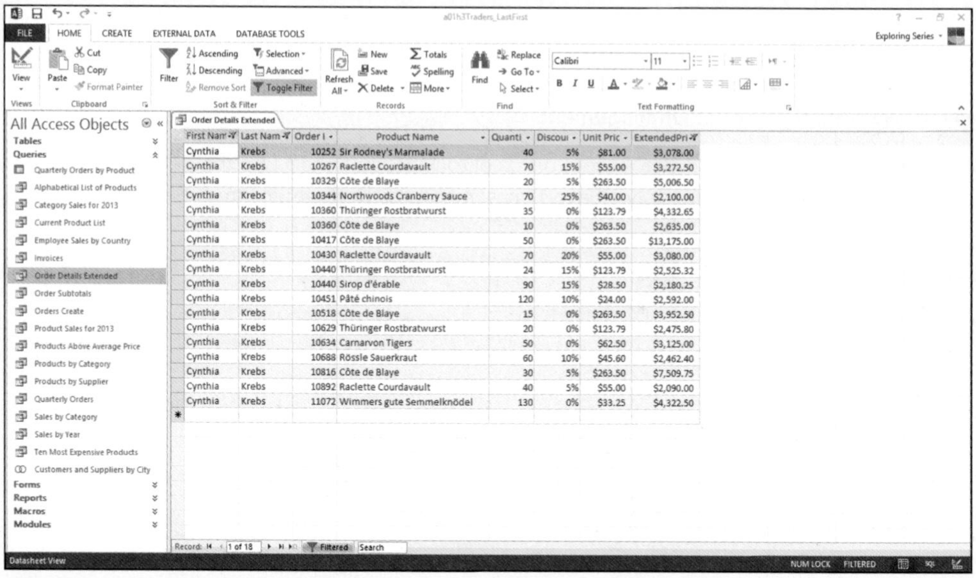

FIGURE 1.24 Query Results with Your Name and Extended Price >$2,000

a. Reposition the Shippers table beneath the Orders table by dragging it to the right by its table name. Reposition the Categories table beneath the Order Details table by dragging it to the right by its table name.

   Tables may be repositioned to make it easier to see the join lines creating the relationships.

b. Click **Show Table** in the Relationships group on the RELATIONSHIPS TOOLS DESIGN tab.

   The Show Table dialog box opens. It shows you the eight tables that are available in the database. If you look in the Relationships window, you will see that all eight tables are open in the relationships diagram.

c. Click the **Queries tab** in the Show Table dialog box.

   All of the queries created from the tables in the database are listed in the Show Table dialog box. You could add all of the queries to the Relationships window. Things might become cluttered, but you could tell at a glance from where the queries get their information.

d. Close the Show Table dialog box.

e. Click the **Shutter Bar Open/Close button** in the Navigation Pane to open the Navigation Pane, if necessary.

f. Click **All Access Objects** on the Navigation Pane and click **Tables and Related Views.**

   You now see each table and all the queries, forms, and reports that are based on each table. If a query is created using more than one table, it appears multiple times in the Navigation Pane.

g. Close the Relationships window. Save the changes to the design. Click **All Tables** on the Navigation Pane and click **Object Type.**

h. Collapse the Tables group in the Navigation Pane, expand the **Queries** group, and then double-click the **Order Details Extended query.**

i. Click **Advanced** in the Sort & Filter group, select **Filter by Form,** click in the first row under the Last Name field, and then select your last name.

j. Scroll right (or press **Tab**) until the Extended Price field is visible. Click in the first row in the Extended Price field and type **>2000**.

The Extended Price field shows the purchased amount for each item ordered. If an item sold for $15 and a customer ordered 10, the Extended Price would display $150.

k. Click **Toggle Filter** in the Sort & Filter group. Examine the filtered results.

Your comparison operator, >2000, identified 18 items ordered where the extended price exceeded $2,000.

l. Close the Order Details Extended query by clicking the **Close (X) button**. Click **Yes** to save changes.

m. Open the Order Details Extended query again.

The filter disengages when you close and reopen the object. However, because you opted to save the changes before closing, the filter has been stored with the query. You may reapply the filter at any time by clicking the Toggle Filter command (until the next filter replaces the current one).

n. Click **Toggle Filter** in the Sort & Filter group. Compare your results to Figure 1.24.

o. Save and close the query.

STEP 3 >> ENFORCE REFERENTIAL INTEGRITY

You need an additional relationship created between the Orders table and the Customers table. You create the relationship and enforce referential integrity. Refer to Figure 1.25 as you complete Step 3.

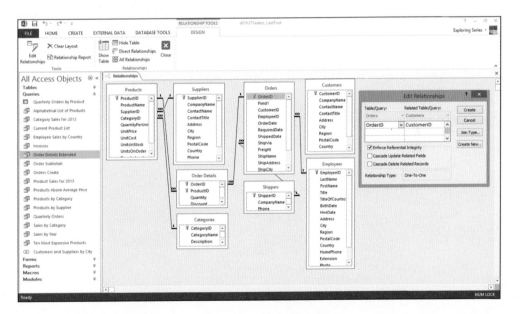

FIGURE 1.25 Relationship Created Between Orders Table and Customers Table

a. Click the **DATABASE TOOLS tab** and click **Relationships** in the Relationships group.

b. Locate the CustomerID field in the Orders table and drag it to the CustomerID field (primary key) in the Customers table.

The Edit Relationships dialog box opens. It shows that the Table/Query is from the Customers table and the related Table/Query comes from the Orders table. The relationship type is displayed at the bottom of the dialog box and indicates that this will be a One-To-Many relationship.

c. Click **Enforce Referential Integrity**.

Access will now ensure that data cannot be entered into the related table (Orders) unless it first exists in the primary table (Customers).

d. Click **Create**.

A join line displays between the Orders and Customers tables.

e. Click the **FILE tab** and click **Compact & Repair Database**. Click **Yes** if asked if you want to save changes to the layout of Relationships.

f. Click the **FILE tab**, click **Save As**, and then click **Save Database As** under *File Types* if necessary. Double-click **Back Up Database** in the Advanced group to open the Save As dialog box.

g. Verify the *Save in* folder displays the location where you want your backup file saved and click **Save**.

A duplicate copy of the database is saved with the default file name that is the original file name followed by the current date.

h. Exit Access.

Access Database Creation

Now that you have examined the fundamentals of an Access database and explored the power of relational databases, it is time to create one! In this section, you explore the benefits of creating a database using each of the methods discussed in the next section.

Creating a Database

When you first start Access, the Backstage view opens and provides you with three methods for creating a new database. These methods are:

- Creating a custom Web app
- Creating a blank desktop database
- Creating a database from a template

Creating a ***custom Web app*** enables you to create a database that you can build and then use and share with others through the Web. Creating a blank desktop database lets you create a database specific to your needs. Rather than starting from scratch by creating a blank desktop database, you may want to use a template to create a new database. An Access ***template*** is a predefined database that includes professionally designed tables, forms, reports, and other objects that you can use to jumpstart the creation of your database.

Figure 1.26 shows the options for creating a custom Web app, a blank desktop database, and multiple templates from which you can select the method for which you want to create a database.

FIGURE 1.26 Backstage View with Database Creation Options

Create a Web Application Using a Template

Creating a Web app (application) is new in Access 2013. An Access Web app is a new type of database that lets you build a browser-based database application— you can create a database in the cloud that you and others can access and use simultaneously. This requires that you use a host server such as SharePoint (a Web application platform developed by Microsoft) or Office 365 (a cloud service edition of SharePoint).

To create a Web app, click *Custom web app* in the Backstage view, give your app a name, and then choose a location. Once you click Create, a blank database opens. You then create the tables that will serve as the foundation of your database. The easiest way to add a table is to use the Access library of Table Templates. Each of the templates in the library includes tables, fields, and views that you will need to create an app. Some templates also include related tables.

As an alternative to creating a Web app from scratch, you can select a Web app template from the Backstage view. These templates are fully functional Web databases. Click one of the Web app template tiles and an introduction screen appears that previews the datasheet, provides a description of the purpose of the datasheet, lets you know the download size of the database, and even displays how users like you have rated the database. You give the app a name and select the Web location where the app is to be saved. Finally, you create the app. When you have completed the database, click Launch App in the View group on the Home tab. You can then use it and share it on the Web. Figure 1.27 shows the introduction screen for the Asset tracking template. This template requires SharePoint so that you can share content with others.

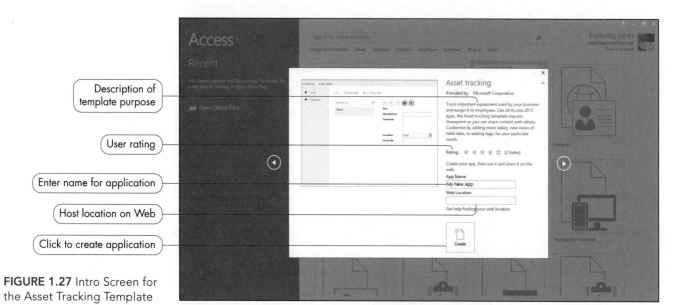

Description of template purpose

User rating

Enter name for application

Host location on Web

Click to create application

FIGURE 1.27 Intro Screen for the Asset Tracking Template

Create a Blank Desktop Database

To create a blank desktop database specific to your needs, click *Blank desktop database* in the Backstage view. Access opens to a blank table in Datasheet view where you can add data. You can refine the table in Design view. You would then create additional tables and objects as necessary. To create a blank desktop database, do the following:

1. Open Access or click the FILE tab to open the Backstage view and click New.
2. Click the *Blank desktop* database tile.
3. Enter the file name for the file in the text box, click the Browse button to navigate to the folder where you want to store the database file, and then click OK.
4. Click Create.
5. Enter data in the empty table that displays.

Create a Desktop Database Using a Template

Using a template to start a database saves you a great deal of creation time. Working with a template can also help a new Access user become familiar with database design. Templates are available from the Backstage view, where you can select from a variety of templates or search online for more templates.

Access also provides templates for desktop use. To create a desktop database from a template, do the following:

STEP 1 ›
1. Open Access or click the FILE tab to open the Backstage view and click New.
2. Click the database template you want to use.
3. Enter the file name for the file in the text box, click the Browse button to navigate to the folder where you want to store the database file, and then click OK.

4. Click Create to download the template.
5. Open the database and click Enable Content in the Security Warning message bar if you trust the source of the database.

Once the database is open, you may see a Getting Started page that includes links you can use to learn more about the database. A new Access user can gain valuable information by watching any associated videos and clicking provided hyperlinks. When finished reviewing the learning materials, close the Getting Started page to view the database. Figure 1.28 displays the Getting Started page included with the *Desktop task management* template. Two videos are provided to aid you in using and modifying the database. Because this database contains a Contacts table, there is a hyperlink to a wizard that will import contacts from Microsoft Outlook (if you use Microsoft Outlook). Links are available that will connect you with experts, enable you to get free advice from a forum, and get more help from Microsoft .com. The Getting Started page also includes a button you can click to open a survey that provides feedback to Microsoft. Close the Getting Started page to return to the database.

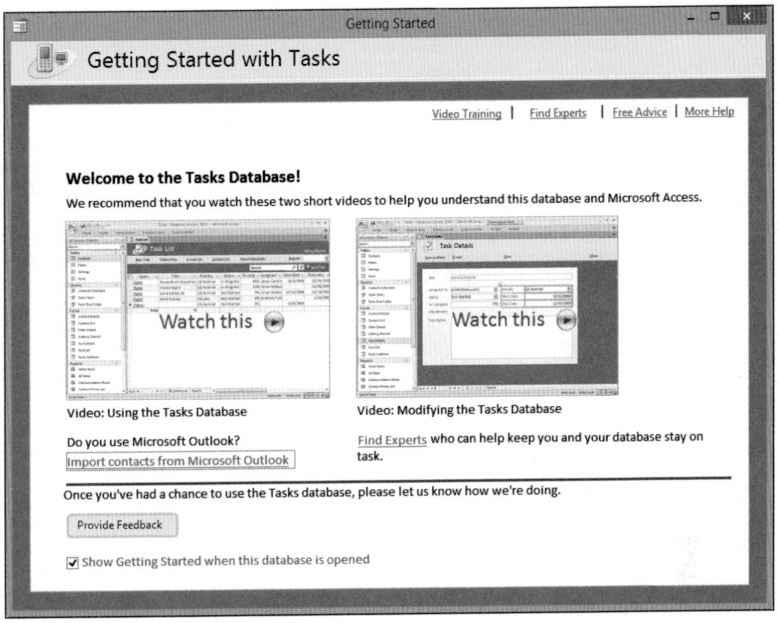

FIGURE 1.28 Getting Started Page for Desktop Task Management Template

STEP 2»
Because you downloaded a template, some objects will have already been created. You can work with these objects just as you did in the first three sections of this chapter. For example, you can enter data directly into any existing table in the database by opening the table, clicking in the first empty field, typing the data, tabbing to the next empty field, and then typing the data for the next field. You can also open any form that is part of the downloaded template and enter the data directly in the forms. Some templates will include queries and reports. Edit any object to meet your requirements.

STEP 3»
Once the database is opened, review the objects listed in the Navigation Pane. Change the Navigation Pane category from Object Type to *Tables and Related Views* to become familiar with the relationships between the tables and other database objects. Note the tables and the objects that are based on them.

After noting the objects in the database, open the Relationships window to see the connections between them. Once you are familiar with the database design, you can enter your data.

Figure 1.29 displays the open Task Management database with the Navigation Pane set to display *Tables and Related Views*. The Tasks table displays with its related queries, forms, and reports. The Relationships window shows the relationship between the Contacts table and the Tasks table.

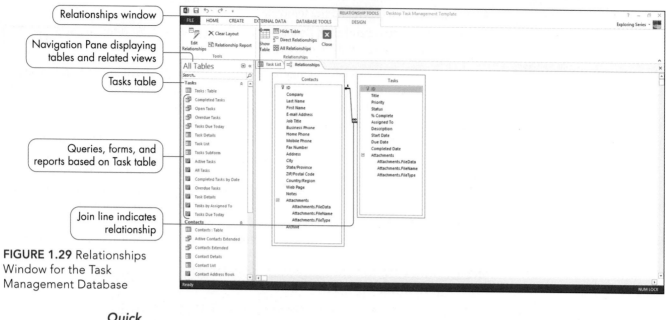

- Relationships window
- Navigation Pane displaying tables and related views
- Tasks table
- Queries, forms, and reports based on Task table
- Join line indicates relationship

FIGURE 1.29 Relationships Window for the Task Management Database

Quick Concepts ✓

1. Name the three methods for creating a new database. *p. 119*

2. What is a custom Web app, and what is required to build a custom Web app? *p. 119*

3. What are two benefits of using a template to create a database? *p. 120*

Hands-On Exercises

4 Access Database Creation

After working with the Northwind Traders database on the job, you decide to use Access to create a personal contact database. Rather than start from scratch, you use an Access Contact Manager desktop template to jumpstart your database creation. A Web app is not necessary because you do not want to share your contacts with others.

Skills covered: Create a Desktop Database Using a Template • Add Records to a Downloaded Desktop Database Template • Explore the Database Objects in a Downloaded Desktop Database Template

---

STEP 1 >> CREATE A DESKTOP DATABASE USING A TEMPLATE

You locate an Access desktop template that you can use to create your personal contact database. This template not only allows you to store names, addresses, telephone numbers, and other information, but also lets you categorize your contacts, send e-mail messages, and create maps of addresses. You download and save the template. Refer to Figure 1.30 as you complete Step 1.

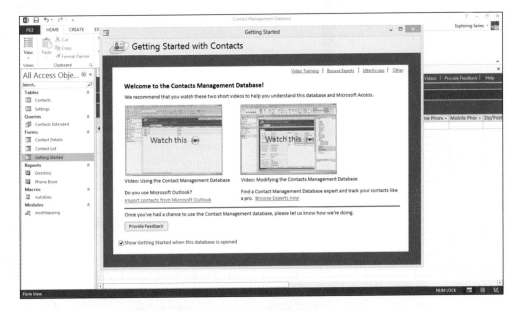

FIGURE 1.30 Desktop Contacts Intro Screen

a. Open Access. Click the Contacts link in the Suggested searches list. Click *Desktop contacts* from the available contacts.

   The Create Intro Screen page for the Desktop contacts database opens.

b. Click the **Browse icon** to navigate to the folder where you are saving your files, enter **a01h4Contacts_LastFirst** as the file name, and then click **OK**.

c. Click **Create** to download the template.

d. Click **Enable Content** on the Security Warning message bar.

> **TROUBLESHOOTING:** If the Getting Started page does not display, click Getting Started in the Forms category on the Navigation Pane.

TROUBLESHOOTING: The Getting Started page opens every time you open the Contacts Management database. To close this page until you want to view it again, clear the *Show Getting Started when this database is opened* check box at the bottom-left corner of the dialog box before closing the Getting Started page.

e. Close the Getting Started page.

The database displays with the Contact List table open.

STEP 2 ❯❯ ADD RECORDS TO A DOWNLOADED DESKTOP DATABASE TEMPLATE

Because the database opens in the Contact List form, you decide to begin by entering a contact—your dentist—in the form. Refer to Figure 1.31 as you complete Step 2.

Step d: Open your dentist's record

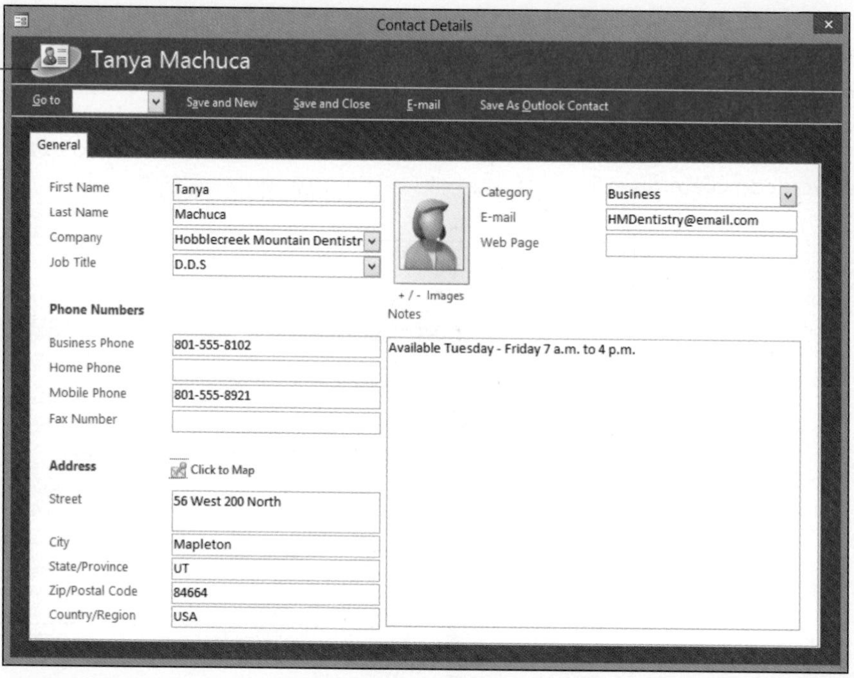

FIGURE 1.31 Contact Details Form

a. Click in the empty first field of the first row. Enter the following information, pressing **Tab** between each entry. Do not press Tab after entering the ZIP/Postal Code.

Field Name	Value to Type
First Name	Tanya
Last Name	Machuca
Company	Hobblecreek Mountain Dentistry
Job Title	D.D.S.
Category	Business (select from list)
E-mail Address	HMDentistry@email.com
Business Phone	801-555-8102
Home Phone	(leave blank)
Mobile Phone	801-555-8921
ZIP/Postal Code	84664

b. Click **Save and Close.**

c. Double-click **Contact List** in the Forms group on the Navigation Pane.

d. Click **Open** in the first field of Dr. Machuca's record.

Open is a hyperlink to a different form in the database. The Contact Details form opens, displaying Dr. Machuca's information. More fields are available for you to use to store information.

e. Enter the following additional information to the record:

Field Name	Value to Type
Street	56 West 200 North
City	Mapleton
State/Province	UT
Country/Region	USA
Notes	Available Tuesday - Friday 7 a.m. to 4 p.m.

f. Click the **Click to Map hyperlink** to view a map to Dr. Machuca's office. Close the map.

Bing displays a map to the address in the record. You can get directions, locate nearby businesses, and use many other options.

g. Click **Save and Close** in the top center of the form to close the Contact Details form.

The record is saved.

h. Click **New Contact** beneath the Contact List title bar.

The Contact Details form opens to a blank record.

i. Enter the following information for a new record, pressing **Tab** to move between fields. Some fields will be blank.

Field Name	Value to Type
First Name	Rowan
Last Name	Westmoreland
Company	Phoenix Aesthetics
Job Title	Aesthetician
Mobile Phone	801-555-2221
Street	425 North Main Street
City	Springville
State/Province	UT
ZIP/Postal Code	84663
Category	Personal
E-mail Address	Rowan55W5@email.com
Notes	Recommended by Michelle

j. Click **Save and Close.**

STEP 3 ›› EXPLORE THE DATABASE OBJECTS IN A DOWNLOADED DESKTOP DATABASE TEMPLATE

You explore the objects created by the template so that you understand the organization of the database. Refer to Figure 1.32 as you complete Step 3.

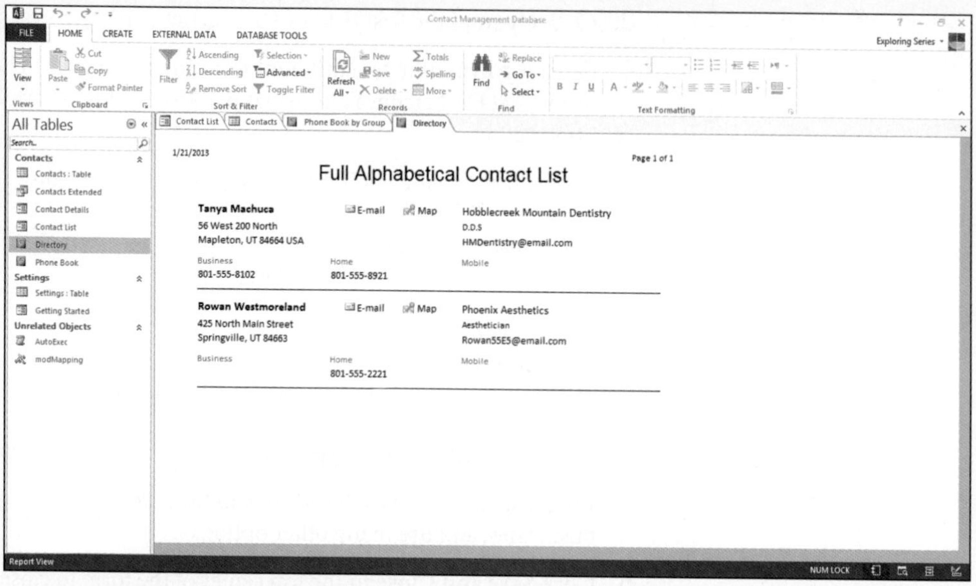

FIGURE 1.32 Directory Form

a. Double-click the **Contacts table** in the Navigation Pane to open it.

The information you entered using the Contact List form and the Contact Details form displays in the Contacts table.

b. Click the **Reports group** in the Navigation Pane to expand the list of reports, if necessary.

The list of reports contained in the database file opens.

c. Double-click **Phone Book** in the Navigation Pane to open it.

The Phone Book report opens displaying the contact name and phone information organized by category.

d. Double-click the **Directory report** in the Navigation Pane to open it.

The Directory report opens, displaying a full alphabetical contact list. The Directory report was designed to display more fields than the Phone Book, but it is not organized by category.

e. Click **All Access Objects** on the Navigation Pane and select **Tables and Related Views**.

You can now see the objects that are based on the Contacts table.

f. Right-click the **Directory report tab** and click **Close All**.

g. Exit Access and submit your work based on your instructor's directions.

Chapter Objectives Review

After reading this chapter, you have accomplished the following objectives:

1. Understand database fundamentals.

- A database is a collection of data organized as meaningful information that can be accessed, managed, stored, queried, sorted, and reported.
- Organize information in a database and recognize Access objects: An Access database is a structured collection of six types of objects—tables, forms, queries, reports, macros, and modules.
- The foundation of a database is its tables, the objects in which data is stored. Each table in the database is composed of records, and each record is in turn comprised of fields.
- The primary key in a table is the field (or combination of fields) that makes every record in a table unique.
- Examine the Access interface: Objects are organized and listed in the Navigation Pane. Access also uses a Tabbed Documents interface in which each object that is open has its own tab.
- Explore Access views: The Datasheet view enables the user to view, add, edit, and delete records, whereas the Design view is used to create and modify a table's design by specifying the fields it will contain, the fields' data types, and their associated properties.
- Open an Access file and work with Content Security: When a database is opened from a location that has not been designated as a trusted location or that does not have a digital signature from a publisher you can trust, Access displays a message bar with a security warning. Click the Enable Content button if you trust the database's source.

2. Use an existing database.

- Understand the difference between working in storage and memory: Access works primarily from storage. Records can be added, modified, or deleted in the database, and as the information is entered it is automatically saved.
- Add, edit, and delete records: A pencil icon displays in the row selector box to indicate when you are in editing mode. Moving to another record or clicking Save on the Quick Access Toolbar saves the changes.
- To add a new record, click *New (blank) record* on the navigation bar. To delete a record, click the row selector and click Delete in the Records group on the Home tab.
- Save As, Compact and Repair, and Back Up Access files: *Compact and Repair* reduces the size of the database, and Back Up creates a duplicate copy of the database.

3. Sort table data on one or multiple fields.

- Sorting changes the order of information, and information may be sorted by one or more fields.

4. Create, modify, and remove filters.

- A filter is a set of criteria that is applied to a table to display a subset of records in that table.
- *Filter by Selection* displays only the records that match the selected criteria.
- *Filter by Form* displays records based on multiple criteria and enables the user to apply logical operators and use comparison operators.

5. Know when to use Access or Excel to manage data.

- Use Access to manage data when you require multiple related tables to store your data; have a large amount of data; need to connect to and retrieve data from external databases; need to group, sort, and total data based on various parameters; and/or have an application that requires multiple users to connect to one data source.
- Use Excel to manage data when you need one worksheet to handle all of your data; have mostly numeric data; require subtotals and totals in your worksheet; want to primarily run a series of "what if" scenarios on your data; and/or need to create complex charts and/or graphs.

6. Understand relational power.

- Use the Relationships window: A relationship is a connection between two tables using a common field. The benefit of a relationship is to efficiently combine data from related tables for the purpose of creating queries, forms, and reports.
- Enforce referential integrity: Enforcing referential integrity when setting a table relationship ensures that data cannot be entered into a related table unless it first exists in the primary table.

7. Create a database.

- Create a Web application using a template: Creating a custom Web app enables you to create a database that you can build and use and share with others through the Web.
- Creating a blank desktop database: Creating a blank desktop database lets you create a database specific to your needs.
- Create a desktop database using a template: A template is a predefined database that includes professionally designed tables, forms, reports, and other objects that you can use to jumpstart the creation of your database.

Key Terms Matching

Match the key terms with their definitions. Write the key term letter by the appropriate numbered definition.

a. Back Up Database
b. Compact and Repair
c. Custom Web app
d. Datasheet view
e. Design view
f. Field
g. Filter by Form
h. Filter by Selection
i. Form
j. Navigation Pane
k. Object

l. Primary key
m. Query
n. Record
o. Relational database management system (RDBMS)
p. Relationship
q. Report
r. Sort
s. Table
t. Template

1. _____ View that enables you to add, edit, and delete the records of a table. **p. 88**

2. _____ An Access object that enables you to enter, modify, or delete table data. **p. 86**

3. _____ An Access utility that reduces the size of the database and can repair a corrupt database. **p. 93**

4. _____ A main component that is created and used to make a database function. **p. 85**

5. _____ A filtering method that displays records based on multiple criteria **p. 104**

6. _____ A system that uses the relational model to manage groups of data (tables) and rules (relationships) between tables. **p. 112**

7. _____ A database that can be built, used, and shared with others through the use of a host server. **p. 119**

8. _____ An object that contains professional-looking formatted information from underlying tables or queries. **p. 86**

9. _____ An object used to store data, and the foundation of every database. **p. 85**

10. _____ An Access utility that creates a duplicate copy of the database. **p. 93**

11. _____ A predefined database that includes professionally designed tables, forms, reports, and other objects. **p. 119**

12. _____ A filtering method that displays only records that match selected criteria. **p. 103**

13. _____ A connection between two tables using a common field. **p. 111**

14. _____ A method of listing records in a specific sequence. **p. 102**

15. _____ View that enables you to create tables, add and delete fields, and modify field properties. **p. 90**

16. _____ An Access interface element that organizes and lists the database objects in a database. **p. 85**

17. _____ A question you ask that can help you find and retrieve table data meeting conditions you specify. **p. 86**

18. _____ The smallest data element in a table, such as first name, last name, address, or phone number. **p. 85**

19. _____ Complete set of all the fields (data elements) about one person, place, event, or concept. **p. 85**

20. _____ The field (or combination of fields) that uniquely identifies each record in a table. **p. 90**

Multiple Choice

1. Which sequence represents the hierarchy of terms, from smallest to largest?

   (a) Database, table, record, field
   (b) Field, record, table, database
   (c) Record, field, table, database
   (d) Field, record, database, table

2. You edit several records in an Access table. When should you execute the Save command?

   (a) Immediately after you edit a record
   (b) When you close the table
   (c) Once at the end of the session
   (d) Records are saved automatically; the save command is not required.

3. Which of the following is *not* true of an Access database?

   (a) Short Text, Number, AutoNumber, and Currency are valid data types.
   (b) Every record in a table has the same fields as every other record.
   (c) Every table in a database contains the same number of records as every other table.
   (d) Each table should contain a primary key; however, a primary key is not required.

4. Which of the following is *true* regarding the record selector box?

   (a) An orange border surrounds the record selector box and the active record.
   (b) A pencil symbol indicates that the current record already has been saved.
   (c) An asterisk indicates the first record in the table.
   (d) An empty square indicates that the current record is selected.

5. Which of the following will be accepted as valid during data entry?

   (a) Adding a record with a duplicate primary key
   (b) Entering text into a numeric field
   (c) Entering numbers into a text field
   (d) Omitting an entry in a required field

6. You have finished an Access assignment and wish to turn it in to your instructor for evaluation. As you prepare to transfer the file, you discover that it has more than doubled in size. You should:

   (a) Delete extra tables or reports or fields to make the file smaller.

   (b) Zip the database file prior to sending it to your instructor.
   (c) Compact and repair the database before sending it to your instructor.
   (d) Turn it in; the size does not matter.

7. Which of the following conditions is available through *Filter by Selection*?

   (a) Equals condition
   (b) Delete condition
   (c) AND condition
   (d) OR condition

8. An Employees table is open in Datasheet view. You want to sort the names alphabetically by last name and then by first name (e.g., Smith, Andrew). To do this, you must:

   (a) First sort ascending on first name and then on last name.
   (b) First sort descending on first name and then on last name.
   (c) First sort ascending on last name and then on first name.
   (d) First sort descending on last name and then on first name.

9. Which of the following is *not* true when creating relationships between tables?

   (a) Join lines create a relationship between two tables.
   (b) The common fields used to create a relationship must both be primary keys.
   (c) The data types of common fields must be the same.
   (d) Enforcing referential integrity ensures that data cannot be entered into a related table unless it first exists in the primary table.

10. All of the following statements are *true* about creating a database *except*:

    (a) Creating a custom Web app requires that you use a host server.
    (b) When creating a blank desktop database, Access opens to a blank table in Datasheet view.
    (c) Using a template to create a database saves time because it includes predefined objects.
    (d) The objects provided in a template cannot be modified.

Practice Exercises

1 Hotel Rewards

FROM SCRATCH

The Lakes Hotel and Conference Center caters to upscale business travelers and provides stylish hotel suites, sophisticated meeting and reception facilities, and state-of-the-art media equipment. The hotel is launching a rewards club to help the marketing department track the purchasing patterns of its most loyal customers. All of the hotel transactions will be stored in an Access database. Your task is to create a member table and enter sample customers. You will practice filtering on the table data. This exercise follows the same set of skills as used in Hands-On Exercises 1 and 2 in the chapter. Refer to Figure 1.33 as you complete this exercise.

ID	LastName	FirstName	Address	City	Stat	Zip	Phone	DateOfMembership
1	Guerassio	Janine	1012 TRADERS TRAIL	GRAHAM	NC	27253		1/26/2015
2	Gutierrez	Antonio	102 PENNYPACKER CT	ELIZABETH CITY	NC	27909	555-387-6394	1/29/2016
3	Sigman	Hanni	1922 WRIGHTSVILLE AVE	CARY	NC	27512	555-784-8851	7/30/2016
4	O'Brien	Lovie	3413 KISTLER COURT	WILMINGTON	NC	28409	555-227-8335	2/13/2015
5	Ratanaphruks	Kritika	4444 LLOYD CT	RALEIGH	NC	27609		3/18/2014
6	Koski	Janice	3904 HUNT CHASE CT	RALEIGH	NC	27612		7/3/2016
7	Tulowiecki	Jerry	775 BEAR RIDGE TRAIL	RALEIGH	NC	27607	555-762-9373	5/21/2016
8	Yingling	Bev	PO BOX 7045	SALISBURY	NC	28146		2/17/2014
9	Gray	Bob	100 BIRDIE COURT	RALEIGH	NC	27612	555-787-7688	9/1/2015
10	Hauser	Bob	10008 WHITESTONE RD	RALEIGH	NC	27612	555-783-8286	3/1/2015
(New)								

FIGURE 1.33 Enter Data into the Members Table

a. Open Access and click **Blank desktop database**.

b. Type **a01p1Rewards_LastFirst** in the **File Name box**. Click the **Browse icon**. Navigate to the location where you are saving your files in the File New Database dialog box, click **OK** to close the dialog box, and then click **Create** to create the new database.

c. Click **View** in the Views group on the TABLE TOOLS FIELDS tab to switch to Design view. Type **Members** in the **Save As dialog box** and click **OK**.

d. Type **LastName** under the ID field and press **Tab**. Accept **Short Text** as the Data Type. Type **FirstName** in the third row and press **Tab**. Accept **Short Text** as the Data Type.

e. Type the next five fields into the Field Name column: **Address**, **City**, **State**, **Zip**, and **Phone**. Accept **Short Text** as the Data Type for each of these fields.

f. Type **DateOfMembership** as the last Field Name and select **Date/Time** as the Data Type.

g. Click **View** in the Views group to switch to Datasheet view. Click **Yes** to save the table. Type the data as shown in Figure 1.33. Increase the column widths to fit the data as necessary. Press **Tab** to move to the next field.

h. Find a record that displays *Raleigh* as the value in the City field. Click **Raleigh** to select that data value.

i. Click **Selection** in the Sort & Filter group on the HOME tab. Select **Equals "Raleigh"**.

j. Find a record that displays *27612* as the value in the Zip field. Click **27612** to select that data value.

k. Click **Selection** in the Sort & Filter group on the HOME tab. Select **Equals "27612"**.

l. Click any value in the FirstName field. Click **Ascending** in the Sort & Filter group on the HOME tab. Click any value in the LastName field. Click **Ascending** in the Sort & Filter group on the HOME tab.

m. Click the **FILE tab**, click **Print**, and then click **Print Preview** to preview the sorted and filtered table.

n. Click **Close Print Preview** in the Close Preview group.

o. Close the table and save the changes.

p. Click the **FILE tab** and click **Compact and Repair Database** under *Advanced*.

q. Click the **FILE tab**, click **Save As**, and then double-click **Back Up Database**.

r. Click **Save** to accept the default backup file name with today's date.

s. Click the **FILE tab** and click **Exit** (to exit Access). Submit the database based on your instructor's directions.

The Custom Coffee Company provides coffee, tea, and snacks to offices in Miami. Custom Coffee also provides and maintains the equipment for brewing the beverages. The firm has a reputation for providing outstanding customer service. To improve customer service even further, the owner recently purchased an Access database to keep track of customers, orders, and products. This database will replace the Excel spreadsheets currently maintained by the office manager. The Excel spreadsheets are out of date, and they do not allow for data validation while data is being entered. The company hired you to verify and enter all the Excel data into the Access database. This exercise follows the same set of skills as used in Hands-On Exercises 1–3 in the chapter. Refer to Figure 1.34 as you complete this exercise.

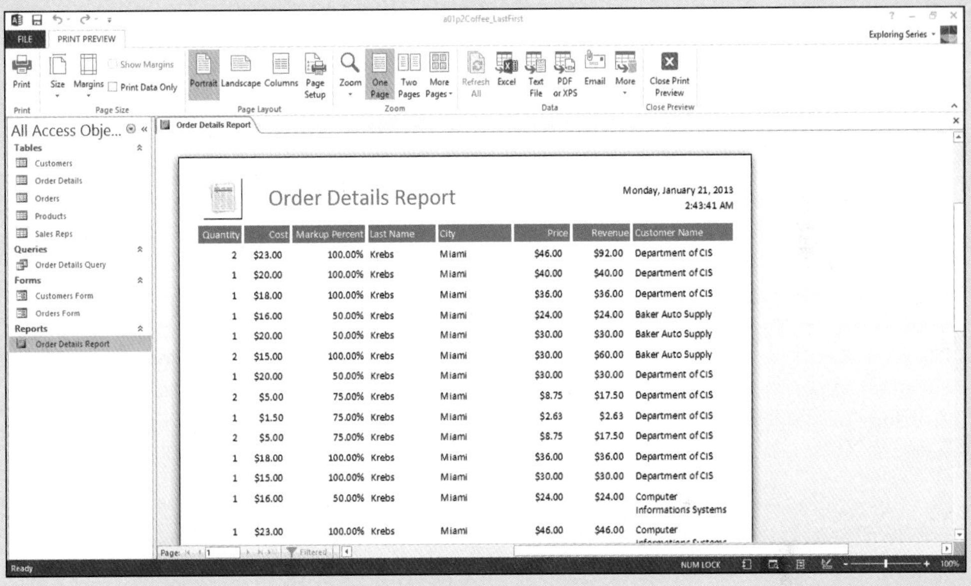

FIGURE 1.34 Order Details Report Filtered for *YourName* and *Miami*

a. Open the *a01p2Coffee* file and save the database as **a01p2Coffee_LastFirst**.

b. Click the **DATABASE TOOLS tab** and click **Relationships** in the Relationships group. Review the table relationships. Take note of the join line between the Customers and Orders tables.

c. Click **Close** in the Relationships group.

d. Double-click the **Sales Reps table** in the Navigation Pane to open it. Replace *YourName* with your name in both the LastName and FirstName fields. For example, as the Access author, I used the name Cynthia Krebs in place of FirstName LastName. Close the table by clicking the **Close (X) button** on the right side of the Sales Reps window.

e. Double-click the **Customers Form** to open it. Click **New (blank) record** in the navigation bar at the bottom of the window. Add a new record by typing the following information; press **Tab** after each field.

Customer Name:	*your name* Company
Contact:	*your name*
Email:	yourname@email.com
Address1:	123 Main St
Address2:	(leave blank)
City:	Miami
State:	FL
Zip Code:	33133
Phone:	(305) 555-1234

Fax: (leave blank)
Service Start Date: 01/17/2016
Credit Rating: A
Sales Rep ID: 2

Note the pencil in the top-left margin of the form window. This symbol indicates the new record has not been saved. Press **Tab**. The pencil symbol disappears, and the new customer is automatically saved to the table.

f. Close the Customers Form.

g. Double-click the **Orders Form** to open it. Click **New (blank) record** in the navigation bar at the bottom of the window. Add a new record by typing the following information:

Customer ID: 15 (Access will convert it to C0015)
Payment Type: Cash (select using the arrow)
Comments: Ship this order in 2 days
Product ID: 4 (Access will convert it to P0004)
Quantity: 2

h. Add a second product using the following information:

Product ID: 6 (Access will convert it to P0006)
Quantity: 1

i. Close the form.

j. Double-click the **Order Details Report** to open it in Report view. Click your name in the Last Name field, click **Selection** in the Sort & Filter group, and then click **Equals "Your Name"**.

k. Right-click **Miami** in the City field and select **Equals "Miami"** from the shortcut menu.

l. Click the **FILE tab**, click **Print**, and then click **Print Preview**.

m. Click **Close Print Preview** in the Close Preview group. Close the report.

n. Click the **FILE tab** and click **Compact & Repair Database**.

o. Click the **FILE tab**, click **Save As**, and then double-click **Back Up Database**. Use the default backup file name.

p. Close Access. Submit based on your instructor's directions.

3 Camping Trip

FROM
SCRATCH

You and your friends have decided to spend your annual reunion camping at the Wawona Campground in Yosemite National Park. Wawona Campground is an extremely popular campground. Campground reservations are available in blocks of one month at a time, up to five months in advance, on the 15th of each month at 7 AM Pacific time. Nearly all reservations are filled the first day they become available, usually within seconds or minutes after 7 AM. Realizing that making reservations is a high-priority, critical task, and that there are many other tasks that must be completed before you can have a successful trip, your group decides to use the Access Task Management Database to begin getting organized for their trip on September 15, 2015. Other tasks can be entered at a later time. This exercise follows the same set of skills as used in Hands-On Exercises 3 and 4 in the chapter. Refer to Figures 1.35–1.38 as you complete this exercise.

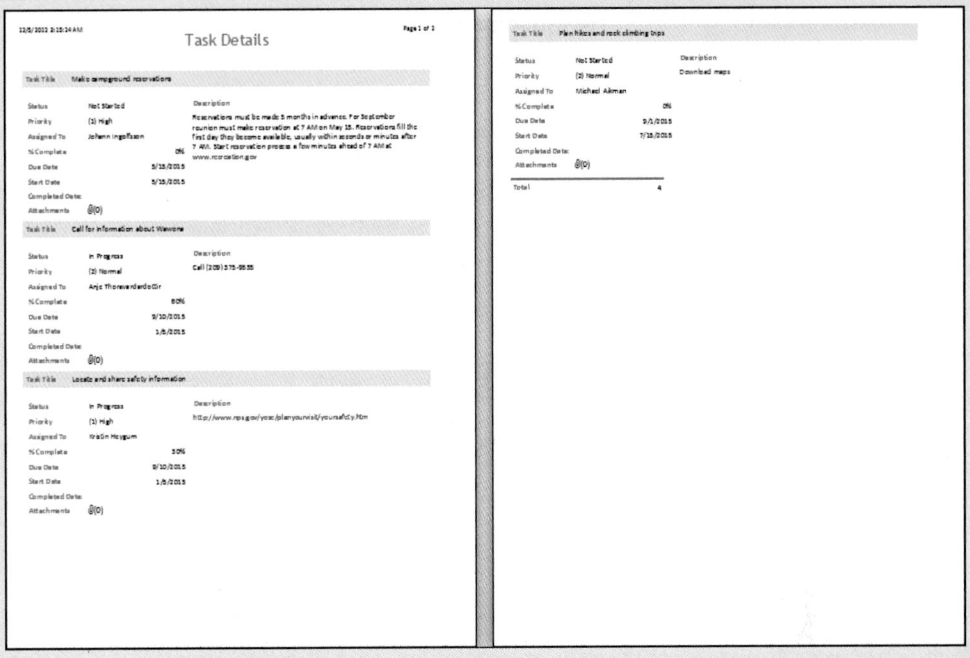

FIGURE 1.35 Task Details Report

a. Open Access and click the **Desktop task management template** in the Access Backstage view.

b. Type **a01p3Camping_LastFirst** in the **File name box**. Click the **Browse icon**. Navigate to the location where you are saving your files in the File New Database dialog box, click **OK** to close the dialog box, and then click **Create** to create the new database.

c. Click the **Watch this arrow** for the *Using the Tasks Database* template video on the left side of the Getting Started page. If the Getting Started page does not open, open the Getting Started form in the Forms group in the Navigation Pane. Click **Watch this>>** and watch the video. Close the video when you have finished watching it. Click **Close** again to return to the *Getting Started with Tasks* page.

d. Remove the check in the *Show Getting Started when this database is opened* check box so that the page does not automatically display in the future. If you want to view Getting Started again, you can click **Getting Started** in the Forms category on the Navigation Pane. Click the **Close (X) button**.

e. Click **Relationships** in the Relationships group on the DATABASE TOOLS tab and note the relationship between the Contacts table and the Tasks table. Close the Relationships window.

f. Double-click **Contact List** in the Forms category on the Navigation Pane. Type the information for each field in the Contact list form using the information displayed in Figure 1.36, pressing **Tab** between each field.

FIGURE 1.36 Contact List

g. Close the Contact List form. The Task List form displays because it was the form open when you downloaded the database.

> **TROUBLESHOOTING:** If the Task List form does not display, double-click the Task List form in the Navigation Pane to open it.

h. Click the **Shutter Bar Open/Close button** to close the Navigation Pane, which enables you to see more table fields.

i. Enter the information for each field in the Task List form using the information displayed in Figure 1.37. In the Priority field, Status field, and Assigned To field, click the arrow and select the list of options. When typing the Start Date and Due Date, type the date and add **7 AM** after the date. Although the date does not show in the table, it is required.

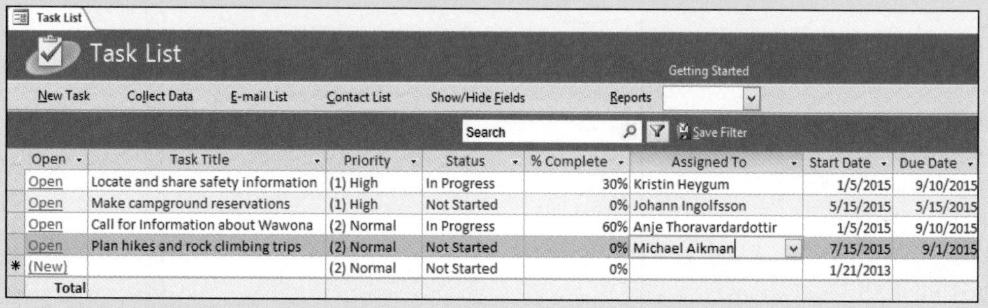

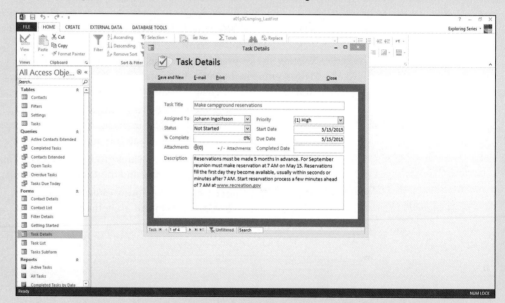

FIGURE 1.37 Task List Form

j. Close the Tasks table and click the **Shutter Bar Open/Close button** to open the Navigation Pane.

k. Double-click **Task Details** in the Forms category in the Navigation Pane.

l. Refer to Figure 1.38 to enter the information in the **Description box** and close the Task Details form.

FIGURE 1.38 Description in Task Details Form

m. Refer to Figure 1.35 and continue entering the descriptions for each of the records.

n. Double-click **Task Details** in the Reports category in the Navigation Pane to view the report displaying the details about the tasks you have created. Scroll down to see all tasks.

o. Click the **FILE tab**, click **Print**, and then click **Print Preview**.

p. Click **Two Pages** in the Zoom group on the Print Preview tab. Note the report format groups the information by Task Title.

q. Click **Close Print Preview** in the Close Preview group. Close the report.

r. Click the **FILE tab** and click **Compact & Repair Database**.

s. Click the **FILE tab**, click **Save As**, and then double-click **Back Up Database**. Use the default backup file name.

t. Close Access. Submit based on your instructor's directions.

1 Home Sales

FROM SCRATCH

You are the senior partner in a large, independent real estate firm that specializes in home sales. Most of your time is spent supervising the agents who work for your firm. The firm needs to create a database to hold all of the information on the properties it has listed. You will use the database to help find properties that match the goals of your customers. You will create the database, create two tables, add data to both tables, and create a relationship. Refer to Figure 1.39 as you complete this exercise.

ID	DateListed	DateSold	ListPrice	SalesPrice	SqFeet	Beds	Baths	Address	SubDivision	Agent	Style	Construction	Garage	YearBuilt
1	5/28/2015		$246,000.00		1928	2	2	1166 Avondale	3	1	Ranch	Brick	1 Car Attached	2010
2	7/22/2015		$263,600.00		1896	2	2	1684 Riverdale	3	2	2 Story	Frame	1 Car Attached	2009
3	6/7/2015		$270,000.00		2026	2	2	1166 So;verdate	3	4	Split Level	Stone	2 Car Attached	2007
4	6/7/2015		$298,000.00		1672	1	1	4520 Oakdale	3	3	Ranch	Brick	1 Car Attached	1997
5	6/22/2015		$312,000.00		2056	2	2	1838 Hillendale	3	4	Split Level	Frame	2 Car Attached	2003
6	7/24/2015		$339,600.00		2456	3	3	1255 Copperdale	3	5	Ranch	Brick	2 Car Attached	2008
7	6/22/2015		$339,600.00		2539	3	3	1842 Gardendale	3	3	2 Story	Stone	1 Car Detached	1983
8	8/12/2015		$239,600.00		2032	2	3	1605 Lakedale	3	2	Split Foyer	Frame	Carport	2002
9	6/22/2015		$379,000.00		2540	3	2	1775 Jerrydale	3	1	Ranch	Brick	3 Car Attached	2014
10	6/23/2015	9/14/2015	$172,500.00	$168,000.00	2030	3	2	213 Merrydale	3	3	Ranch	Stone	1 Car Attached	2010
* (New)			$0.00	$0.00	0	0	0		0	0				0

FIGURE 1.39 Properties Table

a. Open Access and click **Blank desktop database**. Type **a01m1Homes_LastFirst** in the **File Name box**. Click **Browse** and navigate to the location where you are saving your files. Click **OK** to close the dialog box and click **Create** to create the new database.

b. Switch to Design view. Type **Properties** in the **Save As dialog box** and click **OK**.

c. Type **DateListed** under the ID field and press **Tab**. Select **Date/Time** as the Data Type.

d. Type the remainder of the fields and Data Types as shown:

Field Name	Data Type
DateSold	Date/Time
ListPrice	Currency
SalesPrice	Currency
SqFeet	Number
Beds	Number
Baths	Number
Address	Short Text
SubDivision	Number
AgentID	Number
Style	Short Text
Construction	Short Text
Garage	Short Text
YearBuilt	Number

e. Switch to Datasheet view. Type the first 10 records as shown in Figure 1.39.

f. Open the *a01m1Properties.xlsx* workbook file in Excel. Click **row 2**, press and hold the **left mouse button**, and then drag through **row 70** so that all the data rows are selected. Click **Copy** in the Clipboard group on the HOME tab. Click **Yes** to save the data to the Clipboard when prompted. Close the Excel file.

g. Return to Access and click on the **asterisk (*)** on the first new row of the Properties table. Click **Paste** in the Clipboard group to paste all 69 rows into the Properties table. Save and close the table.

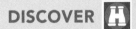
DISCOVER

h. Click **Table** in the Tables group on the CREATE tab. Click **View** in the Views group on the TABLE TOOLS FIELDS tab to switch to Design view. Save the table as **Agents**. Change the primary key from ID to **AgentID**. Add the following fields and switch to Datasheet view. Save changes to the table design when prompted.

Field Name	Data Type
FirstName	Short Text
LastName	Short Text
Title	Short Text

i. Enter the following data in the Agents table and close the table.

AgentID	FirstName	LastName	Title
1	Kia	Hart	Broker
2	Keith	Martin	Agent
3	Kim	Yang	Agent
4	Steven	Dougherty	Agent in Training
5	Angela	Scott	Agent in Training
6	Juan	Resario	President

j. Click the **DATABASE TOOLS tab** and click **Relationships** in the Relationships group. Add both tables to the Relationships window and close the Show Table dialog box.

k. Drag the bottom border of the Properties table downward until all fields display. Drag the **AgentID field** from the Agents table and drop it onto the **AgentID field** in the Properties table. Click the **Enforce Referential Integrity check box** in the Edit Relationships dialog box to activate it. Click **Create** and close the Relationships window. Click **Yes** to save your changes.

l. Open the **Properties** table. Click **Advanced** in the Sort & Filter group and click **Filter By Form**. Set the criteria to identify properties with a list price less than $300,000 and with two bedrooms. (You will use the expression <300000 for the criteria of the list price.) Display the results and sort by ascending list price. Save and close the table.

m. Compact, repair, and back up the database.

n. Exit Access. Submit the database based on your instructor's directions.

2 National Conference

The Association of Higher Education will host its National Conference on your campus next year. To facilitate the conference, the information technology department has replaced last year's Excel spreadsheets with an Access database containing information on the rooms, speakers, and sessions. Your assignment is to create a room itinerary that will list all of the sessions, dates, and times for each room. The list will be posted on the door of each room for the duration of the conference. Refer to Figure 1.40 as you complete this exercise.

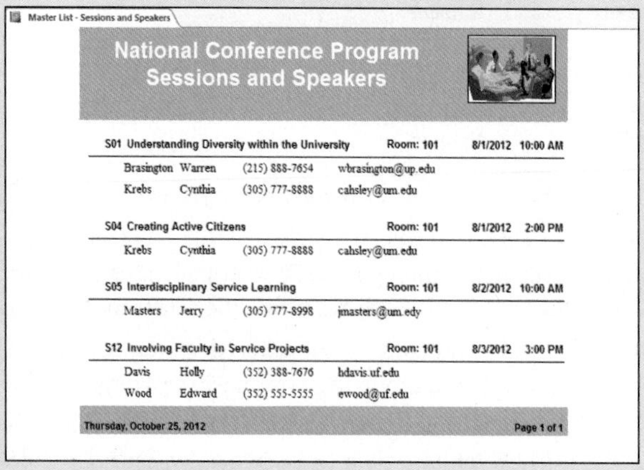

FIGURE 1.40 Sessions and Speakers Report—Room 101

a. Open the *a01m2NatConf* file and save the database as **a01m2NatConf_LastFirst**.

b. Open the Relationships window.

c. Review the objects in the database to see if any of the existing objects will provide the room itinerary information displayed in Figure 1.40.

d. Open the SessionSpeaker table. Scroll to the first blank record at the bottom of the table and enter a new record using SpeakerID **99** and SessionID **09**. (Note: Speaker 99 does not exist.) How does Access respond? Close the dialog box, recognizing that you are not saving this record. Close the SessionSpeaker table. In the Relationships window, right-click the join line between the Speakers table and SessionSpeaker table and click **Delete**. Click **Yes** to permanently delete the selected relationship from the database. Close the Relationships window. Open the SessionSpeaker table and enter the same record again. How does Access respond this time? Close the SessionSpeaker table.

e. Open the Speakers table. Find and replace *YourName* with your name. Close the Speakers table.

f. Open the Speaker–Session Query and apply a filter to identify the sessions where you or Holly Davis are the speakers. Use *Filter by Form* and the Or tab. (Nine records should display.)

g. Sort the filtered results in ascending order by the RoomID field and save and close the query.

h. Open the Master List–Sessions and Speakers report. Right-click the **Master List–Sessions and Speakers tab** and select **Report View**.

i. Apply a filter that limits the report to sessions in Room 101 only.

j. Click the **FILE tab**, click **Print**, and then click **Print Preview**. Compare the report to Figure 1.40 and make any corrections necessary. Close Print Preview and close the report.

k. Compact and repair the database.

l. Back up the database. Use the default backup file name.

m. Exit Access. Submit based on your instructor's directions.

3 Used Cell Phones for Sale

You and a few of your classmates decide to start a new business selling used cell phones, MP3 players, and accessories. You will use an Access database to track your inventory. To begin, one person in your group will locate the Access database for this exercise, complete steps b through f, and then post the database to a SkyDrive folder. The next person in your group will retrieve the revised database and also complete steps b through f (and so on until everyone has completed steps b through f). After everyone has completed steps b through f, you will retrieve the database again and complete step g. At the completion of this exercise, each person will submit his or her own Word document containing the answers to the questions below.

a. Open the *a01m3Phones* database and save it as **a01m3PhonesGroupX_LastFirst**. (Replace *X* with the number assigned to your group by your instructor.)

b. Open the Inventory table and review the records in the table. Take note of the data in the TypeOfDevice column. Close the table and open the DeviceOptions table. Review the data and close the table.

c. Open the Relationships window. What is the benefit of the relationship between the Inventory table and the DeviceOptions table? Create a Word document with both the question and your answer. After you complete this exercise, you will submit this Word document to your instructor using the file name **a01m3PhonesAnswers_LastFirst**. Close the Relationships window.

d. Open the Inventory Form and add the information about your cell phone to the table (or search the Internet for any model if you do not have a cell phone) in the first new blank record. Enter your name in the SellerName field. With your information showing in the form, take a screenshot of the form using the Snipping Tool. Paste the image into the Word document you created in step c. Close the form.

e. Open the Inventory Report by Manufacturer in Report view. Filter the records for only items that have not been sold. Take a screenshot using the Snipping Tool and paste the image into the Word document. Close the report, close the database, and then exit Access.

f. Create a folder on your SkyDrive account named **Exploring Access** and share the folder with other members in your group and the instructor. Upload the database to this new folder and notify another person in your group. The next person will complete steps b through f, and then the next person, until all group members have added their information.

g. After all the new phone records have been added, each person in the group should download the **a01m3PhonesGroupX** database again and use filters to answer the following questions. Add the questions and your answers to the Word document you created.

1. How many phones are still for sale? _____
2. How many phones are made by Apple or Samsung? _____
3. How many phones were sold in the first half of 2013? _____ List the ID numbers _____
4. Sort the phones from lowest to highest asking price. Which phone is the least expensive? _____ Most expensive? _____
5. How many items are not phones? _____

h. Use e-mail or text messaging to communicate with the other members in your group if you have any questions.

i. Submit the Word document based on your instructor's directions.

Beyond the Classroom

Northwind Revenue Report

RESEARCH CASE

Open the *a01b2NWind* file and save the database as **a01b2NWind_LastFirst**. Open the Employees table and replace *YourName* with your first and last names. Before you can filter the Revenue report, you need to update the criterion in the underlying query to match the dates in the database. Right-click the **Revenue query** in the Navigation Pane and click **Design view** in the shortcut menu. Scroll to the right until you see *OrderDate*. Right-click in the **Criteria row** under *OrderDate* and click **Zoom**. Change the criterion to **Between#1/1/ 2015#And#3/31/2015#** and click **OK**. Click **Run** in the Results group on the Query Tools Design tab and save the query. Open the Revenue report. Use the tools that you have learned in this chapter to filter the report for only your sales of Confections. Close the report. Compact, repair, and back up your database and exit Access.

Lugo Computer Sales

DISASTER RECOVERY

You are having trouble with an Access 2013 database. One of the employees accidentally changed the CustomerID of Lugo Computer Sales. This change caused a problem in one of the relationships. Open the *a01b3Recover* file and save the database as **a01b3Recover_LastFirst**. Open the Customers and Orders tables and examine the data. Change the Lugo Computer Sales CustomerID in the Customers table back to the original number of 6. Reset the relationship between the Customers table and the Orders table and enforce referential integrity. Compact, repair, and back up your database and exit Access. Submit the database based on your instructor's directions.

Financial Literacy

SOFT SKILLS CASE

The Cambridge Resources Group stated that surveyed executives ranked the "toll on productivity caused by financial stress" as one of the "most critical unaddressed issues in the workplace today." Dr. E. Thomas Garman*, the president of Personal Finance Employee Education Foundation, stated that "60% of employees live paycheck to paycheck" and that research shows that "those with more financial distress report poor health; financially distressed workers (40–50%) report that their financial problems cause their health woes; and that positive changes in financial behaviors are related to improved health."

Tracking your income and your expenses enables you to see where your money is going. With this information you can create a budget that will help you reach your goals. To aid you with this process, Microsoft created a downloadable Personal Account Ledger template. This database includes a form that enables you to record transactions; reports to display transactions, expenses by category, and income by category; and a tax report. Open *a01b4Ledger*, a database based on the Microsoft Personal Account Ledger, and save it as **a01b4Ledger_LastFirst**. Use the Account Transaction List to enter your income and expenses for the previous month. Then view the Income by Category report and the Expenses by Category report. Compact, repair, and back up your database and exit Access. Submit the database based on your instructor's directions.

* Employee Financial Wellness slideshare presentation, http://www.slideshare.net/irwink/Employee-Financial-Wellness, by Dr. E. Thomas Garman, President, Personal Finance Employee Education Foundation.

Your boss expressed concern about the accuracy of the inventory reports in the bookstore. He needs you to open the inventory database, make modifications to some records, and determine if the changes you make carry through to the other objects in the database. You will make changes to a form and verify those changes in a table, a query, and a report. When you have verified that the changes update automatically, you will compact and repair the database and make a backup of it.

Database File Setup

You will open an original database file and save the database with a new name, replace an existing author's name with your name, create a table, create table relationships, sort, and apply a filter by selection.

a. Open the *a01c1Books* file and save the database as **a01c1Books_LastFirst**.

b. Create a new table in Design view. Save the table as **Publishers**. Change the primary key from ID to **PubID** with a Data Type of **Short Text**. Add the following fields and switch to Datasheet view. Save changes to the table design when prompted.

Field Name	Data Type
PubName	Short Text
PubAddress	Short Text
PubCity	Short Text
PubState	Short Text
PubZIP	Short Text

c. Enter the following data in the Publishers table and close the table.

PubID	PubName	PubAddress	PubCity	PubState	PubZIP
BB	Bantam Books	1540 Broadway	New York	NY	10036
FS	Farrar, Straus and Giroux	12 Union Square West	New York	NY	10003
KN	Knopf	299 Park Avenue	New York	NY	10171
LB	Little, Brown and Company	1271 Avenue of the Americas	New York	NY	10020
PH	Pearson/ Prentice Hall	1 Lake Street	Upper Saddle	NJ	07458
SS	Simon & Schuster	100 Front Street	Riverside	NY	08075

d. Open the Maintain Authors form.

e. Navigate to Record 7 and replace *YourName* with your name.

f. Add a new Title: **Technology in Action**. The ISBN is **0-13-148905-4**, the PubID is **PH**, the PublDate is **2015**, the Price is $89.95 (just type **89.95**, no $), and StockAmt is **95** units. Move to any other record to save the new record. Close the form.

g. Open the Maintain Authors form again and navigate to Record 7. The changes are there because Access works from storage, not memory. Close the form again.

Sort a Query and Apply a Filter by Selection

You need to reorder a detail query so that the results are sorted alphabetically by the publisher name.

a. Open the Publishers, Books, and Authors Query.

b. Click in any record in the PubName column and sort the field in ascending order.

c. Check to make sure that four books list you as the author.

d. Click your name in the Author's Last Name field and filter the records to show only your books.

e. Close the query and save the changes.

View a Report

You need to examine the Publishers, Books, and Authors Report to determine if the changes you made in the Maintain Authors form appear in the report.

a. Open the Publishers, Books, and Authors Report.

b. Check to make sure that the report shows four books listing you as the author.

c. View the layout of the report in Print Preview.

d. Close the report.

Filter a Table

You need to examine the Books table to determine if the changes you made in the Maintain Authors form carried through to the related table. You also will filter the table to display books published after 2010 with fewer than 100 copies in inventory.

a. Open the Books table.

b. Use *Filter by Form* to create a filter that will identify all books published after 2010 with fewer than 100 items in stock.

c. Apply the filter and preview the filtered table.

d. Close the table and save the changes.

Compact and Repair a Database and Back Up a Database

Now that you are satisfied that any changes made to a form or query carry through to the table, you are ready to compact, repair, and back up your file.

a. Compact and repair your database.

b. Create a backup copy of your database, accept the default file name, and save it.

c. Exit Access. Submit based on your instructor's directions.

Tables and Queries in Relational Databases

Designing Databases and Extracting Data

OBJECTIVES | AFTER YOU READ THIS CHAPTER, YOU WILL BE ABLE TO:

1. Design a table p. 142
2. Create and modify tables p. 146
3. Share data p. 157
4. Establish table relationships p. 160
5. Create a single-table query p. 171
6. Specify query criteria for different data types p. 173

7. Understand query sort order p. 177
8. Run, copy, and modify a query p. 177
9. Use the Query Wizard p. 178
10. Create a multitable query p. 184
11. Modify a multitable query p. 185

CASE STUDY | Bank Audit

During a year-end review, a bank auditor uncovers mishandled funds at Commonwealth Federal Bank in Wilmington, Delaware. In order to analyze the data in more detail, the auditor asks you to create an Access database so he can enter the compromised accounts, the associated customers, and the involved employees. Once the new database is created and all the data are entered, you will help the auditor answer questions by creating and running queries.

As you begin, you realize that some of the data are contained in Excel spreadsheets. After discussing this with the auditor, you decide importing these data directly into the new database would be best. Importing from Excel into Access is commonplace and should work well. Importing will also help avoid errors that are associated with data entry. Once the Excel data have been imported, you will use queries to determine which data do not belong in the database. Unaffected records will be deleted.

This chapter introduces the Bank database case study to present the basic principles of table and query design. You will use tables and forms to input data, and you will create queries and reports to extract information from the database in a useful and organized way. The value of that information depends entirely on the quality of the underlying data—the tables.

Table Design, Creation, and Modification

Good database design begins with the tables. Tables provide the framework for all of the activities you perform in a database. If the framework is poorly designed, the rest of the database will be poorly designed as well. Whether you are experienced in designing tables or just learning how, the process should not be done haphazardly. You should follow a systematic approach when creating tables for a database. This process will take practice; however, over time, you will begin to see the patterns and eventually see the similarities among all databases.

In this section, you will learn the principles of good table design. You will review essential guidelines used when creating tables. After developing and testing the table design on paper, you will implement that design in Access. The first step is to list all the tables you need for the database and list all the fields in each table. While you learned to create tables in the previous chapter, in this chapter, you will learn to refine them by changing the properties of various fields. You will also be introduced to the concept of data validation. You want to make sure the data entered into the database are valid for the field and valid for the organization. Allowing invalid data into the tables will only cause problems later.

Designing a Table

Recall that a table is a collection of records, with each record made up of a number of fields. During the table design process, think of the specific fields you need in each table; list the fields under the correct table and assign each field a data type (such as short text, number, or date) as well as its size (length) or format. The order of the fields within the table and the specific field names are not significant because they can be changed later. What is important is that the tables contain all necessary fields so that the system can produce the required information.

For example, consider the design process necessary to create a database for a bank. Most likely you have a bank account and know that the bank maintains data about you. Your bank has your name, address, phone number, and Social Security number. It also knows what accounts you have (checking, savings, money market), if you have a credit card with that bank, and what its balance is. Additionally, your bank keeps information about its branches around the city or state. If you think about the data your bank maintains, you could make a list of the categories of data needed to store that information. These categories for the bank—customers, accounts, branches—become the tables in the bank's database. A bank's customer list is an example of a table: It contains a record for each bank customer.

After the tables have been identified, add the necessary fields using these six guidelines. (These guidelines are discussed in detail in the following paragraphs.)

- Include the necessary data.
- Design for now and for the future.
- Store data in their smallest parts.
- Add calculated fields to a table.
- Design to accommodate date arithmetic.
- Link tables using common fields.

Figure 2.1 shows a customer table and two other tables found in a sample bank database. It also lists fields that would be needed in each table record.

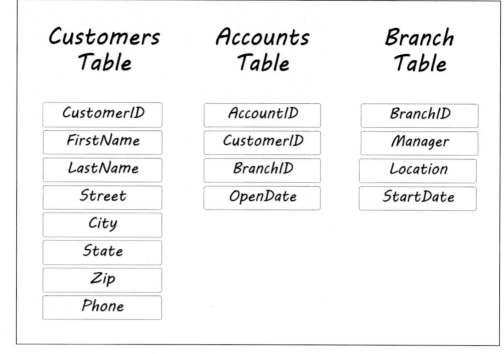

FIGURE 2.1 Rough Draft of Tables and Fields in a Sample Database

Include Necessary Data

A good way to determine what data are necessary in tables is to consider the output you need. It will probably be necessary for you to create professional-looking reports for others, so begin by creating a rough draft of the reports you will need. Then design tables that contain the fields necessary to create those reports. In other words, ask yourself what information will be expected from the system and determine the data required to produce that information. Consider, for example, the tables and fields in Figure 2.1. Is there required information that could not be generated from those tables?

- You can determine which branch a customer uses because the Accounts table includes the CustomerID and the BranchID.
- You can determine who manages a particular branch and which accounts are located there because the Branch table contains the Manager and Location fields.
- You can determine how long a customer has banked with the branch because the date he or she opened the account is stored in the Accounts table.
- You cannot generate the monthly bank statement. In order to generate a customer bank statement (showing all deposits and withdrawals for the month), you would need to add an additional table—an Account Activity table.
- You cannot e-mail a customer because the Customers table does not contain an E-mail field.

If you discover a missing field, such as the E-mail field, you can insert a row anywhere in the appropriate table and add the missing field. The databases found in a real bank are more complex, with more tables and more fields; however, the concepts illustrated here apply both to our sample bank database and to real bank databases.

Design for Now and for the Future

As the data requirements of an organization evolve over time, the information systems that hold the data must change as well. When designing a database, try to anticipate the future needs of the system and build in the flexibility to satisfy those demands. For example, when you add a text field, make sure that the number of characters allocated is sufficient to accommodate future expansion. On the other hand, if you include all the possible fields that anyone might ever need, you could drive up the cost of the database. Each additional field can increase the cost of the database, because it will require additional employee time to enter and maintain the data. The additional fields will also require more storage space, which you will need to calculate, especially when working with larger databases. Good database design must balance the data collection needs of the company with the cost associated with collection and storage. Plans must also include the frequency and cost necessary to modify and update the database.

Suppose you are designing a database for a college. You would need to store each student's name, address, and phone number. You would also need to store multiple phone numbers for most students—a cell phone number, a work number, and an emergency number. As a database designer, you will need to design the tables to accommodate multiple entries for similar data.

Store Data in Their Smallest Parts

The table design in Figure 2.1 divides a customer's name into two fields (FirstName and LastName) to reference each field individually. You might think it easier to use a single field consisting of both the first and last name, but that approach is too limiting. Consider a list of customers stored as a single field:

- Sue Grater
- Rick Grater
- Nancy Gallagher
- Harry Weigner
- Barb Shank
- Pete Shank

The first problem in this approach is the lack of flexibility: You could not easily create a salutation for a letter of the form *Dear Sue* or *Dear Ms. Gallagher* because the first and last names are not accessible individually.

A second difficulty is that the list of customers cannot be easily displayed in alphabetical order by last name because the last name begins in the middle of the field. The names could easily be alphabetized by first name because the first name is at the beginning of the field. However, the most common way to sort names is by the last name, which can be done more efficiently if the last name is stored as a separate field.

Think of how an address might be used. The city, state, and postal code should always be stored as separate fields. Any type of mass mailing requires you to sort on ZIP codes to take advantage of bulk mail. Other applications may require you to select records from a particular state or postal code, which can be done more efficiently if you store the data as separate fields. Often database users enter the postal code, and the database automatically retrieves the city and state information. You may need to direct a mailing only to a neighborhood or to a single street. The guideline is simple: Store data in their smallest parts.

Add Calculated Fields to a Table

A *calculated field* produces a value from an expression or function that references one or more existing fields. Access enables you to store calculated fields in a table using the calculated data type. An example of a calculated field can be found in the bank database. Suppose the bank pays its customers 1.0% interest on the principal each month. A calculated field, such as Monthly Interest, could store the expression Principal × 0.01. The interest amount would then appear on the customer's monthly bank statement.

Storing calculated data in a table enables you to add the data easily to queries, forms, and reports without the trouble of an additional calculation. Storing calculated data in a table may increase the size of the database slightly, but the benefits may outweigh this drawback. In the chapters ahead, you will examine calculations and calculated fields in greater detail. You will learn when to add calculated fields to a table and when to avoid them.

Design to Accommodate Date Arithmetic

Calculated fields are frequently created with numeric data, as the preceding Monthly Interest field example illustrates. You can also create calculated fields using date/time data. If you want to store the length of time a customer has been a customer, you would first create a field to hold the start date for each customer. Next, you would create a calculated field that contains an expression that subtracts the start date from today's date. The resulting calculation would store the number of days each customer has been a customer. Divide the results by 365 to convert days to years. If you want to calculate days to years and account for leap year, you could divide the results by 365.25.

This same concept applies to bank accounts; a bank is likely to store the OpenDate for each account in the Accounts table, as shown in Figure 2.1. Using this date, you can subtract the open date from today's date and calculate the number of days the account has been open. (Again, divide the results by 365 to convert to years.) If you open the Accounts table at least one day later, the results of the calculated field will be different.

A person's age is another example of a calculated field using date arithmetic—the date of birth is subtracted from today's date and the result is divided by 365. It might seem easier to store a person's age rather than the birth date to avoid the calculation. But that would be a mistake because age changes over time and would need to be updated each time age changes. Storing the date of birth is much better because the data remains **constant**. You can use **date arithmetic** to subtract one date from another to find out the number of days, months, or years that have lapsed between them. You can also add or subtract a constant from a date.

Plan for Common Fields Between Tables

As you create the tables and fields for the database, keep in mind that the tables will be joined in relationships using common fields. Draw a line between common fields to indicate the joins, as shown in Figure 2.2. These join lines will be created in Access when you learn to create table relationships later in the chapter. For now, you should name the common fields the same and make sure they have the same data type. For example, CustomerID in the Customers table will join to the CustomerID field in the Accounts table. CustomerID must have the same data type (in this case number/long integer) in both tables; otherwise, the join line will not be allowed.

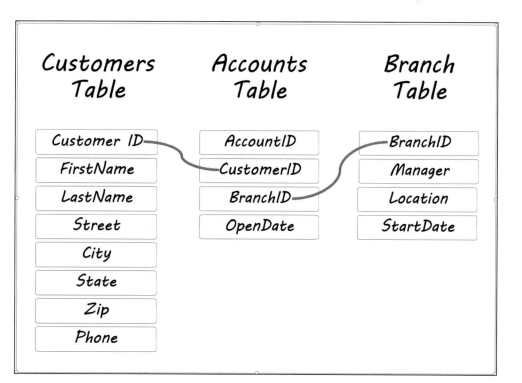

FIGURE 2.2 Create Relationships Using Common Fields

Avoid *data redundancy*, which is the unnecessary storing of duplicate data in two or more tables. You should avoid duplicate information in multiple tables in a database, because errors may result. Suppose the customer address data were stored in both the Customers and Accounts tables. If a customer moved to a new address, it is possible that the address would be updated in only one of the two tables. The result would be inconsistent and unreliable data. Depending on which table served as the source for the output, either the new or the old address might be given to someone requesting the information. Storing the address in only one table is more reliable.

Creating and Modifying Tables

Tables can be created in a new blank database or in an existing database. You can create a table by:

STEP 1 ≫
- Typing a field name in a row in Design view.
- Entering table data into a new row in Datasheet view.
- Importing data from another database or application such as Excel.

Regardless of how a table is first created, you can always modify it later to include a new field or change an existing field. Figure 2.3 shows a table created by entering fields in Design view.

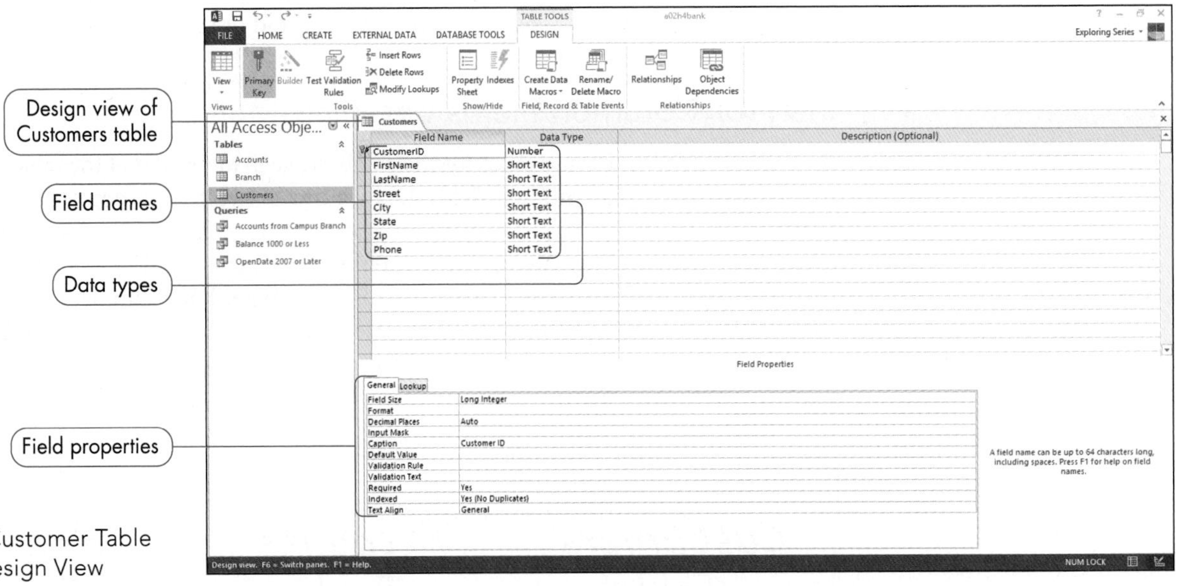

FIGURE 2.3 Customer Table Created in Design View

STEP 4 ≫
When you add a new field in Design view, the field must be given a field name to identify the data it holds. The field name should be descriptive of the data and can be up to 64 characters in length, including letters, numbers, and spaces. Database developers use *CamelCase notation* for field names. Instead of spaces in multiword field names, use uppercase letters to distinguish the first letter of each new word, for example, ProductCost or LastName. It is best to avoid spaces in field names, because spaces can cause problems when creating the other objects—such as queries, forms, and reports—based on tables.

Fields may be renamed either in Design view or in Datasheet view. In Design view, double-click the field name you want to change, type the new field name, and then click Save on the Quick Access Toolbar. To rename a field in Datasheet view, double-click the field selector of the field that you want to rename, type the new field name, and then press Enter.

Fields can be also be deleted in Design view or Datasheet view. To delete a field in Datasheet view, select the field or fields you want to delete and press Delete. To delete fields in Design view, do the following:

1. Click the Record Selector of the field you want to delete to select it.
2. Click Delete Rows in the Tools group.

3. Click Yes in the message box that appears if you want to permanently delete the field(s). Click No if you do not want to delete the field(s).
4. Click Yes in the second message box that will appear if the selected field you are deleting is a primary key. Click No if you do not want to delete the primary key.

> **TIP Freeze Fields in an Access Database**
>
> To keep a field viewable while you are scrolling through a table, select the field or fields you want to freeze, right-click, and then click Freeze Fields. If you want the field(s) to remain frozen when you are finished working, save the changes when you close the table. To unfreeze all fields, right-click the field(s) and select Unfreeze All Fields.

Determine Data Type

Every field also has a ***data type*** property that determines the type of data that can be entered and the operations that can be performed on that data. Access recognizes 12 data types. Table 2.1 lists these data types, their uses, and examples of the data type.

TABLE 2.1 Data Types and Uses

Data Type	Description	Example
Short Text	Stores alphanumeric data, such as a customer's name or address. It can contain alphabetic characters, numbers, and/or special characters (e.g., an apostrophe in O'Malley). Social Security numbers, telephone numbers, and postal codes should be designated as text fields since they are not used in calculations and often contain special characters such as hyphens and parentheses. A short text field can hold up to 255 characters. Formerly Text data type.	2184 Walnut Street
Long Text	Lengthy text or combinations of text and numbers, such as several sentences or paragraphs; used to hold descriptive data. Formerly Memo data type.	A description of product packaging
Number	Contains a value that can be used in a calculation, such as the number of credits a course is worth. The contents are restricted to numbers, a decimal point, and a plus or minus sign.	12
Date/Time	Holds dates or times and enables the values to be used in date or time arithmetic.	10/31/2016 1:30:00 AM
Currency	Used for fields that contain monetary values.	$1,200
AutoNumber	A special data type used to assign the next consecutive number each time you add a record. The value of an AutoNumber field is unique for each record in the file.	1, 2, 3
Yes/No	Assumes one of two values, such as Yes or No, True or False, or On or Off (also known as a Boolean). For example, is a student on the Dean's list: Yes or No.	Yes
OLE Object	Contains an object created by another application. OLE objects include spreadsheets, pictures, sounds, and graphics.	JPG image
Hyperlink	Stores a Web address (URL) or the path to a folder or file. Hyperlink fields can be clicked to retrieve a Web page or to launch a file stored locally.	http://www.keithmast.com
Attachment	Used to store multiple images, spreadsheet files, Word documents, and other types of supported files.	An Excel workbook
Calculated	The results of an expression that references one or more existing fields.	[IntRate] + 0.25
Lookup Wizard	Creates a field that enables you to choose a value from another table or from a list of values by using a list box or a combo box.	Customers table with an AccountID field that looks up the Account ID from an Accounts table

Establish a Primary Key

STEP 2 As you learned earlier, the primary key is the field (or combination of fields) that uniquely identifies each record in a table. Access does not require that each table have a primary key. However, good database design usually includes a primary key in each table. You should select unique and infrequently changing data for the primary key. For example, a complete address (street, city, state, and postal code) may be unique but would not make a good primary key because it is subject to change when someone moves.

You probably would not use a person's name as the primary key, because several people could have the same name. A customer's account number, on the other hand, is unique and is a frequent choice for the primary key, as in the Customers table in this chapter. The primary key can be easily identified in many tables—for example, a PartNumber in a parts table, the ISBN in the book database of a bookstore, or a StudentID that uniquely identifies a student. When no primary key occurs naturally, you can create a primary key field with the AutoNumber data type. The *AutoNumber* data type is a number that automatically increments each time a record is added.

In Figure 2.4, the book's ISBN is the natural primary key for the book table because no two book titles can have the same ISBN. This field uniquely identifies the records in the table. Figure 2.5 depicts the Speakers table, where no unique field can be identified from the data. Because of this, you can add the SpeakerID field with an AutoNumber data type. Access automatically numbers each speaker record sequentially with a unique ID as each record is added.

ISBN provides a unique identifier

Books

ISBN	AuthorID	Title	Publisher ID	PublDate	Price	StockAmt	Click to Add
0-275-41199-7	13	Blackhills Farm	KN	2010	$18.87	28	
0-316-06943-4	15	The Black Box	LB	2012	$16.79	375	
0-316-15391-5	15	Chasing the Dime	LB	2003	$51.75	400	
0-316-15405-9	15	City of Bones	LB	2007	$20.76	94	
0-316-15407-5	15	A Darkness More than Midnight	LB	2002	$20.76	432	
0-374-23713-1	12	Presumed Innocent	GC	2011	$9.99	180	
0-394-49821-6	13	Interview with the Vampire	KN	1976	$19.57	371	
0-553-38398-0	16	True Blue	BB	2003	$7.50	492	
0-553-58102-3	16	Follow the Stars Home	BB	2001	$6.99	496	
0-670-02356-6	16	Little Night: A Novel	PD	2012	$14.48	113	
0-679-45449-7	13	Blood and Gold	KN	2005	$18.87	640	
0-684-80408-5	11	Reaching for Glory	SS	2006	$24.00	480	
0-684-80415-5	17	Computer Wisdom	SS	2006	$23.50	75	
0-684-80416-5	17	Computer Wisdom II	SS	2011	$28.00	27	
0-684-85351-5	14	Hearts in Atlantis	SS	2012	$28.00	528	
0-742095692-X	12	Personal Injuries	FS	2004	$27.00	403	
0-743-21137-5	14	From a Buick 8	SS	2004	$16.80	368	
1-451-62728-2	14	11/22/63	SS	2011	$18.81	225	
1-931-91704-3	11	The Presidents of the United States of America	WH	2009	$11.01	265	

FIGURE 2.4 Books Table with a Natural Primary Key

SpeakerID (AutoNumber data type) is the primary key

Speakers

SpeakerID	First Name	Last Name	Address	City	Sta	Zip Co	Phone Numl	Email	AreaOfExpertise	Click to Add
1	Cynthia	Krebs	10000 SW 59 Court	Miami	FL	33146	(305) 777-8888	cahsley@um.edu	Student Life	
2	Warren	Brasington	9470 SW 25 Street	Philadelphia	PA	19104	(215) 888-7654	wbrasington@up.edu	Residence Halls	
3	James	Shindell	14088 Malaga Avenue	Miami	FL	33146	(305) 773-4343	jshindell@um.edu	Administration	
4	Edward	Wood	400 Roderigo Avenue	Gainesville	FL	32611	(352) 555-5555	ewood@uf.edu	Student Life	
5	Kristine	Park	9290 NW 59 Steet	Athens	GA	30602	(706) 777-1111	kpark@ug.edu	Student Life	
6	William	Williamson	108 Los Pinos Place	Tuscaloosa	AL	35487	(205) 888-4554	wwilliamson@ua.edu	Deans' Office	
7	Holly	Davis	8009 Riviera Drive	Gainesville	FL	32611	(352) 388-7676	hdavis.uf.edu	Residence Halls	
8	David	Tannen	50 Main Street	Philadelphia	PA	19104	(215) 777-2211	dtannen@up.edu	Student Life	
9	Jeffrey	Jacobsen	490 Bell Drive	Athens	GA	30602	(706) 388-9999	jjacobsen@ug.edu	Wellness	
10	Jerry	Masters	2000 Main Highway	Miami	FL	33146	(305) 777-8998	jmasters@um.edy	Wellness	
11	Kevin	Kline	2980 SW 89 Street	Gainesville	FL	32611	(352) 877-8900	kkline@uf.edu	Student Life	
12	Jessica	Withers	110 Center Highway	Athens	GA	30602	(706) 893-8872	jwithers@ug.edu	Wellness	
13	Betsy	Allman	2987 SW 14 Avenue	Philadelphia	PA	19104	(215) 558-7748	ballman@up.edu	Counseling Center	
14	Mary	Miller	1008 West Marine Road	Miami	FL	33146	(305) 877-4993	mmiller@um.edu	Student Life	
15	Nancy	Vance	1878 W. 6 Street	Gainesville	FL	32611	(352) 885-4330	nvance@uf.edu	Counseling Center	
16	George	Jensen	42-15 81 Street	Elmhurst	NY	11373	(718) 555-6666	gjensen@school.edu	Residence Halls	
* (New)										

Next record will be assigned SpeakerID 17

Record: 17 of 17 | No Filter | Search

NUM LOCK

FIGURE 2.5 Speakers Table with an AutoNumber Primary Key

Explore a Foreign Key

A *foreign key* is a field in one table that is also the primary key of another table. The CustomerID is the primary key in the Customers table. It serves to uniquely identify each customer. It also appears as a foreign key in a related table. For example, the Accounts table contains the CustomerID field to establish which customer owns the account. A CustomerID can appear only once in the Customers table, but it may appear multiple times in the Accounts table (when viewed in Datasheet view) because one customer may own multiple accounts (checking, money market, home equity). Therefore, the CustomerID is the primary key in the Customers table and a foreign key in the Accounts table.

If you were asked to create an Access database for the speakers at a national conference, you would create a database with the tables Speakers and SessionSpeaker. You would add a primary key field to the Speakers table (SpeakerID) along with a speaker's FirstName and LastName fields; you would also add two fields to the SessionSpeaker table (SpeakerID and SessionID). The SpeakerID field in the Speakers table is a primary key and would not allow duplicates; the SpeakerID field in the SessionSpeaker table is a foreign key and would allow duplicates so that a speaker may speak more than once at the conference. The SpeakerID in the SessionSpeaker table enables you to join the two tables in a relationship. Figure 2.6 shows portions of the Speakers and SessionSpeaker tables.

SpeakerID is the primary key of the Speakers table (no duplicates)

SpeakerID is a foreign key in the Session Speaker table so speakers can be assigned multiple sessions

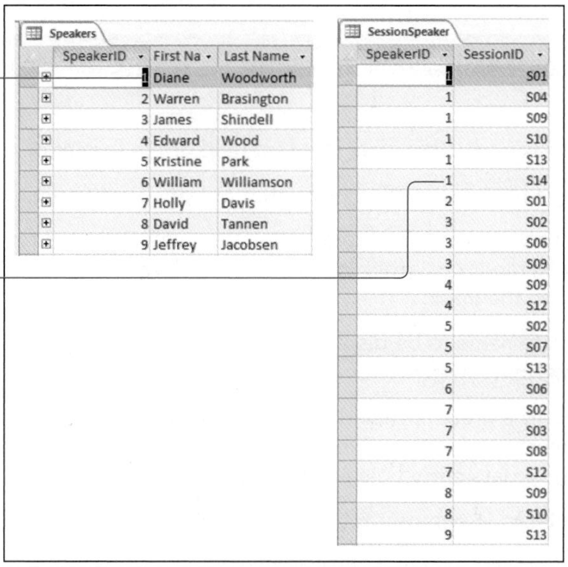

FIGURE 2.6 Two Tables Illustrating Primary and Foreign Keys

Work with Field Properties

STEP 3 »

While a field's data type determines the type of data that can be entered and the operations that can be performed on that data, it is its *field properties* that determine how the field looks and behaves.

Field Size is a commonly changed field property. A field with a *short text data type* can hold up to 255 characters; however, you can limit the characters by reducing the field size property. For example, you would limit the State field to only two characters because all state abbreviations are two letters. A field with a *number data type* can be set to Integer to display the field contents as integers from –32,768 to 32,768 or to Long Integer for larger values.

You can set a *caption property* to create a label more readable than a field. The caption displays at the top of a table or query column in Datasheet view and when the field is used in a report or form. For example, a field named ProductCostPerUnit could have the caption *Per Unit Product Cost*. Even if a caption is used, however, you must use the actual field name, ProductCostPerUnit, in any calculation.

> ## TIP: Best Fit Columns
>
> If a field name is cut off in Datasheet view, you can adjust the column width by positioning the pointer on the vertical border on the right side of the column. When the pointer displays as a two-headed arrow, double-click the border. You can also click More in the Records group on the Home tab. Select Field Width and click Best Fit in the Column Width dialog box.

Set the validation rule property to restrict data entry in a field to ensure the correct type of data are entered or that the data do not violate other enforced properties. The *validation rule* checks the data entered when the user exits the field. If the data entered violate the validation rule, an error message displays and prevents the invalid data from being entered into the field. For example, if you have set the data type for a field as Number and then try to enter text in the field, you will receive an error message telling you that the value you entered does not match the Number data type in the column.

The field properties are set to default values according to the data type, but you can modify them if necessary. Common property types are defined in Table 2.2.

TABLE 2.2 Common Access Table Property Types and Descriptions

Property Type	Description
Field Size	Determines the maximum characters of a text field or the format of a number field.
Format	Changes the way a field is displayed or printed but does not affect the stored value.
Input Mask	Simplifies data entry by providing literal characters that are typed for every entry, such as hyphens in a Social Security Number or slashes in a date. It also imposes data validation by ensuring that data entered conform to the mask.
Caption	Enables an alternate name to be displayed other than the field name; alternate name appears in datasheets, forms, and reports.
Default Value	Enters automatically a predetermined value for a field each time a new record is added to the table. For example, if most customers live in Los Angeles, the default value for the City field could be set to Los Angeles to save data entry time and accuracy.
Validation Rule	Requires data entered to conform to a specified rule.
Validation Text	Specifies the error message that is displayed when the validation rule is violated.
Required	Indicates that a value for this field must be entered.
Allow Zero Length	Allows entry of zero length text strings ("") in a Hyperlink, or Short or Long Text fields.
Indexed	Increases the efficiency of a search on the designated field.
Expression	Used for calculated fields only. Enters the expression you want Access to evaluate and store.
Result Type	Used for calculated fields only. Enters the format for the calculated field results.

Enter Table Records in Datasheet View

STEP 5 ›》 While Design view is used to create and modify the table structure by enabling you to add and edit fields and set field properties, Datasheet view is used to add, edit, and delete records. As you have learned, the Datasheet view of an Access table resembles an Excel spreadsheet and displays data in a grid format—rows represent records and columns represent fields. Datasheet view indicates the current record using a gold border; you can select a record by clicking the record selector on the left side of each record. Use the new blank record (marked with an asterisk) at the end of the table to add a new record.

In Hands-On Exercise 1, you will create a new database and enter fields into a table. Then you will switch to the table's Design view to add additional fields and modify selected field properties of various fields within the table. Finally, you will enter data in the table in Datasheet view.

Quick
Concepts ✓

1. What is meant by "Design for now and the future" when designing database fields? ***p. 143***

2. What is the difference between a primary key and a foreign key? ***p. 149***

3. What is a field property? Which field property creates a more readable label that displays in the top row in Datasheet view and in forms and reports? ***p. 149***

Hands-On Exercises

Watch the Video for this Hands-On Exercise!

MyITLab® HOE1 Training

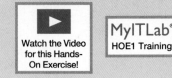

1 Table Design, Creation, and Modification

Assisting the bank auditor at Commonwealth Federal Bank as he investigates the mishandled funds will be a great opportunity for you to showcase your Access skills. Be sure to check your work each step of the way, because your work will come under substantial scrutiny. Do a good job with this Access project and more opportunities might come your way.

Skills covered: Create a Table in Datasheet View • Delete a Field and Set a Table's Primary Key • Work with Field Properties • Create a New Field in Design View • Modify the Table in Datasheet View

STEP 1 » CREATE A TABLE IN DATASHEET VIEW

You create a new desktop database to store information about the mishandled funds database. You enter the data for the first record (BranchID, Manager, and Location). Refer to Figure 2.7 as you complete Step 1.

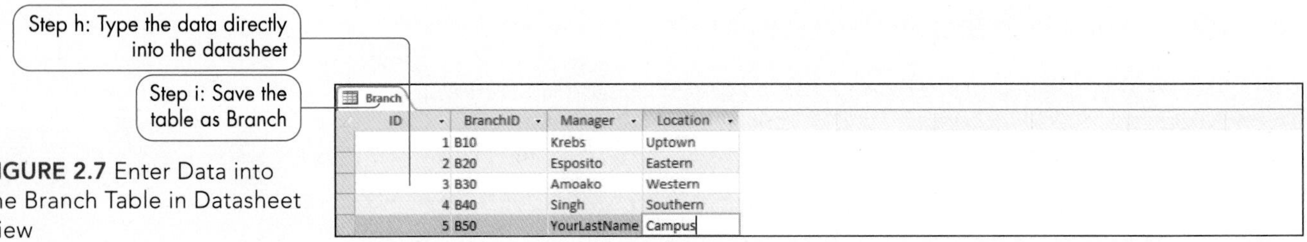

Step h: Type the data directly into the datasheet
Step i: Save the table as Branch
Branch
ID
BranchID
Manager
Location
1 B10 Krebs Uptown
2 B20 Esposito Eastern
3 B30 Amoako Western
4 B40 Singh Southern
5 B50 YourLastName Campus

FIGURE 2.7 Enter Data into the Branch Table in Datasheet View

a. Start Microsoft Office Access 2013 and click **Blank desktop database**.

b. Type **a02h1Bank_LastFirst** into the **File Name box**.

c. Click **Browse** to find the folder location designated by your instructor and click **OK**. Click **Create** to create the new database.

   Access will create the new database named *a02h1Bank_LastFirst* and a new table will automatically open in Datasheet view.

d. Click **Click to Add** and select **Short Text** as the Data type.

   Click to Add changes to *Field1*. *Field1* is selected to make it easier to change the field name.

e. Type **BranchID** and press **Tab**.

   A list of Data types for the third column opens so that you can select the data type for the third column.

f. Select **Short Text**, type **Manager**, and then press **Tab**.

g. Select **Short Text**, type **Location**, and then click in the first column next to the New Record asterisk.

h. Enter the data for the new table as shown in Figure 2.7, letting Access assign the ID field for each new record. Replace *YourLastName* with your own last name.

   Entering data in Datasheet view provides an easy way to create the table initially. You can now modify the table in Design view as described in the next several steps.

i. Click **Save** on the Quick Access Toolbar. Type **Branch** in the **Save As dialog box** and click **OK**.

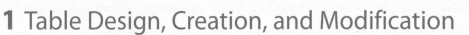

STEP 2 » DELETE A FIELD AND SET A TABLE'S PRIMARY KEY

It is possible to modify tables even after data have been entered; however, pay attention to the messages from Access after you make a design change. In this step, you will be modifying the Branch table. You examine the design of the table and realize that the BranchID field is a unique identifier, making the ID field redundant. You delete the ID field and make the BranchID field the primary key field. Refer to Figure 2.8 as you complete Step 2.

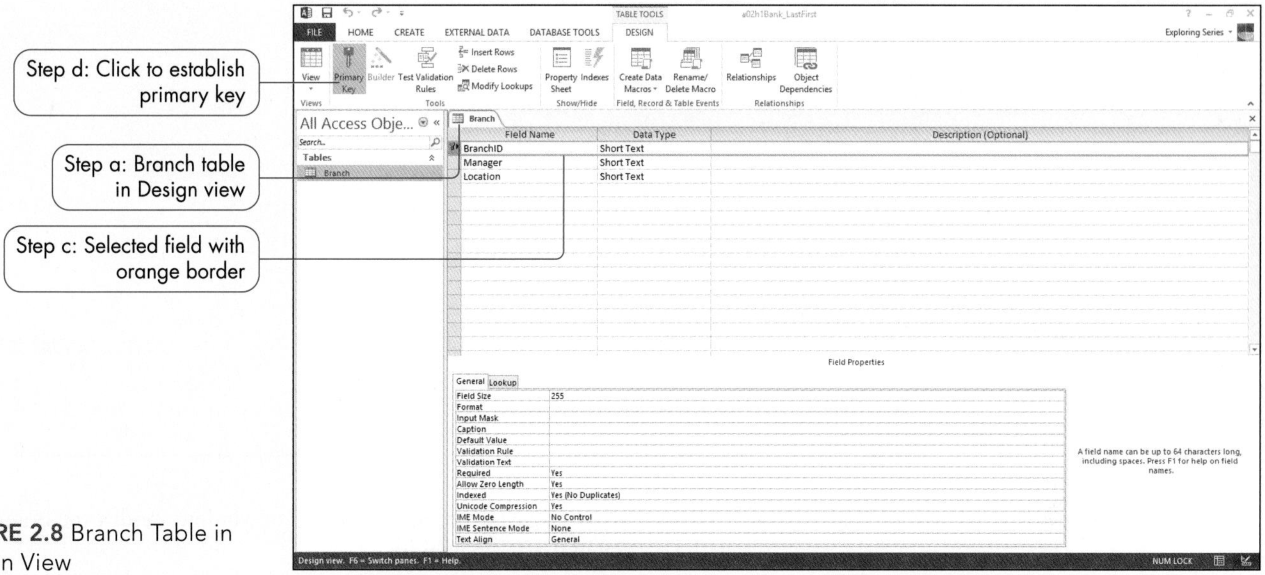

FIGURE 2.8 Branch Table in Design View

a. Click **View** in the Views group to switch to the Design view of the Branch table.

The Field Name for each of the four fields displays along with the Data Type.

b. Click the **ID field** to select it, if necessary. Click **Delete Rows** in the Tools group. Click **Yes** to both warning messages.

Access responds with a warning that you are about to permanently delete a field and a second warning that the field is the primary key. You delete the field because you will set the BranchID field as the primary key.

c. Click the **BranchID field,** if necessary.

The cell field name now has a orange border, as shown in Figure 2.8.

d. Click **Primary Key** in the Tools group on the DESIGN tab.

You set the BranchID as the primary key. The Indexed property in the *Field Properties* section at the bottom of the design window displays *Yes (No Duplicates)*.

e. Click **Save** on the Quick Access Toolbar to save the table.

TIP Shortcut Menu

You can right-click a row selector to display a shortcut menu to copy a field, set the primary key, insert or delete rows, or to access field properties. Use the shortcut menu to make these specific changes to the design of a table.

STEP 3 ›› WORK WITH FIELD PROPERTIES

You need to modify the table design further to comply with the bank auditor's specifications. Be aware of messages from Access that indicate you may lose data. Refer to Figure 2.9 as you complete Step 3.

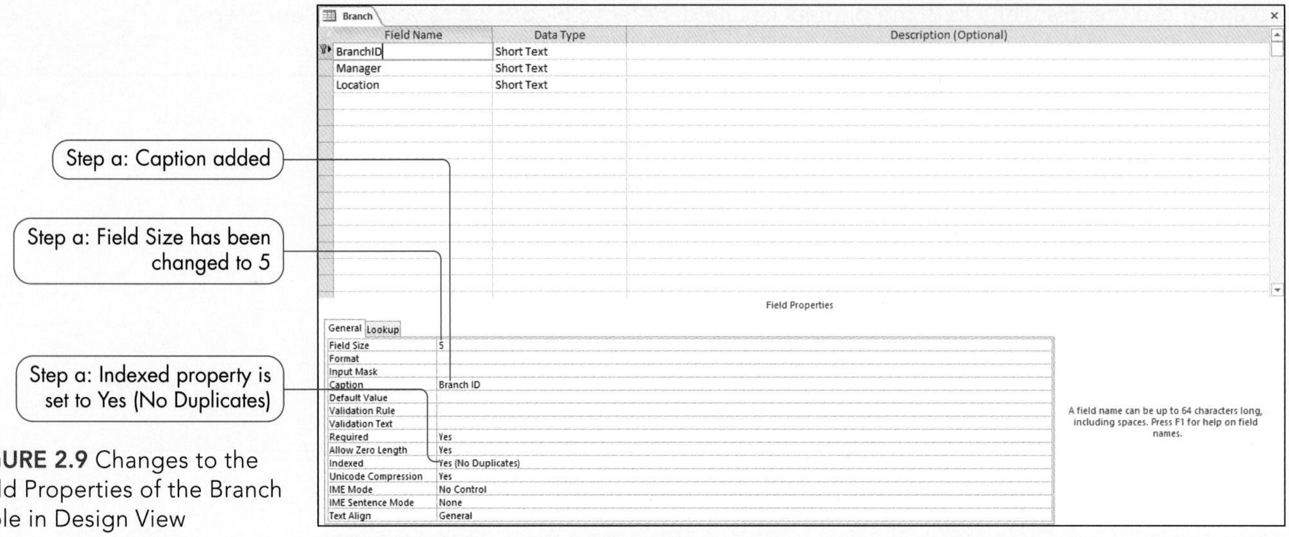

Step a: Caption added

Step a: Field Size has been changed to 5

Step a: Indexed property is set to Yes (No Duplicates)

FIGURE 2.9 Changes to the Field Properties of the Branch Table in Design View

a. Click the **BranchID field name** in the top section of the design window; modify the BranchID field properties in the bottom of the design window.

- Click in the **Field Size property** and change *255* to **5**.
- Click in the **Caption property** and type **Branch ID**. Make sure *Branch* and *ID* have a space between them.
  A caption provides a more descriptive field name. It will appear as the column heading in Datasheet view.
- Check the Indexed property; confirm it is *Yes (No Duplicates)*.

b. Click the **Manager field name** at the top of the window; modify the following field properties:

- Click in the **Field Size property** and change *255* to **30**.
- Click in the **Caption property** and type **Manager's Name**.

c. Click the **Location field name** and modify the following field properties:

- Click in the **Field Size property** and change *255* to **30**.
- Click in the **Caption property** and type **Branch Location**.

STEP 4 ›› CREATE A NEW FIELD IN DESIGN VIEW

You notify the auditor that a date field is missing in your new table. Modify the table to add the new field. The data can be entered at a later time. Refer to Figure 2.10 as you complete Step 4.

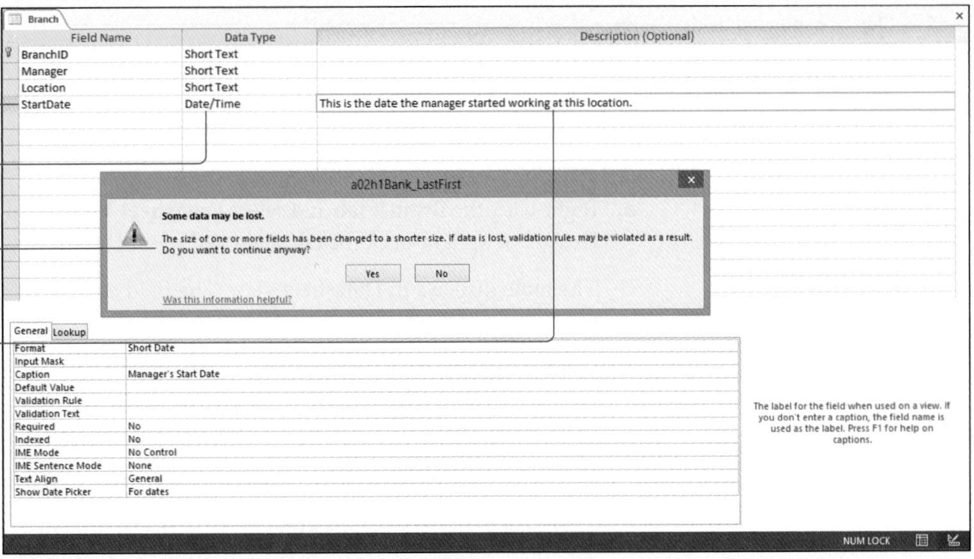

Step a: New field added

Step b: Date/Time data type added

Step f: Message indicating the field size was reduced

Step c: Description added

FIGURE 2.10 Adding a New Field to the Branch Table

a. Click in the first blank row below the Location field name and type **StartDate**.

You added a new field to the table.

b. Press **Tab** to move to the Data Type column. Click the **Data Type arrow** and select **Date/Time**.

> **TIP** **Keyboard Shortcut for Data Types**
>
> You also can type the first letter of the data type, such as d for Date/Time, s for Short Text, or n for Number. To use the keyboard shortcut, click on the field name and press Tab to advance to the Data Type column. Next, type the first letter of the data type.

c. Press **Tab** to move to the Description column and type **This is the date the manager started working at this location.**

d. Click the **Format property**, click the arrow, and then select **Short Date** from the list of date formats.

e. Click in the **Caption property** and type **Manager's Start Date**.

f. Click **Save** on the Quick Access Toolbar.

A warning dialog box opens to indicate that "Some data may be lost" because the size of the BranchID, Manager, and Location field properties were shortened. It asks if you want to continue anyway. Always read the Access warning! In this case, you can click Yes to continue because you know that the existing data are no longer than the new field sizes.

g. Click **Yes** in the warning box.

STEP 5 ≫ MODIFY THE TABLE IN DATASHEET VIEW

As you work with the auditor, you will modify tables in the bank database from time to time. To modify the table, you will need to switch between Design view and Datasheet view. Refer to Figure 2.11 as you complete Step 5.

Branch ID	Manager's Name	Branch Location	Manager's Start Date	Click to Add
B10	Krebs	Uptown	12/3/2014	
B20	Esposito	Eastern	6/18/2013	
B30	Amoako	Western	3/13/2011	
B40	Singh	Southern	9/15/2014	
B50	YourLastName	Campus	10/11/2016	

FIGURE 2.11 Start Dates Added to the Branch Table

a. Right-click the **Branch tab** and select **Datasheet View** from the shortcut menu. (To return to Design view, right-click the tab again and select Design view.)

The table displays in Datasheet view. The field captions display at the top of the columns, but they are cut off.

b. Double-click the border between *Branch ID* and *Manager's Name*, the border between *Manager's Name* and *Branch Location*, the border between *Branch Location* and *Manager's Start Date*, and the border after *Manager's Start Date*.

The columns shrink or expand to display the best fit for the field name.

c. Click inside the **Manager's Start Date** in the first record and click the **Calendar** next to the date field. Use the navigation arrows to find and select **December 3, 2014** from the calendar.

You can also enter the dates by typing them directly into the StartDate field.

d. Type the start date directly in each field for the rest of the managers, as shown in Figure 2.11.

e. Click the **Close (X) button** at the top-right corner of the datasheet, below the Ribbon.

> **TROUBLESHOOTING:** If you accidentally click the Close (X) button on top of the Ribbon, you will exit Access completely. To start again, launch Access and click the first file in the Recent list.

f. Double-click the **Branch table** in the Navigation Pane to open the table. Check the start dates.

The start dates are still there even though you did not save your work in the previous step. Access saves the data to your storage location as soon as you move off the current record or close an object.

g. Click the **FILE tab**, click **Print**, and then click **Print Preview**.

Occasionally, users will print an Access table. However, database developers usually create reports to print table data.

h. Click **Close Print Preview** and close the Branch table.

i. Keep the database open if you plan to continue with Hands-On Exercise 2. If not, close the database and exit Access.

Multiple-Table Databases

In Figure 2.1, the sample bank database contains three tables—Customers, Accounts, and Branch. You created one table, the Branch table, in the previous section using the Datasheet view and modified the table fields in Design view. You will create the two remaining tables using a different method—importing data from Excel. In this section, you will learn how to import data from Excel, modify tables, create indexes, create relationships between tables, and enforce referential integrity.

Sharing Data

Most companies store some type of data in Excel spreadsheets. Often, the data stored in those spreadsheets can be more efficiently managed in an Access database. Fortunately, Access provides you with a wizard that guides you through the process of importing data from Excel. The wizard can also guide you as you import data from other Access databases. You can import tables, queries, forms, reports, pages, macros, and modules from another database.

Import an Excel Spreadsheet

STEP 1 Figures 2.12 through 2.17 show the steps of the Get External Data – Excel Spreadsheet feature. Launch the feature by clicking the External Data tab and clicking Excel in the Import & **STEP 2** Link group. Figure 2.12 shows the first screen of the Get External Data – Excel Spreadsheet feature. In this step, you specify the source of the data. Locate the Excel file you want to import by clicking Browse. Then choose between three options for the incoming data: *Import the source data into a new table in the current database*; *Append a copy of the records to the table*, which adds the data to an existing table; or *Link to the data source by creating a linked table*, which creates a link to the Excel source. Importing or appending data stores a copy of the data in Access, whereas linking the data keeps the data in the original file and Access retrieves the data each time the database is opened.

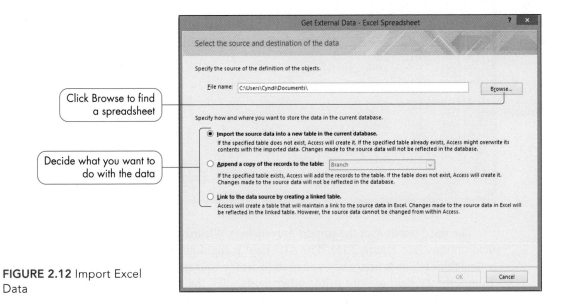

Click Browse to find a spreadsheet

Decide what you want to do with the data

FIGURE 2.12 Import Excel Data

After you locate and select an Excel workbook, accept the default option (*Import the source data into a new table in the current database*) and click OK. The Import Spreadsheet Wizard dialog box launches and displays a list of the worksheets in the specified workbook. Select the worksheet you want to import and click Next. Figure 2.13 shows the Accounts worksheet selected. The bottom of the Import Spreadsheet Wizard dialog box displays a preview of the data stored in the specified worksheet.

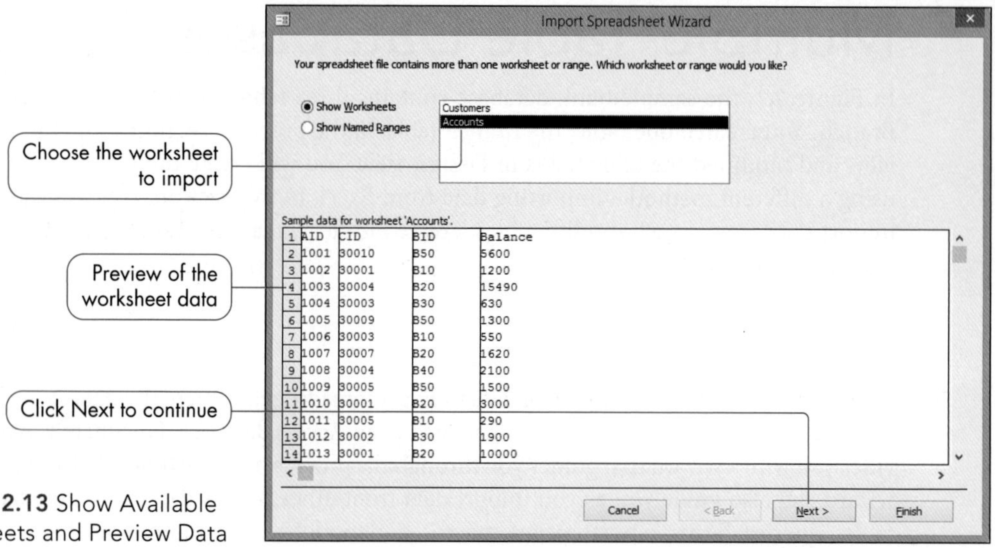

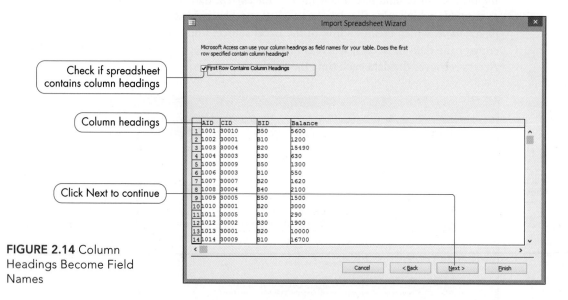

Choose the worksheet to import

Preview of the worksheet data

Click Next to continue

FIGURE 2.13 Show Available Worksheets and Preview Data

Although a well-designed spreadsheet may include descriptive column headings that can be used as field names, not all spreadsheets are ready to import. You may have to revise the spreadsheet before importing it. The second window of the Import Spreadsheet Wizard dialog box contains a check box that enables you to convert the first row of column headings to field names in Access (see Figure 2.14). If a column heading row exists in the spreadsheet, check the box. If no column headings exist, leave the check box unchecked, and the data will import using Field1, Field2, Field3, and so forth as the field names.

Check if spreadsheet contains column headings

Column headings

Click Next to continue

FIGURE 2.14 Column Headings Become Field Names

The third window of the Import Spreadsheet Wizard dialog box enables you to specify field options (see Figure 2.15). The AID field is highlighted in this figure. Because it will become this table's primary key, you need to set the Indexed Property to *Yes (No Duplicates)*. To modify the field options of the other fields, click the Field Name column heading and make the changes. Not all Access table properties are supported by the wizard. You may need to open the table in Design view after importing it to make any additional field property changes.

TIP Retrieve Data Quickly with Indexing

When you set the primary key in Access, the ***indexed property*** is automatically set to *Yes (No Duplicates)*. The indexed property setting enables quick sorting in primary key order and quick retrieval based on the primary key. For non–primary key fields, it may be beneficial to set the Indexed property to *Yes (Duplicates OK)*. Again, Access uses indexing to sort and retrieve data quickly based on the indexed field. As a general rule, indexed fields are usually foreign keys and are numeric.

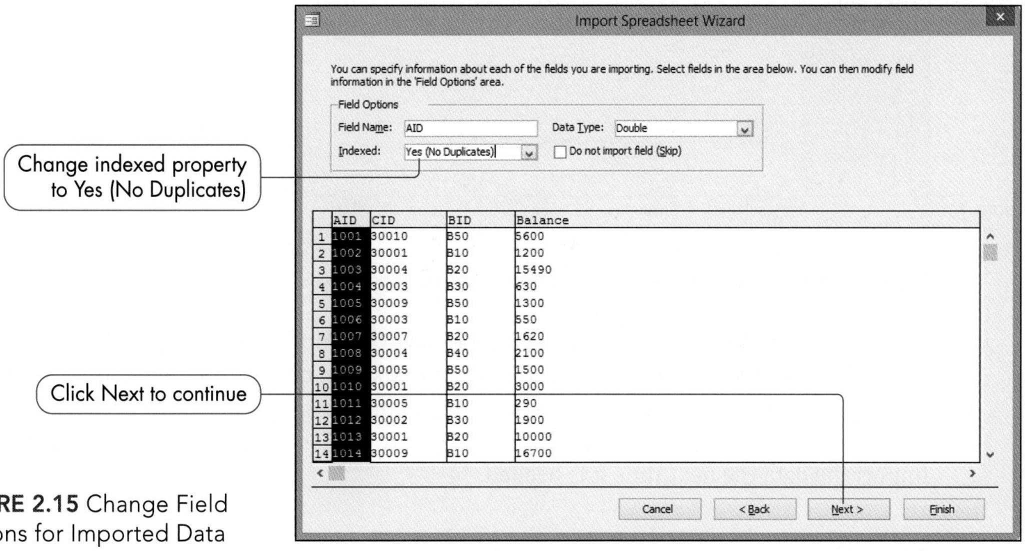

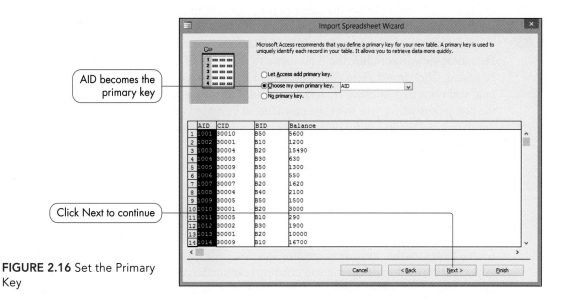

FIGURE 2.15 Change Field Options for Imported Data

The fourth window of the Import Spreadsheet Wizard dialog box enables you to choose a primary key before the import takes place (see Figure 2.16). If the option *Let Access add primary key* is selected, Access will generate an AutoNumber field and designate it as the primary key. Otherwise, you can designate a field to be the primary key or choose to have no primary key. In the import depicted in the Figure 2.16, the Excel data have a unique identifier (AID) that will become the table's primary key.

FIGURE 2.16 Set the Primary Key

Use the final window of the Import Spreadsheet Wizard to name the Access table. If the worksheet in the Excel workbook was named, Access uses the worksheet name as the table name (see Figure 2.17).

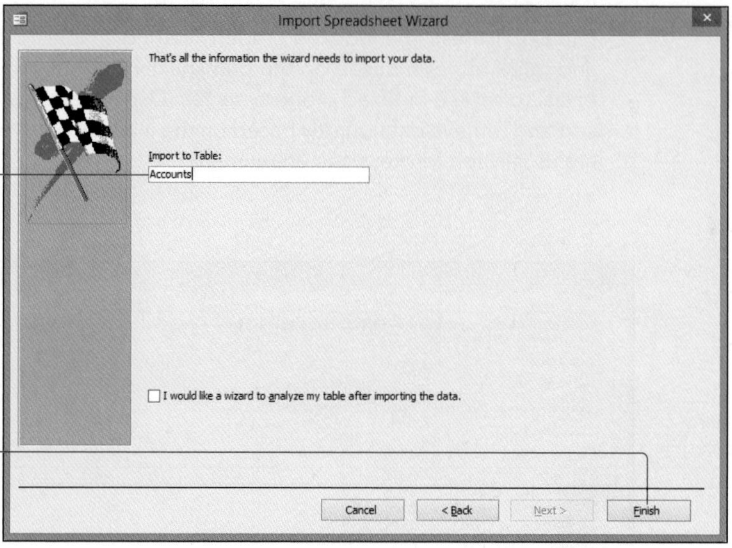

Type the table name

Click Finish to import the data

FIGURE 2.17 Enter a Table Name

Finally, the Wizard will ask if you wish to save the import steps. If the same worksheet is imported from Excel to Access on a recurring basis, you could save the parameters and use them again. To save the import steps, such as the indexing option and any new field names, click Save Import Steps in the Save Import Steps group. Saving the import steps will help you import the data the next time it is needed.

Modify an Imported Table's Design and Add Data

STEP 3 Importing data saves typing and prevents errors that may occur while entering data, but modifications will usually be required. After you have imported a table, open the table and examine the design to see if changes need to be made. You may need to modify the table by renaming fields so that they are more meaningful. To rename a field in Datasheet view, right-click the arrow next to the field name and click Rename Field. Type the new field name. To rename a field in Design view, select the field name and type the new name. In the bank example, you would change the name of the AID field to AccountID. Switch to Design view to modify the data type and field size.

STEP 4 You may need to add new fields or delete unnecessary fields. To add a new field in Datasheet view, right-click the field name to the right of where you want the new field to be added. Click Insert Field. To delete a field in Datasheet view, right-click the name of the field you want to delete and click Delete Field. To create a new field in Design view, click in the row below where you want the new field to be added and click Insert Rows in the Tools group on the Design tab. To delete a row in Design view, click in the row you want to delete and click Delete Rows in the Tools group on the Design tab. After making the modifications, you can add any data needed to the table.

Establishing Table Relationships

As previously discussed, the benefit of a relationship is to efficiently combine data from related tables for the purpose of creating queries, forms, and reports. Because this is such an important concept in designing and creating relational databases, this chapter reviews creating relationships and enforcing referential integrity. To ensure you are creating redundancy, you should store like data items together in the same table. In the example we are using, the customer data are stored in the Customers table. The Branch table stores data about the bank's branches, management, and locations. The Accounts table stores data about account ownership and balances.

STEP 5 » Once you have created the tables by storing like data items together, you will be able to recognize that some tables have common fields with others. Our Accounts table shares a common field with the Customers table—the CustomerID. It also shares a common field with the Branch table—BranchID. These common fields can be used to establish relationships between two tables.

Once you determine the common fields, you drag the field name from one table to the field name on the table you want to be joined.

Figure 2.18 shows the Bank database with relationships created by joining common fields.

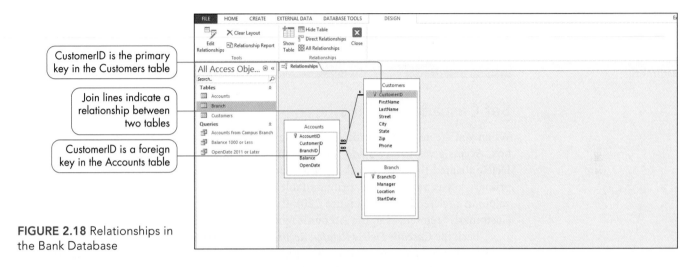

CustomerID is the primary key in the Customers table

Join lines indicate a relationship between two tables

CustomerID is a foreign key in the Accounts table

FIGURE 2.18 Relationships in the Bank Database

The primary key of a table plays a significant role when setting relationships. You cannot join two tables unless a primary key has been set in the primary table. In our Bank database, the CustomerID has been set as the primary key in the Customers table. Therefore, a relationship can be set between the Customers table and the Accounts table. Similarly, the Branch table can be joined to the Accounts table because BranchID has been set as the primary key in the Branch table.

The other side of the relationship join line is most often a foreign key of the related table. A foreign key is a field in one table that is also the primary key of another table. In the previous example, CustomerID in the Accounts table is a foreign key; BranchID in the Accounts table is a foreign key. Relationships between tables will almost always be set using primary and foreign keys.

Establish Referential Integrity

When you create a relationship in Access, the Edit Relationships dialog box displays. The first check box, Enforce Referential Integrity, should be checked in most cases. Remember, **referential integrity** enforces rules in a database that are used to preserve relationships between tables when records are changed.

STEP 6 » When referential integrity is enforced, you cannot enter a foreign key value in a related table unless the primary key value exists in the primary table. In the case of the Bank database, a customer's account information (which includes CustomerID) cannot be entered into the Accounts table unless the customer information is first entered into the Customers table. If you attempt to enter an account prior to entering the customer information, an error will appear, as shown in Figure 2.19. When referential integrity is enforced, you cannot delete a record in one table if it has related records.

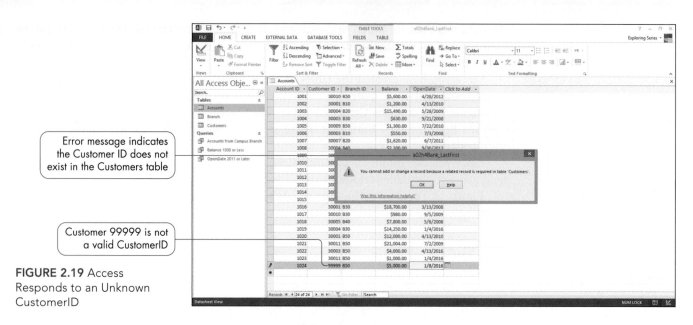

Error message indicates the Customer ID does not exist in the Customers table

Customer 99999 is not a valid CustomerID

FIGURE 2.19 Access Responds to an Unknown CustomerID

Set Cascade Options

When you create a relationship in Access and click the Enforce Referential Integrity check-box, Access gives you two additional options: Cascade Update Related Fields and Cascade Delete Related Records. Check the *Cascade Update Related Fields* option so that when the primary key is modified in a primary table, Access will automatically update all foreign key values in a related table (see Figure 2.20). If a CustomerID is updated for some reason, all the CustomerID references in the Accounts table will automatically be updated.

Check the *Cascade Delete Related Records* option so that when the primary key is deleted in a primary table, Access will automatically delete all records in related tables that reference the primary key (see Figure 2.20). If one branch of a bank closes and its record is deleted from the Branch table, any account that still remains with this branch would be deleted. Access will give a warning first and enable you to avoid the action. This may be a desired business rule, but it should be set with caution.

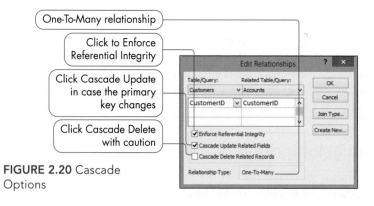

One-To-Many relationship

Click to Enforce Referential Integrity

Click Cascade Update in case the primary key changes

Click Cascade Delete with caution

FIGURE 2.20 Cascade Options

Establish a One-to-Many Relationship

Figure 2.20 also shows that the relationship that will be created will be a one-to-many rela-tionship. Access provides three different relationships for joining your data: one-to-one, one-to-many, and many-to-many. The most common type by far is the one-to-many relationship. A *one-to-many relationship* is established when the primary key value in the primary table can match many of the foreign key values in the related table.

For example, a bank customer will be entered into the Customers table once and only once. The primary key value, which is also the customer's CustomerID number, might be 1585. That same customer could set up a checking, savings, and money market account.

With each account, the CustomerID (1585) is required and therefore will occur three times in the Accounts table. The value appears once in the Customers table and three times in the Accounts table. Therefore, the relationship between Customers and Accounts would be described as one to many.

Table 2.3 lists and describes all three types of relationships you can create between Access tables.

TABLE 2.3 Relationship Types

Relationship Type	Description
One-to-Many	The primary key table must have only one occurrence of each value. For example, each customer must have a unique identification number in the Customers table, or each employee must have a unique EmployeeID in the Employee table. The foreign key field in the second table may have repeating values. For example, one customer may have many different account numbers, or one employee can perform many services.
One-to-One	Two different tables use the same primary key. Exactly one record exists in the second table for each record in the first table. Sometimes security reasons require a table be split into two related tables. For example, anyone in the company can look in the Employee table and find the employee's office number, department assignment, or telephone extension. However, only a few people need to have access to the employee's network login password, salary, Social Security number, performance review, or marital status. Tables containing this information would use the same unique identifier to identify each employee.
Many-to-Many	This is an artificially constructed relationship giving many matching records in each direction between tables. It requires construction of a third table called a junction table. For example, a database might have a table for employees and one for projects. Several employees might be assigned to one project, but one employee might also be assigned to many different projects. When Access connects to databases using Oracle or other software, you find this relationship type.

Figure 2.21 shows the Relationships window for the Bank database and all the relationships created using referential integrity. The join line between the CustomerID field in the Customers table and the CustomerID field in the Accounts table indicates that a one-to-many relationship has been set. You can rearrange the tables by dragging the tables by the title bar. You can switch the positions of the Branch and Accounts tables in the Relationships window without changing the relationship itself.

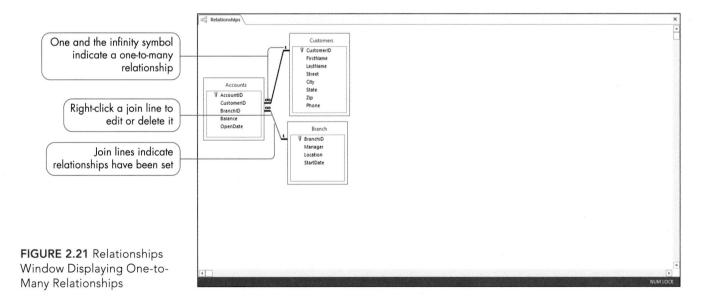

FIGURE 2.21 Relationships Window Displaying One-to-Many Relationships

When you right-click on a table's title bar in the Relationships window, the shortcut menu offers you a chance to open the table in Design view. This is a convenient feature because if you want to link one table to another table, the joined fields must have the same data type. This shortcut enables you to check the fields and revise them if necessary if a table contains a field with the wrong data type.

In the following Hands-On Exercise, you will create two additional tables in the Bank database by importing data from an Excel spreadsheet and from an Access database. You will establish and modify field properties. Then you will connect the newly imported data to the Branch table by establishing relationships between the tables.

Quick
Concepts ✓

1. Describe a scenario that may require you to import Excel data into Access. ***p. 157***

2. What is the purpose of setting a relationship between two tables? ***p. 160***

3. Why would you enforce referential integrity when setting a relationship? ***p. 161***

4. Give an example of two database tables that would contain a one-to-many relationship. Describe the relationship. ***pp. 162–163***

Hands-On Exercises

Watch the Video for this Hands-On Exercise!

MyITLab®
HOE2 Training

2 Multiple-Table Databases

You created a new Bank database, and you created a new Branch table. Now you are ready to import additional tables—one from an Excel spreadsheet and one from an Access database. Assume that the data are formatted correctly and are structured properly so that you can begin the import process.

Skills covered: Import Excel Data • Import Data from an Access Database • Modify an Imported Table's Design and Add Data • Add Data to an Imported Table • Establish Table Relationships • Test Referential Integrity

STEP 1 >> IMPORT EXCEL DATA

You and the auditor have discovered several of Commonwealth's files that contain customer data. These files need to be analyzed, so you decide to import the data into Access. In this exercise, you import an Excel spreadsheet into the Bank database. Refer to Figure 2.22 as you complete Step 1.

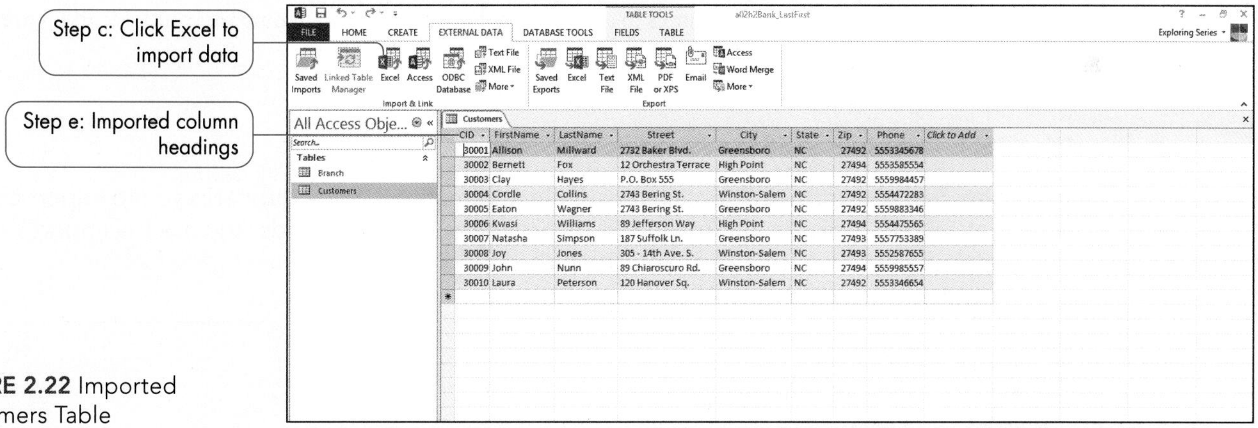

Step c: Click Excel to import data

Step e: Imported column headings

FIGURE 2.22 Imported Customers Table

a. Open *a02h1Bank_LastFirst* if you closed it at the end of Hands-On Exercise 1. Click the **FILE tab**, click **Save As**, and then click **Save As** in the *Save Database As* section. Type **a02h2Bank_LastFirst**, changing *h1 to h2*. Click **Save**.

b. If necessary, click **Enable Content** below the Ribbon to indicate you trust the contents of the database

> **TROUBLESHOOTING:** If you make any major mistakes in this exercise, you can close the file, open *a02h1Bank_LastFirst* again, and then start this exercise over.

c. Click the **EXTERNAL DATA tab** and click **Excel** in the Import & Link group to launch the Get External Data – Excel Spreadsheet feature. Select the **Import the source data into a new table in the current database option**, if necessary.

d. Click **Browse** and go to the student data folder. Select the *a02h2Customers* workbook. Click **Open** and click **OK** to open the Import Spreadsheet Wizard.

e. Ensure that the *First Row Contains Column Headings* check box is checked to tell Access that column headings exist in the Excel file.

The field names CID, FirstName, LastName, Street, City, State, ZIP, and Phone will import from Excel along with the data stored in the rows in the worksheet. The field names will be modified later in Access.

f. Click **Next**.

g. Ensure that *CID* is displayed in the Field Name box in Field Options. Click the **Indexed arrow** and select **Yes (No Duplicates)**. Click **Next**.

The CID (CustomerID) will become the primary key in this table. It needs to be a unique identifier, so we must change the properties to no duplicates.

h. Click the **Choose my own primary key option**. Make sure that the CID field is selected. Click **Next**.

The final screen of the Import Spreadsheet Wizard asks you to name your table. The name of the Excel worksheet was Customers, and Access defaults to the worksheet name. It is an acceptable name.

i. Click **Finish** to accept the Customers table name.

A dialog box opens asking if you wish to save the steps of this import to use again. If this were sales data that was collected in Excel and updated to the database on a weekly basis, saving the import steps would save time. You do not need to save this example.

j. Click the **Close (X) button**.

The new table displays in the Navigation Pane and resides in the Bank database.

k. Open the imported Customers table in Datasheet view and double-click the border between each of the field names to adjust the columns to Best fit. Compare your table to Figure 2.22.

l. Close the table.

STEP 2 》 IMPORT DATA FROM AN ACCESS DATABASE

The Customers spreadsheet that you imported contains customer information. The auditor asks you to import an Access database table that contains account information related to the mishandled funds. You use the Import Wizard to import the database table. Refer to Figure 2.23 as you complete Step 2.

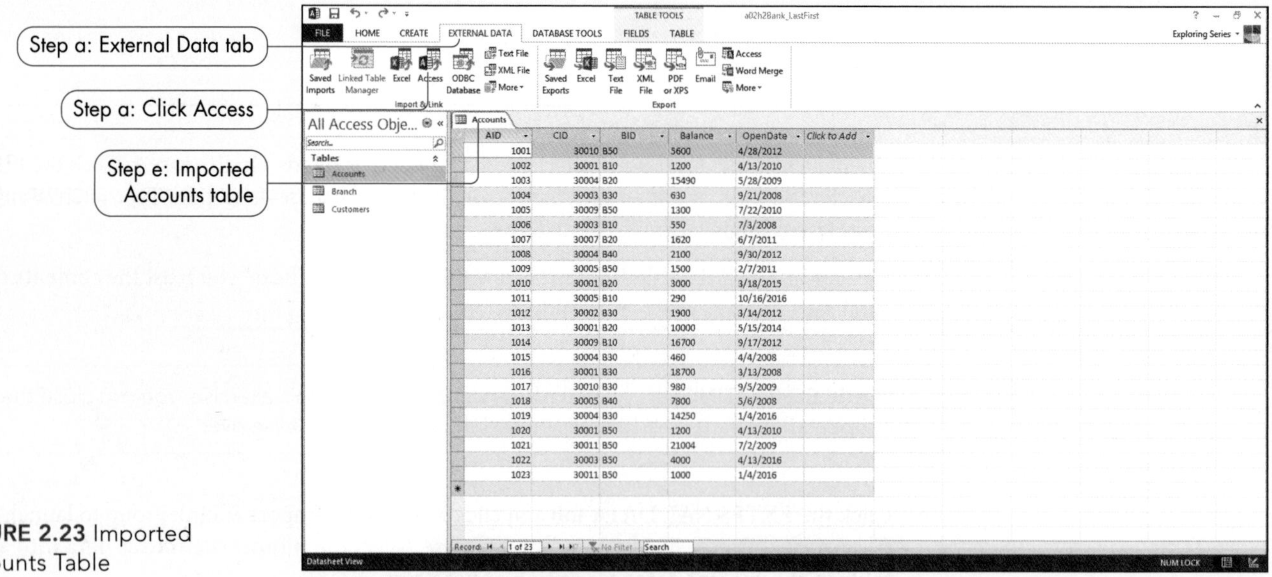

FIGURE 2.23 Imported Accounts Table

a. Click the **EXTERNAL DATA tab** and click **Access** in the Import & Link group to launch the Get External Data – Access Database feature. Select the **Import tables, queries, forms, reports, macros, and modules into the current database option**, if necessary.

b. Click **Browse** and go to the student data folder. Select the *a02h2Accounts* database. Click **Open** and click **OK** to open the Import Objects dialog box.

The Accounts table is active; you will import this table.

c. Ensure that the Accounts table is selected and click **OK**.

d. Click **Close** on the Save Import Steps dialog box.

The Navigation Pane contains three tables: Accounts, Branch, and Customers.

e. Open the imported Accounts table in Datasheet view and compare it to Figure 2.23.

STEP 3 》 MODIFY AN IMPORTED TABLE'S DESIGN AND ADD DATA

When importing tables from either Excel or Access, the fields may have different data types and property settings than required to create table relationships. You need to modify the tables so that each field has the correct data type and field size. Refer to Figure 2.24 as you complete Step 3.

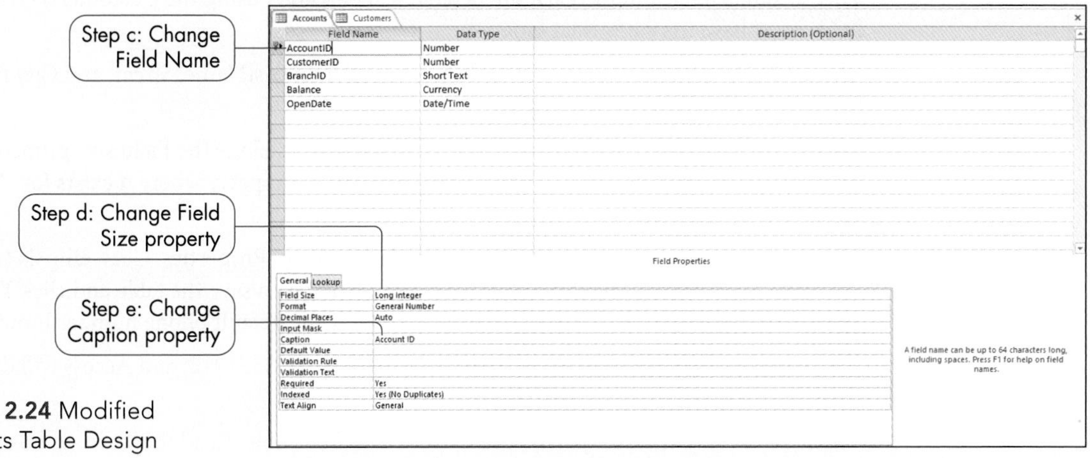

FIGURE 2.24 Modified Accounts Table Design

a. Right-click the **Accounts table** in the Navigation Pane.

b. Click **Design View** to open the table in Design view.

The Accounts table displays with the primary key AID selected.

c. Change the AID field name to **AccountID**.

d. Change the Field Size property to **Long Integer** in the Field Properties at the bottom of the Design window.

Long Integer ensures that there will be enough numbers as the number of customers grows over time and may exceed 32,768 (the upper limit for Integer values).

e. Type **Account ID** in the **Caption property box** for the AccountID field. The caption contains a space between *Account* and *ID*.

f. Change the CID field name to **CustomerID**.

g. Change the Field Size property to **Long Integer** in the Field Properties at the bottom of the Design window.

You can select the Field Size option using the arrow, or you can type the first letter of the option you want. For example, type l for Long Integer or s for Single. Make sure the current option is completely selected before you type the letter.

h. Type **Customer ID** in the **Caption property box** for the CustomerID field. The caption contains a space between *Customer* and *ID*.

i. Click the **BID field**. Change the BID field name to **BranchID**.

j. Type **5** in the **Field Size property box** in the Field Properties.

k. Type **Branch ID** in the **Caption property box** for the Branch ID field.

l. Change the Data Type of the Balance field to **Currency**.

The Currency data type is used for fields that contain monetary values.

m. Change the Data Type of the OpenDate field to **Date/Time** and add **Short Date** in the Format field property. Type **Open Date** in the **Caption property box**.

The OpenDate field stores the date that each account was opened.

n. Click **View** in the Views group to switch to Datasheet view. Read the messages and click **Yes** twice.

In this case, it is OK to click Yes because the shortened fields will not cut off any data. Leave the table open.

o. Right-click the **Customers table** in the Navigation Pane and select **Design View** from the shortcut menu.

p. Change the CID field name to **CustomerID**. Change the Field Size property of the CustomerID field to **Long Integer** and add a caption, **Customer ID**. Take note of the intentional space between *Customer* and *ID*.

The Accounts table and the Customers table will be joined using the CustomerID field. Both fields must have the same data type.

q. Change the Field Size property to **20** for the FirstName, LastName, Street, and City fields. Change the Field Size for State to **2**.

r. Change the data type for ZIP and Phone to **Short Text**. Change the Field size property to **15** for both fields. Remove the @ symbol from the Format property where it exists for all fields in the Customers table.

s. Click the **Phone field name** and click **Input Mask** in Field Properties. Click **ellipsis (...)** on the right side to launch the Input Mask Wizard. Click **Yes** to save the table and click **Yes** to the *Some data may be lost* warning. Click **Finish** to apply the default phone number Input Mask.

The phone number input mask enables users to enter 6105551212, and Access will display it as (610)555-1212.

t. Click **Save** to save the design changes to the Customers table. Read the warning box and click **Yes**.

STEP 4 ≫ ADD DATA TO AN IMPORTED TABLE

Now that you have created the Access tables, you add records. You may also need to update and delete records if you and the auditor decide the information is no longer needed. Refer to Figure 2.25 as you complete Step 4.

Step b: Enter yourself as a new customer

FIGURE 2.25 Customers Table Displaying Your Information

Cust	FirstName	LastName	Street	City	State	Zip	Phone	Click to Add
30001	Allison	Millward	2732 Baker Blvd.	Greensboro	NC	27492	(555) 334-5678	
30002	Bernett	Fox	12 Orchestra Terrace	High Point	NC	27494	(555) 358-5554	
30003	Clay	Hayes	P.O. Box 555	Greensboro	NC	27492	(555) 998-4457	
30004	Cordie	Collins	2743 Bering St.	Winston-Salem	NC	27492	(555) 447-2283	
30005	Eaton	Wagner	2743 Bering St.	Greensboro	NC	27492	(555) 988-3346	
30006	Kwasi	Williams	89 Jefferson Way	High Point	NC	27494	(555) 447-5565	
30007	Natasha	Simpson	187 Suffolk Ln.	Greensboro	NC	27493	(555) 775-3389	
30008	Joy	Jones	305 - 14th Ave. S.	Winston-Salem	NC	27493	(555) 258-7655	
30009	John	Nunn	89 Chiaroscuro Rd.	Greensboro	NC	27494	(555) 998-5557	
30010	Laura	Peterson	120 Hanover Sq.	Winston-Salem	NC	27492	(555) 334-6654	
30011	YourName	YourName	800 University Ave.	High Point	NC	27494	(555) 447-1235	

a. Click **View** in the Views group to display the Customers table in Datasheet view.

The asterisk at the bottom of the table data in the row selector area is the indicator of a place to enter a new record.

b. Click the **Customer ID field** in the record after *30010*. Type **30011**. Fill in the rest of the data using your information as the customer. You may use a fictitious address and phone number.

Note the phone number format. The input mask you set formats the phone number.

c. Close the Customers table. The Accounts table tab is open.

> **TROUBLESHOOTING:** If the Accounts table is not open, double-click Accounts in the Navigation Pane.

d. Locate the new record indicator—the * in the row selector—and click in the **Account ID column**. Type **1024**. Type **30011** as the Customer ID and **B50** as the Branch ID. Type **14005** for the Balance field value. Type **8/7/2015** for the OpenDate.

e. Add the following records to the Accounts table:

Account ID	Customer ID	Branch ID	Balance	Open Date
1025	30006	B40	$11,010	3/13/2013
1026	30007	B20	$7,400	5/1/2014

f. Close the Accounts table; keep the database open.

STEP 5 ❯❯ ESTABLISH TABLE RELATIONSHIPS

The tables for the bank investigation have been designed. Now you will need to establish connections between the tables. Look at the primary and foreign keys as a guide. Refer to Figure 2.26 as you complete Step 5.

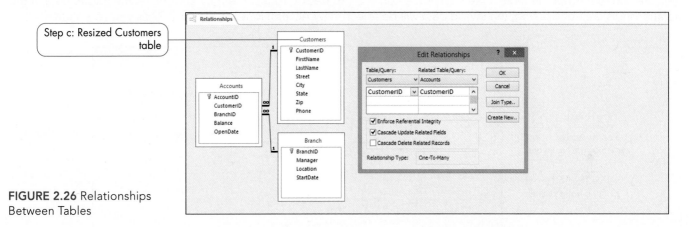

FIGURE 2.26 Relationships Between Tables

a. Click the **DATABASE TOOLS tab** and click **Relationships** in the Relationships group.

The Relationships window opens and the Show Table dialog box appears.

> **TROUBLESHOOTING:** If the Show Table dialog box does not open, click Show Table in the Relationships group on the Relationships Tools Design tab.

b. Double-click each of the three tables displayed in the Show Table dialog box to add them to the Relationships window. (Alternatively, click a table and click **Add**.) Click **Close** in the Show Table dialog box.

> **TROUBLESHOOTING:** If you have a duplicate table, click the title bar of the duplicated table and press Delete.

c. Resize the Customers table box so all of the fields are visible. Arrange the tables as shown in Figure 2.26.

d. Drag the **BranchID field** in the Branch table onto the BranchID field in the Accounts table. The Edit Relationships dialog box opens. Click the **Enforce Referential Integrity** and **Cascade Update Related Fields check boxes**. Click **Create**.

A black line displays, joining the two tables. It has a 1 at the end near the Branch table and an infinity symbol on the end next to the Accounts table. You have established a one-to-many relationship between the Branch and Accounts tables.

e. Drag the **CustomerID field** in the Customers table onto the CustomerID field in the Accounts table. The Edit Relationships dialog box opens. Click the **Enforce Referential Integrity** and **Cascade Update Related Fields check boxes**. Click **Create**.

You have established a one-to-many relationship between the Customers and Accounts tables. A customer will have only a single CustomerID number. The same customer may have many different accounts: Savings, Checking, CDs, and so forth.

> **TROUBLESHOOTING:** If you get an error message when you click Create, verify that the data types of the joined fields are the same. To check the data types from the Relationships window, right-click the title bar of a table and select Table Design from the shortcut menu. Modify the data type and field size of the join fields if necessary.

    f. Click **Save** on the Quick Access Toolbar to save the changes to the relationships. Close the Relationships window.

STEP 6 ≫ TEST REFERENTIAL INTEGRITY

The design of the Bank database must be 100% correct; otherwise, data entry may be compromised. Even though you are confident that the table relationships are correct, you decide to test them by entering some invalid data. If the relationships are not working, the invalid data will be rejected by Access. Refer to Figure 2.27 as you complete Step 6.

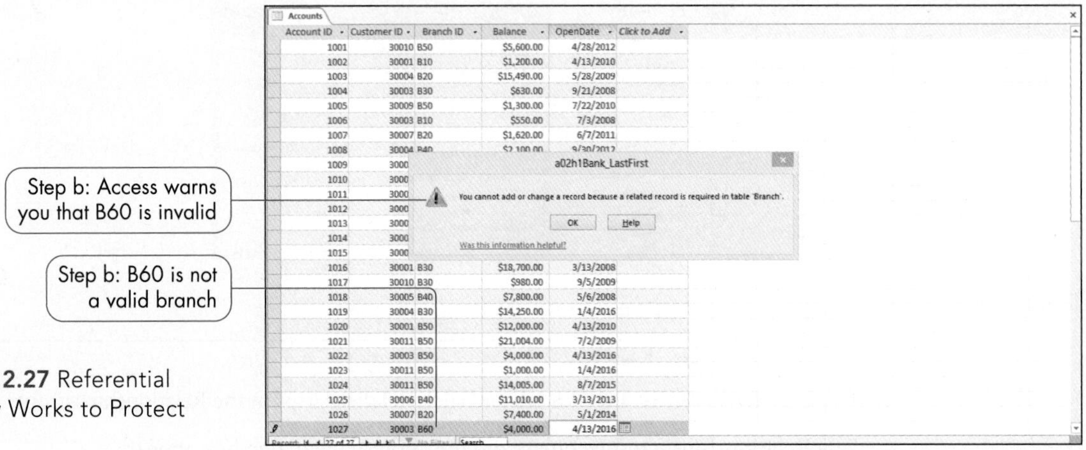

Step b: Access warns you that B60 is invalid

Step b: B60 is not a valid branch

FIGURE 2.27 Referential Integrity Works to Protect Data

    a. Double-click the **Accounts table** to open it in Datasheet view.

    b. Add a new record, pressing **Tab** after each field: Account ID: **1027**, Customer ID: **30003**, Branch: **B60**, Balance: **4000**, OpenDate: **4/13/2016**.

    You attempted to enter a nonexistent BranchID and were not allowed to make that error. A warning message is telling you that a related record in the Branch table is required because the Accounts table and the Branch table are connected by a relationship with Enforce Referential Integrity checked.

    c. Click **OK**. Double-click the **Branch table** in the Navigation Pane and examine the data in the BranchID field. Notice the Branch table has no B60 record. Close the Branch table.

    d. Replace *B60* with **B50** in the new Accounts record and press **Tab** three times. As soon as the focus moves to the next record, the pencil symbol disappears and your data are saved.

    You successfully identified a BranchID that Access recognizes. Because referential integrity between the Accounts and Branch tables has been enforced, Access looks at each data entry item in a foreign key and matches it to a corresponding value in the table where it is the primary key. In step b, you attempted to enter a nonexistent BranchID and were not allowed to make that error. In step d, you entered a valid BranchID. Access examined the index for the BranchID in the Branch table and found a corresponding value for B50.

    e. Close the Accounts table. Reopen the Accounts table; you will find that the record you just entered for 1027 has been saved. Close the table.

    You have established a one-to-many relationship between the Customers and Accounts tables. A customer will have only a single CustomerID number. The same customer may have many different accounts: Savings, Checking, CDs, and so forth.

    f. Close all open tables, if necessary.

    g. Keep the database open if you plan to continue with Hands-On Exercise 3. If not, close the database and exit Access.

Single-Table Queries

If you wanted to see which customers currently have an account with a balance over $5,000, you could find the answer by creating an Access query. A *query* enables you to ask questions about the data stored in a database and then provides the answers to the questions by providing subsets or summaries of data. Because data are stored in tables in a database, you always begin a query by asking, "Which table holds the data I want?" For the question about account balances over $5,000, you would reference the Accounts table. If you want to invite customers in a certain ZIP code to the Grand Opening of a new branch, you could create a query based on the Customers table.

You use the *Query Design view* to create queries. The Query Design view is divided into two parts: The top portion displays the tables, and the bottom portion (known as the query design grid) displays the fields and the criteria. You select only the fields you want arranged in the order that you want the resulting data displayed. The design grid also enables you to sort the records based on one or more fields. You can also create calculated fields to display data based on expressions that use the fields in the underlying table. For example, you could calculate the monthly interest earned on each bank account.

In this section, you will use the Query Design view and the Query Wizard to create queries that display only data that you select. Multitable queries will be covered in the next section.

Creating a Single-Table Query

You can create a single-table query in two ways—by using the Simple Query Wizard or the Query Design tool in the Queries group on the Create tab. The Query Design tool is the most flexible way to create a query. You can add criteria to a query while in the Query Design view. After you design a query, you can display the results of the query by switching to Datasheet view. A query's datasheet looks and acts like a table's datasheet, except that it is usually a subset of the records found in the entire table. The subset shows only the records that match the criteria that were added in the query design. The subset may contain different sorting of the records than the sorting in the underlying table. Datasheet view allows you to enter a new record, modify an existing record, or delete a record. Any changes made in Datasheet view are reflected in the underlying table that the query is based upon.

STEP 3 Be aware that query results display the actual records that are stored in the underlying table(s). Being able to correct an error immediately while it is displayed in query results is an advantage. You save time by not having to close the query, open the table, find the error, fix it, and then run the query again. However, you should use caution when editing records in query results since you will be changing the table data.

Create a Single-Table Select Query

The Query Design tool is used to create *select queries*, a type of query that displays only the records that match criteria entered in Query Design view. To create a select query using the Query Design tool, do the following:

STEP 2
1. Click the CREATE tab.
2. Click Query Design in the Queries group.
3. Select the table you need in your query from the Show Table dialog box.
4. Click Add to add the table to the top section of the query design and close the Show Table dialog box.
5. Drag the fields needed from the table to the query design grid (or alternatively, double-click the field names); then add criteria and sorting options.
6. Click Run in the Results group to show the results in Datasheet view.

Use Query Design View

The Query Design view consists of two parts. The top portion contains tables with their respective field names. If a query contains more than one table, the join lines between tables will be displayed as they were created in the Relationships window.

The bottom portion (known as the query design grid) contains columns and rows. Each field in the query has its own column and contains multiple rows. The rows permit you to control the query results.

- The **Field row** displays the field name.
- The **Table row** displays the data source.
- The **Sort row** enables you to sort in ascending or descending order.
- The **Show row** controls whether the field will be displayed in the query results.
- The **Criteria row** is used to set the rules that determine which records will be selected, such as customers with account balances greater than $5,000.

Figure 2.28 displays the query design grid with the Show Table dialog box open. The Accounts table has been added from the Show Table dialog box. Figure 2.29 shows the Design view of a sample query with four fields, with a criterion set for one field and sorting set on another. The results of the query are shown in Datasheet view, as shown in Figure 2.30.

TIP **Examine the Records**

An experienced Access user always examines the records returned in the query results. Verify that the records in the query results match the criteria that you specified in Design view. As you add additional criteria, the number of records returned will usually decrease.

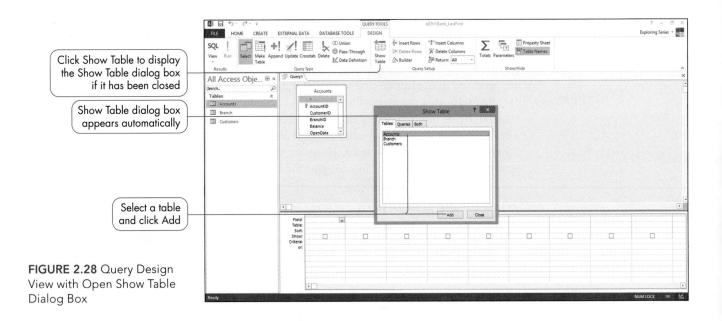

Click Show Table to display the Show Table dialog box if it has been closed

Show Table dialog box appears automatically

Select a table and click Add

FIGURE 2.28 Query Design View with Open Show Table Dialog Box

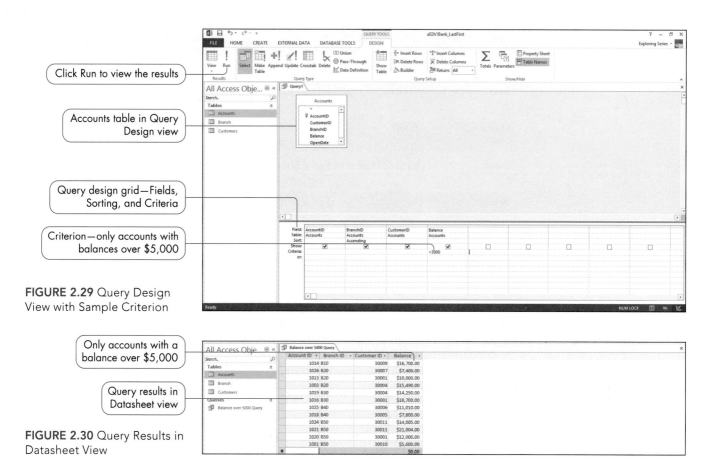

Click Run to view the results

Accounts table in Query Design view

Query design grid—Fields, Sorting, and Criteria

Criterion—only accounts with balances over $5,000

FIGURE 2.29 Query Design View with Sample Criterion

Only accounts with a balance over $5,000

Query results in Datasheet view

FIGURE 2.30 Query Results in Datasheet View

When you developed the tables, you toggled between the Design view and Datasheet view. Similarly, you will toggle between Design view and Datasheet view when you create queries. Use Design view to specify the criteria; you can use the results that display in Datasheet view to answer a question or to make a decision about the organization. Use Datasheet view to see the results of your query. Each time you need to fine-tune the query, switch back to Design view, make a change, and then test the results in Datasheet view. After you are satisfied with the query results, you may want to save the query so it can become a permanent part of the database and can be used later.

Specifying Query Criteria for Different Data Types

When specifying the criteria for a query, you may need to include a **delimiter**—a special character that surrounds a criterion's value. The delimiter needed is determined by the field data type, and Access will automatically enter the delimiter for you for some data types. Text fields require quotation marks before and after the text. Access automatically adds the quotation marks around text, but to ensure that the correct delimiter is used, you may want to include the delimiters yourself.

Use plain digits (no delimiter) for the criteria of a numeric field, currency, or AutoNumber. You can enter numeric criteria with or without a decimal point and with or without a minus sign. Commas and dollar signs are not allowed.

When the criterion is in a date field, you enclose the criterion in pound signs, such as #10/14/2016#. Access accepts a date with or without the pound signs, but if you enter 1/1/2016 without the pound signs, Access will automatically add the pound signs when you move to another column in the design grid. The date value can be entered using any allowed format, such as February 2, 2016, 2/2/2016, or 2-Feb-16. You enter criteria for a Yes/No field as Yes or No. See Table 2.4 for query criteria and examples.

TABLE 2.4	Query Criteria	
Data Type	Criteria	Example
Text	"Harry"	For a FirstName field, displays only text that matches Harry exactly.
Numeric	5000	For a Quantity field, displays only numbers that match 5000 exactly.
Date	#2/2/2015#	For a ShippedDate field, shows orders shipped on February 2, 2015.
Yes/No	Yes	For a Discontinued field, returns records where the check box is selected.

Use Wildcards

Suppose you want to search for the last name of a customer, but you are not sure how to spell the name; however, you know that the name starts with the letters Sm. You can use a wildcard to search for the name. *Wildcards* are special characters that can represent one or more characters in a text value. A question mark is a wildcard that stands for a single character in the same position as the question mark, whereas an asterisk is a wildcard that stands for any number of characters in the same position as the asterisk. Use brackets to match any single character within the brackets, or use an exclamation mark inside brackets to match any character not in the brackets. Use the pound sign to match any single numeric character.

You can enter wildcard characters in the Criteria row of a query. Therefore, if you wanted to search for just names that start with the letters Sm, you can specify the criterion in the LastName field as Sm*. All last names that begin with Sm would display. For example, H?ll will return Hall, Hill, and Hull, whereas S*nd will return Sand, Stand, and StoryLand. Table 2.5 shows more query examples that use wildcards.

TABLE 2.5	Query Criteria Using Wildcards			
Character	Description		Example	Result
*	Matches for any number of characters in the same position as the asterisk		Sm*	Small, Smiley, Smith, Smithson
?	Matches for a single character in the same position as the question mark		H?ll	Hall, Hill, Hull
[ ]	Matches any single character within the brackets		F[ae]ll	Fall and Fell, but not Fill or Full
[!]	Matches any character not in the brackets		F[!ae]ll	Fill and Full, but not Fall or Fell

Use Comparison Operators in Queries

A comparison operator, such as equal (=), not equal (<>), greater than (>), less than (<), greater than or equal to (>=), and less than or equal to (<=), can be used in the criteria of a query. Comparison operators enable you to limit the query results to only those records that meet the criteria. For example, if you only want to see accounts that have a balance greater than $5,000, you would type >5000 in the Criteria row. Table 2.6 shows more comparison operator examples as well as other sample expressions.

TABLE 2.6 Comparison Operators in Queries

Expression	Example
=10	Equals 10
<>10	Not equal to 10
>10	Greater than 10
>=10	Greater than or equal to 10
<10	Less than 10
<=10	Less than or equal to 10

Work with Null

Sometimes finding what is missing is an important part of making a decision. For example, if you need to know which orders have been completed but not shipped, you would create a query to find the orders with a missing ShipDate. Are there missing phone numbers or addresses for some of your customers? Create a query to find customers with a missing PhoneNumber. The term that Access uses for a blank field is *null*. Table 2.7 gives two illustrations of when to use the null criterion in a query.

TABLE 2.7 Establishing Null Criteria Expressions

Expression	Description	Example
Is Null	Use to find blank fields	For an Employee field in the Customers table when the customer has not been assigned a sales representative.
Is Not Null	Used to find fields with data	For a ShipDate field; a value inserted indicated the order was shipped to the customer.

Establish AND, OR, and NOT Criteria

Remember the earlier question, "Which customers currently have an account with a balance over $5,000?" This question was answered by creating a query with a single criterion, as shown in Figure 2.29. At times, questions are more specific and require queries with multiple criteria. For example, you may need to know "Which customers from the Eastern branch currently have an account with a balance over $5,000?" To answer this question, you need to specify criteria in multiple fields using the *AND logical operator*. When the criteria are in the same row of the query design grid, Access interprets the instructions using the AND operator. This means that the query results will display only records that match *all* criteria.

When you have multiple sets of criteria and you need to satisfy one set only, use the *OR logical operator*. The query results will display records that match any of the specified criteria. To use the OR operator, type your expression into the Criteria row, separating the criteria with the OR operator. Table 2.8 shows an example of an OR operator created using this method. You can also type the first expression into the Criteria row and then type the subsequent expression by using the Or row in the design grid. Figure 2.31b displays an example of an OR operator using this method.

The *NOT logical operator* returns all records except the specified criteria. For example, "Not Eastern" would return all accounts except those opened at the Eastern branch.

TABLE 2.8 AND, OR, and NOT Queries

Logical Operator	Example	Result
AND	"Eastern" AND "Campus"	For a Branch field, returns all records for the Eastern and Campus branches.
AND	>5000 AND <10000	For a Balance field, returns all accounts with a balance greater than $5,000 and less than $10,000.
OR	5000 OR 10000	For a Balance field, returns all accounts with a balance of exactly $5,000 or $10,000.
NOT	Not "Campus"	For a Branch field, returns all records except those in the Campus branch.

The first example in Figure 2.31 shows a query with an AND logical operator (criteria on the same row are implicitly joined by AND). It will return all of the B20 branch accounts with balances over $5,000. (Both conditions must be met for the record to be included.) The second example in Figure 2.31 shows a query with an OR logical operator. It will return all of the B20 branch accounts regardless of balance plus all accounts at any branch with a balance over $5,000. (One condition must be met for a record to be included.) The third example in Figure 2.31 shows a query that uses the NOT logical operator. It will return all of the accounts—excluding the B20 branch—with a balance over $5,000. The last example in Figure 2.31 shows a query that combines AND and OR logical operators. The top row will return B20 branch accounts with a balance over $5,000, and the second row will return B30 branch accounts with a balance over $15,000.

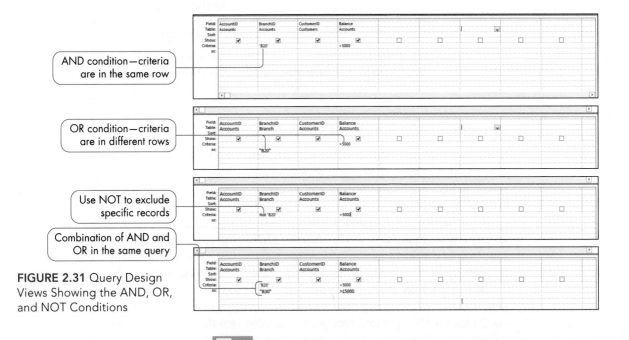

AND condition—criteria are in the same row

OR condition—criteria are in different rows

Use NOT to exclude specific records

Combination of AND and OR in the same query

FIGURE 2.31 Query Design Views Showing the AND, OR, and NOT Conditions

TIP Finding Values in a Date Range

To find the values contained within a data range, use the > (greater than) and < (less than) operators. For example, to find the values of a date after January 1, 2015, and before December 31, 2015, use the criterion >1/1/2015 and <12/31/2015. You can also use the BETWEEN operator. For example BETWEEN 1/1/2015 and 12/31/2015.

Understanding Query Sort Order

The *query sort order* determines the order of records in a query's Datasheet view. You can change the order of records by specifying the sort order in the Design view. When you want to sort using more than one field, the sort order is determined from left to right. The order of columns should be considered when first creating the query. For example, a query sorted by LastName and then by FirstName must have those two fields in the correct order in the design grid. You can change the order of the query fields in the design grid to change the sort order of the query results.

STEP 2 » To change the order of fields, select the column you want to move by clicking the column selector. Release the mouse, then click again and drag the selected field to its new location. To insert additional columns in the design grid, select a column and click Insert Columns in the Query Setup group. The inserted column will insert to the left of the selected column. To delete a column, click the column selector to select the column and click the Delete Columns button on the Design tab or press Delete on the keyboard.

Running, Copying, and Modifying a Query

Several ways exist to run a query. One method is to click Run in the Results group when you are in Design view. Another method is to locate the query in the Navigation Pane and double-click it. A similar method is to select the query and press Enter.

After you create a query, you may want to create a duplicate copy to use as the basis for creating a similar query. Duplicating a query saves time when you need the same tables and fields but with slightly different criteria.

Run a Query

After you create a query and save it, you can run it directly from the Design view. You run a query by clicking the Run command (the red exclamation point) in the Results group on the Query Tools Design tab. You can also run a query from the Navigation Pane. Locate the query you want to run and double-click the query. The results will display as a tab in the main window.

Copy a Query

Sometimes you have a one-of-a-kind question about your data. You would create a query to answer this question and then delete the query. However, sometimes you need a series of queries in which each query is similar to the first. For example, you need a list of accounts in each branch. In a case like this, you create a query for one branch and then save a copy of the query and give it a new name. Finally, you would change the criteria to match the second branch. To accomplish this, do the following:

1. Open the query you want to copy.
2. Click the FILE tab and click Save As.
3. Click Save Object As in the *File Types* section.
4. Ensure Save Object As is selected in the *Database File Types* section and click Save As.
5. Type the name you want to use for the new query in the Save As dialog box and click OK (see Figure 2.32).
6. Switch to Design view and modify the query criteria.

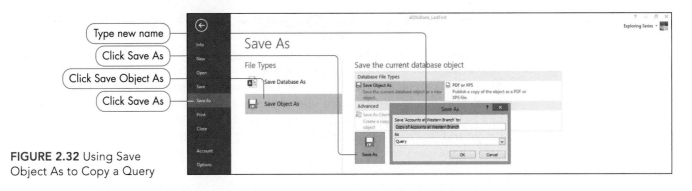

FIGURE 2.32 Using Save Object As to Copy a Query

You can also right-click the original query in the Navigation Pane and click Copy. Click in the Navigation Pane again and click Paste. Type a name for the new query in the Paste As dialog box.

Using the Query Wizard

STEP 1▶ You may also create a query using the Query Wizard. Like all of the Microsoft wizards, the *Simple Query Wizard* guides you through the query design process. The wizard is helpful for creating basic queries that do not require criteria. After the query is created using the Wizard, you can switch to Design view and add criteria manually. Even if you initiate the query with a wizard, you will need to learn how to modify it in Design view. Often, copying an existing query and making slight modifications to its design is much faster than starting at the beginning with the wizard. You also will need to know how to add additional tables and fields to an existing query when conditions change. To launch the Query Wizard, click the Create tab and click Query Wizard in the Queries group (see Figure 2.33).

FIGURE 2.33 Launching the Query Wizard

Select the Simple Query Wizard in the Query Wizard dialog box, as shown in Figure 2.34.

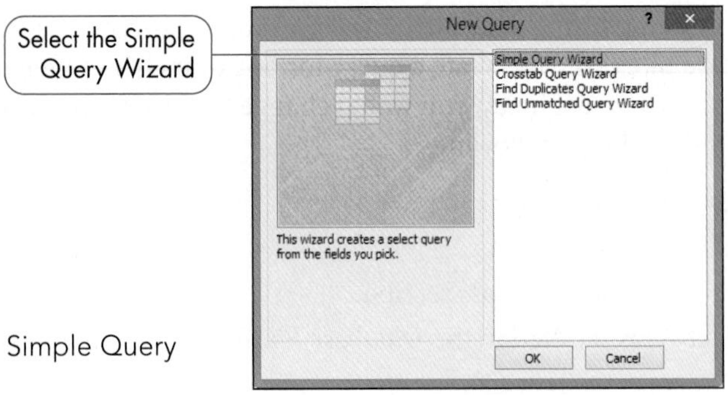

FIGURE 2.34 Simple Query Wizard

In the first step of the Simple Query Wizard dialog box, you specify the tables or queries and fields needed in your query. When you select a table from the Tables/Queries arrow (queries can also be based on other queries), a list of the table's fields displays in the Available Fields list box. See Figures 2.35 and 2.36.

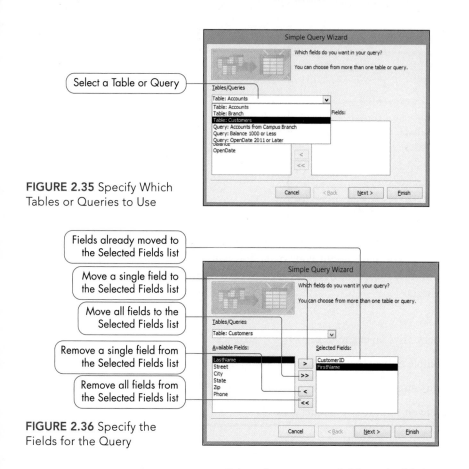

Select a Table or Query

FIGURE 2.35 Specify Which Tables or Queries to Use

Fields already moved to the Selected Fields list

Move a single field to the Selected Fields list

Move all fields to the Selected Fields list

Remove a single field from the Selected Fields list

Remove all fields from the Selected Fields list

FIGURE 2.36 Specify the Fields for the Query

Select the necessary fields and add them to the Selected Fields list box using the directional arrows shown in Figure 2.36.

In the next screen (shown in Figure 2.37), you choose between a detail and a summary query. The detail query shows every field of every record in the result. The summary query enables you to group data and view only summary records. For example, if you were interested in the total funds deposited at each of the bank branches, you would set the query to Summary, click Summary Options, and then click Sum on the Balance field. Access would then sum the balances of all accounts for each branch.

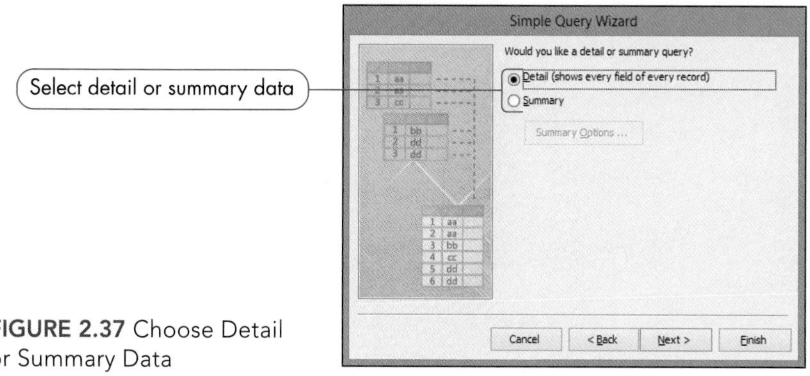

Select detail or summary data

FIGURE 2.37 Choose Detail or Summary Data

The final dialog box of the Simple Query Wizard asks for the name of the query. Assign a descriptive name to your queries so that you know what each does by looking at the query name. See Figure 2.38.

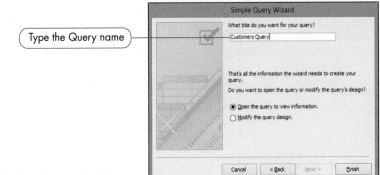

Type the Query name

FIGURE 2.38 Name the Query

The next Hands-On Exercise enables you to create and run queries in order to find answers to questions you have about your data. You will use the Query Wizard to create a basic query and modify the query in Query Design view by adding an additional field and by adding query criteria.

Quick Concepts ✓

1. Define a query. Give an example. *p. 171*

2. Give an example of how to use the criteria row to find certain records in a table. *p. 172*

3. When would you need to use the "is null" and "is not null" criteria? *p. 175*

4. When would you want to copy a query? *p. 177*

Hands-On Exercises

Watch the Video for this Hands-On Exercise!

MyITLab®
HOE3 Training

3 Single-Table Queries

The tables and table relationships have been created, and some data have been entered. Now, you need to begin the process of analyzing the bank data for the auditor. You will do so using queries. You decide to begin with the Accounts table.

Skills covered: Create a Query Using a Wizard • Specify Query Criteria and Query Sort Order • Change Query Data

STEP 1 ≫ CREATE A QUERY USING A WIZARD

You decide to start with the Query Wizard, knowing you can always alter the design of the query later in Query Design view. You will show the results to the auditor using Datasheet view. Refer to Figure 2.39 as you complete Step 1.

Step b: Click Query Wizard

Step 3: Selected fields

Account ID	Customer ID	Branch ID	Balance
1001	30010	B50	$5,600.00
1002	30001	B10	$1,200.00
1003	30004	B20	$15,490.00
1004	30003	B30	$630.00
1005	30009	B50	$1,300.00
1006	30003	B10	$550.00
1007	30007	B20	$1,620.00
1008	30004	B40	$2,100.00
1009	30005	B50	$1,500.00
1010	30001	B20	$3,000.00
1011	30005	B10	$290.00
1012	30002	B30	$1,900.00
1013	30001	B20	$10,000.00
1014	30009	B10	$16,700.00
1015	30004	B30	$460.00
1016	30001	B30	$18,700.00
1017	30010	B30	$980.00
1018	30005	B40	$7,800.00
1019	30004	B30	$14,250.00
1020	30001	B50	$12,000.00
1021	30011	B50	$21,004.00
1022	30003	B50	$4,000.00
1023	30011	B50	$1,000.00
1024	30011	B50	$14,005.00
1025	30006	B40	$11,010.00
1026	30007	B20	$7,400.00
1027	30003	B50	$4,000.00

FIGURE 2.39 Query Results Before Criteria Are Applied

a. Open *a02h2Bank_LastFirst* if you closed it at the end of Hands-On Exercise 2. Save the database as **a02h3Bank_LastFirst**, changing *h2* to *h3*.

b. Click the **CREATE tab** and click **Query Wizard** in the Queries group to launch the New Query wizard.

   The New Query Wizard dialog box opens. Simple Query Wizard is selected by default.

c. Click **OK**.

d. Verify that *Table: Accounts* is selected in the Tables/Query box.

e. Select **AccountID** from the **Available Fields list** and click >. Repeat the process with CustomerID, BranchID, and Balance.

   The four fields should now display in the Selected Fields list box.

f. Click **Next**.

g. Confirm *Detail* is selected and click **Next**.

h. Name the query **Accounts from Campus Branch**. Click **Finish**.

   This query name describes the data in the query results. Your query should have four fields: AccountID, CustomerID, BranchID, and Balance. The Navigation bar indicates 27 records meet the query criteria.

STEP 2 ≫ SPECIFY QUERY CRITERIA AND QUERY SORT ORDER

The auditor indicated that the problem seems to be confined to the Campus branch. You use this knowledge to revise the query to display only Campus accounts. Refer to Figure 2.40 as you complete Step 2.

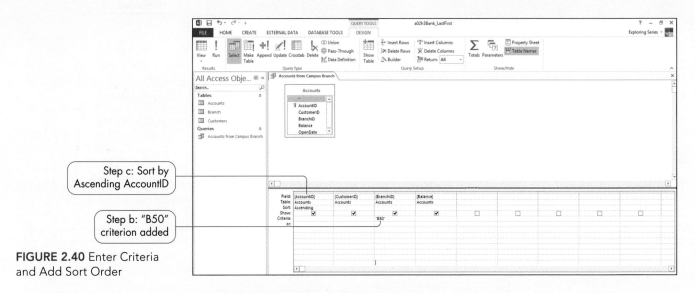

Step c: Sort by Ascending AccountID

Step b: "B50" criterion added

FIGURE 2.40 Enter Criteria and Add Sort Order

a. Click the **HOME tab** and click **View** in the Views group to view the Accounts from Campus Branch query in Design view.

   You have created the Campus Branch Customers query to view only those accounts at the Campus branch. However, other branches' accounts also display. You need to limit the query results to only the records of interest.

b. Click in the **Criteria row** (fifth row) in the BranchID column and type **B50**.

   B50 is the BranchID for the Campus branch. Access queries are not case sensitive; therefore, b50 and B50 will produce the same results. Access adds quotation marks around text criteria.

c. Click in the **Sort row** (third row) in the AccountID column and select **Ascending**.

d. Click **Run** in the Results group.

   You should see nine records, all from Branch B50, in the query results.

STEP 3 ≫ CHANGE QUERY DATA

When the query results are on the screen, the auditor notices that some of the data are incorrect, and one of the accounts is missing. From your experience with Access, you explain to the auditor that the data can be changed directly in a query rather than switching back to the table. Refer to Figure 2.41 as you complete Step 3.

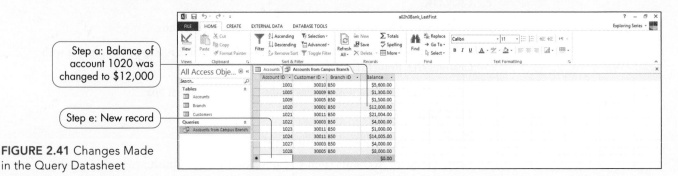

Step a: Balance of account 1020 was changed to $12,000

Step e: New record

FIGURE 2.41 Changes Made in the Query Datasheet

a. Click on the **Balance field** in the record for account 1020. Change *$1,200* to **$12,000**. Press **Enter**. Save and close the query.

You are modifying the record directly in the query results.

b. Double-click the **Accounts table** in the Navigation Pane to open it.

Only one account shows a $12,000 balance. The Account ID is 1020 and the Customer ID is 30001. The change you made in the Accounts table from the Campus Branch query datasheet automatically changed the data stored in the underlying table.

c. Open the Customers table. Find the name of the customer whose CustomerID is 30001. Note that the account belongs to Allison Millward. Close the Customers table.

d. Add a new record to the Accounts table with the following data: **1028** (Account ID), **30005** (Customer ID), **B50** (Branch ID), **8/4/2016** (Open Date), and $8,000 (Balance). Press **Tab**.

> **TROUBLESHOOTING:** If the Accounts table is not open, double-click Accounts in the Navigation Pane.

The new record is added to the Accounts table.

e. Double-click the **Accounts from Campus Branch query** in the Navigation Pane.

Customer 30005 now shows two accounts: one with a balance of $1,500 and one with a balance of $8,000.

f. Close the Accounts from Campus Branch query and close the Accounts table.

g. Keep the database open if you plan to continue with Hands-On Exercise 4. If not, close the database and exit Access.

Multitable Queries

Multitable queries contain two or more tables. They enable you to take advantage of the relationships that have been set in your database. When you need to extract information from a database with a query, most times you will need to pull the data from multiple tables to provide the answers you need. One table may contain the core information that you need, while another table may contain the related data that makes the query relevant to the users.

For example, the sample bank database contains three tables: Customers, Accounts, and Branch. You connected the tables through relationships in order to store data efficiently and enforce consistent data entry. The Accounts table lists the balances of each account at the bank—the key financial information. However, the Accounts table does not list the contact information of the owner of the account. Therefore, the Customers table is needed to provide the additional information.

Creating a Multitable Query

STEP 2 》 Creating a multitable query is similar to creating a single-table query; however, choosing the right tables and managing the table relationships will require some additional skills. First, you should only include related tables in a multitable query. ***Related tables*** are tables that are joined in a relationship using a common field. As a rule, related tables should already be established when you create a multitable query. Using Figure 2.42 as a guide, creating a query with the Accounts and Branch tables would be acceptable, as would using Accounts and Customers tables, or Accounts, Branch, and Customers tables. All three scenarios include related tables. Creating a query with the Branch and Customers tables would not be acceptable because these tables are *not* directly related. To create a multitable query, do the following:

1. Click the CREATE tab.
2. Click Query Design in the Queries group.
3. Select the table you need in your query from the Show Table dialog box.
4. Click Add to add the table to the top section of the query design.
5. Select the next table you want to add to the query and click Add. Continue selecting and adding tables to the top section of the query design until all the tables you need display.
6. Drag the fields needed from the tables to the query design grid (or alternatively, double-click the field names); then add criteria and sorting options.
7. Click Run in the Results group to show the results in Datasheet view.

> **TIP Print the Relationship Report to Help Create a Multitable Query**
>
> When creating a multitable query, you should only include related tables. As a guide, you can print the Relationship Report in the Tools group on the Relationship Tools Design tab when the Relationships window is open. This report will help you determine which tables are related in your database.

Refer to Figure 2.31 (the top image) showing the results of the query "Which customers from the Campus branch have an account with a balance over $5,000?" To make this report more understandable to others, we can modify the query by adding the Branch Location (in place of the BranchID) and the Customer LastName (in place of the CustomerID). To make these changes, we would need to add the Branch table (which contains the Location field) and the Customers table (which contains the LastName field) to the query design.

Add Additional Tables to a Query

STEP 1 ⟫ To modify a saved query, open the query in Design view. If you wanted to change the Balance Over $5000 query as discussed earlier, first open the query in Design view. To add additional tables to a query, open the Navigation Pane (if necessary) and drag tables directly into the top portion of the query design grid. For example, the Branch and Customers tables were added to the query, as shown in Figure 2.42. The join lines between tables indicate that relationships were previously set in the Relationships window.

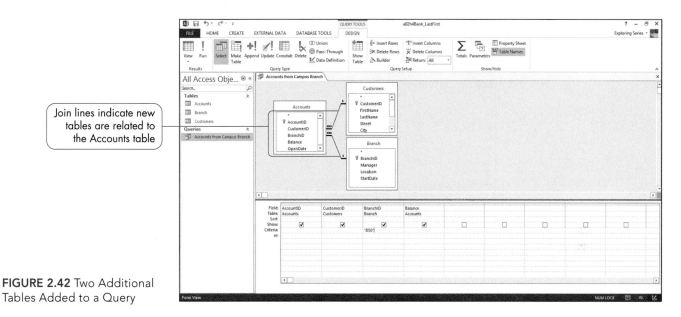

Join lines indicate new tables are related to the Accounts table

FIGURE 2.42 Two Additional Tables Added to a Query

Modifying a Multitable Query

STEP 3 ⟫ After creating a multitable query, you may find that you did not include all of the fields you needed, or you may find that you included fields that are unnecessary and complicate the results. You may find that other fields could be included that would make the results more understandable to others. To modify multitable queries, you use the same techniques you learned for single-table queries. Add tables using the Show Table dialog box; remove tables by clicking the unwanted table and pressing Delete. Add fields by double-clicking the field you want; remove fields by clicking the column selector and pressing Delete. Join lines between related tables should display automatically in a query if the relationships were previously established, as shown in Figure 2.42.

> **TIP Changes in Multitable Queries Do Not Affect Relationships**
>
> When you add two or more tables to a query, join lines appear automatically. You can delete the join lines in a query with no impact on the relationships themselves. Deleting a join line only affects the relationships in the individual query. The next time you create a query with the same tables, the join lines will be restored. And, if you open the Relationships window, you will find the join lines intact.

Add and Delete Fields in a Multitable Query

In Figure 2.43, three tables, as well as the join lines between the tables, display in the top pane of the Query Design view. All the fields from each of the tables are now available to be used in the query design grid. Figure 2.43 shows that Location (from the Branch table) replaced BranchID and LastName (from the Customers table) replaced CustomerID to make the results more useful. The BranchID was deleted from the query; therefore, the "B50" criterion was removed as well. "Campus" was added to the Location field's criteria row in order to extract the same results. Because criteria values are not case sensitive, typing "campus" is the same as typing "Campus," and both will return the same results. The results of the revised query are shown in Figure 2.44.

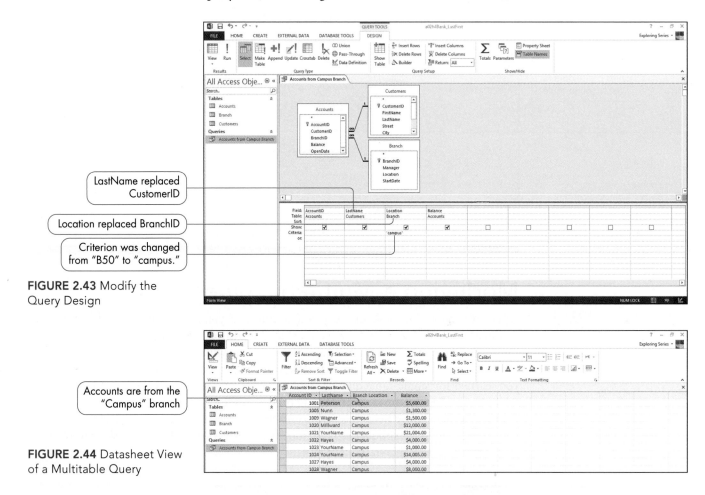

LastName replaced CustomerID

Location replaced BranchID

Criterion was changed from "B50" to "campus."

FIGURE 2.43 Modify the Query Design

Accounts are from the "Campus" branch

FIGURE 2.44 Datasheet View of a Multitable Query

Add Join Lines in a Multitable Query

In Figure 2.45, two tables are added to the query design, but no join line connects them. The results of the query will be unpredictable and will display more records than expected. The Customers table contains 11 records, and the Branch table contains 5 records. Because Access does not know how to interpret the unrelated tables, the results will show 55 records—every possible combination of customer and branch (11 × 5). See Figure 2.46.

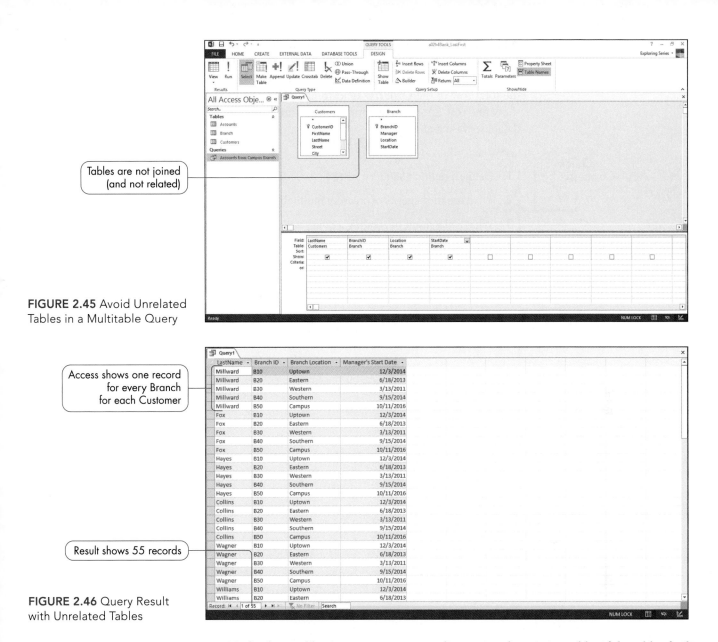

FIGURE 2.45 Avoid Unrelated Tables in a Multitable Query

Tables are not joined (and not related)

Access shows one record for every Branch for each Customer

Result shows 55 records

FIGURE 2.46 Query Result with Unrelated Tables

To fix this problem, you can create join lines using the existing tables if the tables facilitate this by having common fields. In a situation like this, in which there are no common fields, you must add an additional table that will provide a join between all three tables. In the Branch query, you can add the Accounts table, which will facilitate a join between the two existing tables, Customers and Branch. As soon as the third table is added to the query design, the join lines appear automatically, as shown in Figure 2.43.

Over time, your database will grow, and additional tables will be added. Occasionally, new tables are added to the database but not added to the Relationships window. When queries are created with the new tables, join lines will not be established. When this happens, add join lines to the new tables. Or you can create temporary join lines in the query design. These join lines will provide a temporary relationship between two tables and enable Access to interpret the query properly.

Get Answers Using a Multitable Query

STEP 4» You can get key information from your database using a multitable query. For example, if you want to know how many orders each customer placed since the database was created, you would create a new query and add the Customers and Orders tables to the Query Design view. After you verify that the join lines are correct, you add the CustomerID field from the Customers table and the OrderID field from the Order table to the query design grid.

When you run the query, the results show duplicates in the CustomerID column because customers place multiple orders. Then return to the Query Design view and click Totals in the Show/Hide group. Both columns show the Group By option in the Total row. Change the total row of the OrderID field to Count and run the query again. This time the results show one row for each customer and the number of orders each customer placed since the database was created.

Quick
Concepts ✓

1. Define a multitable query. *p. 184*

2. What are the benefits of creating multitable queries? *p. 184*

3. What is the result of creating a query with two unrelated tables? *p. 186*

4. Describe the purpose adding a join line in a multitable query. *p. 187*

4 Multitable Queries

Based on the auditor's request, you will need to evaluate the data further. This requires creating queries that are based on multiple tables rather than on a single table. You decide to open an existing query, add additional tables, and then save the query with a new name.

Skills covered: Add Additional Tables to a Query • Create a Multitable Query • Modify a Multitable Query • Get Answers Using a Multitable Query

STEP 1 》 ADD ADDITIONAL TABLES TO A QUERY

The previous query was based on the Accounts table, but now you need to add information to the query that is in the Branch and Customers tables. You will need to add the Branch and Customers tables to the query. Refer to Figure 2.47 as you complete Step 1.

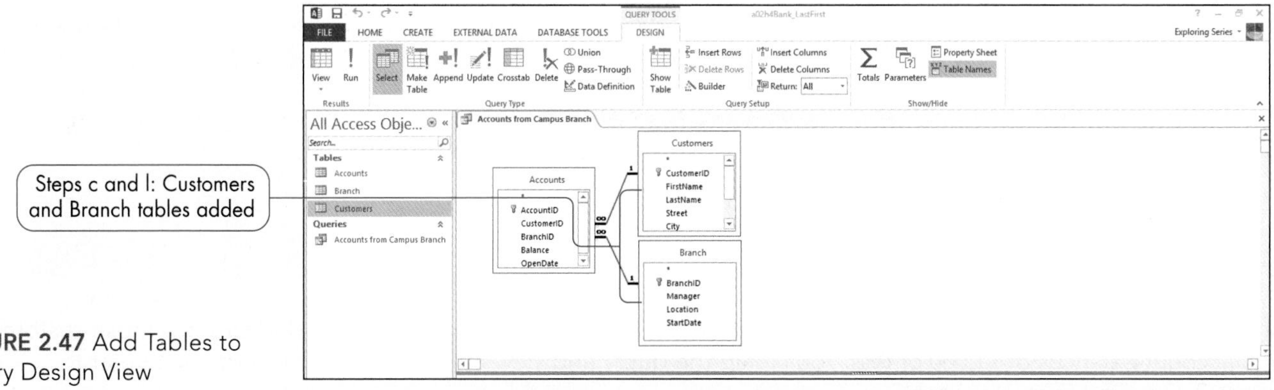

Steps c and l: Customers and Branch tables added

FIGURE 2.47 Add Tables to Query Design View

a. Open *a02h3Bank_LastFirst* if you closed it at the end of Hands-On Exercise 3. Save the database as **a02h4Bank_LastFirst**, changing *h3* to *h4*.

b. Right-click the **Accounts from Campus Branch query** in the Navigation Pane and select **Design View** from the shortcut menu.

c. Drag the **Branch table** from the Navigation Pane to the top pane of the query design grid next to the Accounts table.

   A join line connects the Branch table to the Accounts table. The query inherits the join lines from the relationships created in the Relationships window.

d. Drag the **Location field** from the Branch table to the first empty column in the design grid.

   The Location field should be positioned to the right of the Balance column.

e. Click the **Show check box** under the BranchID field to clear the check box and hide this field in the results.

   The BranchID field is no longer needed because the Location field provides the same information. Because you unchecked the BranchID show check box, the BranchID field will not display the next time the query is opened.

f. Delete the B50 criterion in the BranchID field.

g. Type **Campus** as a criterion in the Location field and press **Enter**.

   Access adds quotation marks around *Campus* for you; quotes are required for text criteria. You are substituting the Location criterion *(Campus)* in place of the BranchID criterion (B50).

h. Remove Ascending from the AccountID sort row. Click in the **Sort row** of the Balance field. Click the arrow and select **Descending**.

i. Click **Run** in the Results group.

The BranchID field does not display in the Datasheet view because you hid the field in step e. Only Campus accounts should display in the datasheet (10 records). Next, you will add the Customer LastName and delete the CustomerID from the query.

j. Save the changes to the query design.

k. Click **View** in the Views group to return to the Design view.

The BranchID field no longer displays on the field as it has been hidden.

l. Drag the **Customers table** from the Navigation Pane to the top section of the query design grid and reposition the tables so that the join lines are not blocked (see Figure 2.47).

The one-to-many relationship lines automatically connect the Customers table to the Accounts table (similar to step c on the previous page).

m. Drag the **LastName field** in the Customers table to the second column in the design grid.

The LastName field should be positioned to the right of the AccountID field.

n. Click the column selector in the CustomerID field to select it. Press **Delete**.

The CustomerID field is no longer needed in the results because we added the LastName field.

o. Click **Run** in the Results group.

The last names of the customers now display in the results.

p. Save and close the query.

STEP 2 ≫ CREATE A MULTITABLE QUERY

After discussing the query results with the auditor, you realize that another query is needed to show those customers with account balances of $1,000 or less. You create the query and view the results in Datasheet view. Refer to Figure 2.48 as you complete Step 2.

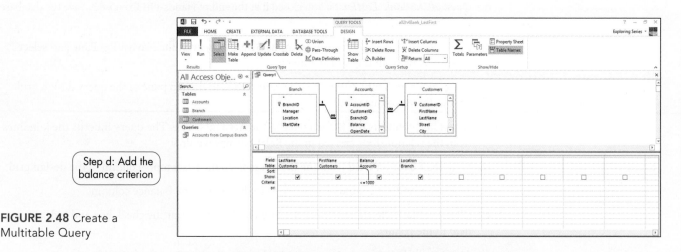

Step d: Add the balance criterion

FIGURE 2.48 Create a Multitable Query

a. Click the **CREATE tab** and click **Query Design** in the Queries group.

b. Double-click the **Branch table name** in the Show Table dialog box and double-click **Accounts** and **Customers** to add all three to the Query Design view. Click **Close** in the Show Table dialog box.

Three tables were added to the query.

c. Double-click the following fields to add them to the design grid: **LastName**, **FirstName**, **Balance**, and **Location**.

d. Type **<=1000** in the **Criteria row** of the Balance column.

e. Click **Run** in the Results group to see the query results.

Six records that have a balance of $1,000 or less display.

f. Click **Save** on the Quick Access Toolbar and type **Balance 1000 or Less** as the Query Name in the **Save As dialog box**. Click **OK**.

STEP 3 ›› MODIFY A MULTITABLE QUERY

The auditor requests additional changes to the Balance 1000 or Less query you just created. You will modify the criteria to display the accounts that were opened after January 1, 2011, with balances of $2,000 or less. Refer to Figure 2.49 as you complete Step 3.

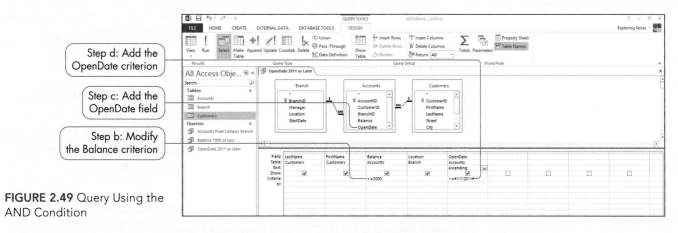

FIGURE 2.49 Query Using the AND Condition

a. Click **View** in the Views group to switch the *Balance 1000 or Less* query to Design view.

b. Type **<=2000** in place of *<=1000* in the **Criteria row** of the Balance field.

c. Double-click the **OpenDate field** in the Accounts table in the top section of the Query Design view to add it to the first blank column in the design grid.

d. Type **>=1/1/2011** in the **Criteria row** of the OpenDate field to extract only accounts that have been opened since January 2011.

After you type the expression and then move to a different column, Access will add the # symbols around the date automatically.

e. Click **Run** in the Results group to display the results of the query.

Five records display in the query results.

f. Click the **FILE tab**, click **Save As**, click **Save Object As**, and then click **Save As**. Type **OpenDate 2011 or Later** as the query name. Click **OK**.

g. Click **View** in the Views group to return to the Design view of the query.

h. Click in the **Sort row** of the OpenDate field and select **Ascending**.

i. Click **Run** in the Results group.

The records are sorted from the earliest open date after January 1, 2011, to the most recent open date.

j. Save and close the query.

STEP 4 » GET ANSWERS USING A MULTITABLE QUERY

The auditor wants to know the number of accounts each customer has opened. You create a query using a Totals row to obtain these data. Refer to Figure 2.50 as you complete Step 4.

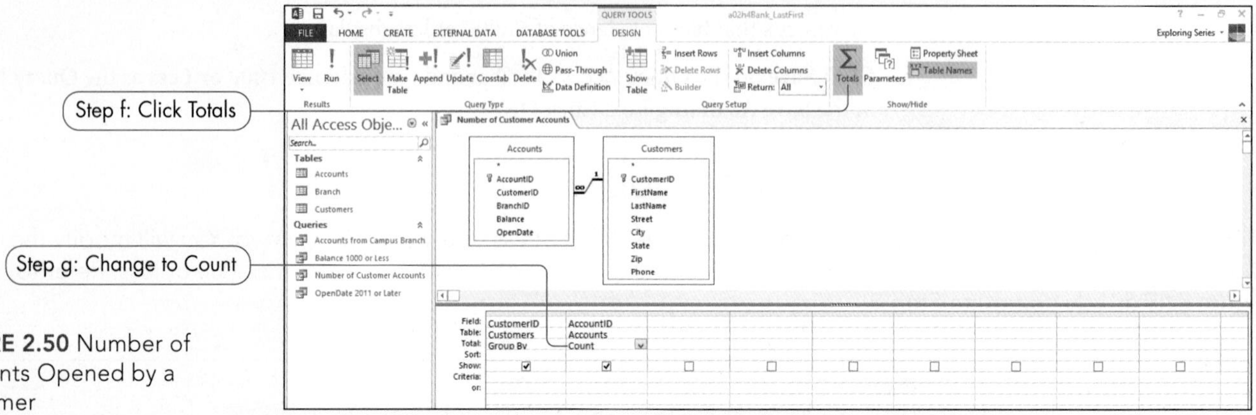

FIGURE 2.50 Number of Accounts Opened by a Customer

a. Click the **CREATE tab** and click **Query Design** in the Queries group.

b. Add the Accounts table and the Customers table to the top section of the Query Design view. Click **Close** in the Show Table dialog box.

c. Double-click the **CustomerID** in the Customers table in the top section of the Query Design view to add it to the first blank column in the design grid and double-click the **AccountID** in the Accounts table to add it to the second column.

d. Click **Run** in the Results group.

The results show there are 28 records. Every account a customer has opened is displayed. The auditor only wants the total number of accounts a customer has, so you need to modify the query.

e. Click **View** in the Views group to return to the Design view of the query.

f. Click **Totals** in the Show/Hide group.

Both columns show the Group By option in the Total row.

g. Click **Group By** in the Total row of the AccountID field and select **Count**.

h. Click **Run** in the Results group.

The results show one row for each customer and the number of accounts each customer has opened since the database was created.

i. Click **Save** on the Quick Access Toolbar and type **Number of Customer Accounts** as the query name. Close the query.

j. Submit based on your instructor's directions and close Access.

Chapter Objectives Review

After reading this chapter, you have accomplished the following objectives:

1. Design a table.

- Include necessary data: Consider the output requirements when creating table structure. Determine the data required to produce the expected information.
- Design for now and for the future: When designing a database, try to anticipate the future needs of the system and build in the flexibility to satisfy those demands.
- Store data in its smallest parts: Store data in its smallest parts to make it more flexible. Storing a full name in a Name field is more limiting than storing a first name in a separate FirstName field and a last name in a separate LastName field.
- Add calculated fields to a table: A calculated field produces a value from an expression or function that references one or more existing fields. Storing calculated data in a table enables you to add the data easily to queries, forms, and reports without the trouble of an additional calculation.
- Design to accommodate date arithmetic: Calculated fields are frequently created with numeric data. You can use date arithmetic to subtract one date from another to find out the number of days, months, or years that have lapsed between them. You can also add or subtract a constant from a date.
- Plan for common fields between tables: Tables are joined in relationships using common fields. Name the common fields with the same name and make sure they have the same data type.

2. Create and modify tables.

- Create tables: Create tables in Datasheet view or Design view. You can also import data from another database or an application such as Excel.
- Determine data type: Data type properties determine the type of data that can be entered and the operations that can be performed on that data. Access recognizes 12 data types.
- Establish a primary key: The primary key is the field that uniquely identifies each record in a table.
- Explore a foreign key: A foreign key is a field in one table that is also the primary key of another table.
- Work with field properties: Field properties determine how the field looks and behaves. Examples of field properties are the field size property and the caption property.
- Enter table records in Datasheet view: Datasheet view is used to add, edit, and delete records. Design view is used to create and modify the table structure by enabling you to add and edit fields and set field properties.

3. Share data.

- Import data: You can import data from other applications such as an Excel spreadsheet or import data from another database by using the Import Wizard.
- Modify an imported table's design and add data: After importing a table, examine the design and make necessary modifications. Modifications may include changing a field name, adding new fields, or deleting unnecessary fields.

4. Establish table relationships.

- Set relationships in the Relationships window: Use Show Table to add tables to the Relationships window. Drag a field name from one table to the corresponding field name in another table to join the tables.
- Establish referential integrity: Referential integrity enforces rules in a database that are used to preserve relationships between tables when records are changed.
- Set cascade options: The Cascade Update Related Fields option ensures that when the primary key is modified in a primary table, Access will automatically update all foreign key values in a related table. The Cascade Delete Related Records option ensures that when the primary key is deleted in a primary table, Access will automatically delete all records in related tables that reference the primary key.
- Establish a one-to-many relationship: A one-to-many relationship is established when the primary key value in the primary table can match many of the foreign key values in the related table. One-to-one and many-to-many are also relationship possibilities, but one-to-many relationships are the most common.

5. Create a single-table query.

- Create a single-table select query: A single-table select query uses fields from one table to display only those records that match certain criteria.
- Use Query Design view: Use Query Design view to create and modify a query. The top portion of the view contains tables with their respective field names and displays the join lines between tables. The bottom portion, known as the query design grid, contains columns and rows that you use to control the query results.

6. Specify query criteria for different data types.

- Different data types require different syntax: Date fields are enclosed in pound signs (#) and text fields in quotations (""). Numeric and currency fields require no delimiters.
- Use wildcards: Wildcards are special characters that can represent one or more characters in a text value. A question mark is a wildcard that stands for a single character in the same position as the question mark, while an asterisk is a wildcard that stands for any number of characters in the same position as the asterisk.
- Use comparison operators in queries: Comparison operators such as equal (=), not equal (<>), greater than (>), less than (<), greater than or equal to (>=), and less than or equal to (<=) signs can be used in the criteria of a query to limit the query results to only those records that meet the criteria.

- Work with null: Access uses the term *null* for a blank field. Null criteria can be used to find missing information.
- Establish AND, OR, and NOT criteria: The AND, OR, and NOT logical operators are used when queries require multiple criteria. The AND logical operator returns only records that meet all criteria. The OR logical operator returns records meeting any of the specified criteria. The NOT logical operator returns all records except the specified criteria.

7. Understand query sort order.

- Query sort order: The query sort order determines the order of records in a query's Datasheet view. You can change the order of records by specifying the sort order in Design view.
- Determining sort order: The sort order is determined from the order of the fields from left to right. Move the field columns to position them in left to right sort order.

8. Run, copy, and modify a Query.

- Run a query: To obtain the results for a query, you must run the query. To run the query, click Run in the Results group when you are in Design view. Another method is to locate the query in the Navigation Pane and double-click it. A similar method is to select the query and press Enter.
- Copy a query: To save time, after specifying tables, fields, and conditions for one query, copy the query, rename it, and then modify the fields and criteria in the second query.

9. Use the Query Wizard.

- Create a query using the Query Wizard: The Query Wizard is an alternative method for creating queries. It enables you to select tables and fields from lists. The last step of the wizard prompts you to save the query.

10. Create a multitable query.

- Creating a multitable query: Multitable queries contain two or more tables enabling you to take advantage of the relationships that have been set in your database.
- Add additional tables to a query: Open the Navigation Pane and drag the tables from the Navigation Pane directly into the top section of the Query Design view.

11. Modify a multitable query.

- Add and delete fields in a multitable query: Multitable queries may need to be modified. Add fields by double-clicking the field name in the table you want; remove fields by clicking the column selector and pressing Delete.
- Add join lines in a multitable query: If the tables have a common field, create join lines by dragging the field name of one common field onto the field name of the other table. Or you can add an additional table that will provide a join between all three tables.
- Get answers using a multitable query: Use the total row options of a field such as Count to get answers.

Key Terms Matching

Match the key terms with their definitions. Write the key term letter by the appropriate numbered definition.

a. AND logical operator
b. AutoNumber
c. CamelCase notation
d. Caption property
e. Cascade Update Related Fields
f. Criteria row
g. Data redundancy
h. Data type
i. Field property
j. Foreign key

k. Multitable query
l. Number data type
m. Null
n. One-to-many relationship
o. OR logical operator
p. Query
q. Referential Integrity
r. Simple Query Wizard
s. Sort row
t. Wildcard

1. _____ A special character that can represent one or more characters in the criterion of a query. **p. 174**

2. _____ A characteristic of a field that determines how a field looks and behaves. **p. 149**

3. _____ Returns only records that meet all criteria. **p. 175**

4. _____ A row in the Query Design view that determines which records will be selected. **p. 172**

5. _____ Determines the type of data that can be entered and the operations that can be performed on that data. **p. 147**

6. _____ Used to create a more readable label that displays in the top row in Datasheet view and in forms and reports. **p. 149**

7. _____ Enables you to ask questions about the data stored in a database. **p. 171**

8. _____ The term *Access* uses to describe a blank field. **p. 175**

9. _____ A data type that is a number that automatically increments each time a record is added. **p. 148**

10. _____ The unnecessary storing of duplicate data in two or more tables. **p. 146**

11. _____ A data type that can store only numerical data. **p. 149**

12. _____ A relationship established when the primary key value in the primary table can match many of the foreign key values in the related table. **p. 162**

13. _____ A field in one table that is also the primary key of another table. **p. 149**

14. _____ An option that directs Access to automatically update all foreign key values in a related table when the primary key value is modified in a primary table. **p. 162**

15. _____ Rules in a database that are used to preserve relationships between tables when records are changed. **p. 161**

16. _____ Uses no spaces in multiword field names, but uses uppercase letters to distinguish the first letter of each new word. **p. 146**

17. _____ A row in the Query Design view that enables you to reorder data in ascending or descending order. **p. 172**

18. _____ Contains two or more tables, enabling you to take advantage of the relationships that have been set in your database. **p. 184**

19. _____ Returns records meeting any of the specified criteria. **p. 175**

20. _____ Provides dialog boxes to guide you through the query design process. **p. 171**

Multiple Choice

1. All of the following are suggested guidelines for table design *except*:

   (a) Include all necessary data.

   (b) Store data in its smallest parts.

   (c) Avoid date arithmetic.

   (d) Link tables using common fields.

2. Which of the following determines the type of data that can be entered and the operations that can be performed on that data?

   (a) Field properties

   (b) Data type

   (c) Caption property

   (d) Normalization

3. When entering, deleting, or editing table data:

   (a) The table must be in Design view.

   (b) The table must be in Datasheet view.

   (c) The table may be in either Datasheet or Design view.

   (d) Data may only be entered in a form.

4. When importing data into Access, which of the following statements is *true*?

   (a) The Import Wizard only works for Excel files.

   (b) The Import Wizard is found on the Create tab.

   (c) You can assign a primary key while you are importing Excel data.

   (d) The wizard will import the data in one step after you select the file.

5. The main reason to enforce referential integrity in Access is to:

   (a) Limit the number of records in a table.

   (b) Make it possible to delete records.

   (c) Keep your database safe from unauthorized users.

   (d) Keep invalid data from being entered into a table.

6. An illustration of a one-to-many relationship would be a:

   (a) Person changes his/her primary address.

   (b) Customer may have multiple orders.

   (c) Bank branch location has an internal BranchID code.

   (d) Balance field is totaled for all accounts for each person.

7. A query's specifications providing instructions about which records to include must be entered on the:

   (a) Table row of the query design grid.

   (b) Show row of the query design grid.

   (c) Sort row of the query design grid.

   (d) Criteria row of the query design grid.

8. When adding Value criteria to the Query Design view, the value you enter must be delimited by:

   (a) Nothing ().

   (b) Pound signs (#).

   (c) Quotes (" ").

   (d) At signs (@).

9. It is more efficient to make a copy of an existing query rather than create a new query when which of the following is *true*?

   (a) The existing query contains only one table.

   (b) The existing query and the new query use the same tables and fields.

   (c) The existing query and the new query have the exact same criteria.

   (d) The original query is no longer being used.

10. Which of the following is *true* for the Query Wizard?

    (a) You can only select tables as a source.

    (b) No criteria can be added.

    (c) Fields from multiple tables are not allowed.

    (d) You do not need a summary.

Practice Exercises

1 Our Corner Bookstore

FROM SCRATCH

Tom and Erin Mullaney own and operate a bookstore in Philadelphia, Pennsylvania. Erin asked you to help her create an Access database because of your experience in this class. You believe that you can help her by creating a database and importing the Excel spreadsheets they use to store the publishers and the books that they sell. You determine that a third table—for authors—is also required. Your task is to design and populate the three tables, set the table relationships, and enforce referential integrity. If you have problems, reread the detailed directions presented in the chapter. This exercise follows the same set of skills as used in Hands-On Exercises 1 and 2 in the chapter. Refer to Figure 2.51 as you complete this exercise.

FIGURE 2.51 Books Relationships Window

a. Open Access and click **Blank desktop database**. Type **a02p1Books_LastFirst** in the **File Name box**. Click **Browse** to locate your student data files folder in the File New Database dialog box, click **OK** to close the dialog box, and then click **Create** to create the new database.

b. Type **11** in the **Click to Add column** and click **Click to Add**. The field name becomes *Field1*, and *Click to Add* now appears as the third column. Click in the third column, type **Benchloss**, and then press **Tab**. The process repeats for the fourth column; type **Michael R.** and press **Tab** twice.

c. The cursor returns to the first column where *(New)* is selected. Press **Tab**. Type the rest of the data using the following table. These data will become the records of the Author table.

ID	Field1	Field2	Field3
1	11	Brenchloss	Michael R.
(New)	12	Turow	Scott
	13	Rice	Anne
	14	King	Stephen
	15	Connelly	Michael
	16	Rice	Luanne
	17	*your last name*	*your first name*

d. Click **Save** on the Quick Access Toolbar. Type **Author** in the **Save As dialog box** and click **OK**.

e. Click **View** in the Views group to switch to the Design view of the Author table.

f. Select **Field1**—in the second row—in the top portion of the table design and type **AuthorID** to rename the field. In the *Field Properties* section in the lower portion of the table design, type **Author ID** in the **Caption property box** and verify that *Long Integer* displays for the Field Size property.

g. Select **Field2** and type **LastName** to rename the field. In the *Field Properties* section in the bottom portion of the Design view, type **Author's Last Name** in the **Caption property box** and type **20** as the field size.

h. Select **Field3** and type **FirstName** to rename the field. In the *Field Properties* section in the bottom portion of the table design, type **Author's First Name** as the caption and type **15** as the field size.

i. Click the **ID field row selector** (which shows the primary key) to select the row and click **Delete Rows** in the Tools group. Click **Yes** twice to confirm both messages.

j. Click the **AuthorID row selector** and click **Primary Key** in the Tools group to reset the primary key.

k. Click **Save** on the Quick Access Toolbar to save the design changes. Click **Yes** to the *Some data may be lost* message. Close the table.

l. Click the **EXTERNAL DATA tab** and click **Excel** in the Import & Link group to launch the Get External Data – Excel Spreadsheet feature. Verify the *Import the source data into a new table in the current database* option is selected, click **Browse**, and then go to the student data folder. Select the *a02p1Books* workbook, click **Open**, and then click **OK**. This workbook contains two worksheets. Follow these steps:

- Select the **Publishers worksheet** and click **Next**.
- Click the **First Row Contains Column Headings check box** and click **Next**.
- Select the **PubID field**, click the **Indexed arrow**, select **Yes (No Duplicates)**, and then click **Next**.
- Click the **Choose my own primary key arrow**, select **PubID**, if necessary, and then click **Next**.
- Accept the name *Publishers* for the table name, click **Finish**, and then click **Close** without saving the import steps.

m. Repeat the Import Wizard to import the Books worksheet from the *a02p1Books* workbook into the Access database. Follow these steps:

- Select the **Books worksheet** and click **Next**.
- Ensure the *First Row Contains Column Headings* check box is checked and click **Next**.
- Click on the **ISBN column**, set the Indexed property box to **Yes (No Duplicates)**, and then click **Next**.
- Click the **Choose my own primary key arrow**, select **ISBN** as the primary key field, and then click **Next**.
- Accept the name *Books* as the table name. Click **Finish** and click **Close** without saving the import steps.

n. Right-click the **Books table** in the Navigation Pane and select **Design View**. Make the following changes:

- Change the PubID field name to **PublisherID**.
- Change the Caption property to **Publisher ID.**
- Change the PublisherID Field Size property to **2**.
- Click the **ISBN field** and change the Field Size property to **13**.
- Change the AuthorCode field name to **AuthorID**.
- Change the AuthorID Field Size property to **Long Integer**.
- Click the **ISBN field row selector** (which shows the primary key) to select the row. Drag the row up to the first position.
- Click **Save** on the Quick Access Toolbar to save the design changes to the Books table. Click **Yes** to the *Some data may be lost* warning.
- Close the table.

o. Right-click the **Publishers table** in the Navigation Pane and select **Design View**. Make the following changes:

- Change the PubID field name to **PublisherID**.
- Change the PublisherID Field Size property to **2**.
- Change the Caption property to **Publisher's ID.**
- Change the Field Size property to **50** for the PubName and PubAddress fields.
- Change the Pub Address field name to **PubAddress** (remove the space).
- Change the PubCity Field Size property to **30**.
- Change the PubState Field Size property to **2**.
- Change the Pub ZIP field name to **PubZIP** (remove the space).
- Click **Save** on the Quick Access Toolbar to save the design changes to the Publishers table. Click **Yes** to the *Some data may be lost* warning. Close all open tables.

p. Click the **DATABASE TOOLS tab** and click **Relationships** in the Relationships group. Click **Show Table** if necessary. Follow these steps:

- Double-click each table name in the Show Table dialog box to add it to the Relationships window and close the Show Table dialog box.
- Drag the **AuthorID field** from the Author table onto the AuthorID field in the Books table.

- Click the **Enforce Referential Integrity** and **Cascade Update Related Fields check boxes** in the Edit Relationships dialog box. Click **Create** to create a one-to-many relationship between the Author and Books tables.
- Drag the **PublisherID field** from the Publishers table onto the PublisherID field in the Books table.
- Click the **Enforce Referential Integrity** and **Cascade Update Related Fields check boxes** in the Edit Relationships dialog box. Click **Create** to create a one-to-many relationship between the Publishers and Books tables.
- Click **Save** on the Quick Access Toolbar to save the changes to the Relationships window and click **Close**.

q. Click the **FILE tab** and click **Close** to exit Access.

r. Submit based on your instructor's directions.

2 Morgan Insurance Company

The Morgan Insurance Company offers a full range of insurance services in four locations: Miami, Boston, Chicago, and Philadelphia. They store all of the firm's employee data in an Excel spreadsheet. This file contains employee name and address, job performance, salary, and title. The firm is converting from Excel to Access. A database file containing two of the tables already exists; your job is to import the employee data from Excel for the third table. Once imported, you need to modify field properties and set new relationships. The owner of the company, Victor Reed, is concerned that some of the Atlanta and Boston salaries may be below the guidelines published by the national office. He asks that you investigate the salaries of the two offices and create a separate query for each city. If you have problems, reread the detailed directions presented in the chapter. This exercise follows the same set of skills as used in Hands-On Exercises 2–4 in the chapter. Refer to Figure 2.52 as you complete this exercise.

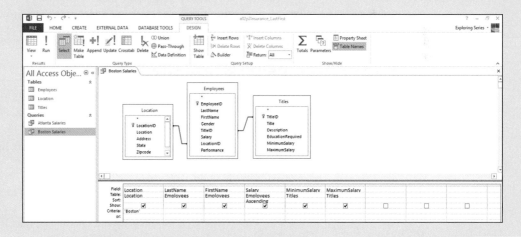

FIGURE 2.52 Boston Salaries Query Design

a. Open *a02p2Insurance*. Click the **FILE tab**, click **Save As**, and then click **Save As** again to save the database as **a02p2Insurance_LastFirst**. Double-click the **Location table** and look at the contents to become familiar with the field names and the type of information stored in the table. Repeat with the Titles table.

b. Click the **EXTERNAL DATA tab**, click **Excel** in the Import & Link group, and then do the following:
- Click **Browse** and locate the *a02p2Employees* workbook in your student data files location. Select the file, click **Open**, and then click **OK**.
- Select the **Employees worksheet**, if necessary, and click **Next**.
- Click the **First Row Contains Column Headings check box** and click **Next**.
- Click the **Indexed arrow** for the EmployeeID field, select **Yes (No Duplicates)**, and then click **Next**.

- Click **Choose my own primary key arrow**, select the **EmployeeID** as the primary key, and then click **Next**.
- Accept the name *Employees* for the table name, click **Finish**, and then click **Close** without saving the import steps.

c. Double-click the **Employees table** in the Navigation Pane, click the **HOME tab**, and then click **View** in the Views group to switch to the Design view of the Employees table. Make the following changes:
- Click the **LastName field** and change the Field Size property to **20**.
- Change the Caption property to **Last Name**.
- Click the **FirstName field** and change the Field Size property to **20**.
- Change the Caption property to **First Name**.
- Click the **LocationID field** and change the Field Size property to **3**.
- Change the Caption property to **Location ID**.
- Click the **TitleID field** and change the Field Size property to **3**.
- Change the Caption property to **Title ID**.
- Change the Salary field data type to **Currency** and change *General Number* in the Format property in field properties to **Currency**.
- Save the design changes. Click **Yes** to the *Some data may be lost* warning.

d. Click **View** in the Views group to view the Employees table in Datasheet view and examine the data. Click any record in the Title ID and click **Ascending** in the Sort & Filter group on the HOME tab. Multiple employees are associated with the T01, T02, T03, and T04 titles.

e. Double-click the **Titles table** in the Navigation Pane to open it in Datasheet view. Notice the T04 title is not in the list.

f. Add a new record in the first blank record at the bottom of the Titles table. Use the following data:
- Type **T04** in the **TitleID field**.
- Type **Senior Account Rep** in the **Title field**.
- Type **A marketing position requiring a technical background and at least three years of experience** in the **Description field**.
- Type **Four-year degree** in the **Education Requirements field**.
- Type **45000** in the **Minimum Salary field**.
- Type **75000** in the **Maximum Salary field**.

g. Close all tables. Click **Yes** if you are asked to save changes to the Employees table.

h. Click the **DATABASE TOOLS tab** and click **Relationships** in the Relationships group. Click **Show Table** if necessary. Follow these steps:
- Double-click each table name in the Show Table dialog box to add them to the Relationships window and close the Show Table dialog box.
- Adjust the height of the tables so that all fields display.
- Drag the **LocationID field** in the Location table onto the LocationID field in the Employees table.
- Click the **Enforce Referential Integrity** and **Cascade Update Related Fields check boxes** in the Edit Relationships dialog box. Click **Create** to create a one-to-many relationship between the Location and Employees tables.
- Drag the **TitleID field** in the Titles table onto the TitleID field in the Employees table.
- Click the **Enforce Referential Integrity** and **Cascade Update Related Fields check boxes** in the Edit Relationships dialog box. Click **Create** to create a one-to-many relationship between the Titles and Employees tables.
- Click **Save** on the Quick Access Toolbar to save the changes to the Relationships window and close the Relationships window.

i. Click the **CREATE tab** and click the **Query Wizard** in the Queries group. Follow these steps:
- Select **Simple Query Wizard** and click **OK**.
- Select **Table: Employees** in the Tables/Queries box, if necessary.
- Double-click **LastName** in the **Available Fields list** to move it to the Selected Fields list.
- Double-click **FirstName** in the **Available Fields list** to move it to the Selected Fields list.

- Double-click **LocationID** in the **Available Fields list** to move it to the Selected Fields list.
- Click **Next**.
- Select the **Detail (shows every field of every record) option**, if necessary, and click **Next**.
- Type **Employees Location** as the query title and click **Finish**.

j. Click the **CREATE tab** and click the **Query Wizard** in the Queries group. Follow these steps:

- Select **Simple Query Wizard** and click **OK**.
- Select **Table: Location** in the Tables/Queries box.
- Double-click **Location** in the **Available Fields list** to move it to the Selected Fields list.
- Select **Table: Employees** in the Tables/Queries box.
- Double-click **LastName**, **FirstName**, and **Salary**.
- Select **Table: Titles** in the Tables/Queries box.
- Double-click **MinimumSalary** and **MaximumSalary**. Click **Next**.
- Select the **Detail (shows every field of every record) option**, if necessary, and click **Next**.
- Type **Atlanta Salaries** as the query title and click **Finish**.

k. Click the **HOME tab** and click **View** to switch to the Design view of the Atlanta Salaries Query. In the Criteria row of the Location field, type **Atlanta**. Click in the **Sort row** in the Salary field and select **Ascending**. Click **Run** in the Results group on the DESIGN tab. Visually inspect the data to see if any of the Atlanta employees have a salary less than the minimum or greater than the maximum when compared to the published salary range. These salaries will need to be updated later. Save and close the query.

l. Right-click on the **Atlanta Salaries query** in the Navigation Pane and select **Copy**. Right-click a blank area in the Navigation Pane and select **Paste**. In the Paste As dialog box, type **Boston Salaries** for the query name. Click **OK**.

m. Right-click on the **Boston Salaries query** in the Navigation Pane and select **Design View**. In the Criteria row of the Location field, replace *Atlanta* with **Boston**. Click **Run** in the Results group on the DESIGN tab. Visually inspect the data to see if any of the Boston employees have a salary less than the minimum or greater than the maximum when compared to the published salary range. Save and close the query.

n. Click the **FILE tab** and click **Close** to exit Access.

o. Submit based on your instructor's directions.

Mid-Level Exercises

1 My Game Collection

ANALYSIS CASE

Over the years, you have collected quite a few video games, so you cataloged them in an Access database. After opening the database, you create two tables—one to identify the game system that plays your game and the other to identify the category or genre of the game. Then, you will join each table in a relationship so that you can query the database. Refer to Figure 2.53 as you complete this exercise.

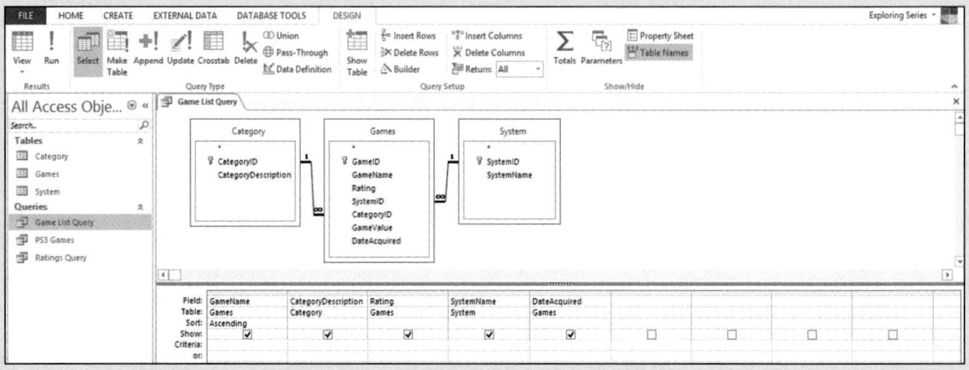

FIGURE 2.53 Game List Query

a. Open *a02m1Games* and save the database as **a02m1Games_LastFirst**. Open the *Games* table and review the fields containing the game information.

b. Click the **CREATE tab** and click **Table Design** in the Tables group. To save time, you opened Table Design to create the fields for a new table rather than creating a table and switching to Design View.

c. Type **SystemID** for the first Field Name and select **Number** as the Data Type.

d. Type **SystemName** for the second Field Name and accept **Short Text** as the Data Type.

e. Change to Design view. Delete the ID row. Make **SystemID** the primary key and change the Data Type to **AutoNumber**. Add the caption **System ID**.

f. Change the SystemName Field Size property to **15**. Add the caption **System Name**, making sure there is a space between System and Name. Save the table as **System**, saving the changes to the table design. Switch to Datasheet view.

g. Add the system names to the System table as shown below, letting Access use AutoNumber to create the SystemID field. Close the table.

System ID	System Name
1	XBOX 360
2	PS3
3	Wii
4	NES
5	PC Game
6	Nintendo 3DS

h. Click the **CREATE tab** and click **Table Design** in the Tables group. Delete the existing ID row. Type **CategoryID** for the first Field Name and select **AutoNumber** as the Data Type. Set the CategoryID as the **Primary Key**.

i. Type **CategoryDescription** for the second Field Name and accept **Short Text** as the Data Type. Change the Field Size property to **25**. Add the caption **Category Description**, making sure there

j. Add the category descriptions to the Category table as shown below, letting Access use AutoNumber to create the CategoryID field. Close the table.

CategoryID	Category Description
1	Action
2	Adventure
3	Arcade
4	Racing
5	Rhythm
6	Role-playing
7	Simulation
8	Sports

k. Click the **DATABASE TOOLS tab** and click **Relationships** in the Relationships group. Add all three tables to the Relationships window and close the Show Table dialog box. Create a one-to-many relationship between CategoryID in the Category table and CategoryID in the Games table. Enforce referential integrity and cascade update related fields.

l. Create a one-to-many relationship between SystemID in the System table and SystemID in the Games table. Enforce referential integrity and cascade update related fields. Close the Relationships window, saving changes.

m. Use the Query Wizard to create a simple query using the Games table. Use the following fields in the query: GameName, Rating. Save the query using the title **Ratings Query**.

n. Switch to Query Design view. Sort the rating field in ascending order and run the query. Close the query, saving the changes to the design of the Ratings Query.

o. Create a multitable query in Design view using all three tables. Use the following fields: GameName, CategoryDescription, Rating, SystemName, and DateAcquired.

p. Sort the query in Ascending order by GameName and run the query. Save the query as **Game List Query** and close the query.

q. Copy the **Game List Query** and paste it in the Navigation Pane using the name **PS3 Games**. Modify the query in Design view by using **PS3** as the criteria for SystemName. Remove the sort by GameName and sort in ascending order by CategoryDescription. The query results should include 7 records.

r. Close the PS3 Games query, saving the changes to the design.

s. Assume you are going home for Thanksgiving and you want to take your Wii gaming system and games home with you—but you only want to take home games with a rating of Everyone. Create a query named **Thanksgiving Games** that shows the name of the game, its rating, the category description of the games, and the system name. The results of the query will tell you which games to pack.

t. Submit based on your instructor's directions.

2 The Prestige Hotel

The Prestige Hotel chain caters to upscale business travelers and provides state-of-the-art conference, meeting, and reception facilities. It prides itself on its international, four-star cuisine. Last year, it began a member reward club to help the marketing department track the purchasing patterns of its most loyal customers. All of the hotel transactions are stored in the database. Your task is to help the managers of the Prestige Hotel in Denver and Chicago identify their customers who stayed in a room last year and who had three persons in their party. Refer to Figure 2.54 as you complete this exercise.

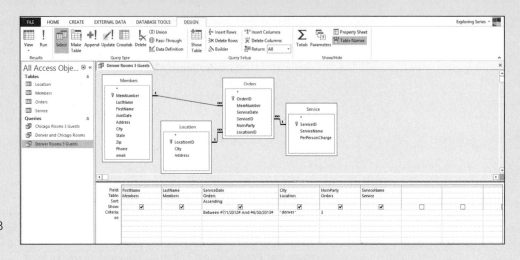

FIGURE 2.54 Denver Rooms 3 Guests Query

a. Open *a02m2Hotel* and save the file as **a02m2Hotel_LastFirst**. Review the data contained in the three tables. Specifically, look for the tables and fields containing the information you need: dates of stays in Denver suites, the members' names, and the numbers in the parties.

b. Import the location data from the Excel file *a02m2Location* into your database as a new table. The first row does contain column headings. Set the LocationID Indexed property to **Yes (No Duplicates)** and set the Data Type to **Long Integer**. Select the **LocationID field** as the primary key. Name the table **Location**. Do not save the import steps.

c. Open the Relationships window and create a relationship between the Location table and the Orders table using the LocationID field. Enforce referential integrity and select **Cascade Update Related Fields**. Create a relationship between the Orders and Members tables using the MemNumber field, ensuring that you enforce referential integrity and cascade update related fields. Create a relationship between the Orders and Service tables using the ServiceID field, ensuring that you enforce referential integrity and cascade update related fields. Save and close the Relationships window.

d. Open the Members table and find Bryan Gray's name. Replace his name with your own first and last names. Use Find to locate Nicole Lee's name and replace it with your name. Close the table.

DISCOVER e. Create a query using the following fields: ServiceDate (Orders table), City (Location table), NoInParty (Orders table), ServiceName (Service table), FirstName (Members table), and LastName (Members table). Set the criteria to limit the output to **Denver**. Use the Between command to only show services from **7/1/2012** to **6/30/2013**. Set the Number in Party criterion to **3**. Sort the results in ascending order by the Service Date. Compare your query to Figure 2.54.

f. Run the query and examine the number of records in the status bar at the bottom of the query. It should display *154*. If your number of records is different, examine the criteria.

g. Change the order of the query fields so that they display as FirstName, LastName, ServiceDate, City, NoInParty, and ServiceName.

h. Save the query as **Denver Rooms 3 Guests**. Close the query and copy and paste it, renaming the new query **Chicago Rooms 3 Guests**; one of your colleagues in Chicago asked for your help in analyzing the guest data.

i. Open the Chicago Rooms 3 Guests query in Design view and change the criterion for Denver to **Chicago**. Run and save the changes. You should have 179 results.

DISCOVER j. Combine the two previous queries into a third query named **Denver and Chicago Rooms 3 Guests**. Use the criteria from the two individual queries to create a combination AND–OR condition. The records in the combined query should equal the sum of the records in the two individual queries (333 records).

k. Submit based on your instructor's directions.

3 | Used Cell Phones for Sale

COLLABORATION CASE

ANALYSIS CASE

You and a few of your classmates started a new business selling used cell phones, MP3 players, and accessories. You have been using an Access database to track your inventory. You decide to improve the data entry process by adding three additional tables. After the new tables are added and the relationships set, you will create several queries to analyze the data. In order to collaborate with the other members of your group, you will post an Access database and two Excel files to a SkyDrive folder. At the completion of this exercise, each person will submit his or her own Word document containing the answers to the questions below.

a. Open the *a02m3Phones* database and save the file as **a02m3Phones_GroupX**. Close the database. (This step will be completed by only one person in your group. Replace *X* with the number assigned to your group by your instructor.) Create a folder on your SkyDrive account named **Exploring Access** and share the folder with the other members in your group and the instructor. Upload the database to this new folder and notify the other members in your group.

★ b. Download the database from the Exploring Access SkyDrive folder created in step a and save it locally as **a02m3Phones_GroupX_LastFirst**. (Everyone in the group will complete this step.) Open the database, open the Inventory table, and than review the records in the table. Take note of the data in the TypeOfDevice column; this field is joined to the DeviceOptions table, and the *enforce referential integrity* option has been set. Only the options in the DeviceOptions table are allowed to be entered. What other fields in this table could be joined to a table in the same way? Type your answer into a Word document named **a02m3Phones_Answers_LastFirst**.

c. Import the data in the *a02m3Carriers* Excel spreadsheet into a new table named **Carriers**. Let Access add a primary key field (ID). Open the table and verify that the data imported correctly. Change the ID field to **CarrierID**. Save and close the Carriers table.

d. Open the Inventory table in Design view and add a new field under the Carrier field named **CarrierID**. Set the Data Type to **Number**. Save and close the table. Open the Relationships window and the Carriers table. Create a relationship between the Carriers table and the Inventory table using the CarrierID field. Enforce referential integrity. Take a screen shot of the Relationships window using the Snipping Tool and paste the image into the Word document you created in step b. Close the Relationships window.

e. Open the Inventory table and the Carriers table. Using the CarrierID field in the Carriers table, enter the correct CarrierID into each record in the Inventory table.

f. Repeat steps c, d, and e for the fields Manufacturer and Color. To do this, one member of the group must create an Excel spreadsheet named **a02m3Manufacturers**, which contains all the manufacturers found in the Inventory table. Another member of the group must create an Excel spreadsheet named **a02m3Colors**, which contains all the colors found in the Inventory table. Both of these Excel spreadsheets must be saved to the Exploring Access folder created in step a so all members can access the data.

g. Create relationships between the tables based on common fields. Take a screen shot of the Relationships window using the Snipping Tool and paste the image into the Word document. Close the Relationships window.

DISCOVER

h. After all the new tables have been added, each person in the group should create all of the following queries. Make sure the text fields from the supporting tables appear in the queries (not the ID fields). Save each query as noted below. Take a screen shot of the datasheet of each query using the Snipping Tool and paste the image into the Word document.

   1. Display all the phones that are still for sale (SellDate is Null). Save as **qry1 Phones For Sale**.

   2. Display all the phones that are not made by Apple. Save as **qry2 Not Apple Phones**.

   3. List the Manufacturer and Model and asking price of sold phones; also include phones that are less than $50. Sort by asking price; only include tables that are required. Save as **qry3 Phones Sold or less than $50**.

   4. Display the phones that were purchased before 4/1/2012. Exclude the sold phones. Sort by purchase date. Save as **qry4 Obsolete Phones**.

i. Use e-mail or text messaging to communicate with other members in your group if you have any questions.

j. Exit all applications. Submit both the Word document and the database based on your instructor's directions.

Beyond the Classroom

Database Administrator Position

RESEARCH CASE →

FROM SCRATCH

You arrive at Secure Systems, Inc., for a database administrator position interview. After meeting the human resources coordinator, you are given a test to demonstrate your skills in Access. You are asked to create a database from scratch to keep track of all the candidates for the positions currently open at Secure Systems. Use the Internet to search for information about database management. One useful site is published by the federal government's Bureau of Labor Statistics. It compiles an Occupational Outlook Handbook describing various positions, the type of working environment, the education necessary, salary information, and the projected growth. The Web site is http://www.bls.gov/ooh. After researching the database administrator position requirement, create a database using these requirements:

a. Name the database **a02b2Admin_LastFirst**.

b. Create three tables including these fields: Candidates (CandidateID, FirstName, LastName, Phone, Email), JobOpenings (Job OpeningID, JobName, Required Skill, HourlyPayRate, DataPosted, Supervisor), and Interviews (InterviewSequenceID, CandidateID, JobOpeningID, InterviewedBy, DateOfInterview, Rank).

c. Set the table relationships.

d. Add 10 candidates—yourself and 9 other students in your class.

e. Add the Database Administrator job and four other sample jobs.

f. Add eight sample interviews—four for the Database Administrator position and four others. Rank each candidate on a scale of 1 to 5 (5 is highest).

g. Create a query that lists the LastName, FirstName, JobOpeningID, InterviewedBy, DateofInterview, and Rank fields. Display only Database Administrator interviews with a ranking of 4 or 5. Sort by last name and first name. Run the query.

h. Compact and repair the database. Close Access. Submit based on your instructor's directions.

May Beverage Sales

DISASTER RECOVERY +

A coworker called you into his office, explained that he was having difficulty with Microsoft Access 2013, and asked you to look at his work. Open *a02b3Traders* and save it as **a02b3Traders_LastFirst**. It contains two queries, *May 2015 Orders of Beverages and Confections* and *2015 Beverage Sales by Ship Country*. The May 2015 Orders of Beverages and Confections query is supposed to have only information from May 2015. You find other dates included in the results. Change the criteria to exclude the other dates. The 2015 Beverage Sales by Ship Country query returns no results. Check the criteria in all fields and modify so that the correct results are returned. After you find and correct the error(s), compact and repair the database. Close Access. Submit based on your instructor's directions.

Conflict Database

SOFT SKILLS S

After watching the Conflict: Sexual Harassment video, search the Web for the Equal Employment Opportunities Commission (EEOC) government site. Open the EEOC site and read the *About EEOC: Overview* information. Open a Word document and save it as **a02b4Harrassment_Answers_LastFirst**. Type a paragraph about the responsibilities of the EEOC.

Locate the *EEOC Laws, Regulations, Guidance & MOUs* page. The *Discrimination by Type* section includes a list of hyperlinks to discrimination type pages—pages that include laws, regulations and policy guidance, and also fact sheets, Q&As, best practices, and other information organized by basis of discrimination. Select a discrimination link and review the material on the page. Type two to three additional paragraphs in the Word document to summarize what you have read. Be sure to use good grammar, punctuation, and spelling in your document. Save the Word document and submit based on your instructor's directions.

Capstone Exercise

The Morris Arboretum in Chestnut Hill, Pennsylvania, tracks donors in Excel. They also use Excel to store a list of plants in stock. As donors contribute funds to the Arboretum, they can elect to receive a plant gift from the Arboretum. These plants are both rare plants and hard-to-find old favorites, and they are part of the annual appeal and membership drive to benefit the Arboretum's programs. The organization has grown, and the files are too large and inefficient to handle in Excel. Your task will be to begin the conversion of the files from Excel to Access.

Create a New Database

You need to examine the data in the Excel worksheets to determine which fields will become the primary keys in each table and which fields will become the foreign keys. Primary and foreign keys are used to form the relationships between tables.

a. Open the *a02c1Donors* Excel workbook.

b. Open the *a02c1Plants* Excel workbook.

c. Examine the data in each worksheet and identify the column that will become the primary key in an Access table. Identify the foreign keys in each table.

d. Create a new, blank database named **a02c1Arbor_ LastFirst**.

Create a New Table

Use the new blank table created automatically by Access to hold the donations as they are received from the donors.

a. Switch to Design view and save the table as **Donations**.

b. Add the remaining field names in Design view. Note: The data for this table will be added later in this exercise.

- Change *ID* to **DonationID** with the **AutoNumber Data Type**.

- Add **DonorID** (a foreign key) with the **Number Data Type** and a field size of **Long Integer**.

- Add **PlantID** (a foreign key) as **Number Data** and a field size of **Long Integer**.

- Enter two additional fields with an appropriate data type and field properties. Hint: You need the date of donation and the amount of donation.

c. Verify the primary key is *DonationID*.

d. Save the table. Close the table.

Import Data from Excel

You need to use the Import Spreadsheet Data Wizard twice to import a worksheet from each Excel workbook into Access. You need to select the worksheets, specify the primary keys, set the indexing option, and name the newly imported tables (see Figures 2.12 through 2.17).

a. Click the **EXTERNAL DATA tab** and click **Excel** in the Import & Link group.

b. Locate and select the *a02c1Donors* workbook.

c. Set the DonorID field Indexed option to **Yes (No Duplicates)**.

d. Select **DonorID** as the primary key when prompted.

e. Accept the table name *Donors*.

f. Import the *a02c1Plants* file, set the **ID field** as the primary key, and then change the indexing option to **Yes (No Duplicates)**.

g. Accept the table name *Plants*.

h. Open each table in Datasheet view to examine the data.

i. Change the ID field name in the Plants table to **PlantID**.

Create Relationships

You need to create the relationships between the tables using the Relationships window. Identify the primary key fields in each table and connect them with their foreign key counterparts in related tables. Enforce referential integrity and cascade and update related fields.

a. Open the Donors table in Design view and change the Field Size property for DonorID to **Long Integer** so it matches the Field Size property of DonorID in the Donations table.

b. Open the Plants table in Design view and change the Field Size property for PlantID to **Long Integer** so it matches the Field Size property for PlantID in the Donations table.

c. Close the open tables and open the Relationships window.

d. Add the three tables to the Relationships window using the Show Table dialog box. Close the Show Tables dialog box.

e. Drag the **DonorID field** in the Donors table onto the DonorID field in the Donations table. Enforce referential integrity and cascade and update related fields. Drag the **PlantID field** from the Plants table onto the PlantID field of the Donations table. Enforce referential integrity and check the **Cascade Update Related Fields option**.

f. Close the Relationships window and save your changes.

Add Sample Data to the Donations Table

Add 10 records to the Donations table.

a. Add the following records to the Donations table.

Donation ID	Donor ID	Plant ID	Date Of Donation	Amount Of Donation
10	8228	611	3/1/2015	$150
18	5448	190	3/1/2015	$15
6	4091	457	3/12/2015	$125
7	11976	205	3/14/2015	$100
1	1000	25	3/17/2015	$120
12	1444	38	3/19/2015	$50
2	1444	38	4/3/2015	$50
4	10520	49	4/12/2015	$460
5	3072	102	4/19/2015	$450
21	1204	25	4/22/2015	$120

b. Sort the Donations table by the AmountOfDonation field in descending order.

Use the Query Wizard

Use the Query Wizard to create a query of all donations greater than $100 in the Donations table. Use the following guidelines:

a. Include the DonorID and AmountOfDonation fields.

b. Name the query **Donations Over 100**.

c. Add criteria to include only donations of more than $100.

d. Sort by ascending AmountOfDonation.

e. Save and close the query.

Create a Query in Design View

You need to create a query that identifies the people who made a donation after April 1, 2015. The query should list the date of the donation, donor's full name (LastName, FirstName), phone number, the amount of the donation, and name of the plant they want. Sort the query by date of donation, then by donor last name. This list will be given to the Arboretum staff so they can notify the donors that a plant is ready for pickup.

a. Click the **CREATE tab** and click **Query Design** in the Queries group.

b. Add the tables and fields necessary to produce the query as stated previously. Name the query **Plant Pickup List**.

c. Run and print the query from Datasheet view.

Modify a Query in Design View

a. Copy the Plant Pickup List query on the Navigation Pane and paste it using **ENewsletter** as the query name.

b. Open the ENewsletter query in Design view and delete the DateofDonation column.

c. Add the ENewsletter field to the design and set it to sort in Ascending order. Position the ENewsletter field on the grid so that the query sorts first by ENewsletter and then by LastName.

d. Compact and repair the database. Close Access.

e. Submit based on your instructor's directions.

Customize, Analyze, and Summarize Query Data

Yuri Arcurs/Shutterstock

CHAPTER

3

Creating and Using Queries to Make Decisions

OBJECTIVES | AFTER YOU READ THIS CHAPTER, YOU WILL BE ABLE TO:

1. Create a calculated field in a query p. 212
2. Format and save calculated results p. 215
3. Create expressions with the Expression Builder p. 223

4. Use built-in functions in Access p. 225
5. Add aggregate functions to datasheets p. 233
6. Create queries with aggregate functions p. 234

CASE STUDY | Housing Slump Means Opportunity for College Students

Two students from Passaic County Community College (PCCC) decided they would take advantage of the declining housing market. After taking several business courses at PCCC and a weekend seminar in real estate investing, Donald Carter and Matthew Nevoso were ready to test their skills in the marketplace. Don and Matt had a simple strategy—buy distressed properties at a significant discount, then resell the properties for a profit one year later when the market rebounds.

As they drove through the surrounding neighborhoods, if they noticed a For Sale sign in a yard, they would call the listing agent and ask for the key information such as the asking price, the number of bedrooms, square feet, and days on the market. Because they were just starting out, they decided to target houses that were priced at $150,000 or below and only houses that had been on the market at least six months.

For the first two months, they gathered lots of information and began to get a feel for the houses and prices in the area. Some neighborhoods were definitely more distressed than others! But they still had not made any offers. The two PCCC investors realized they needed a more scientific approach to finding an investment property. Based on a tip from the real estate seminar, they decide to create a database using Access 2013, using data from free lists of homes for sale. They would then like to use Access to help them find houses that meet their criteria. Once the data is in Access, you can help Don and Matt easily identify the qualifying properties. This new database approach should help them become more successful and hopefully help them acquire their first investment property.

Calculations and Expressions

One reason you might choose Excel over a program like Word is for the ability to perform calculations. At first glance, you may not see an obvious location for you to enter a calculation in Access. However, Access includes many of the same built-in calculations and functions that Excel does.

So, why do you need to create calculated fields? Similar to Excel, there are going to be times when you have to process data into information. For example, it could be as simple as needing to calculate a paycheck amount. If you have one field storing the number of hours worked and another field storing the hourly pay rate, you would be able to multiply them together to get the total amount the person is owed. Basic calculations such as these can be done using a query, so you do not have to rely on doing calculations by hand, which can lead to mistakes.

Unfortunately, calculations may not always be that easy. We did not consider some of the common deductions, such as Social Security, Medicare/FICA, federal and state income taxes, unemployment insurance, and possibly union dues. Some of these may be a flat rate, and others may be calculated based on your paycheck amount.

Expressions go beyond simple mathematical functions. Access includes extremely powerful logical functions as well. For example, your employees will claim a certain number of allowances. Based on the number of allowances an employee claims, the amount deducted from the paycheck will be different. This advanced topic will not be covered in this chapter.

When working with Access, there will be times when you need to create arithmetic calculations—using expressions and functions—in your database. In Access 2013, you can add calculations to tables, queries, forms, and reports. Often, rather than storing a calculated value, you would instead store the components of it and calculate the field when necessary. For example, if you have a list price and amount ordered, you would not need to also store the total amount due, because this is the list price multiplied by the amount ordered. Calculating fields rather than storing them will reduce the likelihood of errors and inconsistencies and also save space, as you are storing less information.

In this section, you will learn about the order of operations and how to create a calculated field in a query.

Creating a Calculated Field in a Query

When creating a query, in addition to using fields from tables, you may also need to create a calculation based on the fields from one or more tables. For example, a table might contain the times when employees clock in and out of work. You could create a calculated field (as defined in an earlier chapter) to determine, or calculate, how many hours each employee worked by subtracting the ClockIn field from the ClockOut field. You create calculated fields in the Design view of a query. A formula used to calculate new fields from the values in existing fields is known as an *expression*. An expression can consist of a number of different elements to produce the desired output. The elements used in an expression may include the following:

- Identifiers (the names of fields, controls, or properties)
- Arithmetic operators (for example, *, /, +, or –)
- Functions (built-in functions like Date or Pmt)
- Values that do not change, known as *constants* (numbers such as 30 or 0.5)

You can use calculations to create a new value based on an existing field, verify data entered, set grouping levels in reports, or help set query criteria.

Understand the Order of Operations

The *order of operations* determines the sequence by which operations are calculated in an expression. You may remember PEMDAS from a math class, or the mnemonic device "Please Excuse My Dear Aunt Sally." Evaluate expressions in parentheses first, then exponents, then multiplication and division, and, finally, addition and subtraction. Table 3.1 shows some examples of the order of operations. You must have a solid understanding of these rules in order to create calculated fields in Access. Access, like Excel, uses the following symbols:

- Parentheses   ( )
- Exponentiation   ^
- Multiplication   *
- Division   /
- Addition   +
- Subtraction   –

TABLE 3.1   Examples of Order of Operations

Expression	Order to Perform Calculations	Output
=2+3*3	Multiply first and then add.	11
=(2+3)*3	Add the values inside the parentheses first and then multiply.	15
=2+2^3	Evaluate the exponent first, $2^3=2*2*2$ (or 8). Then add.	10
=10/2+3	Divide first and then add.	8
=10/(2+3)	Add first to simplify the parenthetical expression and then divide.	2
=10*2–3*2	Multiply first and then subtract.	14

Build Expressions with Correct Syntax

Expressions are entered in the first row of the query design grid. You must follow the correct *syntax*, which dictates the structure and components required to perform the necessary calculations in an equation or evaluate expressions. You can create expressions to perform calculations using field names, constants, and functions. If you use a field name, such as Balance, in an expression, you must spell the field name correctly; otherwise, Access displays an error. Access ignores spaces in calculations.

For example, if you worked at a company that was planning on allowing customers to pay off their balance in 12 monthly payments, you would divide the balance by 12. However, let's say you wanted to add a 3.5% surcharge. In this case, you would multiply the balance by 0.035 (3.5%) and then divide that total by 12. An example of an expression with correct syntax is:

STEP 1

Balance*0.035/12

If you type the preceding function into a line in a query and save the query, you may be surprised to see Access add a few things to the line (see Figure 3.1):

Expr1: [Balance]*0.035/12

Access made a few changes to your entry. First, it removed extra spaces. Secondly, Access added brackets [ ] around the Balance field, which Access uses to indicate a field name. In addition, you see that Access added *Expr1:* to the start of the line. This is how Access assigns a column heading to this field. If you were to run the query, the column heading would be *Expr1*. As this is not a descriptive name, it would probably be better to include your own title. If you wanted to name this column MonthlySurcharge, you would start the expression with the name, followed by a colon, followed by the expression:

MonthlySurcharge: Balance*0.035/12

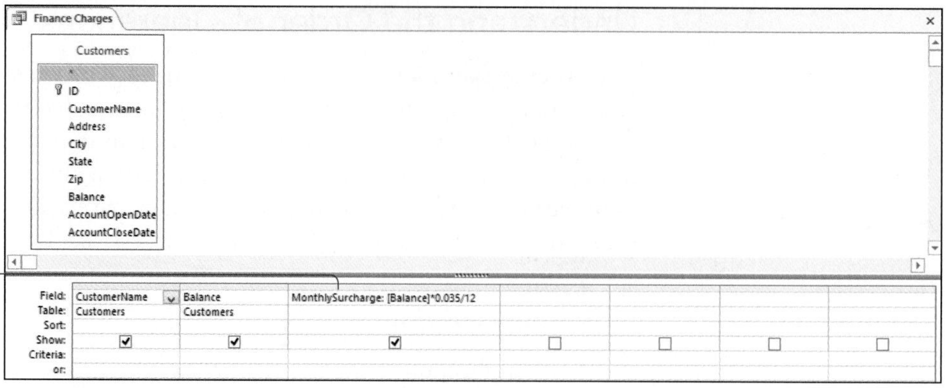

Field calculates monthly surcharge

FIGURE 3.1 Calculated Field in a Query Design

TIP Avoid Spaces in Calculated Field Names

Although you can use spaces in calculated field names, it is a good habit not to use spaces. For example, use NewPrice: [Price]*1.1 rather than New Price: [Price]*1.1. If you avoid spaces in calculated field names, it will be easier to reference these fields in other queries, related forms, and related reports. If you want a column heading to have spaces in it, you should set the Caption property, which will be discussed later in this section.

Again, if you saved the query, Access would add brackets around the Balance field.

In calculated fields, the parts of the formula are usually a constant (for example, 0.035 and 12 in the preceding example), a field name (for example, Balance), or another calculated field. Figure 3.1 shows the MonthlySurcharge field, calculated by multiplying the Balance field by 0.035 (or 3.5%) and dividing by 12. This calculation shows what a customer would pay as a monthly surcharge if you offered him or her the monthly payments and added a 3.5% fee.

The arithmetic operators, the * symbol (multiply) and the / symbol (divide), first multiply [Balance] by 0.035 and then divide the result by 12. There is no real issue in this example with order of operations because the order of operations states that multiplication and division are at the same level of precedence. In other words, if you state 12*3/3, whether you do the multiplication or division first, the result will be exactly the same (12).

The query results, as shown in Figure 3.2, display a decimal number in the MonthlySurcharge column. Notice the results are not formatted well. This will be addressed later in this section.

Finance Charges

CustomerName	Balance	MonthlySurcharge
Terri Mccoy	$24,286.00	70.8341666666667
Willie Mann	$47,041.00	137.202916666667
Michael Warren	$26,888.00	78.4233333333333
Tammy Mason	$28,255.00	82.4104166666667
Ashley Smith	$38,108.00	111.148333333333
Paul Johnson	$38,664.00	112.77
Leroy Morrison	$8,070.00	23.5375
Phyllis Daniel	$19,166.00	55.9008333333333
Ryan Weaver	$34,000.00	99.1666666666667
Aaron Jordan	$39,889.00	116.342916666667
Howard Hernandez	$2,296.00	6.69666666666667
Francisco Byrd	$17,146.00	50.0091666666667
Jacob Santos	$49,218.00	143.5525
Willie Anderson	$40,940.00	119.408333333333
Oscar Porter	$12,064.00	35.1866666666667
Evelyn Moore	$42,199.00	123.080416666667
Cheryl Carr	$40,620.00	118.475
Ana Keller	$49,509.00	144.40125
Glenn Brewer	$24,820.00	72.3916666666667
Peter Dean	$48,987.00	142.87875
Sheila Turner	$32,572.00	95.0016666666667
Jason Rodgers	$28,864.00	84.1866666666667
Joel Gonzales	$31,350.00	91.4375
Dolores Hayes	$13,745.00	40.0895833333333
Nancy Daniels	$4,639.00	13.5304166666667
Vivian Cannon	$24,358.00	71.0441666666667

MonthlySurcharge shows many digits

FIGURE 3.2 Results of a Calculated Field in a Query

Another example of when to use a calculated field is calculating a price increase for a product or service. Suppose you need to calculate a 10% price increase on certain products you sell. You could name the calculated field NewPrice and use the expression (CurrentPrice) + (CurrentPrice × 0.10). The first segment represents the current price, and the second segment adds an additional 10%. (Recall that to get 10% of a number, you would multiply by 0.10.) The expression would be entered into the query design grid as follows:

NewPrice: [CurrentPrice] + [CurrentPrice]*0.10

Note that if you are adept at math, you may find other ways to calculate this increase.

> ## TIP Use Zoom (Shift+F2) to View Long Expressions
>
> To see the entire calculated field expression, click the field in Query Design view and press Shift+F2. A new window will appear to enable you to easily see and edit the entire contents of the cell. Access refers to this window as the Zoom dialog box, as shown in Figure 3.3.
>
> Zoom can also be used in a number of other contexts. If you are ever having trouble viewing the entirety of a text box, try using Shift+F2 to expand it. Once you are done modifying a field, click the X in the top-right corner of the Zoom dialog box.

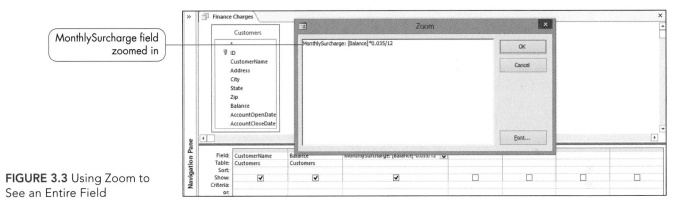

MonthlySurcharge field zoomed in

FIGURE 3.3 Using Zoom to See an Entire Field

Formatting and Saving Calculated Results

In the previous example, we saw inconsistent results in the formatting, with some results showing only two decimal places and others showing many decimal places. In Figure 3.2, the MonthlySurcharge field was extremely difficult to read. Part of the purpose of queries is to perform calculations, but an overlooked portion of that is the formatting. You can create a clever calculation, but if it is not labeled and formatted correctly, it may leave your users confused. Spending a few moments formatting your output will make your query more usable.

There is a way to give Access instructions as to how to format the field. You can use the **Property Sheet** to do so. The Property Sheet enables you to change settings such as number format, number of decimal places, and caption, among many others. You can select a predefined format (for example, currency), change the number of decimal places, and also change the caption, as you did in the earlier chapter on tables. To format the calculated results:

STEP 2»
1. Open the query in Design view.
2. Click in the calculated field cell (the cell you just created).
3. On the QUERY TOOLS DESIGN tab, click Property Sheet in the Show/Hide group.
4. To change the format, click the *Format property* arrow and select your desired format. For numeric fields, the Decimal Places property will allow you to choose exactly how many decimal places display.

5. To change the caption, click in the text box next to the caption and type your desired column heading. This will override the column name, much like the caption property does for a field name in a table, as shown in a previous chapter.

Formats vary based on the data type. A currency field will have options related to number format, whereas a date/time field will have options related to changing the display of the date and/or time. Figure 3.4 shows the Property Sheet options related to a numeric field.

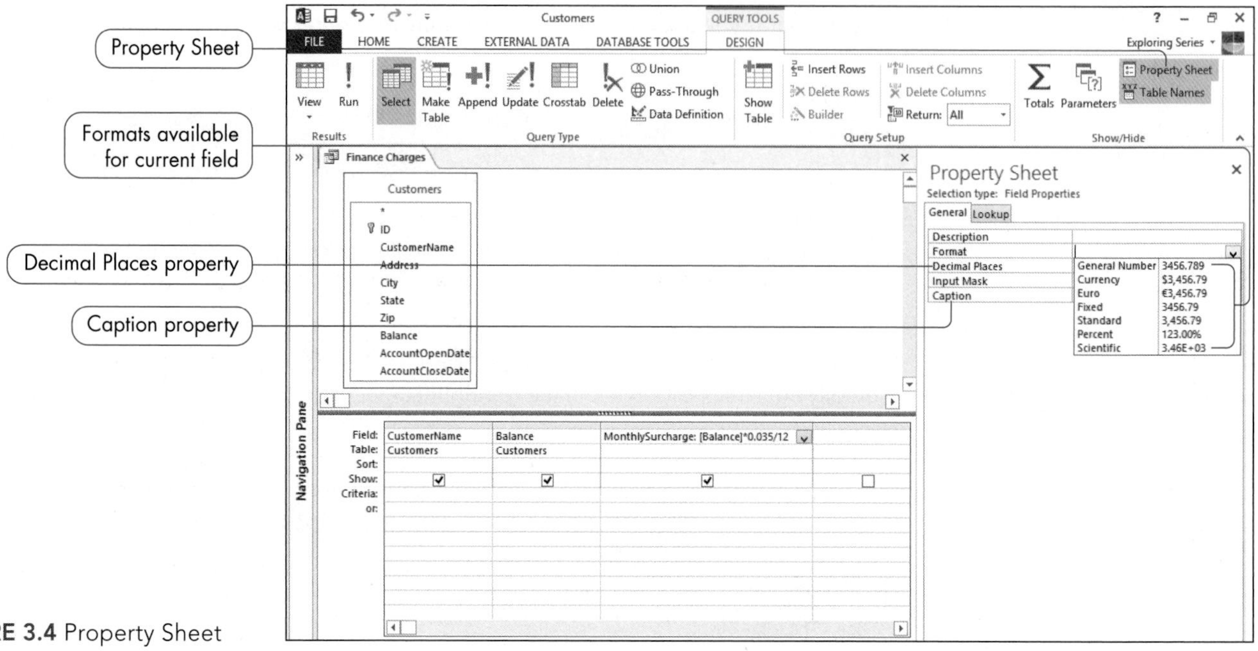

FIGURE 3.4 Property Sheet

Recover from Common Errors

A number of common errors can occur while creating calculated fields. Access may not provide as much assistance as you may be used to in cases like this. The following are three common errors that occur when you begin creating formulas.

STEP 3 ▶▶

- Forgetting the colon between the column title and the formula
  - A correct formula would look like this:

    Expr1: [Balance]*0.035/12

    If you forget the colon, the formula looks like this instead:

    Expr1 [Balance]*0.035/12

    and you will get an error about invalid syntax.
- Typing a field name incorrectly
  - If your field name is Balance and you mistype it, you will not get an error until you attempt to run the query. You may end up with a formula that looks like this:

    Expr1: [Baalnce]*0.035/12

  - When you run the query, you will be prompted by Access to give a value for Baalnce.
- Forgetting the order of operations
  - If you do not check your formulas, you may get bad values. For example, the following would not produce the expected output:

    Expr2: [NumberOfDays] + 7/365

  - If you need addition to be done before division, you must remember the parentheses:

    Expr2: ([NumberOfDays] + 7)/365

Verify Calculated Results

STEP 4 » After your query runs, look at the field values in the Datasheet view and look at the calculated values. Ask yourself, "Does the data make sense?" Assume you are calculating a mortgage payment for a $300,000 house, with monthly payments for 20 years. If your formula is incorrect, you may end up calculating a monthly payment such as $30,000. If you look at your data, you should say to yourself, "Does it make sense for me to pay $30,000 a month for a mortgage?" or perhaps "Does it make sense that, on a $300,000 loan, my total repayment is $7,200,000 ($30,000 a month times 12 months a year times 20 years)?" In a real-world scenario, you will not be given step-by-step directions, and you will need to apply critical thinking skills to your work. Access will calculate exactly what you tell it to calculate, even if you make logical errors in the calculation. Although it will catch some errors, it will not catch or note logic errors.

Use a calculator to manually calculate some of the results in the calculated fields and compare the answers to the datasheet results. Another method to verify the results is to copy and paste all or part of the datasheet into Excel. Recreate the calculations in Excel and compare the answers to the query results in Access. The Access calculated field, the calculator, and the Excel calculations should all return identical results.

In the first Hands-On Exercise, you will create a query with a calculated field, format the results, learn how to recover from common errors, and verify your results.

Quick
Concepts ✓

1. Briefly describe the order of operations. Give an example of how order of operations makes a difference in a calculation. *p. 213*

2. When might you need a calculated field in a query? Give an example. *p. 212*

3. Define syntax. How does Access respond to incorrect syntax? *p. 213*

4. Why is it important to verify calculated results? *p. 217*

Hands-On Exercises

Watch the Video for this Hands-On Exercise!

MyITLab®
HOE1 Training

1 Calculations and Expressions

Using the data from the homes for sale lists that Don and Matt acquired, you are able to help them target properties that meet their criteria. As you examine the data, you discover other ways to analyze the properties. You create several queries and present your results to the two investors for their comments.

Skills covered: Create a Query with a Calculated Field • Format and Save Calculated Results • Recover from Common Errors • Verify the Calculated Results

STEP 1 ≫ CREATE A QUERY WITH A CALCULATED FIELD

You begin your analysis by creating a query using the Properties and Agents tables. The Properties table contains all the properties the investors will evaluate; the Agents table contains a list of real estate agents who represent the properties' sellers. In this exercise, add the fields you need and only show properties that have not been sold. Refer to Figure 3.5 as you complete Step 1.

Price Per Sq Ft

First Name	Last Name	List Price	Square Feet	Sold	PricePerSqFt
StudentFirst	StudentLast	$109,140.00	1133	No	96.3283318623124
Bill	Sabey	$119,990.00	1202	No	99.8252911813644
Anny	Almonte	$122,220.00	1235	No	98.9635627530364
Robert Allen	Dickey	$129,780.00	1132	No	114.646643109541
Bill	Sabey	$136,680.00	1375	No	99.4036363636364
Karean	Eissler	$138,990.00	1276	No	108.926332288401
Anny	Almonte	$140,693.00	1490	No	94.4248322147651
Karean	Eissler	$140,904.00	1301	No	108.304381245196
Anny	Almonte	$150,200.00	1652	No	90.9200968523002
StudentFirst	StudentLast	$163,737.00	1476	No	110.932926829268
StudentFirst	StudentLast	$164,436.00	1850	No	88.8843243243243
Pradeep	Rana	$166,530.00	1676	No	99.3615751789976
StudentFirst	StudentLast	$166,552.00	1623	No	102.619839802834
Anny	Almonte	$166,800.00	1598	No	104.380475594493
Anny	Almonte	$168,354.00	1651	No	101.970926711084
StudentFirst	StudentLast	$168,504.00	1625	No	103.694769230769
Anny	Almonte	$172,458.00	1798	No	95.916573971079
Bill	Sabey	$174,230.00	1771	No	98.3794466403162
StudentFirst	StudentLast	$174,720.00	1694	No	103.140495867769
Robert Allen	Dickey	$174,720.00	1610	No	108.521739130435
Anny	Almonte	$174,720.00	1667	No	104.811037792442
Robert Allen	Dickey	$175,560.00	1562	No	112.394366197183
StudentFirst	StudentLast	$177,984.00	1707	No	104.267135325132
Bill	Sabey	$179,712.00	1854	No	96.9320388349515
Bill	Sabey	$182,385.00	2014	No	90.5585898709037
Anny	Almonte	$183,312.00	1721	No	106.51481696688
Anny	Almonte	$184,473.00	1791	No	103

Record: 1 of 213 | No Filter | Search

Step i: Sorted in ascending order by ListPrice field

Step h: Only unsold properties shown

Step j: 213 records

FIGURE 3.5 Query Results for Properties NOT Sold

a. Open *a03h1Property*. Save the database as **a03h1Property_LastFirst**.

> **TROUBLESHOOTING:** Throughout the remainder of this chapter and textbook, click Enable Content whenever you are working with student files.

> **TROUBLESHOOTING:** If you make any major mistakes in this exercise, you can delete the *a03h1Property_LastFirst* file, repeat step a above, and then start this exercise over.

b. Open the Agents table and replace *Angela Scott* with your name. Close the table.

c. Click the **CREATE tab** and click **Query Design** in the Queries group to create a new query.

The Show Table dialog box opens so you can specify the table(s) and/or queries to include in the query design.

d. Select the **Agents table** and click **Add**. Select the **Properties table** and click **Add**. Close the Show Table dialog box.

e. Double-click the **FirstName** and **LastName fields** in the Agents table to add them to the design grid.

f. Double-click the **ListPrice, SqFeet,** and **Sold fields** in the Properties table to add them to the query design grid.

g. Click **Run** in the Results group to display the results in Datasheet view.

You should see 303 properties in the results.

h. Switch to Design view. Type **No** in the Criteria row of the Sold field.

i. Select **Ascending** from the Sort row of the ListPrice field.

j. Click **Run** to see the results.

You only want to see properties that were not sold. There should now be 213 properties in the datasheet.

k. Click **Save** on the Quick Access Toolbar and type **Price Per Sq Ft** as the Query Name in the Save As dialog box. Click **OK**.

l. Switch to Design view. Click in the top row of the first blank column of the query design grid and use **Shift+F2** to show the Zoom dialog box. Type **PricePerSqFt: ListPrice/SqFeet** and click **OK**.

Access inserts square brackets around the fields for you. The new field divides the values in the ListPrice field by the values in the SqFeet field. The : after *PricePerSqFt* is required.

m. Click **Run** in the Results group to view the results.

The new calculated field, PricePerSqFt, is displayed. Compare your results to those shown in Figure 3.5.

> **TROUBLESHOOTING:** If you see pound signs (#####) in an Access column, use the vertical lines between column indicators to increase the width.

> **TROUBLESHOOTING:** If, when you run the query, you are prompted for PricePerSqFt, cancel and return to Design view. Ensure you have entered the formula from step l to the field line of the query, not the criteria line.

---

n. Save the changes to the query and close the query.

Don and Matt would like the field formatted differently. You will change the format to Currency and add a caption to the calculated field. Refer to Figure 3.6 as you complete Step 2.

> Steps d–e: PricePerSqFt field formatted as Currency with added caption

First Name	Last Name	List Price	Square Feet	Sold	Price Per Sq Ft
StudentFirst	StudentLast	$109,140.00	1133	No	$96.33
Bill	Sabey	$119,990.00	1202	No	$99.83
Anny	Almonte	$122,220.00	1235	No	$98.96
Robert Allen	Dickey	$129,780.00	1132	No	$114.65
Bill	Sabey	$136,680.00	1375	No	$99.40
Karean	Eissler	$138,990.00	1276	No	$108.93
Anny	Almonte	$140,693.00	1490	No	$94.42
Karean	Eissler	$140,904.00	1301	No	$108.30
Anny	Almonte	$150,200.00	1652	No	$90.92
StudentFirst	StudentLast	$163,737.00	1476	No	$110.93
StudentFirst	StudentLast	$164,436.00	1850	No	$88.88
Pradeep	Rana	$166,530.00	1676	No	$99.36
StudentFirst	StudentLast	$166,552.00	1623	No	$102.62
Anny	Almonte	$166,800.00	1598	No	$104.38
Anny	Almonte	$168,354.00	1651	No	$101.97
StudentFirst	StudentLast	$168,504.00	1625	No	$103.69
Anny	Almonte	$172,458.00	1798	No	$95.92
Bill	Sabey	$174,230.00	1771	No	$98.38
StudentFirst	StudentLast	$174,720.00	1694	No	$103.14
Robert Allen	Dickey	$174,720.00	1610	No	$108.52
Anny	Almonte	$174,720.00	1667	No	$104.81
Robert Allen	Dickey	$175,560.00	1562	No	$112.39
StudentFirst	StudentLast	$177,984.00	1707	No	$104.27
Bill	Sabey	$179,712.00	1854	No	$96.93
Bill	Sabey	$182,385.00	2014	No	$90.56
Anny	Almonte	$183,312.00	1721	No	$106.51
Anny	Almonte	$184,473.00	1791	No	$103.00

FIGURE 3.6 Results of Calculated Field Creation

a. Make a copy of the Price Per Sq Ft query. Name the copy **Price Per Sq Ft Formatted**.

b. Open the Price Per Sq Ft Formatted query in Design view.

c. Click in the **PricePerSqFt calculated field cell**. Click **Property Sheet** in the Show/Hide group on the DESIGN tab.

The Property Sheet displays on the right side of your screen.

d. Click the **Format box**. Click the **Format property arrow** and select **Currency**.

e. Click in the **Caption box** and type **Price Per Sq Ft**. Press **Enter**. Close the Property Sheet.

f. Click **Run** to view your changes.

The calculated field values are formatted as Currency, and the column heading displays *Price Per Sq Ft* instead of *PricePerSqFt*.

g. Save the changes to the query.

STEP 3 » RECOVER FROM COMMON ERRORS

A few errors arise as you test the new calculated fields. You check the spelling of the field names in the calculated fields because that is a common mistake. Refer to Figure 3.7 as you complete Step 3.

First Name	Last Name	List Price	Square Feet	Sold	Price Per Sq Ft	Wrong Price Per Sq Ft
StudentFirst	StudentLast	$109,140.00	1133	No	$96.33	$100.00
Bill	Sabey	$119,990.00	1202	No	$99.83	$100.00
Anny	Almonte	$122,220.00	1235	No	$98.96	$100.00
Robert Allen	Dickey	$129,780.00	1132	No	$114.65	$100.00
Bill	Sabey	$136,680.00	1375	No	$99.40	$100.00
Karean	Eissler	$138,990.00	1276	No	$108.93	$100.00
Anny	Almonte	$140,693.00	1490	No	$94.42	$100.00
Karean	Eissler	$140,904.00	1301	No	$108.30	$100.00
Anny	Almonte	$150,200.00	1652	No	$90.92	$100.00
StudentFirst	StudentLast	$163,737.00	1476	No	$110.93	$100.00
StudentFirst	StudentLast	$164,436.00	1850	No	$88.88	$100.00
Pradeep	Rana	$166,530.00	1676	No	$99.36	$100.00
StudentFirst	StudentLast	$166,552.00	1623	No	$102.62	$100.00
Anny	Almonte	$166,800.00	1598	No	$104.38	$100.00
Anny	Almonte	$168,354.00	1651	No	$101.97	$100.00
StudentFirst	StudentLast	$168,504.00	1625	No	$103.69	$100.00
Anny	Almonte	$172,458.00	1798	No	$95.92	$100.00
Bill	Sabey	$174,230.00	1771	No	$98.38	$100.00
StudentFirst	StudentLast	$174,720.00	1694	No	$103.14	$100.00
Robert Allen	Dickey	$174,720.00	1610	No	$108.52	$100.00
Anny	Almonte	$174,720.00	1667	No	$104.81	$100.00
Robert Allen	Dickey	$175,560.00	1562	No	$112.39	$100.00
StudentFirst	StudentLast	$177,984.00	1707	No	$104.27	$100.00
Bill	Sabey	$179,712.00	1854	No	$96.93	$100.00
Bill	Sabey	$182,385.00	2014	No	$90.56	$100.00
Anny	Almonte	$183,312.00	1721	No	$106.51	$100.00
Anny	Almonte	$184,473.00	1791	No	$103.00	$100.00

Record: 1 of 213 — No Filter — Search

Step g: Same results ($100.00) for every record

FIGURE 3.7 Results of a Misspelled Field Name

a. Switch to Design view of the Price Per Sq Ft Formatted query. Scroll to the first blank column of the query design grid and click in the top row.

b. Use **Shift+F2** to display the Zoom dialog box. Type **WrongPricePerSqFt: xListPrice/ xSqFeet**. Click the **OK button** in the Zoom dialog box.

Be sure that you added the extra *x*'s to the field names. You are intentionally misspelling the field names to see how Access will respond. Access inserts square brackets around the field names for you.

c. Click **Property Sheet** in the Show/Hide group of the DESIGN tab. Click the **Format box**. From the menu, select **Currency**. Click in the **Caption box** and type **Wrong Price Per Sq Ft**. Close the Property Sheet.

d. Click **Run** in the Results group.

You should see the Enter Parameter Value dialog box. The dialog box indicates that Access does not recognize xListPrice in the tables defined for this query in the first record. When Access does not recognize a field name, it will ask you to supply a value.

e. Type **100000** in the first parameter box. Press **Enter** or click **OK**.

Another Enter Parameter Value dialog box displays, asking that you supply a value for xSqFeet. Again, this error occurs because the tables defined for this query do not contain an xSqFeet field.

f. Type **1000** in the second parameter box and press **Enter**.

The query has the necessary information to run and returns the results in Datasheet view.

g. Examine the results of the calculation for *Wrong Price Per Sq Ft*. You may have to scroll right to see the results.

All of the records show 100 because you entered the values 100000 and 1000, respectively, into the parameter boxes. The two values are treated as constants and give the same results for all the records.

h. Return to Design view. Press **Shift+F2** to zoom. Correct the errors in the WrongPricePerSqFt field by changing the formula to **WrongPricePerSqFt: [ListPrice]/ [SqFeet]**. Click the **Close (X) button** in the top-right corner of the Zoom dialog box to close it.

i. Run and save the query. Close the query.

The calculated values in the last two columns should be the same.

STEP 4 >> VERIFY THE CALCULATED RESULTS

Because you are in charge of the Access database, you decide to verify your data prior to showing it to the investors. You use two methods to check your calculations: estimation and checking your results using Excel. Refer to Figure 3.8 as you complete Step 4.

Step e: Column G results should match first 10 results in column F

	First Name	Last Name	List Price	Square Feet	Sold	PricePerSqFt	
2	StudentFirst	StudentLast	$109,140.00	1133	FALSE	96.32833186	$96.33
3	Bill	Sabey	$119,990.00	1202	FALSE	99.82529118	$99.83
4	Anny	Almonte	$122,220.00	1235	FALSE	98.96356275	$98.96
5	Robert Allen	Dickey	$129,780.00	1132	FALSE	114.6466431	$114.65
6	Bill	Sabey	$136,680.00	1375	FALSE	99.40363636	$99.40
7	Karean	Eissler	$138,990.00	1276	FALSE	108.9263323	$108.93
8	Anny	Almonte	$140,693.00	1490	FALSE	94.42483221	$94.42
9	Karean	Eissler	$140,904.00	1301	FALSE	108.3043812	$108.30
10	Anny	Almonte	$150,200.00	1652	FALSE	90.92009685	$90.92
11	StudentFirst	StudentLast	$163,737.00	1476	FALSE	110.9329268	$110.93

FIGURE 3.8 Results Validated in Excel

a. Open the Price Per Sq Ft query in Datasheet view. Examine the PricePerSqFt field.

One of the ways to verify the accuracy of the calculated data is to ask yourself if the numbers make sense.

b. Locate the second record with *Bill Sabey* as the listing agent, an asking price of *$119,990*, and square footage of *1202*. Ask yourself if the calculated value of *$99.83* makes sense.

The sale price is $119,990, and the square footage is 1202. You can verify the calculated field easily by rounding the two numbers (to 120,000 and 1,200) and dividing the values in your head (120,000 divided by 1,200 = 100) to verify that the calculated value, $99.83 per square foot, makes sense.

TROUBLESHOOTING: If the second record is not the one listed above, ensure you have sorted the query by the List Price in ascending order, as specified in Step 1i.

c. Open a new, blank workbook in Excel and switch to Access. Drag over the record selector for the first 10 records (the tenth record has a list price of $163,737). Click **Copy** in the Clipboard group on the HOME tab.

You will verify the calculation in the first 10 records by pasting the results in Excel.

d. Switch to Excel and, click **Paste** in the Clipboard group on the HOME tab.

The field names display in the first row, and the 10 records display in the next 10 rows. The fields are located in columns A–F. The calculated field results are pasted in column F as values rather than as a formula.

TROUBLESHOOTING: If you see pound signs (#####) in an Excel column, use the vertical lines between column indicators to increase the width.

e. Type **=C2/D2** in **cell G2** and press **Enter**. Copy the formula from **cell G2** and paste it into **cells G3 to G11**.

The formula divides the list price by the square feet. Compare the results in columns F and G. The numbers should be the same, except for a slight difference due to rounding.

TROUBLESHOOTING: If the values differ, look at both the Excel and Access formulas. Determine which is correct, and then find and fix the error in the incorrect formula.

f. Save the Excel workbook as **a03Property_LastFirst**. Exit Excel.

g. Keep the database open if you plan to continue with the next Hands-On Exercise. If not, close the database and exit Access.

The Expression Builder and Functions

In the last Hands-On Exercise, you calculated the price per square foot for real estate properties. That simple calculation helped you to evaluate all the properties on the investment list. You were able to type the expression manually.

When you encounter more complex expressions, you can use the ***Expression Builder*** tool to help you create more complicated expressions. When you create an expression in the field cell, you must increase the column width to see the entire expression. The Expression Builder's size enables you to easily see complex formulas and functions in their entirety. In addition, it provides easy access to objects, operators, functions, and explanations for functions.

In this section, you will learn how to create expressions using the Expression Builder. You also will learn how to use built-in functions.

Creating Expressions with the Expression Builder

Launch the Expression Builder while in the query design grid to assist with creating a calculated field (or other expression). (See "Launch the Expression Builder" later in this section for directions.) The Expression Builder helps you create expressions by supplying you with the fields, operators, and functions you need to create them. When you use the Expression Builder to help you create expressions, you can eliminate spelling errors in field names. Another advantage is when you are inserting functions; functions require specific arguments in a specific order. When you insert a function using the Expression Builder, the builder gives you placeholders that tell you which values belong where.

You may not always need the Expression Builder. As you become familiar with programs like Access, some of the more common tasks may become second nature to you. Rather than clicking to find what you need, you may be able to do your day-to-day work without the aid of the Expression Builder. However, when working with a less familiar calculation, having this tool gives you extra support.

Though you will learn about the Expression Builder in queries in this chapter, this tool can be used in many other areas. You can also use the Expression Builder when working with forms and reports. For example, if you need to perform a calculation in a form or report, you can launch the Expression Builder to assist you with this task. The same skills you learn here can be applied there as well.

TIP | Missing Field Names

If you have not yet saved your query, you may not see the names of the fields you are working with. This is especially true of any calculated fields you want to use as part of another expression. If you cannot see a field you need to use, exit the Expression Builder, save the query, and close and reopen the query. Once you reenter the Expression Builder, you should see the missing fields.

Create an Expression

The left column of the Expression Builder dialog box contains Expression Elements (see Figure 3.9), which include the built-in functions, the tables and other objects from the current database, and common expressions. Select an item in this column.

The middle column displays the Expression Categories based on the item selected in the Expression Elements box (see Figure 3.9). For example, when the Built-In Functions item is selected in the Expression Elements box, the available built-in function categories, such as the Math category, are displayed in the Expression Categories box.

The right column displays the Expression Values, if any, for the categories that you selected in the Expression Categories box (see Figure 3.9). For example, if you click Built-In Functions in the Expression Elements box and click Date/Time in the Expression Categories box, the Expression Values box lists all of the built-in functions in the Date/Time category.

You can create an expression by manually typing text in the expression box or by double-clicking the elements from the bottom section in the Expression Builder dialog box. For example, to create a calculated field using the fields in the tables, type the calculated field name and type a colon. Next, click the desired table listed in the Expression Elements section and double-click the field you want. Click the Operators item in the Expression Elements section and choose an operator (such as + or *) from the Expression Categories section (or just type the operator). The Expression Builder is flexible and will enable you to find what you need while still enabling you to modify the expression manually.

Calculated fields are relatively simple to create, and most Access developers can create them without the Expression Builder. The main reason to use the builder for a calculated field is to eliminate spelling errors in field names. Using functions in Access almost always requires the Expression Builder because the syntax of functions can be difficult to remember. When you double-click the Functions command in the Expression Elements box and click Built-In Functions, the Expression Categories box lists all the available functions in Access. The Expression Values box lists the functions in each of the categories. When you find the function you need, double-click it and the function displays in the expression box. You can see the «placeholder text» where the arguments belong; replace each placeholder text with the argument values, either numbers or fields from a table.

Launch the Expression Builder

STEP 1 ⟫ To launch the Expression Builder:

1. Open a query in Design view (or create a new query).
2. Verify the QUERY TOOLS DESIGN tab is selected on the Ribbon.
3. Click the top cell of a blank column (also known as the Field cell, because it appears in the row labeled Field) where you would like your expression to appear.
4. Click Builder in the Query Setup group, and the Expression Builder launches (see Figure 3.9). (You can also launch the Expression Builder by right-clicking the cell where you want the expression and selecting Build from the shortcut menu.)

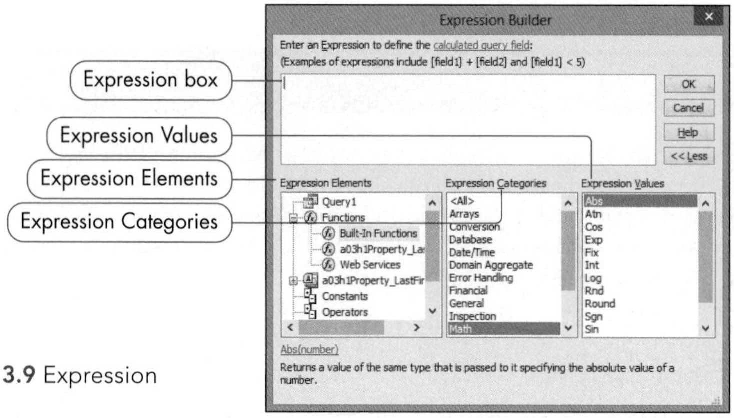

FIGURE 3.9 Expression Builder

5. The top section of the Expression Builder dialog box contains a rectangular area (known as the *expression box*) where you create an expression. You can type your expression in the expression box manually, or you can use the Expression Elements, Expression Categories, and Expression Values in the bottom portion of the Expression Builder. The bottom area allows you to browse for functions, tables, queries, and more. Refer to Figure 3.9.

6. Double-click an item in the *Expression Categories* or *Expression Values* section to add it automatically to the expression box, thus allowing you to use this interface to avoid typographical errors.

7. After you create the expression, click OK to close the Expression Builder window. The expression is then entered into the current cell in the query design grid. From the query design, click Run in the Results group to view the results (in Datasheet view). If the results are incorrect, you can return to Design view and use the Expression Builder again to correct the expression.

Using Built-In Functions in Access

STEP 2 》

Similar to Excel, a number of functions are built into Access. A **function** is a predefined computation that performs a complex calculation. It produces a result based on inputs known as arguments. An **argument** is any data that is needed to produce the output for a function. The term *argument*, outside of computers, can mean a fact. For example, in court, you may have a judge ask a lawyer to present his argument. Similarly, Access will need arguments, or facts, to execute a function. Arguments can be a variable (such as a field name) or a constant (such as a number). Some functions require no arguments, but many require at least one. Some functions have optional arguments, which are not required but may be necessary for your task.

Many of the tasks that are built in are tasks that would otherwise be difficult to perform. If you had to figure out the payment of a loan or determine the year portion of a date without functions, it would not be an easy task.

Once you identify what you need a function to do, you can check the Built-In Functions in the Expression Builder to see if the function exists. If it does, add the function to the expression box and replace the «placeholder text» with the argument values. Functions work the same in Access and Excel and other programming languages (such as Visual Basic). There are nearly 150 built-in functions in Access, and many of them will not apply to the task you are performing. Be aware that if you want to perform complex operations, there may be a function that can do it for you. In cases like this, search engines or Microsoft Help are extremely useful. This chapter will demonstrate one function.

Calculate Payments with the Pmt Function

Figure 3.10 shows the **Pmt function**, which calculates the periodic loan payment given the interest rate per period (for example, monthly), term of the loan (in months), and the original value of the loan (the principal). To use this function, you will need to supply at least three arguments as field names from underlying tables or as constants:

- The first argument is the interest rate per period. Interest rates are usually stated as annual rates, so you will need to convert the annual interest rate to the rate per period. For example, if a loan is paid monthly, you can calculate the rate by dividing the yearly rate by 12.

- The second argument is the number of periods. Because loan terms are usually stated in years, you will need to multiply the number of years by the number of payments per year. For example, a monthly payment would be calculated as the number of years multiplied by 12.

- The third argument is the present value—or principal—of the loan. It is the amount a customer is borrowing.

- The last two arguments—future value and type—are both optional, so they are usually 0 or blank. The future value shows the amount the borrower will owe after the final payment has been made. The type tells Access whether the payment is made at the beginning or the end of the period.

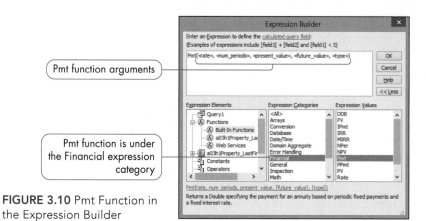

Pmt function arguments

Pmt function is under the Financial expression category

FIGURE 3.10 Pmt Function in the Expression Builder

The following example shows how to use the Pmt function to calculate the monthly payment on a $12,500 loan, at a 5.0% interest rate, with a four-year loan term.

Function: Pmt(*rate, num_periods, present_value, future_value, type*)

Example: Pmt(0.06/12, 5*12, 12500)

The Pmt function will return a negative value (as a loan payment is considered a debit). If you would like to display this as a positive number, you will need to negate it.

Table 3.2 describes the arguments for the Pmt function in more detail.

TABLE 3.2 Arguments of the Pmt Function

Part	Description
( )	Items inside the parentheses are arguments for the function. The arguments are separated by commas. Some arguments are optional; some arguments have a default value. In the Pmt function, the first three arguments are required and the last two are optional.
rate	Required. Expression or value specifying interest rate per period, usually monthly. A mortgage with an annual percentage rate of **6.0%** with monthly payments would have a rate entered as **0.06/12**, since the rate of 6% would be entered as .06, and because there are 12 months in a year. A loan with a 4% interest rate paid quarterly would be expressed as .04/4 for the same reason. A common cause of issues with this function is that people forget to divide the annual percentage rate by the number of periods in a year.
num_periods	Required. Expression or integer value specifying total number of payment periods in the loan. For example, monthly payments on a five-year car loan give a total of 5 * 12 (or 60) payment periods. Quarterly payments on a six-year loan would give a total of 6 * 4 (or 24) payment periods.
present_value	Required. Expression or value specifying the present value of the money you borrow. If you borrow $12,500 for a car, the value would be 12500.
future_value	*Optional* (can be left blank). Expression or value specifying the future value after you've made the final payment. Most consumer loans have a future value of $0 after the final payment. However, if you want to save $50,000 over 18 years for your child's education, then 50000 is the future value. Zero is assumed if left blank.
type	*Optional* (can be left blank). Value (0 or 1) identifying when payments are due. Use 0 if payments are due at the end of the payment period (the default), or 1 if payments are due at the beginning of the period. Zero is assumed if left blank.

In the second Hands-On Exercise, you will practice using the Expression Builder to add and modify a field, and use a built-in function.

Quick Concepts

1. List two benefits of creating expressions with the Expression Builder. ***p. 223***

2. Give an example of a built-in function. ***p. 225***

3. What is an argument in a function? Give an example. ***p. 225***

4. Describe a scenario where you might use the Pmt function. ***p. 225***

Hands-On Exercises

Watch the Video for this Hands-On Exercise!

MyITLab®
HOE2 Training

2 The Expression Builder and Functions

When Don and Matt ask you to calculate the price per bedroom and the price per room for each property, you use the Expression Builder to make the task easier. You also add two additional fields that calculate the days on market and the estimated commission for each property.

Skills covered: Use the Expression Builder to Add and Modify a Field • Use Built-In Functions

STEP 1 ≫ USE THE EXPRESSION BUILDER TO ADD AND MODIFY A FIELD

You create a copy of the Price Per Sq Ft Formatted query from the previous Hands-On Exercise and paste it using a new name. You will add a few more calculated fields to the new query. You will create one calculation to determine the price per bedroom for each house. You will create a second field to calculate the price per room. For this calculation, you will assume that each property has a kitchen, a living room, a dining room, and the listed bedrooms and bathrooms. The calculations you will create are shown in Figure 3.11. Your expected output is shown in Figure 3.12.

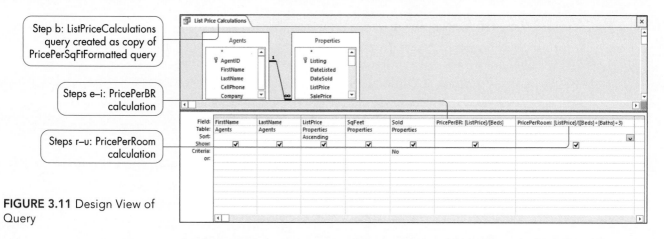

Step b: ListPriceCalculations query created as copy of PricePerSqFtFormatted query

Steps e–i: PricePerBR calculation

Steps r–u: PricePerRoom calculation

FIGURE 3.11 Design View of Query

a. Open *a03h1Property_LastFirst* if you closed it at the end of Hands-On Exercise 1 and save it as **a03h2Property_LastFirst**, changing *h1* to *h2*.

b. Create a copy of the Price Per Sq Ft Formatted query with the name **List Price Calculations**.

   The new query is displayed in the Navigation Pane. The name of the query suggests it should contain calculations based on each property's list price.

c. Open the List Price Calculations query in Design view. Click the **WrongPricePerSqFt field**. Click **Delete Columns** in the Query Setup group on the QUERY TOOLS DESIGN tab.

> **TROUBLESHOOTING:** If instead of the column being deleted, a new row named *Delete* appears on the bottom half of the screen, close the query without saving, open in Design view once more, and ensure you are clicking Delete Columns in the Query Setup group. If you click Delete under Query Type, you will get very different results.

d. Click in the top cell in the PricePerSqFt column and click **Builder** in the Query Setup group.

   The Expression Builder dialog box opens, displaying the current formula.

e. Change the PricePerSqFt field name to **PricePerBR**.

f. Double-click the **[SqFeet] field** in the expression and press **Delete**.

g. Click the **plus sign (+)** under Expression Elements, next to the *a03h2Property_LastFirst* database in the Expression Elements box, to expand the list. Click + next to *Tables* and click the table named **Properties**.

The fields from the Properties table are now listed in the middle column (Expression Categories).

h. Double-click the **Beds field** to add it to the expression box.

The expression now reads *PricePerBR: [ListPrice]/[Properties]![Beds]*.

i. Highlight the **[Properties]! prefix** in front of *Beds* and press **Delete**.

The expression now reads *PricePerBR: [ListPrice]/[Beds]*. As the Beds field name is unique within our query, the table name is not necessary. Removing this makes the query easier to read. If a field named Beds appeared in more than one table in our query, removing the table name would cause problems.

j. Click **OK** and click **Run** to view the query results.

Notice the column heading still reads Price Per Sq Ft. Also notice the column's contents are formatted as Currency. These settings were copied when we copied the query.

k. Switch to Design view and ensure the **PricePerBR field** is selected. Click **Property Sheet** in the Show/Hide group and change the **Caption** to **Price Per Bedroom**. Close the Property Sheet. Run the query and examine the changes.

The PricePerBR column now has an appropriate caption.

l. Switch to Design view. Select the entire **PricePerBR expression**, right-click the selected expression, and then select **Copy**. Right-click in the top cell of the next blank column and select **Paste**.

You will edit the copy so that it reflects the price per room. As stated already, you assume the kitchen, living room, dining room, and the bedrooms and bathrooms will make up the number of rooms. Your final formula would be the list price divided by the total number of rooms, which is the number of bedrooms (in the Beds field), plus the number of bathrooms (found in the Baths field), plus 3 (a constant representing the kitchen, living room, and dining room).

m. Click **Builder** in the Query Setup group.

n. Change the PricePerBR field name to **PricePerRoom**.

o. Add **parentheses** before the [Beds] portion of the formula. Type a **plus sign (+)** after *[Beds]*.

As you want the addition to be done first, the order of operations states we must enclose the addition in parentheses. The expression box should read *PricePerRoom: [ListPrice]/([Beds]+*

p. Click the **plus sign (+)** next to the *a03h2Property_LastFirst* database in the Expression Elements box to expand the list. Click the **plus sign (+)** next to *Tables* and click the **Properties table**.

The fields from the Properties table are now listed in the Expression Categories box.

q. Double-click the **Baths field** to add it to the expression box.

The expression now reads *PricePerRoom: [ListPrice]/([Beds]+[Properties]![Baths]*.

r. Type another plus sign after *[Baths]* and type **3).**

The expression now reads *PricePerRoom: [ListPrice]/([Beds]+[Properties]![Baths]+3).*

s. Delete the [Properties]! portion of the expression and click **OK** to close the Expression Builder.

The expression now reads *PricePerRoom: [ListPrice]/([Beds]+[Baths]+3).*

t. Click **Property Sheet**. Type **Price Per Room** in the **Caption box**. Close the Property Sheet.

u. Run the query. Widen the PricePerRoom column if necessary in order to see all the values.

First Name	Last Name	List Price	Square Feet	Sold	Price Per Bedroom	Price Per Room
StudentFirst	StudentLast	$109,140.00	1133	No	$54,570.00	$18,190.00
Bill	Sabey	$119,990.00	1202	No	$59,995.00	$17,141.43
Anny	Almonte	$122,220.00	1235	No	$61,110.00	$17,460.00
Robert Allen	Dickey	$129,780.00	1132	No	$64,890.00	$18,540.00
Bill	Sabey	$136,680.00	1375	No	$68,340.00	$22,780.00
Karean	Eissler	$138,990.00	1276	No	$69,495.00	$19,855.71
Anny	Almonte	$140,693.00	1490	No	$70,346.50	$20,099.00
Karean	Eissler	$140,904.00	1301	No	$70,452.00	$23,484.00
Anny	Almonte	$150,200.00	1652	No	$75,100.00	$21,457.14
StudentFirst	StudentLast	$163,737.00	1476	No	$81,868.50	$27,289.50
StudentFirst	StudentLast	$164,436.00	1850	No	$82,218.00	$27,406.00
Pradeep	Rana	$166,530.00	1676	No	$83,265.00	$27,755.00
StudentFirst	StudentLast	$166,552.00	1623	No	$83,276.00	$27,758.67
Anny	Almonte	$166,800.00	1598	No	$83,400.00	$27,800.00
Anny	Almonte	$168,354.00	1651	No	$84,177.00	$24,050.57
StudentFirst	StudentLast	$168,504.00	1625	No	$84,252.00	$28,084.00
Anny	Almonte	$172,458.00	1798	No	$86,229.00	$24,636.86
Bill	Sabey	$174,230.00	1771	No	$87,115.00	$29,038.33
StudentFirst	StudentLast	$174,720.00	1694	No	$87,360.00	$29,120.00
Robert Allen	Dickey	$174,720.00	1610	No	$87,360.00	$29,120.00
Anny	Almonte	$174,720.00	1667	No	$87,360.00	$29,120.00
Robert Allen	Dickey	$175,560.00	1562	No	$87,780.00	$25,080.00
StudentFirst	StudentLast	$177,984.00	1707	No	$88,992.00	$29,664.00
Bill	Sabey	$179,712.00	1854	No	$89,856.00	$25,673.14
Bill	Sabey	$182,385.00	2014	No	$45,596.25	$22,798.13
Anny	Almonte	$183,312.00	1721	No	$91,656.00	$30,552.00
Anny	Almonte	$184,473.00	1791	No	$92,236.50	$26,353.29

Record: 1 of 213 | No Filter | Search

Step i: Price Per Bedroom results

Step u: Price Per Room results

FIGURE 3.12 Final Results of Query

v. Save and close the query.

TIP Switching Between Object Views

You can switch between object views quickly by clicking View, or you can click the View arrow and select the desired view from the list. Another way to switch between views is to right-click the object tab and select the view from the shortcut menu.

TIP Expression Builder and Property Sheet

You can launch the Expression Builder by either clicking Builder in the Query Setup group on the Design tab or by right-clicking in the top row of the query design grid and selecting Build. Similarly, you can display the Property Sheet by clicking Property Sheet in the Show/Hide group on the Design tab or by right-clicking the top row of the query design grid and selecting Properties from the shortcut menu.

STEP 2 » USE BUILT-IN FUNCTIONS

Don and Matt feel like they are close to making an offer on a house. They would like to restrict the query to houses that cost $150,000 or less. They would also like to calculate the estimated mortgage payment for each house. You create this calculation using the Pmt function. You will use the Pmt function to calculate an estimated house payment for each of the sold properties. You make the following assumptions: 100% of the sale price will be financed, a 30-year term, monthly payments, and a fixed 6.0% annual interest rate. Refer to Figures 3.13 and 3.14 as you complete Step 2.

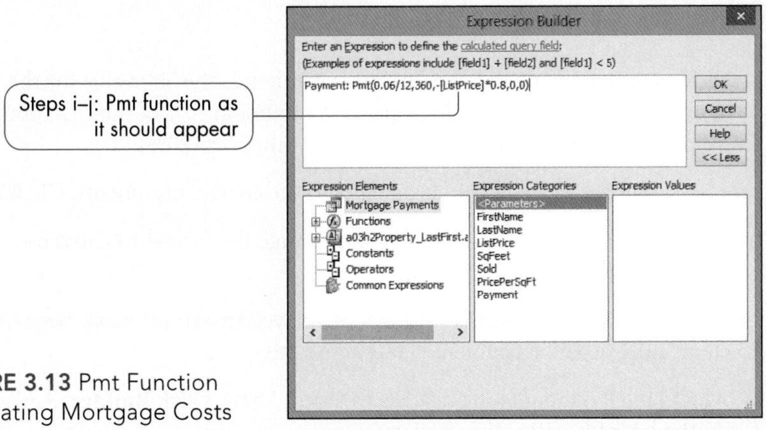

Steps i–j: Pmt function as it should appear

Expression Builder

Enter an Expression to define the calculated query field:
(Examples of expressions include [field1] + [field2] and [field1] < 5)

`Payment: Pmt(0.06/12,360,-[ListPrice]*0.8,0,0)`

OK
Cancel
Help
<< Less

Expression Elements
- Mortgage Payments
- Functions
- a03h2Property_LastFirst.a
- Constants
- Operators
- Common Expressions

Expression Categories
- <Parameters>
- FirstName
- LastName
- ListPrice
- SqFeet
- Sold
- PricePerSqFt
- Payment

Expression Values

FIGURE 3.13 Pmt Function Calculating Mortgage Costs

a. Create a copy of the Price Per Sq Ft Formatted query named **Mortgage Payments**.

The new query is displayed in the Navigation Pane.

b. Right-click **Mortgage Payments** and select **Design View**.

c. Delete the WrongPricePerSqFt field.

The WrongPricePerSqFt field is not needed for this query.

> **TROUBLESHOOTING:** If you do not see the WrongPricePerSqFt field, ensure you copied the correct query.

d. Type <=**150000** in the Criteria row of the ListPrice column. Press **Enter**.

The query, when it is run, will show only the houses that cost $150,000 or less.

e. Click in the top cell of the first blank column. Click **Builder** in the Query Setup group to open the Expression Builder dialog box.

f. Double-click **Functions** in the Expression Elements box and click **Built-In Functions**.

g. Click **Financial** in the Expression Categories box.

h. Double-click **Pmt** in the Expression Values box.

The expression box displays:

Pmt(«rate», «num_periods», «present_value», «future_value», «type»)

i. Position the insertion point before the Pmt function. Type **Payment:** to the left of the Pmt function.

The expression box now displays:

Payment:Pmt(«rate», «num_periods», «present_value», «future_value», «type»)

> **TROUBLESHOOTING:** If you forget to add the calculated field name to the left of the expression, Access will add *Expr1* to the front of your expression for you. You can edit the Expr1 name later, after the Expression Builder is closed.

j. Click each argument to select it and substitute the appropriate information. Make sure there is a comma between each argument.

Argument	Replacement Value
«rate»	0.06/12
«num_periods»	360
«present_value»	[ListPrice]*0.8
«future_value»	0
«type»	0

Note the loan is a 30-year loan with 12 payments per year, hence the 360 value for the number of payments. Also note, Don and Matt plan on financing 80% of the cost, putting 20% down. Therefore, you need to multiply the list price times 0.8 (80%).

k. Examine Figure 3.13 to make sure that you have entered the correct arguments. Click **OK**.

l. Click **OK**. Open the **Property Sheet** for *Payment* and change the format to **Currency**. Close the Property Sheet. **Run** the query.

Notice the payment amounts are negative numbers (displayed in parentheses). You will edit the formula to change the negative payment values to positive.

m. Right-click the **Mortgage Payments tab** and select **Design View**. Click **Builder**. Add a **minus sign** (–) to the left of *[ListPrice]* and click **OK**.

By adding the negative sign in front of the ListPrice field, you ensure the value is displayed as a positive number. The expression now reads *Payment: Pmt(0.06/12,360, –[ListPrice]*0.8,0,0)*.

The calculated field values should now appear as positive values formatted as currency, as shown in Figure 3.14.

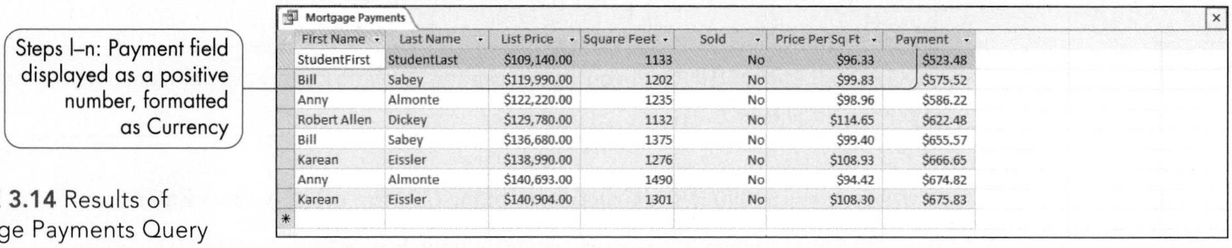

Steps l–n: Payment field displayed as a positive number, formatted as Currency

First Name	Last Name	List Price	Square Feet	Sold	Price Per Sq Ft	Payment
StudentFirst	StudentLast	$109,140.00	1133	No	$96.33	$523.48
Bill	Sabey	$119,990.00	1202	No	$99.83	$575.52
Anny	Almonte	$122,220.00	1235	No	$98.96	$586.22
Robert Allen	Dickey	$129,780.00	1132	No	$114.65	$622.48
Bill	Sabey	$136,680.00	1375	No	$99.40	$655.57
Karean	Eissler	$138,990.00	1276	No	$108.93	$666.65
Anny	Almonte	$140,693.00	1490	No	$94.42	$674.82
Karean	Eissler	$140,904.00	1301	No	$108.30	$675.83

FIGURE 3.14 Results of Mortgage Payments Query

n. Click **OK**. Run the query and examine the results.

The query displays a column containing the calculated monthly mortgage payment, formatted as currency.

o. Save and close the query. Keep the database open if you plan to continue with the next Hands-On Exercise. If not, close the database and exit Access.

Aggregate Functions

Aggregate functions perform calculations on an entire column of data and return a single value. Aggregate functions—such as Sum, Avg, and Count—are used when you need to evaluate a group of record values rather than the individual records in a table or query.

Access refers to aggregate functions as Totals. Totals can be added to the Datasheet view of a query, or they can be added to a query's Design view. Based on the data type, different aggregate functions will be available. Numeric fields are eligible for all of the functions, whereas Short Text fields are not. A list of common aggregate functions is shown in Table 3.4.

A car dealer's monthly inventory report is a good example of a report that might contain aggregate information. The cars would be grouped by model, then by options package and color. At the end of the report, a summary page would list the count of cars in each model for quick reference by the sales reps. In the property database, aggregate information could be grouped by county or by subdivision. For example, the average home price per county could be presented in a query or a report. This would give prospective buyers a good idea of home prices in their target counties. Almost every company or organization that uses a database will require some type of aggregate data.

TABLE 3.4	Common Aggregate Functions	
Function	**Description**	**Use with Data Type(s)**
AVG	Calculates the average value for a column. The function ignores null values.	Number, Currency, Date/Time
COUNT	Counts the number of items in a column. The function ignores null values.	All data types except a column of multivalued lists.
MAXIMUM	Returns the item with the highest value. For text data, the highest value is "Z." The function ignores null values.	Number, Currency, Date/Time, Short Text
MINIMUM	Returns the item with the lowest value. For text data, the lowest value is "a." The function ignores null values.	Number, Currency, Date/Time, Short Text
SUM	Adds the items in a column. Works only on numeric and currency data.	Number, Currency

In this section, you will learn how to create and work with aggregate functions. Specifically, you will learn how to use the Total row and create a totals query.

Adding Aggregate Functions to Datasheets

Aggregate functions are most commonly used in tables, queries, and reports. Occasionally, aggregate functions are also added to the *form footer* section of forms. Aggregate data helps users evaluate the values in a single record as compared to the aggregate of all the records. If you are considering buying a property in Bergen County, New Jersey, for $150,000, and the average price of a property in that county is $450,000, you know you are getting a good deal (or buying a bad property).

Access provides two methods of adding aggregate functions to a query—a *Total row*, which displays the results of the aggregate function as the last row in the Datasheet view of a table or query, and a totals query created in Query Design view.

The first method enables you to add a Total row to the Datasheet view. This method is quick and easy and has the advantage of showing the total information while still showing the individual records. Adding a Total row to a query or table can be accomplished by most users, even those who are not familiar with designing a query. Note the Total row values cannot be modified; you can change the aggregate function displayed there, but you cannot overwrite the numbers.

Add a Total Row in a Query or Table

STEP 1 » Figure 3.15 shows the Total row added to the Datasheet view of a query. You can choose any of the aggregate functions that apply to numeric fields. Follow these steps to add a Total row to a query or table:

1. Ensure you are viewing the query in Datasheet view.
2. Click Totals in the Records group on the HOME tab. The Total row is added at the bottom of the datasheet, below the new record row of the query or table.
3. In the new Total row, you can select one of the aggregate functions by clicking in the cell and clicking the arrow. The list of aggregate functions includes Sum, Avg, Count, and others.

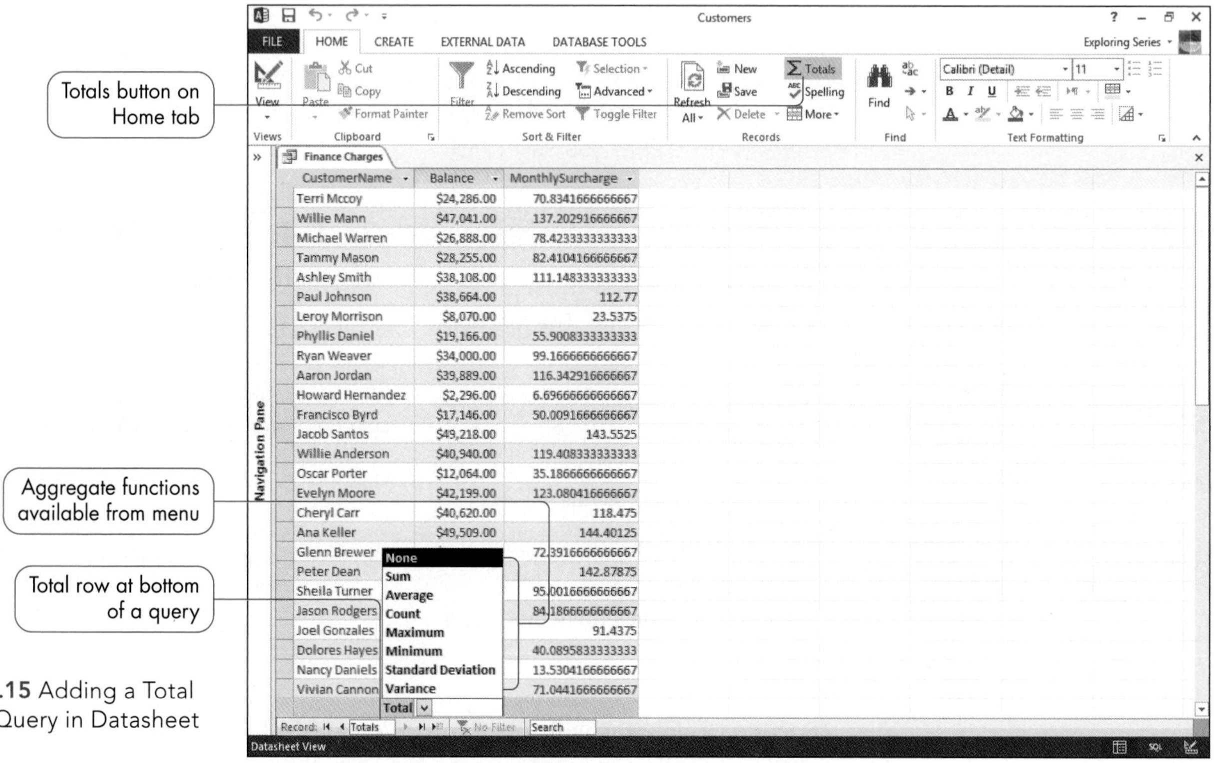

FIGURE 3.15 Adding a Total Row to a Query in Datasheet View

Creating Queries with Aggregate Functions

The second method to display aggregate functions requires you to alter the design of a query and add a Total row in the Query Design view. Once the totals data is assembled, you can use it to make decisions. For example, you can use the Count function to show the number of houses sold. You could also use the Avg function to show the average sale price for houses. This method has the advantage of enabling you to group your data by categories.

Many times, you will need to find some sort of averages for fields, and you may need to do more in-depth statistics than just an overall set as we did in the previous few pages. Instead of wanting to see the average sale price for houses, you may want to see the average sale price by city. Using the total row in the previous example, this is not feasible. Another limitation of the previous example is that I might want to see the average sale price, minimum sale price, and maximum sale price. Using the previous method, we would have to put the sale price field into our query three times, leading to repeated columns.

Instead of showing detail, we can quickly see the overall statistics for the entire table or query. For example, if you want to see the number of listings, average value, and the average size in square feet for all properties in your table, you can run a totals query to get that data and not see details. Instead of doing that, we can create a different type of query to summarize our data.

Create a Basic Totals Query

A **totals query** contains an additional row in the query design grid and is used to display aggregate data when the query is run. Figure 3.16 shows a totals query in Design view, and Figure 3.17 shows the results.

To create a Totals query:

1. Create a query in Design view and add the fields for which you want to get statistics. For example, in the preceding example, we would add the Listing, List Price, and Square Feet fields.

2. Click Totals in the Show/Hide group on the QUERY TOOLS DESIGN tab to display the total row. A new row should display in your query between the Table and Sort options. You will notice it defaults to Group By.

3. For each field, select the menu next to Group By and select the aggregate function you want applied to that field. For example, we want to count the number of listings and average both the list price and square feet values.

4. If you would like to apply specific formats, display the Property Sheet (as we did earlier in this chapter) and adjust the settings for each field.

5. Run the query to see your results.

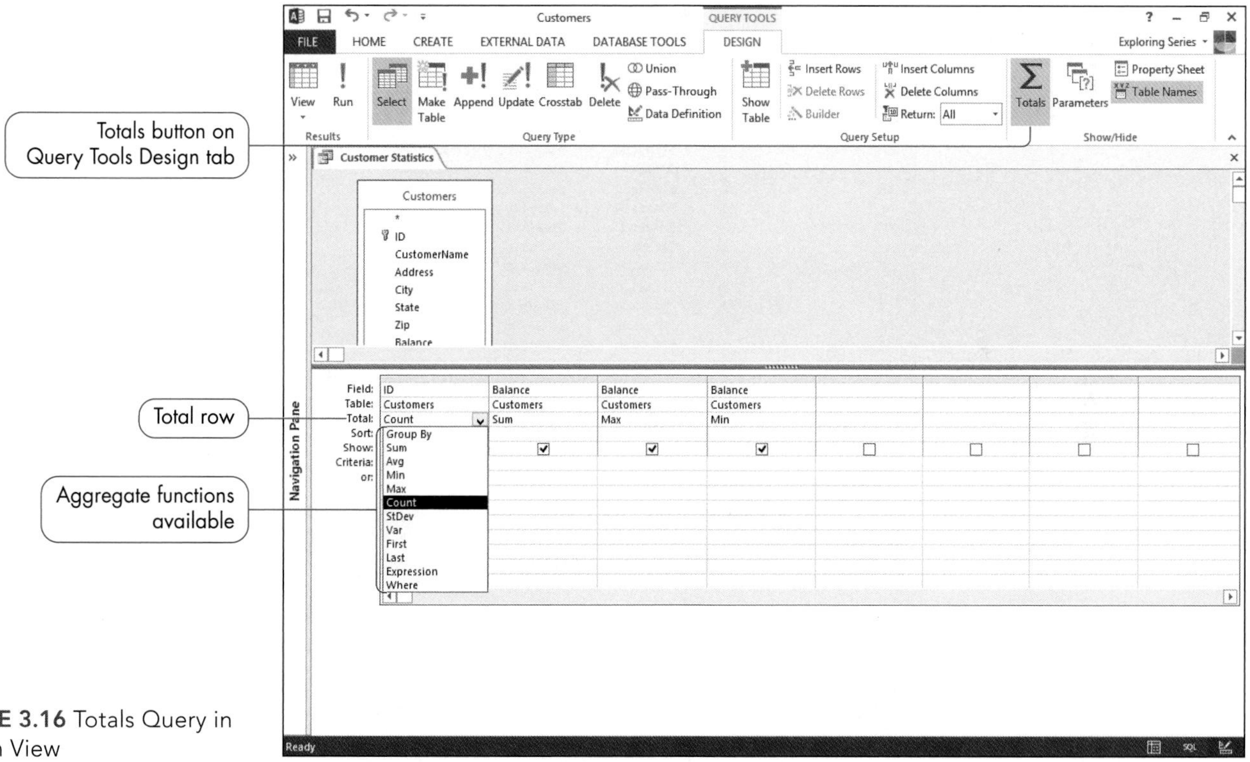

FIGURE 3.16 Totals Query in Design View

FIGURE 3.17 Totals Query Results

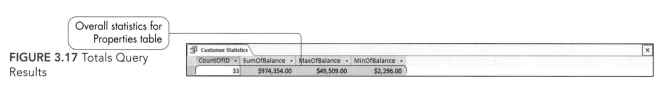

Create a Totals Query with Grouping

Grouping a query allows you to summarize your data by the values of a field. For example, you want to see the results not for the entire table, but instead by state. You can add the State field as a grouping level, and Access will show you the statistics you request for each state.

To group an existing query, add the field you wish to group by to the query in Design view. You would then verify the Total row displays Group By (see Figure 3.18). So if you want to see the results by state, add the State field to the query and leave the Total with the default of Group By. You may want to move this column to the beginning, as it will make your query easier to read.

Figure 3.18 shows the Design view of a totals query with five columns, one of which is the grouping field. Figure 3.19 shows the results of this query.

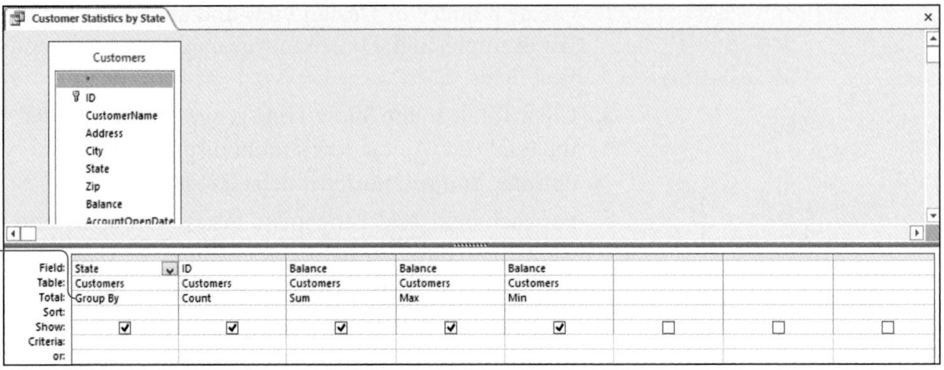

Group By State field

FIGURE 3.18 Totals Query with Grouping Field

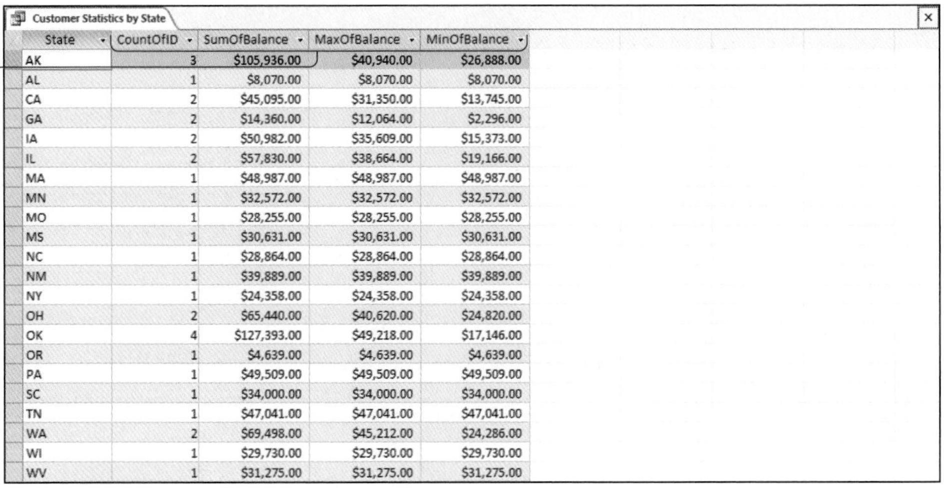

State	CountOfID	SumOfBalance	MaxOfBalance	MinOfBalance
AK	3	$105,936.00	$40,940.00	$26,888.00
AL	1	$8,070.00	$8,070.00	$8,070.00
CA	2	$45,095.00	$31,350.00	$13,745.00
GA	2	$14,360.00	$12,064.00	$2,296.00
IA	2	$50,982.00	$35,609.00	$15,373.00
IL	2	$57,830.00	$38,664.00	$19,166.00
MA	1	$48,987.00	$48,987.00	$48,987.00
MN	1	$32,572.00	$32,572.00	$32,572.00
MO	1	$28,255.00	$28,255.00	$28,255.00
MS	1	$30,631.00	$30,631.00	$30,631.00
NC	1	$28,864.00	$28,864.00	$28,864.00
NM	1	$39,889.00	$39,889.00	$39,889.00
NY	1	$24,358.00	$24,358.00	$24,358.00
OH	2	$65,440.00	$40,620.00	$24,820.00
OK	4	$127,393.00	$49,218.00	$17,146.00
OR	1	$4,639.00	$4,639.00	$4,639.00
PA	1	$49,509.00	$49,509.00	$49,509.00
SC	1	$34,000.00	$34,000.00	$34,000.00
TN	1	$47,041.00	$47,041.00	$47,041.00
WA	2	$69,498.00	$45,212.00	$24,286.00
WI	1	$29,730.00	$29,730.00	$29,730.00
WV	1	$31,275.00	$31,275.00	$31,275.00

Statistics by state

FIGURE 3.19 Query Grouped by State Field

TIP Too Much Grouping

Beware that the more grouping levels you add, the less valuable the data is probably going to be; a typical totals query will group by only a few columns. As the purpose of grouping is to get some sort of aggregate data (such as a sum) for related data, grouping by more fields leads to less data being summarized.

Create a Totals Query with a Condition

Totals queries can provide even better information if you add criteria. For example, if you wanted to see the number of houses, average price, and average square feet for only the unsold properties, grouped by state, you can add the Sold field to the query. You would set the criteria to No to indicate that the Sold field is no. You should select Where from the menu in the Total row for any field you add to which you wish to apply criteria. Figure 3.20 shows a query with a condition added, and Figure 3.21 shows the results. You can compare this to Figure 3.19 to see the change in results.

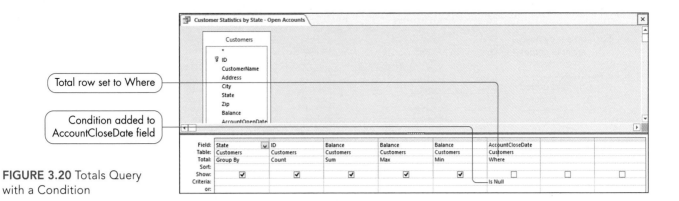

FIGURE 3.20 Totals Query with a Condition

Total row set to Where

Condition added to AccountCloseDate field

FIGURE 3.21 Updated Results of Query

Statistics for open accounts

State	CountOfID	SumOfBalance	MaxOfBalance	MinOfBalance
AK	1	$38,108.00	$38,108.00	$38,108.00
CA	2	$45,095.00	$31,350.00	$13,745.00
GA	1	$2,296.00	$2,296.00	$2,296.00
IL	1	$38,664.00	$38,664.00	$38,664.00
NC	1	$28,864.00	$28,864.00	$28,864.00
OK	2	$66,364.00	$49,218.00	$17,146.00
TN	1	$47,041.00	$47,041.00	$47,041.00
WA	1	$24,286.00	$24,286.00	$24,286.00

Create a Totals Query with Multiple Grouping Levels

At times, you may want to add multiple grouping fields. For example, instead of grouping by State, you might want to group by City. However, if you group by city, customers with the same city name in different states would be grouped together. For example, all 50 states have a location named Greenville. If you grouped by city, all customers with a city of Greenville, regardless of state, would appear as a group. This is probably not your intention. Instead, you probably would want to see results by City and State, and thus would want to add multiple grouping levels. Figure 3.22 shows a second grouping level, and Figure 3.23 shows the results of the query if we group by State and then by City. Notice the multiple Greenville results.

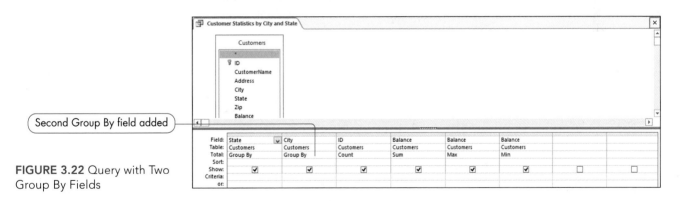

Second Group By field added

FIGURE 3.22 Query with Two Group By Fields

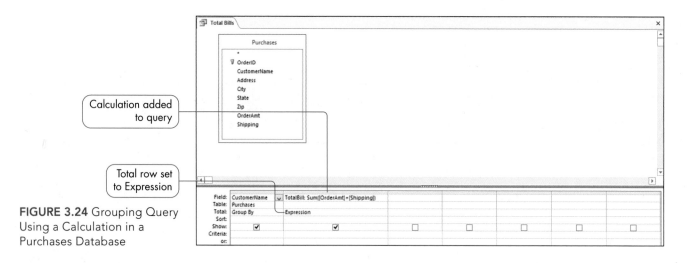

Customer Statistics by City and State					
State	City	CountOfID	SumOfBalance	MaxOfBalance	MinOfBalance
AK	Greenville	2	$67,828.00	$40,940.00	$26,888.00
AK	Kaktovik	1	$38,108.00	$38,108.00	$38,108.00
AL	Greenville	1	$8,070.00	$8,070.00	$8,070.00
CA	Los Angeles	1	$13,745.00	$13,745.00	$13,745.00
CA	San Diego	1	$31,350.00	$31,350.00	$31,350.00
GA	Austell	1	$2,296.00	$2,296.00	$2,296.00
GA	Leary	1	$12,064.00	$12,064.00	$12,064.00
IA	Albert City	1	$15,373.00	$15,373.00	$15,373.00
IA	Iowa City	1	$35,609.00	$35,609.00	$35,609.00
IL	Champaign	2	$57,830.00	$38,664.00	$19,166.00
MA	Southampton	1	$48,987.00	$48,987.00	$48,987.00
MN	Beltrami	1	$32,572.00	$32,572.00	$32,572.00
MO	De Kalb	1	$28,255.00	$28,255.00	$28,255.00
MS	Meridian	1	$30,631.00	$30,631.00	$30,631.00
NC	Raleigh	1	$28,864.00	$28,864.00	$28,864.00
NM	Bard	1	$39,889.00	$39,889.00	$39,889.00
NY	Saint Bonavent	1	$24,358.00	$24,358.00	$24,358.00
OH	Canton	1	$40,620.00	$40,620.00	$40,620.00
OH	Cincinnati	1	$24,820.00	$24,820.00	$24,820.00
OK	Albany	1	$17,146.00	$17,146.00	$17,146.00
OK	Canadian	1	$42,199.00	$42,199.00	$42,199.00
OK	Lahoma	1	$18,830.00	$18,830.00	$18,830.00
OK	Rufe	1	$49,218.00	$49,218.00	$49,218.00
OR	Fall Creek	1	$4,639.00	$4,639.00	$4,639.00
PA	Pine Bank	1	$49,509.00	$49,509.00	$49,509.00
SC	Clemson	1	$34,000.00	$34,000.00	$34,000.00
TN	Auburntown	1	$47,041.00	$47,041.00	$47,041.00

Each state may have multiple entries

City field added to query

FIGURE 3.23 Results of Query with Two Group By Fields

Add a Calculated Field to a Totals Query

STEP 3 ⟫

Once you have created a totals query, you can create calculated fields as you did earlier in the chapter. Often, you will want to apply an aggregate function to an existing field, such as summing up the values in a field. However, there may be times when you would prefer to apply an aggregate function to a calculation rather than a field.

We will use a customer purchases database to demonstrate this. When working with a customer order database, you may have a field for each order containing the total order cost and another field for each order containing the shipping cost. If you use the Sum aggregate function and group by the customer ID, you would have the total amount of their orders, and then as a separate column the total cost of the shipping they have paid. Instead of doing that, you may prefer to first create a calculated field that adds the total order cost and shipping cost for each order, and then group by a CustomerName. You will notice in Figure 3.24 we need to change the total row to Expression. After making that change, your results will resemble Figure 3.25.

Calculation added to query

Total row set to Expression

FIGURE 3.24 Grouping Query Using a Calculation in a Purchases Database

Results are each customer's total bill

CustomerName	TotalBill
Alice Ray	$688.99
Alicia Byrd	$810.50
Amber Ingram	$506.50
Annette Gibson	$720.99
Arthur Powell	$477.99
Beth Vaughn	$203.99
Carla Black	$478.50
Crystal Delgado	$166.99
Esther Bennett	$198.50
Eva Turner	$673.99
Florence Douglas	$633.99
Frances Foster	$317.50
Gina West	$629.99
Gloria Medina	$615.99
Harold Wolfe	$432.50
Heather Davidson	$343.50
Jamie Wheeler	$243.99
Jeanette Griffin	$436.50
Keith Strickland	$349.50
Lawrence Payne	$390.50
Leonard Delgado	$161.50
Lynn Brooks	$363.50
Marvin Santiago	$757.98
Megan Wheeler	$720.99
Phillip Medina	$676.50
Steve Mills	$674.50
Thelma Burgess	$529.99

FIGURE 3.25 Results of Grouping Query with a Calculation in a Purchases Database

In the third Hands-On Exercise, you will add aggregate functions to datasheets, create a totals query, and add grouping, conditions, and calculated fields to totals queries.

Quick Concepts ✓

1. What are the benefits of aggregate functions? Give an example. **p. 233**

2. How do you add a Total row to a datasheet? **p. 234**

3. What is a totals query? **p. 235**

4. What is the difference between a query with a Total row and a totals query? **p. 235**

Hands-On Exercises

3 Aggregate Functions

The investors decide it would be helpful to analyze the property lists they purchased. Some of the lists do not have homes that match their target criteria. The investors will either need to purchase new lists or alter their criteria. You create several totals queries to evaluate the property lists.

Skills covered: Add Aggregate Functions to Datasheets • Create a Totals Query with Grouping and Conditions • Add a Calculated Field to a Totals Query

STEP 1 ≫ ADD AGGREGATE FUNCTIONS TO DATASHEETS

You begin your property list analysis by creating a total row in the Datasheet view of the Mortgage Payments query. This will give you a variety of aggregate information for each column. Refer to Figure 3.26 as you complete Step 1.

Step g: Average of PricePerSqFt

Step f: Count of Listing

Step e: Average of ListPrice

Step c: Total row

First Name	Last Name	List Price	Square Feet	Listing	Sold	Price Per Sq Ft	Payment
StudentFirst	StudentLast	$109,140.00	1133	10004	No	$96.33	$523.48
Bill	Sabey	$119,990.00	1202	10091	No	$99.83	$575.52
Anny	Almonte	$122,220.00	1235	10036	No	$98.96	$586.22
Robert Allen	Dickey	$129,780.00	1132	10028	No	$114.65	$622.48
Bill	Sabey	$136,680.00	1375	10008	No	$99.40	$655.57
Karean	Eissler	$138,990.00	1276	10016	No	$108.93	$666.65
Anny	Almonte	$140,693.00	1490	10069	No	$94.42	$674.82
Karean	Eissler	$140,904.00	1301	10061	No	$108.30	$675.83
Total		$129,799.63		8		$102.60	

Mortgage Payments

FIGURE 3.26 Total Row Added to Query Datasheet

a. Open *a03h2Property_LastFirst* if you closed it at the end of Hands-On Exercise 2 and save it as **a03h3Property_LastFirst**, changing *h2* to *h3*.

b. Right-click the **Mortgage Payments query** in the Navigation Pane and select **Design View**. Drag the **Listing field** from the Properties table to the fifth column.

   The Listing field is now in the fifth column, between the SqFeet and Sold fields. The other columns shift to the right.

> **TROUBLESHOOTING:** If you drag the Listing field to the wrong position, you can drag it again to the correct location.

c. Switch to Datasheet view. Click **Totals**, in the Records group on the HOME tab to display the Total row.

   The Total row displays as the last row of the query results.

d. Click in the cell that intersects the Total row and the List Price column.

e. Click the arrow and select **Average** to display the average value of all the properties that have not sold. Widen the List Price column if you can't see the entire total value.

   The average list price of all properties is $129,799.63.

f. Click the arrow in the Total row in the Listing column and select **Count** from the list.

   The count of properties in this datasheet is 8.

g. Click in the **Total row** in the Price Per Sq Ft column. Click the arrow and select **Average** to display the average price per square foot.

   The average price per square foot is $102.60.

h. Save and close the query.

You create a totals query to help Don and Matt evaluate the properties in groups. Refer to Figure 3.27 and Figure 3.28 as you complete Step 2.

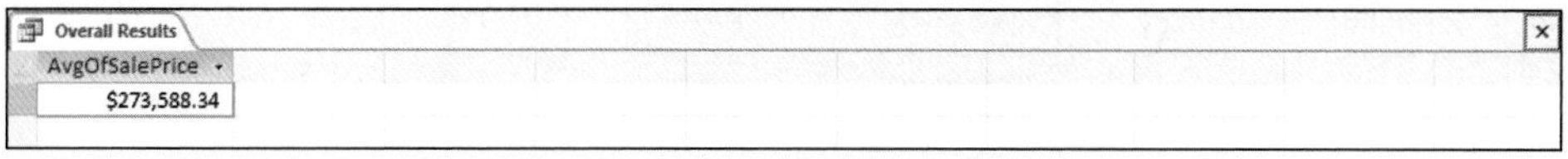

FIGURE 3.27 Overall Results Query

a. Click **Query Design** in the Queries group of the CREATE tab.

You create a new query in Query Design; the Show Table dialog box opens.

b. Add the Properties table from the Show Table dialog box. Close the Show Table dialog box.

c. Add the SalePrice and Sold fields from the Properties table to the query design grid.

d. Click **Totals** in the Show/Hide group of the QUERY TOOLS DESIGN tab to show the Total row.

A new row labeled Totals displays at the bottom of the screen in the design grid, between the Table and Sort rows. Each field will have Group By listed in the new row by default.

e. Click the **Group By arrow** in the SalePrice column Total row and select **Avg.**

f. Click the **Group By arrow** in the Sold column Total row and select **Where**. Type **Yes** in the Criteria row.

This criterion will limit the results to sold houses only.

g. Click in the **SalePrice field** and click **Property Sheet** in the Show/Hide group. Change the SalePrice format to **Currency**. Close the Property Sheet. Run the query and compare your results to Figure 3.27.

The results show an overall average of $273,588.34 for the sold properties in the database.

h. Click **Save** on the Quick Access Toolbar and type **Overall Results** as the Query Name in the Save As dialog box. Click **OK**. Close the query.

i. Click **Query Design** in the Query group of the HOME tab to create a new query.

j. Add the Properties table and the Lists table from the Show Table dialog box. Close the Show Table dialog box.

k. Add the NameOfList field from the Lists table and the SalePrice, Listing, and Sold fields from the Properties table to the query design grid.

l. Click **Totals** on the QUERY TOOLS DESIGN tab in the Show/Hide group to show the Total row.

A new row labeled Total appears at the bottom of the screen in the design grid between the Table and Sort rows.

m. Change the Total row for *SalePrice* to **Avg.**

n. Change the Total row for *Listing* to **Count**.

o. Change the Total row for *Sold* to **Where**. Type **Yes** in the Criteria row.

This criterion will limit the results to sold houses only.

p. Click in the **SalePrice field** and click **Property Sheet** in the Show/Hide group. Change the SalePrice format to **Currency**.

q. Change the caption of the Listing column to **Number Sold**. Run the query and widen the columns as shown in Figure 3.28.

Notice Major Houses has the only average sale price under $200,000. As Don and Matt are hoping to focus on inexpensive properties, they will focus on properties offered by this source. Notice the query results show the number of properties sold in each source, in addition to the average sale price. This will help determine which sources have been more effective.

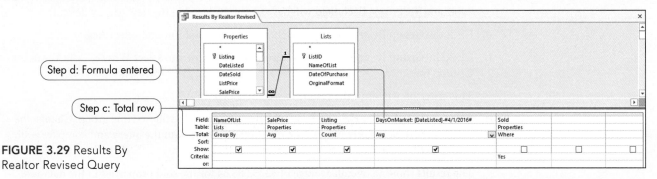

Steps n and q: Count of Listing, with caption of Number Sold

Step k: Grouped by NameOfList

Steps m and p: Average of SalePrice, formatted as Currency

FIGURE 3.28 Totals Query Results

NameOfList	AvgOfSalePrice	Number Sold
Algernon Listings	$297,809.25	24
FastHouse	$306,520.50	5
Houses 4 Sale	$215,356.27	11
Local Listings	$335,638.13	8
Major Houses	$189,291.75	8
Trullo	$279,099.55	18
Wholesaler	$241,016.83	16

r. Click **Save** on the Quick Access Toolbar and type **Results By Realtor** as the Query Name in the Save As dialog box. Click **OK**. Keep the query open for the next step.

STEP 3 ≫ ADD A CALCULATED FIELD TO A TOTALS QUERY

The previous query shows the average value of the properties by realtor. However, Don and Matt learned at the seminar they attended that the longer a property has been on the market, the better your chances of negotiating a better price. You will revise the query to include the average number of days on the market for each realtor. Refer to Figure 3.29 as you complete Step 3.

Step d: Formula entered

Step c: Total row

FIGURE 3.29 Results By Realtor Revised Query

a. Click the **FILE tab**, click **Save As**, and then click **Save Object As**. Click **Save As**, and in the *Save 'Results By Realtor' to:* box, type **Results By Realtor Revised**.

b. Switch to the Datasheet view for the new Results By Realtor Revised query, if necessary.

c. Click **Totals** in the Records group of the HOME tab. Change the Total to **Sum** in the Number Sold column.

The total number of houses sold (90) now displays at the bottom of the Number Sold column.

d. Switch to Design view. In the first blank column, type **DaysOnMarket: [DateListed] – #4/1/2016#** to create a new calculated field. Change the Total row to **Avg**.

The DaysOnMarket field will show the average number of days on the market for each realtor's listings.

e. Display the Property Sheet for the DaysOnMarket field and change the Format property to **Fixed**. Change the Decimal Places property to **0**. Close the Property Sheet.

> **TROUBLESHOOTING:** If you do not see a Decimal Places property immediately beneath the Format property, change the format to Fixed, save and close the query, and then reopen the query. Refer to Figure 3.4 for the location of Decimal Places.

f. Run the query and examine the DaysOnMarket field.

Major Houses listings have an average of 117 days on the market. The combination of inexpensive prices and properties that do not sell quickly may help Don and Matt negotiate with the realtor.

g. Save and close the query.

h. Exit Access. Submit based on your instructor's directions.

Chapter Objectives Review

After reading this chapter, you have accomplished the following objectives:

1. **Create a calculated field in a query.**
   - Calculations can be based on fields, constants, and/or functions.
   - Understand the order of operations: Calculated fields follow the same order of operations as mathematical equations—parentheses, then exponentiation, then multiplication and division, and finally addition and subtraction.
   - Build expressions with correct syntax: Expressions must be written using proper syntax—the rules governing the way you give instructions to Access.

2. **Format and save calculated results.**
   - Calculated results may not have the format you want; change the properties of a calculated field using the Property Sheet.
   - Recover from common errors: Common errors include forgetting the colon in the appropriate location, spelling errors, and misuse of the order of operations.
   - Verify calculated results: Always check the results of your equation; Access will check for syntax errors, but not logic errors.

3. **Create expressions with the Expression Builder.**
   - Expression Builder helps create complex expressions.
   - Create an expression: Expression Builder allows you to choose fields and built-in functions easily, and gives you a larger screen to view your expression.
   - Launch the Expression Builder: Clicking the Builder button will open the tool.

4. **Use built-in functions in Access.**
   - Access includes functions, or predefined computations that perform complex calculations.
   - There are almost 150 built-in functions in Access.

   - Some require arguments: inputs (often fields or constants) given to a function.
   - Calculate payments with the Pmt Function: The Pmt function accepts the rate per term, number of payments, and loan amount and calculates a loan payment.

5. **Add aggregate functions to datasheets.**
   - Aggregate functions perform calculations on an entire column of data and return a single value.
   - Include functions such as Sum, Avg, and Count.
   - Add a total row in a query or table: The total row displays at the bottom of a query or table; it can perform any aggregate function on each column.

6. **Create queries with aggregate functions.**
   - This gives you more control over application of your aggregate functions.
   - Create a basic totals query: Create a query as usual and click the Totals button in Design view.
   - Create a totals query with grouping: Grouping allows you to summarize your data by the values of a field; instead of showing overall averages, add state as a grouping field and see averages for each state.
   - Create a totals query with a condition: Conditions can be added to totals queries, such as only showing listings with the Sold field equal to No.
   - Create a totals query with multiple grouping levels: You can add multiple grouping levels; for example, you could group by State and then by City to get more detailed results.
   - Add a calculated field to a totals query: You can apply an aggregate function to the results of a calculation; for example, subtract a date from today's date to get the number of days a listing is active and calculate the overall average of days listings are active.

Match the key terms with their definitions. Write the key term letter by the appropriate numbered definition.

a. Aggregate Function

b. Argument

c. Constant

d. Expression

e. Expression Builder

f. Function

g. Grouping

h. Order of Operations

i. Pmt Function

j. Property Sheet

k. Syntax

l. Total Row

m. Totals Query

1. _____ A value that does not change. **p. 212**

2. _____ A formula used to calculate new fields from the values in existing fields. **p. 212**

3. _____ Determines the sequence by which operations are calculated in an expression. **p. 213**

4. _____ Dictates the structure and components required to perform the necessary calculations in an equation or evaluate expressions. **p. 213**

5. _____ Enables you to change settings such as number format, number of decimal places, and caption. **p. 215**

6. _____ An Access tool that helps you create more complicated expressions. **p. 223**

7. _____ A predefined computation that performs a complex calculation. Almost 150 are built into Access. **p. 225**

8. _____ Any data needed to produce output for a function. **p. 225**

9. _____ Calculates the periodic loan payment given the interest rate per period, term of the loan in months, and the original value of the loan. **p. 225**

10. _____ Performs calculations on an entire column of data and returns a single value. Includes functions such as Sum, Avg, and Count. **p. 233**

11. _____ Displays aggregate function results as the last row in the Datasheet view of a table or query. **p. 233**

12. _____ Makes an additional row available in the query design grid. Used to display aggregate data when the query is run. **p. 235**

13. _____ Allows you to summarize your data by the values of a field. **p. 235**

Multiple Choice

1. Which of the following correctly identifies the rules for the order of operations?

   (a) Parentheses, exponentiation, addition, subtraction, multiplication, division

   (b) Exponentiation, parentheses, addition, subtraction, multiplication, division

   (c) Addition, subtraction, multiplication, division, exponentiation, parentheses

   (d) Parentheses, exponentiation, multiplication, division, addition, subtraction

2. What is the result of the following expression?
   $(3 * 5) + 7 - 2 - 6 / 2$

   (a) 17

   (b) 7

   (c) 14.5

   (d) 13

3. Which of the following *cannot* be adjusted in the Property Sheet?

   (a) Number of decimal places

   (b) Mathematical expression

   (c) Caption

   (d) Number format (for example, Currency)

4. Which of the following is *not* an aggregate function?

   (a) Pmt

   (b) Avg

   (c) Count

   (d) Min

5. Which of the following can be added to a totals query?

   (a) Conditions

   (b) Grouping fields

   (c) Aggregate functions

   (d) All of the above can be added to a totals query

6. Which statement about a totals query is *true*?

   (a) A totals query is created in Datasheet view.

   (b) A totals query may contain several grouping fields but only one aggregate field.

   (c) A totals query is limited to only two fields, one grouping field and one aggregate field.

   (d) A totals query may contain several grouping fields and several aggregate fields.

7. Which of the following statements is *true*?

   (a) A total order cost would be a common field to group by.

   (b) A last name would be a common field to group by.

   (c) For best results, add as many group by fields as possible.

   (d) None of the above statements is true.

8. After creating a calculated field, you run the query and a Parameter dialog box appears on your screen. How do you respond to the Parameter dialog box?

   (a) Click OK to make the parameter box go away.

   (b) Look for a possible typing error in the calculated expression.

   (c) Type numbers in the Parameter box and click OK.

   (d) Close the query without saving changes. Reopen it and try running the query again.

9. A query contains student names. You run the query and while in Datasheet view, you notice a spelling error on one of the student's names. You correct the error in Datasheet view. Which statement is *true*?

   (a) The name is correctly spelled in this query but will be misspelled in the table and all other queries based on the table.

   (b) The name is correctly spelled in this query and any other queries, but will remain misspelled in the table.

   (c) You cannot edit data in a query.

   (d) The name is correctly spelled in the table and in all queries based on the table.

10. Which of the following about the Total row in the query design grid is *false*?

    (a) The Total row enables you to apply aggregate functions to the fields.

    (b) The Total row does not display by default in all new queries.

    (c) The Total row is located between the Table and Sort rows.

    (d) The Total row cannot be applied to numeric fields.

Practice Exercises

1 Comfort Insurance

The Comfort Insurance Agency is a mid-sized company with offices located across the country. Each employee receives a performance review annually. The review determines employee eligibility for salary increases and the annual performance bonus. The employee data is stored in an Access database, which is used by the human resources department to monitor and maintain employee records. Your task is to calculate the salary increase for each employee; you will also calculate the average salary for each position. This exercise follows the same set of skills as used in Hands-On Exercises 1 and 2 in the chapter. Refer to Figure 3.30 as you complete this exercise.

Last Name	First Name	Performance	Salary	2016 Increase	New Salary
Lacher	Tom	Good	$31,200.00	3.00%	$32,136.00
Fantis	Laurie	Good	$28,000.00	3.00%	$28,840.00
Fleming	Karen	Average	$41,100.00	3.00%	$42,333.00
Mc Key	Boo	Good	$39,600.00	3.00%	$40,788.00
Daniels	Phil	Good	$42,600.00	3.00%	$43,878.00
Park	Johnny	Excellent	$48,400.00	3.00%	$49,852.00
Johnson	Debbie	Excellent	$39,700.00	3.00%	$40,891.00
Drubin	Lolly	Good	$37,000.00	3.00%	$38,110.00
Titley	David	Good	$40,200.00	3.00%	$41,406.00
Grippando	Joan	Average	$26,100.00	3.00%	$26,883.00
Block	Leonard	Excellent	$26,200.00	3.00%	$26,986.00
Mills	Jack	Average	$44,600.00	3.00%	$45,938.00
Nagel	Mimi	Average	$46,200.00	3.00%	$47,586.00
Rammos	Mitzi	Excellent	$32,500.00	3.00%	$33,475.00
Vieth	Paula	Good	$40,400.00	3.00%	$41,612.00
Novicheck	Deborah	Good	$46,800.00	3.00%	$48,204.00
Brumbaugh	Paige	Average	$49,300.00	3.00%	$50,779.00
Abrams	Wendy	Good	$47,500.00	3.00%	$48,925.00
Harrison	Jenifer	Excellent	$44,800.00	3.00%	$46,144.00
Gander	John	Average	$38,400.00	3.00%	$39,552.00
Sell	Mike	Excellent	$43,500.00	3.00%	$44,805.00
Smith	Denise	Average	$45,200.00	3.00%	$46,556.00
Pawley	Eleanor	Excellent	$42,700.00	3.00%	$43,981.00
Harris	Jennifer	Average	$34,900.00	3.00%	$35,947.00
North	Randy	Excellent	$31,700.00	3.00%	$32,651.00
Shuffield	Jan	Good	$33,700.00	3.00%	$34,711.00
Barnes	Jeb	Excellent	$46,900.00	3.00%	$48,307.00

Record: 1 of 311

FIGURE 3.30 Raises and Bonuses Query

a. Open *a03p1Insurance*. Save the database as **a03p1Insurance_LastFirst**.

b. Examine the Relationships for the database. Notice the table structure, relationships, and fields. Once you are familiar with the database, close the Relationships window.

c. Create a new query in Design view. Add the Employees and Titles tables.

d. Add the LastName, FirstName, Performance, and Salary fields from the Employees table to the query. Add the 2016Increase field from the Titles table to the query.

e. Click the top row of the first blank column in the query design grid and type **NewSalary:[Salary]+ [Salary]*[2016Increase]** to create a calculated field that adds the existing salary to the increase. You may opt to use the Expression Builder if you prefer.

f. Click **Run** in the Results group to run the query. Look at the output in the Datasheet view. Verify that your answers are correct. Notice that the fourth column heading displays *2016 Increase*.

This is the caption for the 2016Increase field in the Titles table that was carried over to the query. When a caption exists for a field in the table Design view, the caption also displays in the Query Datasheet view instead of the field name in the query.

g. Switch back to Design view. Click in the **NewSalary calculated field**, display the Property Sheet, and then change the format to **Currency**. Type **New Salary** in the **Caption box**. Close the Property Sheet.

h. Save the query as **Raises and Bonuses**. Close the query.

i. Create a new query in Design view. Add the Employees and Titles tables.

You will create a query to show the average salary by position.

j. Add the TitleName field from the Titles table. From the Employees table, add the Salary field.

k. Display the Total row. Change the Total row for Salary to **Avg**. Leave the TitleName field set to **Group By**.

l. Click the **Salary field** and display the Property Sheet. Change the format for the field to **Currency**.

m. Run the query. Save the query as **Average Salary By Position** and close the query.

n. Exit Access and submit based on your instructor's directions.

2 Analyze Orders

FROM SCRATCH

You are the marketing manager of your company, and you must use the order information from an Access database to analyze sales trends. You need to determine the order revenue for all orders, grouped by Ship Country. The company would also like to check to see if there are order delays related to a specific employee. You must analyze shipping performance based on the number of days it takes to ship each order. This exercise follows the same set of skills as used in Hands-On Exercises 2 and 3 in the chapter. Refer to Figure 3.31 as you complete this exercise.

Shipping Issues

EmployeeID	TimeToShip
1	26
2	47
3	44
4	50
4	29
5	50
6	29
9	80

FIGURE 3.31 Shipping Issues Query

a. Create a new blank desktop database named **a03p2Orders_LastFirst**.
You will be shown a blank table in Datasheet view.

b. Click **View** in the Views group to switch to Design view. Save the table as **Orders**.

c. Change the first Field Name to **OrderID** and change the Data Type to **Number**. Type **CustomerID** in the second row and press **Tab**. Accept **Short Text** as the Data Type. Type **EmployeeID** in the third row and press **Tab**. Select **Number** for the Data Type.

d. Type and format the remainder of the fields as follows:

OrderDate	Date/Time
ShippedDate	Date/Time
ShipVia	Number
Revenue	Currency
ShipCountry	Short Text

e. Click **View** in the Views group to switch to Datasheet view. Click **Yes** to save the table. Add the three records as shown in the following table. Press **Tab** to move to the next field.

Order ID	Customer ID	Employee ID	Order Date	Shipped Date	Ship Via	Revenue	Ship Country
10248	WILMK	5	1/6/2017	1/19/2017	1	$142.86	Belgium
10249	TRADH	6	1/7/2017	1/10/2017	2	$205.38	Germany
10250	HANAR	4	1/10/2017	1/30/2017	2	$58.60	Venezuela

f. Open the *a03p2Orders* Excel file and click **Enable Editing**, if necessary. Click and hold **row 2** and drag through **row 828** so that all of the data rows are selected. Click **Copy** in the Clipboard group.

g. Return to Access and click on the **asterisk** (*) on the fourth row of the Orders table. Click **Paste** in the Clipboard group and click **Yes** to confirm that you want to paste all 827 rows into the Orders table. Save and close the table, and then close the spreadsheet and Excel. If prompted to save the data in the clipboard, click **No**.

h. Click the **CREATE tab** and click **Query Design** in the Queries group to start a new query. The Show Table dialog box opens. Add the Orders table and close the Show Table dialog box.

i. Add EmployeeID to the query and sort the table by EmployeeID in ascending order.

j. Use the Expression Builder to create a new calculated field. Type the following: **TimeToShip: [ShippedDate]-[OrderDate]**

Run the query and verify that TimeToShip is displaying valid values.

k. Switch back to Design view. Add the criteria **>21** to the TimeToShip field. Run the query and compare your results with Figure 3.31.

The results do not show a pattern of one employee's orders being delayed.

l. Save the query as **Shipping Issues**. Close the query.

m. Click the **CREATE tab** and click **Query Design** in the Queries group to start a new query. The Show Table dialog box opens. Add the Orders table and close the Show Table dialog box. Click **Totals** in the Show/Hide group.

n. Insert the ShipCountry and Revenue fields from the Orders table.

o. Verify the value for ShipCountry is set to **Group By** in the Totals row in Design view and verify that the value for the Revenue field is set to **Sum**.

p. Click in the **Revenue field**. Display the Property Sheet and change the caption to **Total Revenue**.

q. Click **Run** to see the results and save the query as **Revenue by Ship Country**. Close the query.

r. Exit Access and submit based on your instructor's directions.

1 Small Business Loans

ANALYSIS
CASE

FROM
SCRATCH

You are the manager of the small business loan department for the U.S. government. You need to calculate the payments for the loans that are currently on the books. To do this, you will need to create a query and add the Pmt function to calculate the loan payments for each loan. You will also summarize each loan by loan type (M=Mortgage, C=Car, and O=Other). Refer to Figure 3.32 as you complete this exercise.

Company	LoanID	Amount	InterestRate	Term	LoanClass	Payment
Jones and Co	1	29,000.00	5.90%	15	M	$243.15
Elements, Inc.	2	23,000.00	5.25%	5	C	$436.68
Godshall Meats, LLC	3	24,000.00	4.50%	3	C	$713.93
Godshall Meats, LLC	4	12,000.00	3.99%	10	O	$121.44
Godshall Meats, LLC	5	60,000.00	5.50%	30	M	$340.67
Elements, Inc.	6	4,000.00	6.50%	5	O	$78.26
Jones and Co	7	43,000.00	5.50%	5	O	$821.35
Jones and Co	8	37,000.00	5.80%	30	M	$217.10
Jones and Co	9	15,000.00	4.75%	3	O	$447.88
Jones and Co	10	8,000.00	5.50%	15	M	$65.37
Godshall Meats, LLC	11	34,000.00	5.00%	3	C	$1,019.01
Godshall Meats, LLC	12	13,000.00	7.99%	5	O	$263.53
Jones and Co	13	46,000.00	6.50%	5	C	$900.04
Godshall Meats, LLC	14	56,000.00	5.99%	15	M	$472.26
Godshall Meats, LLC	15	54,000.00	6.25%	15	M	$463.01
Jones and Co	16	39,000.00	6.50%	15	M	$339.73
Jones and Co	17	21,000.00	6.00%	30	M	$125.91
Godshall Meats, LLC	18	27,000.00	5.50%	3	O	$815.29
Elements, Inc.	19	44,000.00	5.50%	5	C	$840.45
Godshall Meats, LLC	20	22,000.00	6.25%	4	C	$519.20
Godshall Meats, LLC	21	6,000.00	6.75%	4	C	$142.98
Godshall Meats, LLC	22	46,000.00	6.50%	15	M	$400.71
Jones and Co	23	25,000.00	5.00%	15	M	$197.70
Jones and Co	24	11,000.00	5.55%	30	M	$62.80
Jones and Co	25	52,000.00	4.99%	15	M	$410.94
Total		751,000.00	5.74%	12		

FIGURE 3.32 Loan Payments Query Results

a. Open Access and create a new blank desktop database named **a03m1Loans_LastFirst**.
Access will display a table named Table1 with one field, ID.

b. Switch to Design view. Type **Customers** in the **Save As dialog box** and click **OK**.

c. Change the first Field Name to **CustomerID** and accept **AutoNumber** as the Data Type. Type **Company** in the second row and press **Tab**. Accept **Short Text** as the Data Type. Type **FirstName** in the third row and press **Tab**. Accept **Short Text** as the Data Type.

d. Type the remainder of the fields:

LastName	Short Text
City	Short Text
State	Short Text
Zip	Short Text

e. Verify the first field is set as the primary key.

f. Switch to Datasheet view. Click **Yes** to save the table. Add the records as shown in the following table. Note you will allow Access to assign an ID. Once you have entered the records, close the Customers table.

Company	FirstName	LastName	City	State	Zip
Jones and Co	Robert	Paterson	Greensboro	NC	27401
Elements, Inc.	Merve	Kana	Paterson	NJ	07505
Godshall Meats, LLC	Francisco	De La Cruz	Beverly Hills	CA	90210

 **DISCOVER**

g. Click the **External Data tab** and click **Excel** in the Import & Link group. Click **Browse** to locate the *a03m1Loans* spreadsheet. Select the database and click **Open** at the bottom of the dialog box.

h. Ensure the *Import the source data into a new table in the current database option* is selected and click **OK**. Click **Next** three times, until you are asked to add a primary key. From the *Choose my own Primary Key* menu, select **LoanID** (this should be the default option). Click **Next** once more and click **Finish**. Click **Close** in the Save Import Steps dialog box.

i. Open the Loans table in Design view. Select the **InterestRate field** and change the format to **Percent**. Change the field size for the CustomerID field to **Long Integer**. Click **Yes** when prompted that some data may be lost. Save and close the table.

j. Click the **Database Tools tab** and click **Relationships** in the Relationships group. Add both tables to the Relationships window and close the Show Table dialog box.

k. Drag the **CustomerID field** from the Customers table and drop it onto the CustomerID field in the Loans table. Check the **Enforce Referential Integrity check box** in the Edit Relationships dialog box and click **Create**. Save and close the Relationships window.

l. Create a query using the two tables that will calculate the payment amount for each loan. Add the following fields: **Company**, **LoanID**, **Amount**, **InterestRate**, **Term**, and **LoanClass**. Sort the query by LoanID in ascending order. Save the query as **Loan Payments**.

⭐ **m.** Add a calculated field named **Payment** in the first blank column to calculate the loan payment for each loan, using the Expression Builder. Use the Pmt function. Insert the appropriate field names in place of the placeholder arguments. Assume the loans have monthly payments (12 payments per year). Ensure the payment displays as a positive number. Run the query.

The first loan should have a value of approximately $243.15 (the extra decimal places will be removed shortly). Refer to Figure 3.32. If your number does not match up, reexamine your formula.

> **TROUBLESHOOTING:** If you cannot see the fields from your current query, ensure you have saved the query. Try closing and reopening the query.

n. Switch to Design view and change the display to **Currency format**. Run the query again to verify your changes. Compare your results to Figure 3.32.

o. Switch to Datasheet view and add a **Totals row**. Use it to calculate the sum of the amount column, the average interest rate, and the average term. Save and close the query.

p. Create a copy of Loan Payments. Save the new query as **Loan Payments Summary**.

q. Open the Loan Payments Summary query in Design view and rearrange the columns as follows: LoanClass, LoanID, Amount, and InterestRate. Delete columns CompanyName, Term, and Payment. Click **Totals** in the Show/Hide group. Change the Total row from left to right as follows: Group By, Count, Sum, and Avg. Run the query.

As we sorted the previous query by LoanID in Ascending order, this query will have the same sort by default.

r. Switch to Design view and display the Property Sheet. For the LoanID field, change the caption to **Loans**. For the Amount field, change the caption to **Total Amount** and change the format to **Currency**. For the InterestRate field, change the caption to **Avg Interest Rate** and change the format to **Percent**. Run the query. Save and close the query.

s. Exit Access, and submit based on your instructor's directions.

2 | Investment Properties

You are in charge of LGS Investment's database, which contains all of the information on the properties your firm has listed and sold. Your task is to determine the length of time each property was on the market before it sold. You also need to calculate the sales commission from each property sold. Two agents will receive commission on each transaction: the listing agent and the selling agent. You also need to summarize the sales data by employee and calculate the average number of days each employee's sales were on the market prior to selling and the total commission earned by the employees. Refer to Figure 3.33 as you complete this exercise.

Sales Summary by Subdivision

Subdivision	Total Sales	Days on Market	Listing Commission	Selling Commission
The Orchards	$1,288,000.00	22.75	$45,080.00	$32,200.00
Fair Brook	$1,053,900.00	24.75	$36,886.50	$26,347.50
Eagle Valley	$4,012,000.00	39.00	$140,420.00	$100,300.00
Wood	$1,428,650.00	47.91	$50,002.75	$35,716.25
Red Canyon	$3,790,000.00	52.00	$132,650.00	$94,750.00
Total	$11,572,550.00		$405,039.25	$289,313.75

FIGURE 3.33 Sales Summary Query

- **a.** Open *a03m2Homes*. Save the database as **a03m2Homes_LastFirst**.
- **b.** Create a new query, add the necessary tables, and then add the following fields: from the Agents table, add the LastName field; from the Properties table, the DateListed, DateSold, SalePrice, SellingAgent, and ListingAgent fields; and from the SubDivision table, the Subdivision field.
- **c.** Add criteria to the table to ensure the DateSold field is not empty (in other words, properties that have not been sold). Format the SalePrice field as **Currency**. Save the query as **Sales Report**.
- **d.** Create a calculated field using the Expression Builder named **DaysOnMarket** by subtracting DateListed from DateSold. This will calculate the number of days each sold property was on the market when it sold. Add a caption of **Days on Market**.
- **e.** Calculate the commissions for the selling and listing agents using two calculated fields. The listing commission rate is **3.5%** of the sale price, and the selling commission rate is **2.5%** of the sale price. You can type these in directly or use the Expression Builder. Name the newly created fields **ListComm** and **SellComm**. These fields contain similar expressions. They need to be named differently so that the proper agent—the listing agent or the selling agent—gets paid. Add captions and format the fields as **Currency**.
- **f.** Save the query after you verify that your calculations are correct. In Datasheet view, add the Total row. Calculate the average number of days on the market and the sum for the SalePrice and the two commission fields. Save and close the query.
- **g.** Create a copy of the Sales Report query named **Sales Summary by Last Name**. Remove the DateListed, SellingAgent, ListingAgent, and Subdivision fields.
- **h.** Display the Total row. Group by LastName and change the DateSold field Total row to **Where**, so the condition carries over. Show the sum of SalePrice, the average of DaysOnMarket, and the sum for both ListComm and SellComm. Change the caption for the SalePrice field to **Total Sales** and format the DaysOnMarket field as **Fixed**. Run the query. Adjust column widths as necessary.
- **i.** Adjust the Total row in the Datasheet view so it shows the sum of TotalSales. Save the query.
- **j.** (DISCOVER) Create a copy of the Sales Summary by Last Name query named **Sales Summary by Subdivision**. Modify the query so the grouping is based on the Subdivision field, not LastName. Sort the query results so the fewest Days on Market is first and the most Days on Market is last. Limit the results to the top five rows.
- **k.** Exit Access and submit based on your instructor's directions.

3 Political Pollsters

COLLABORATION CASE

You are working with a group that would like to analyze survey results. You are specifically looking for trends in the data based on gender, political affiliation, and income level. To demonstrate the power of Access, you and your group will perform a small survey, add the results to a database, and create some queries to demonstrate how grouping can help get results.

- **a.** Individually, open the *a03t1Survey.docx* file. Collect 10 responses each (unless directed to do otherwise by your instructor). You should try to survey a diverse group of people. You can do this survey via e-mail, Facebook, or another appropriate method. Bring the collected data to your group.
- **b.** Open the *a03t1Survey* database and save the database as **a03t1Survey_GroupName**. Use the Enter New Survey Result form to enter all of your information into the existing database. There are four records to start your database.

c. Open the Questions By Gender query. Notice your average for question 1 is a number between 1 and 3. As your survey document listed Agree as a 3, Neutral as 2, and Disagree as 1, the higher the value, the more strongly people agree with the question. Modify the query so that you display the average of Question2, Question3, Question4, and Question5. Change the format for the new fields to **Fixed**.

d. Create a query named **Questions By Party**, using the Questions By Gender query as a guide, grouping by the PoliticalAffiliation field rather than the Gender field.

e. Create a query named **Questions By Income Level**, using the Questions By Gender query as a guide, grouping by the IncomeLevel field rather than the Gender field.

f. Examine your results. Discuss the results with your group and type up your conclusions in a new Word document named **a03t1SurveyResults_GroupName**. You should be able to make around five conclusions. An example of a conclusion might be that people of lower income levels are less interested in being taxed to support free Internet than people of higher income.

g. Exit Access and Word and submit based on your instructor's directions.

Too Many Digits

RESEARCH CASE

This chapter introduced you to calculated fields. Open the database *a03b2Interest* and save the database as **a03b2Interest_LastFirst**. Open the Monthly Interest query in Datasheet view. Notice the multiple digits to the right of the decimal in the Monthly Interest column; there should only be two digits. Search the Internet to find a function that will resolve this rounding problem. You only want to display two digits to the right of the decimal (even when you click on a Monthly Interest value). Apply your changes to the Monthly Interest field, change the format to **Currency**, and then run the query to test your changes. Save the query as **Monthly Interest Revised**. If you manage to find a solution, add a second column named **MonthlyInterestRounded** that rounds to the nearest dollar. Close the query, close the database, and then exit Access. Submit your work based on your instructor's directions.

Payroll Summary Needed

DISASTER RECOVERY

You were given an Excel spreadsheet that contains paycheck information for your company. Your task is to summarize this data by employee Social Security Number (SSN) and report your results to your supervisor. Open the spreadsheet *a03b3Paychecks* and examine the data. Select all the data and copy the data. You will use Access to summarize the data in this spreadsheet. Open the Access database named *a03b3Payroll* and save it as **a03b3Payroll_LastFirst**. Open the Payroll table, select the first row, and then paste the records. Create a new totals query that summarizes the data by SSN; include the count of pay periods (using the ID field) and the sum of each currency field. Do not include the PayDate field in this query. Create a calculated field named **Total Compensation**, which totals all assets the employees have, including pay, 401(k) retirement, and health benefits. Add appropriate captions to shorten the default captions. Run the query and save it as **Payroll Summary**. Close the query, close the database, and then exit Access. Submit the database based on your instructor's directions.

Customer Service Dialog

SOFT SKILLS CASE

Passaic County Technology Services (PCTS) provides technical support for a number of local companies. Part of their customer service evaluation involves logging how calls are closed and a quick, one-question survey given to customers at the end of a call, asking them to rate their experience from 1 (poor) to 5 (excellent). To evaluate the effectiveness of their operation, they have asked you to create some queries to help evaluate the performance of the company. Open the database *a03b4PCTS* and save the database as **a03b4PCTS_LastFirst**.

1. Create a query to show each technician and his or her effectiveness.
   - List each technician's first and last names, the number of calls, and the average of the customer's satisfaction for all calls assigned to the rep.
   - Format the average in Standard format and sort by the average so the highest average customer satisfaction appears first.
   - Save the query as **Tech Effectiveness**.

2. Create a query to show how effective the company is by call type.
   - List the call type's description (for example, Hardware Support) and the number of calls and average customer satisfaction for all calls of that type.
   - Format the average in Standard format and sort by the average so the highest average customer satisfaction appears first.
   - Save the query as **Call Type Effectiveness**.

3. Create a query to show how satisfied each customer is.

- List the company name and the number of calls and average customer satisfaction for all calls.
- Format the average in Standard format and sort by the average so the highest average customer satisfaction appears first.
- Save the query as **Customer Happiness**.

Now that you have created these queries, your supervisor should be able to quickly determine which technicians have the happiest customers, which call types the company is most effective on, and which customers are less happy than others. Close the queries, close the database, and then exit Access. Submit the database based on your instructor's directions.

Northwind Traders, an international gourmet food distributor, is concerned about shipping delays over the past six months. Review the orders over the past six months and identify any order that was not shipped within 30 days. Each customer that falls within that time frame will be called to inquire about any problems the delay may have caused. In addition, you will create an order summary and an order summary by country.

Database File Setup

Open the food database, use Save As to make a copy of the database, and then use the new database to complete this capstone exercise. You will add yourself to the employee database.

a. Locate and open *a03c1Food* and save the database as **a03c1Food_LastFirst**.

b. Open the Employees table. Add yourself as an employee. Fill in all information, with the hire date as today. Set your *Title* to **Technical Aide**, extension to **1144**, and the Reports To field to **Buchanan, Steven**. Leave the EmployeePicture field blank.

c. Close the Employees table.

Shipping Efficiency Query

You need to create a query to calculate the number of days between the date an order was placed and the date the order was shipped for each order. As you create the query, run the query at several intervals so you can verify that the data look correct. The result of your work will be a list of orders that took more than three weeks to ship. The salespeople will be calling each customer to see if there was any problem with their order.

a. Create a query using Query Design. From the Customers table, include the fields CompanyName, ContactName, ContactTitle, and Phone. From the Orders table, include the fields OrderID, OrderDate, and ShippedDate.

b. Run the query and examine the records. Save the query as **Shipping Efficiency**.

c. Add a calculated field named **DaysToShip** to calculate the number of days taken to fill each order. (*Hint*: The expression will include the OrderDate and the ShippedDate; the results will not contain negative numbers.)

d. Run the query and examine the results. Does the data in the DaysToShip field look accurate? Save the query.

e. Add criteria to limit the query results to include any order that took more than 30 days to ship.

f. Add the Quantity field from the Order Details table and the ProductName field from the Products table to the query. Sort the query by ascending OrderID. When the sales reps contact these customers, these two fields will provide useful information about the orders.

g. Switch to Datasheet view to view the final results. This list will be distributed to the sales reps so they can contact the customers. In Design view, add the caption **Days to Ship** to the DaysToShip field.

h. Save and close the query.

Order Summary Query

You need to create an Order Summary that will show the total amount of each order in one column and the total discount amount in another column. This query will require four tables: Orders, Order Details, Products, and Customers. Query to determine if employees are following the employee discount policy. You will group the data by employee name, count the orders, show the total dollars, and show the total discount amount. You will then determine which employees are following the company guidelines.

a. Create a query using Query Design and add the four tables above. Add the fields OrderID and OrderDate. Set both fields' Total row to **Group By**.

b. Add a calculated field in the third column. Name the field **ExtendedAmount**. This field should multiply the number of items ordered by the price per item. This will calculate the total amount for each order. Format the calculated field as **Currency** and change the caption to **Total Dollars**. Change the Total row to **Sum**.

c. Add a calculated field in the fourth column. Name the field **DiscountAmount**. The field should multiply the number of items ordered, the price per item, and the discount field. This will calculate the total discount for each order. Format the calculated field as **Currency** and add a caption of **Discount Amt**. Change the Total row to **Sum**.

d. Run the query. Save the query as **Order Summary**. Return to Design view.

e. Add criteria to the OrderDate field so only orders made between 1/1/2016 and 12/31/2016 are displayed. Change the Total row to **Where**. This expression will display only orders that were created in 2016.

f. Run the query and view the results. Save and close the query.

Order Financing Query

Northwind is considering offering financing options to their customers with 5% interest, to be paid over 12 months.

a. Create a copy of the Order Summary query named **Order Financing**.

b. Switch to Design view of the new query and remove the DiscountAmount field.

c. Add a new field using the Expression Builder named **SamplePayment**. Insert the Pmt function with the following parameters:

- Use **.05/12** for the rate argument (5% interest, paid monthly)
- Use the number **12** for the num_periods argument (12 months)
- Use the calculated field **ExtendedAmount** for the present_value

d. Change the Total row to **Expression** for the SamplePayment field.

e. Change the Format for the SamplePayment field to **Currency**.

f. Save and close the query.

Order Summary by Country Query

You need to create one additional query based on the Order Summary query you created in a previous step. This new query will enable you to analyze the orders by country.

a. Create a copy of the Order Summary query named **Order Summary by Country**.

b. Replace the OrderID field with the Country field in Design view of the new query.

c. Run the query and examine the summary records; there should be 21 countries listed.

d. Switch to Design view and change the sort order so that the country with the highest ExtendedAmount is first and the country with the lowest ExtendedAmount is last.

e. Run the query and verify the results.

f. Save and close the query.

g. Exit Access and submit based on your instructor's directions.

Creating and Using Professional Forms and Reports

Moving Beyond Tables and Queries

OBJECTIVES | AFTER YOU READ THIS CHAPTER, YOU WILL BE ABLE TO:

1. Create forms using form tools p. 258

2. Use form views p. 265

3. Work with a form layout control p. 268

4. Sort records in a form p. 270

5. Create reports using report tools p. 278

6. Use report views p. 285

7. Modify a report p. 287

8. Sort records in a report p. 290

CASE STUDY | Coffee Shop Starts New Business

The La Vida Mocha coffee shop in Paterson, New Jersey, once was an ordinary coffee shop selling retail coffee, tea, and pastries to its loyal customers in northern New Jersey. Then, in 2012, owner Ryung Park decided to use her knowledge of the coffee industry to sell coffee products to businesses in her area. This new venture grew quickly and soon became 25% of her annual revenue. Realizing that this new business would need more of her time each day, she decided to create an Access database to help track her customer, product, and order information.

With the help of a student from Passaic County Community College, she created a database with tables to hold data for customers, products, sales reps, and orders. She is currently using these tables to enter and retrieve information.

Ryung wants to have one of her employees, Nabil, manage the database. However, she does not want him to work in the tables; she wants him to work with forms. Ryung heard that forms have an advantage over tables because they can be designed to show one record at a time—this will reduce data-entry errors. Ryung would also like to create several reports for her own benefit so she can stay on top of the business by reviewing the reports each week.

You have been hired to help Ryung create the new forms and reports that she needs for the business. She will describe the forms and reports to you in detail and also provide written instructions. You will be expected to work independently to create the forms and reports.

Form Basics

A *form* is a database object that is used to add data into or edit data in a table. Most Access database applications use forms rather than tables for data entry and for looking up information. Three main reasons exist for using forms rather than tables for adding, updating, and deleting data. They are:

- You are less likely to edit the wrong record by mistake.
- You can create a form that shows data from more than one table simultaneously.
- You can create Access forms to match paper forms.

If you are adding data using a table with many columns, you could jump to the wrong record in the middle of a column accidentally. For example, you could enter the data for one record correctly for the first 10 fields but then jump to the row above and overwrite existing data for the remaining field values unintentionally. In this case, two records would have incorrect or incomplete data. A form will not allow this type of error because most forms restrict entry to one record at a time.

Many forms require two tables as their record source. For example, you may want to view a customer's details (name, address, e-mail, phone, etc.) as well as all of the orders he or she has placed. This would require using data from both the Customers and the Orders tables in one form. Similarly, you may want to view the header information for an order while also viewing the detail line items for the order. This would require data from both the Orders and Order Details tables. Both of these examples enable a user to view two record sources at the same time and make changes—additions, edits, or deletions—to one or both sources of data.

Finally, when paper forms are used to collect information, it is a good idea to design the electronic forms to match the paper forms. This will make data entry more efficient and reliable and ease the transition from paper form to computer form. Access forms can be designed to emulate the paper documents already in use in an organization. This facilitates the simultaneous use of both paper forms and electronic data. Databases do not necessarily eliminate paper forms; they supplement and coexist with them.

In this section, you will learn the basics of form design. You will discover multiple methods to create and modify Access forms.

Creating Forms Using Form Tools

Access provides a variety of options for creating forms. There are a number of built-in layouts that you can choose from. Database designers may eventually develop a preference for one or two types of form layouts, but keep in mind you have a lot of options if needed. You will want to find a balance between creating a form that is simple while still powerful enough to be of use.

Access provides 14 different tools for creating forms. You can find these options in the Forms group on the Create tab. The Forms group contains four of the most common form tools (Form, Form Design, Blank Form, and Form Wizard), a list of Navigation forms, and More Forms, as shown in Figure 4.1. Navigation forms provides a list of six templates to create a user interface for a database; the More Forms command lists four additional form tools (Multiple Items, Datasheet, Split Form, and Modal Dialog). Select a table or query, click one of the tools, and Access will create a form using the selected table or query. The most common of these tools, the *Form tool*, is used to create data-entry forms for customers, employees, products, and other primary tables.

FIGURE 4.1 Forms Group on Create Tab

A complete list of all the Form tools available in Access is found in the Form Tools Reference at the end of this section. Many of the tools will be covered in this chapter. Some tools will not be covered, however, because they are not commonly used or because they are beyond the scope of this chapter (e.g., Form Design, Blank Form, Navigation forms, and Modal Dialog form). Use Microsoft Access Help to find more information about Form tools not covered in this chapter.

Ideally, a form should simplify data entry. Creating a form is a collaborative process between the form designer and the form users. This process continues throughout the life of the form, because the data needs of an organization may change. Forms designed long ago to collect information for a new customer account may not have an e-mail field; the form would have to be modified to include an e-mail field. The form designer needs to strike a balance between collecting the information users need to do their jobs and cluttering the form with extraneous fields. The users of the data know what they need and usually offer good feedback about which fields should be on a form. If you listen to their suggestions, your forms will function more effectively, the users' work will be easier, and your data will contain fewer data-entry errors.

After discussing the form with the users, it will help you to create the form in Access if you sketch the form first. After sketching the form, you will have a better idea of which form tool to use to create the form. After the form is created, use the sketch to determine which fields are required and in what the order of fields should be.

Identify a Record Source

Before you create a form, you must identify the record source. A *record source* is the table or query that supplies the records for a form or report. You may also see the record source referred to as a data source in certain help files and instructions. Use a table if you want to include all the records from a single table. Use a query if you need to filter the records in a table, if you need to combine records from two or more related tables, or if you do not want to display all fields.

For example, if a sales rep wants to create a form that displays customers from a single state only—where his customers reside—he should base the form on a query. Or, if a parts manager needs to review only parts with a zero on-hand quantity, he could create a form based on a query that includes only records with on-hand equal to zero.

Use the Form Tool

STEP 1 >> As noted earlier, the Form tool is the most common tool for creating forms. To use the Form tool:

1. Select a table or query from the Navigation Pane
2. On the CREATE tab, in the Forms group, click Form.

Based on that table or query, Access automatically creates a new form. You may need to modify the form slightly, but you can create a stacked layout form in a just one click. A *stacked layout* displays fields in a vertical column. Because this is a form, it will display one record at a time, as shown in Figure 4.2. The other type of layout you may use is a *tabular layout*, which displays data horizontally across the page.

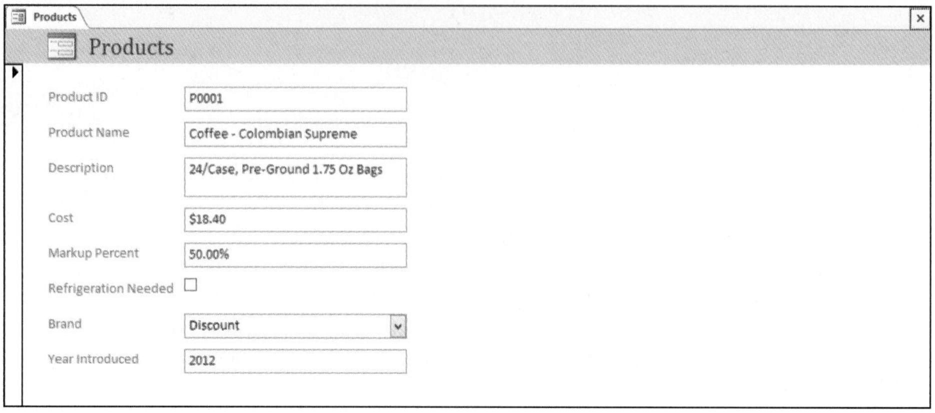

FIGURE 4.2 Form with a Stacked Layout

Understand Controls

Notice in Figure 4.3 that each field has a label on the left and a text box on the right. These are referred to as controls. *Controls* are the text boxes, buttons, boxes, and other tools you use to add, edit, and display the data in a form or report. In Figure 4.3, Product ID, Product Name, Description, and the rest of the field labels are controls. In addition, the boxes containing the values for each field (P0001, Coffee–Colombian Supreme, etc.) are all controls. More specifically, the form locations that hold data are generally text box controls, and the text in front of those, marking what the field means, are label controls.

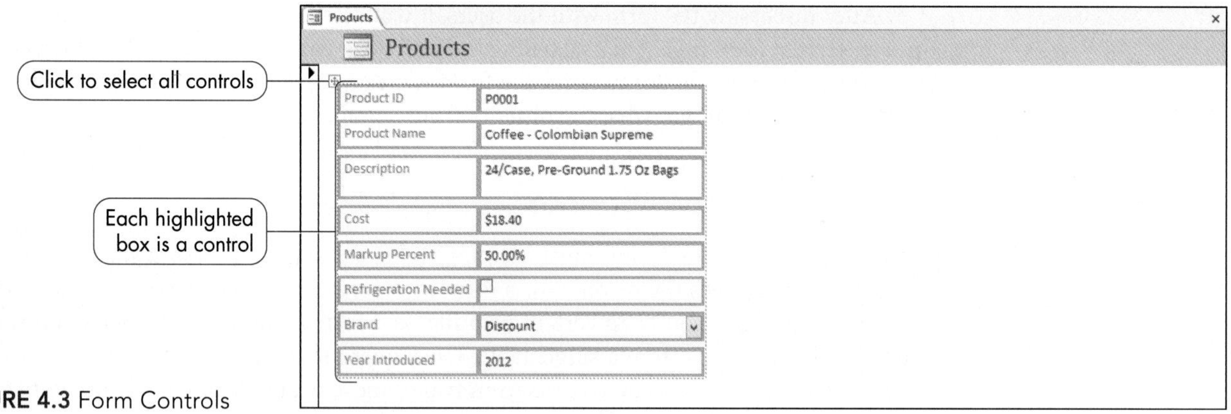

FIGURE 4.3 Form Controls

A *layout control* provides guides to help keep controls aligned horizontally and vertically and give your form a uniform appearance. The fields are all aligned in Figure 4.3 because a layout control keeps them that way. Picture the layout control as a bookcase, with each field being a shelf on the bookcase.

Work with Form Views

There are three different views of a form available. The first, *Form view*, is a simplified interface primarily used for data entry. This view does not enable you to make changes to the layout. As such, the Form view is an excellent way for users to interact with the form. This ensures they do not accidentally change the form layout. Figure 4.4 shows a form in Form view. Notice forms can include features such as drop-down lists.

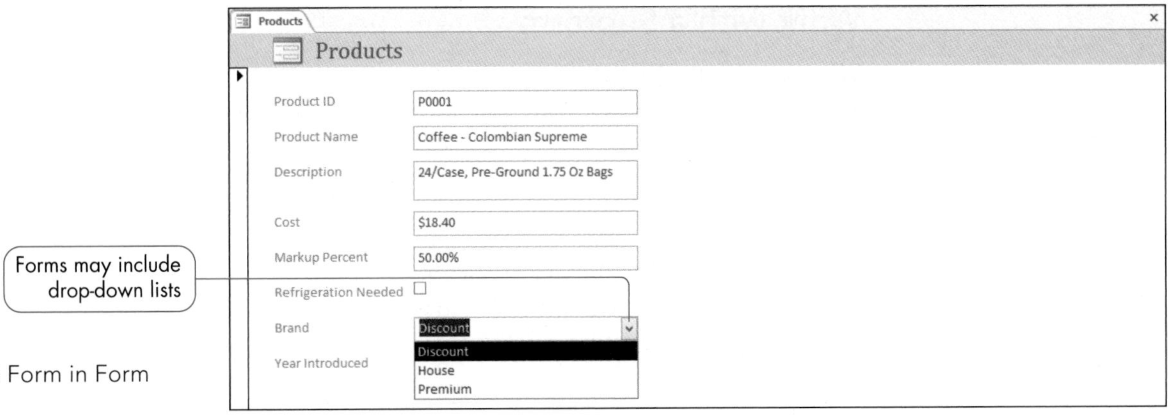

Forms may include drop-down lists

FIGURE 4.4 Form in Form View

The second view, *Layout view*, enables users to make changes to the layout while viewing the data on the form. Reports have a similar view with the same name. This will be discussed later in the chapter. Layout view is useful for testing the functionality of the form and adjusting sizes of fields as needed. In the previous section, you were shown how to create a form using the Form Tool. When you do this, Access opens the form in Layout view ready for customizing. Figure 4.5 shows a form in Layout view.

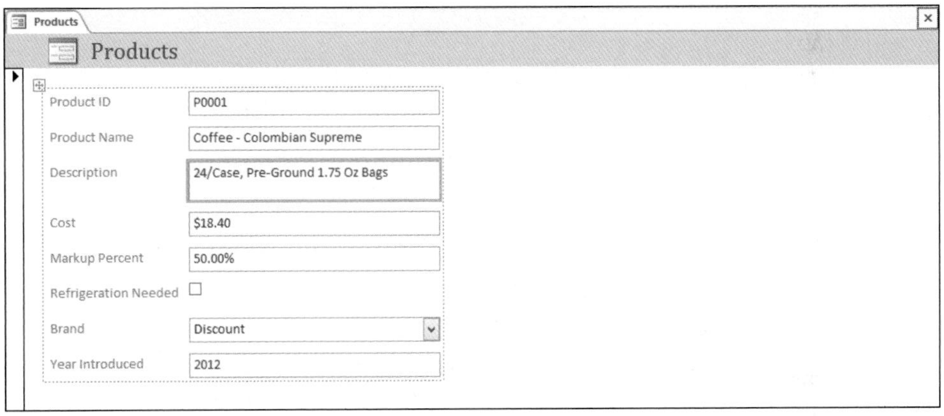

FIGURE 4.5 Form in Layout View

The third view, *Design view*, allows you to change advanced design settings you cannot see in the Layout view, such as a background image. Reports also have a Design view, which will also be discussed later in this chapter. Design view is a much more powerful way of changing the form layout. It is more complex than Layout view, so you would likely use Design view only when you need to perform advanced form layout adjustments. Figure 4.6 shows a form in Design view.

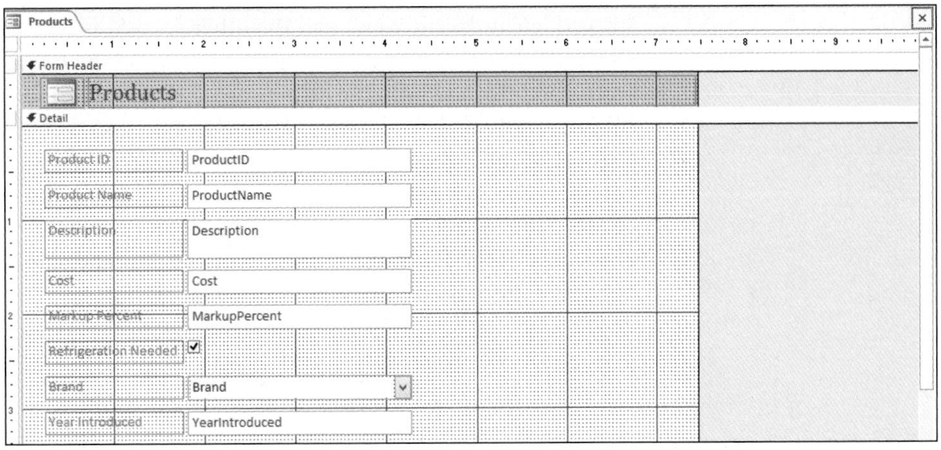

FIGURE 4.6 Form in Design View

These three views will be described in more detail later in this chapter.

Work with a Subform

When you use the Form tool to create a form, Access analyzes the table relationships you created in the database. If the table that the main form is based upon is related to another table through a relationship, then Access automatically adds a subform to the main form. The subform displays records in the related table, generally laid out in a table, similar to an Excel spreadsheet. For example, assume you have sales representatives stored in a SalesReps table and customer information stored in a Customers table. Also assume a relationship exists between the two tables. If you create a new form based on SalesReps using the Form tool, Access will add a Customers subform to the bottom of the main form, showing all customers assigned to each sales representative (see Figure 4.7).

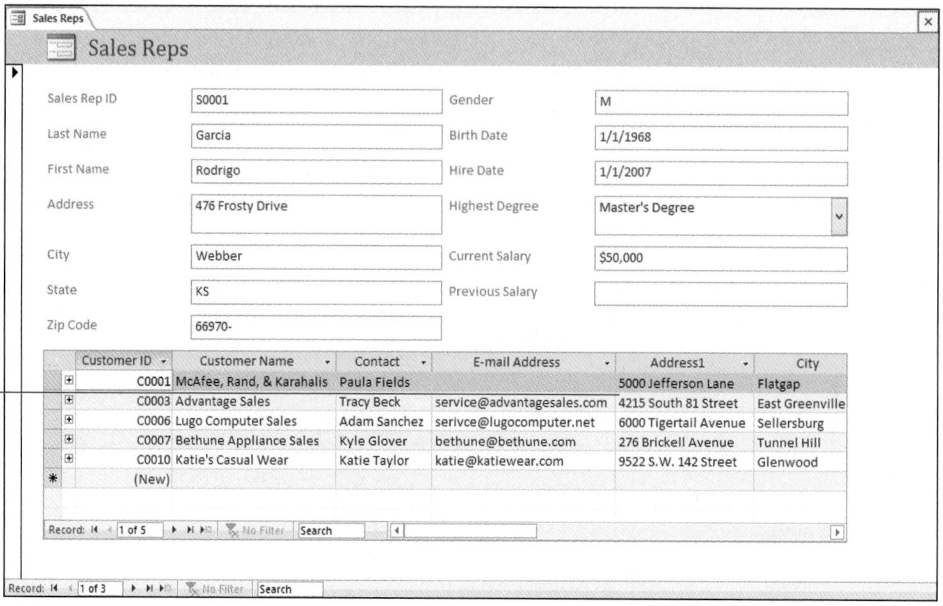

Subform displays related records

FIGURE 4.7 Form with a Subform

At times, you may want the subform as part of your form; at other times, you may want to remove it. To remove a subform from a form:

1. Switch to Design view.
2. Click anywhere inside the subform.
3. Press Delete.

Create a Split Form

A *split form* combines two views of the same record source—one section is displayed in a stacked layout (form view) and the other section is displayed in a tabular layout (datasheet view). By default, the form view is positioned on the top and the datasheet view is displayed on the bottom; however, the form's page orientation can be changed from horizontal to vertical in Layout view. If you select a record in the top half of the form, the same record will be selected in the bottom half of the form and vice versa. For example, if you create a split form based on an Orders table, you can select an Order in the datasheet section and then see the order's information in the *Form view* section (see Figure 4.8). This gives you the option to enter data in the Form view while being able to navigate between orders more quickly. The top and bottom halves are synchronized at all times.

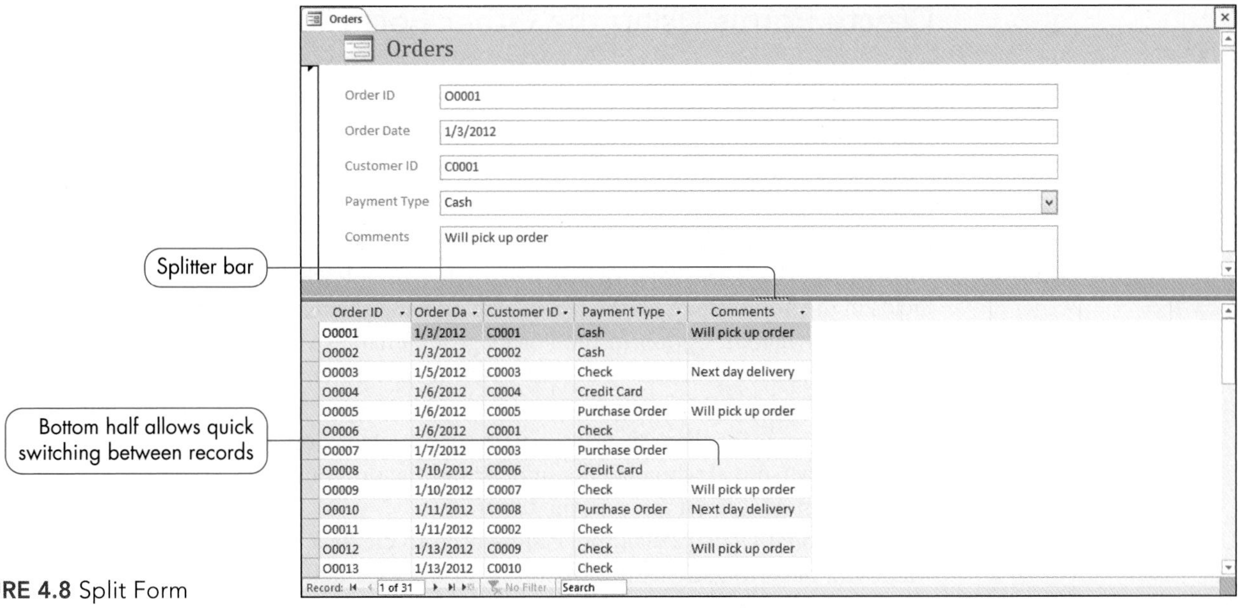

FIGURE 4.8 Split Form

To create a split form, do the following:

1. Select a table or query in the Navigation Pane.
2. Click the CREATE tab.
3. Click More Forms in the Forms group.
4. Select Split Form.

Once you have completed those steps, a new split form displays. You can add, edit, or delete records in either section. The *splitter bar* divides the form into two halves. Users can adjust the splitter bar up or down unless the form designer disables this option.

Create a Multiple Items Form

A *Multiple Items form* displays multiple records in a tabular layout similar to a table's Datasheet view. However, a Multiple Items form gives you more customization options than a datasheet, such as the ability to add graphical elements, buttons, and other controls. Figure 4.9 shows a Multiple Items form created from the Employees table.

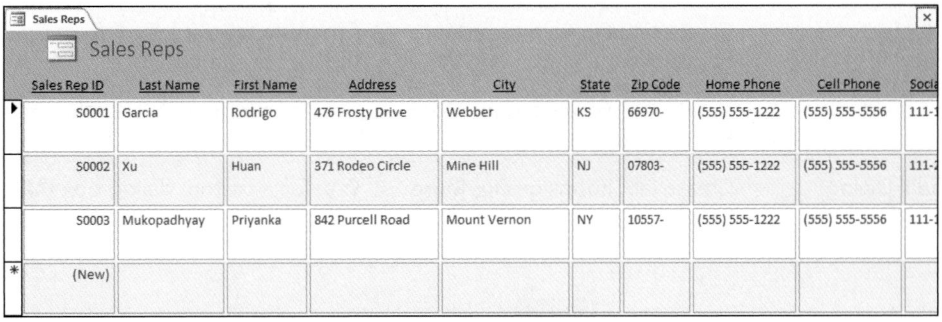

FIGURE 4.9 Multiple Items Form

To create a Multiple Items form, do the following:

1. Select a table or query from the Navigation Pane.
2. Click the CREATE tab.
3. Click More Forms in the Forms group.
4. Select Multiple Items from the list of options.

Create Forms Using the Other Form Tools

A Datasheet form is a replica of a table or query's Datasheet view except that it still retains some of the form properties. Database designers can also use the Datasheet form to display data in a table-like format but change the form properties to not allow a record to be deleted. This would protect the data from accidental damage while still providing the users with the familiar Datasheet view.

The Form Design tool and the Blank Form tools can be used to create a form manually. Click one of these tools and Access will open a completely blank form. Click Add Existing Fields in the Tools group on the Design tab and add the necessary fields.

The Navigation option in the Forms group enables you to create user interface forms that have the look and feel of a Web-based form and enable users to open and close the objects of a database. In other words, you could set up a form that allows users to click on the forms you want them to view. This is an excellent option to simplify the database for data-entry personnel who may not understand the program. These forms are also useful for setting up an Access database on the Internet.

The Modal Dialog Form tool can be used to create a dialog box. This feature is useful when you need to gather information from the user before working with another object. Dialog boxes are common in all Microsoft Office applications.

REFERENCE Form Tools

Form Tool	Location	Use
Form	Create tab, Forms group	Creates a form with a stacked layout displaying all of the fields in the record source.
Form Design	Create tab, Forms group	Create a new blank form in Design view.
Blank Form	Create tab, Forms group	Create a new blank form in Layout view.
Form Wizard	Create tab, Forms group	Answer a series of questions and Access will create a custom form for you.
Navigation	Create tab, Forms group, Navigation button	Create user-interface forms that can also be used on the Internet. Six different Navigation form layouts are available from the drop-down list.
Split Form	Create tab, Forms group, More Forms button	Creates a two-part form with a stacked layout in one section and a tabular layout in the other.
Multiple Items	Create tab, Forms group, More Forms button	Creates a tabular layout form that includes all of the fields from the record source.
Datasheet	Create tab, Forms group, More Forms button	Creates a form that resembles the datasheet of a table or query.
Modal Dialog	Create tab, Forms group, More Forms button	Creates a custom dialog box that forces the user to respond before working with another object.

TIP Print with Caution!

Users can print a form by clicking the File tab and selecting the Print option. However, printing from a form should be done with caution. Forms are not generally designed for printing, so you may end up with hundreds of pages of printouts. A form with a stacked layout of 1,000 records could print thousands of pages unless you choose the Selected Record(s) option in the Print dialog box. The Selected Record(s) option, as shown in Figure 4.10, will only print the current record (or selected records).

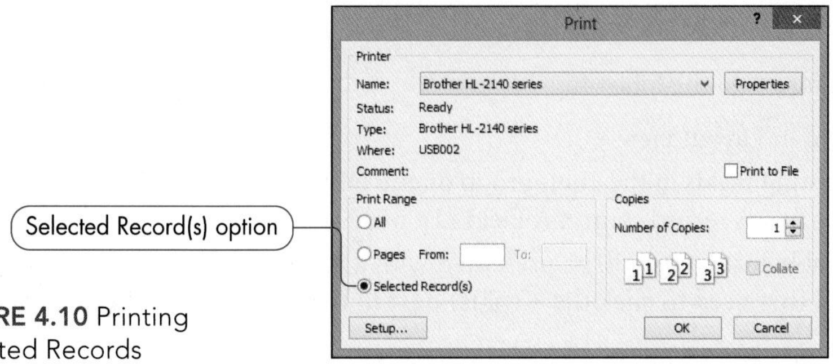

FIGURE 4.10 Printing Selected Records

Using Form Views

Access provides different views for a form, similar to the different views in tables and queries. Tables and queries have Design view and Datasheet view. Most forms have Layout view, Form view, and Design view.

As you work with the form tools to create and modify forms, you will often need to switch between the three form views in Access: Layout view, Form view, and Design view. Most of your design work will be done in Layout view; occasionally, you will switch to Design view to add a more advanced feature, such as a background, or to use a layout option that is otherwise unavailable. Users of the form will only work in Form view. There should be no reason for a user to switch to Layout or Design view. Modifications to the form should be done by the designated form designer.

After a form is generated by a Form tool, you may need to modify it. Commonly, you may add a field, remove a field, change the order of fields, change the width of a field, modify the theme, or modify label text. These changes can be made in a form's Layout view. Advanced changes, such as changing headers or footers or adding a background image, can be made in a form's Design view.

Edit Data in Form View

STEP 2>> Use Form view to add, edit, and delete data in a form; the layout and design of the form cannot be changed in this view. Recall from a previous chapter that you can move from one field to another field by pressing Tab on your keyboard or clicking the desired field with your mouse.

Alter a Form in Layout View

Use Layout view to alter the form design while still viewing the data. You use Layout view to add or delete fields in a form, modify field properties, change the column widths, and enhance a form by adding a color scheme or styling. While you are working in Layout view, you can see the data as it would appear in Form view, but you cannot edit the data in Layout view. Seeing the data in Layout view makes it easier to size controls, for example, to ensure the data is visible. It is good practice to test a form in Form view after making changes in Layout view.

Use the Form Layout Tools Tabs

Forms have a number of options you can use to format. Once you are in Layout or Design view, you will have access to the report layout tools. You have three tabs available:

- Design: Use this tab to make changes to the design of the form, such as adding sorting, changing themes, and inserting additional controls.

- Arrange: Use this tab to change the layout of a form, to move fields, or to insert space.

- Format: Use this tab to change the font; add or remove bolding, italics, or underlining; change font size; change font color or background; adjust text alignment; or add a background image.

Add a Field to a Form

STEP 3 To add a field to a form, do the following:

1. Open the form in Layout view.
2. Click Add Existing Fields in the Tools group on the DESIGN tab to reveal the available fields from the form's record source. A Field List pane appears at the right of your screen.
3. For a single-table form, you will be presented with a list of fields. For a multiple-table form, you will first need to click the + (plus) next to the appropriate table to locate the desired field.
4. Drag the new field to the precise location on the form, using the shaded line (the color may vary, based on your Office configuration) as a guide for the position of the new field. The other fields will automatically adjust to make room for the new field.

Depending on the layout of the form, the shaded line will appear vertically (tabular layouts) or horizontally (stacked).

Delete a Field from a Form

To delete a field, do the following:

1. Switch to Layout view.
2. Click the text box control of the field to be deleted (note the shaded border around the control).
3. Click the Select Row option on the Layout tab in the Rows & Columns group.
4. Press Delete. The other fields will automatically adjust to close the gap around the deleted field.

Adjust Column Widths in a Form

When column widths are adjusted in a form with a stacked layout, all columns will increase and decrease together. Therefore, it is best to make sure that field columns are wide enough to accommodate the widest value in the table. For example, if a form contains information such as a customer's first name, last name, address, city, state, ZIP, phone, and e-mail address, you will need to make sure the longest address and the longest e-mail address are completely visible (because those fields are likely to contain the longest data values).

To decrease column widths in a form with a stacked layout, do the following:

1. Open the form in Layout view.
2. Click the text box control of the first field to select it.
3. Move the mouse over the right border of the field until the mouse pointer turns into a double arrow.
4. Drag the right edge to the left or right until you arrive at the desired width.

You will notice that all the fields change as you change the width of the first field. All fields that are part of the layout will have a standard width. If you wanted to resize one specific field, you would need to remove that field from the layout control. Note that "removing a field from the layout control" does not mean "removing a field from the form." Recall that the layout control keeps each field in place. If you remove a field from the layout control, it stays on the form but can be moved more freely.

Modify Form Controls using the Format Tab

When you view a form in Layout view, the Form Layout Tools tab displays the Design tab, Arrange tab, and Format tab. The Format tab, shown in Figure 4.11, contains a series of commands that enable you change the font, display, and alignment of the controls on a form. This is useful if you need to quickly change the look of one cell. For example, if you have a form that shows the information about the sale of a vehicle, you might want to emphasize the net profit of each transaction.

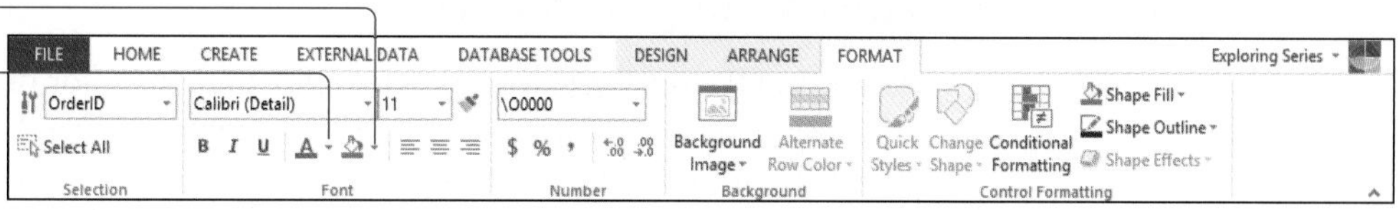

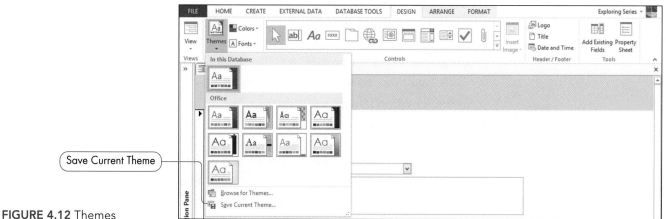

FIGURE 4.11 Format Tab

From this tab, you can change a number of properties. For example, you can perform these tasks, and more:

- Change the font size: Click the Font Size arrow in the Font group.
- Change emphasis: In the Font group, add bold, italics, or underlining.
- Change alignment: In the Font group, choose left, center, or right align.
- Change a control's background color: Click the Background Color arrow (refer to Figure 4.11) and select a color for the background.
- Change a control's font color: Click the Font Color arrow (refer to Figure 4.11) and select a color for the cell's font.
- Change number format: In the Number group, change to currency, percentage, or add commas; increase or decrease decimal places.

Selecting Controls

Controls, as mentioned, include both the labels identifying a field and the text box displaying field values. There may be times you want to select multiple controls. You will notice when you click on one control and click on another that the original control is deselected. If you need to select multiple controls, click on the first control you wish to select, hold down CTRL on your keyboard, and then click on the other controls you wish to select. Once they are selected, you can perform many tasks, such as formatting or deletion.

Add a Theme to a Form

You can apply a theme to a form in order to give the form a more professional finish. A ***theme*** is a defined set of colors, fonts, and graphics that can be applied to a form (or report). Click Themes in the Themes group on the Design tab, select a theme from the Themes Gallery, and Access will apply the theme to the form. Each theme has a name; you can determine the name of a theme by pointing the mouse to a theme and waiting for the tip to pop up, showing the name.

You can apply a theme to a single form or to all the forms in your database that share a common theme. Applying the same theme to all forms will provide a consistent look to your database; most users prefer a consistent theme when using Access forms. The same themes found in Access are also available in Excel, Word, and PowerPoint. Therefore, you can achieve a uniform look across all Office applications. Themes can be customized and saved so that the theme you create can be used again. Click the Save Current Theme command as shown in Figure 4.12 to do so.

Save Current Theme

FIGURE 4.12 Themes

Add Styling to a Form

Modifying the font size of labels, changing the font color of labels, and adding a background color can enhance a form and also make it more usable. It is best to choose a familiar font family, such as Arial or Calibri, for both the form label controls and the text box controls. Apply bold to the labels in order to help the user distinguish labels from the text boxes. You should also consider right-aligning the labels and left-aligning the text box controls to reduce distance between the label and field, as illustrated in Figure 4.13. You may also want to separate the primary key field from the rest of the form by providing a sufficient visual boundary.

One note of caution: Try to avoid what graphic artists refer to as the "ransom note effect." Using too many font families, font sizes, colors, and other effects can take away from your design.

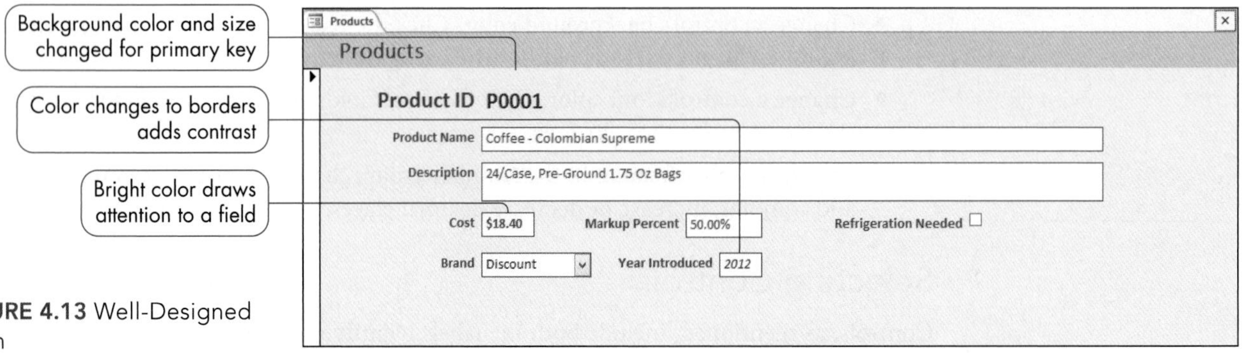

FIGURE 4.13 Well-Designed Form

Working with a Form Layout Control

Whenever you use one of the form tools to create a new form, Access will add a layout control to help align the fields. Recall that the layout control helps keep controls aligned in order to give your form a uniform appearance. The layout control provides structure for the fields but is restrictive. If you wish to have more control over the location of your fields, you can remove the layout control and position the controls manually on the grid.

Modify a Form Using the Arrange Tab

The Arrange tab appears in both Layout view and Design view. Use this tab to change the layout of a form, to move fields up and down, to insert a space above or below your current position, or to insert a space to the left or the right of the current field. To use these commands, first open a form in Layout view or Design view and click the Arrange tab. Next, select a field or fields and click the appropriate command.

The Table group contains commands that enable you to add gridlines to a form's layout, to change a form's layout from stacked to tabular (and vice versa), or to remove a form's layout. The Remove Layout command is only available in Design view.

STEP 4 ⟩⟩   To change the arrangement of a form, do the following:

1. Open the form in Layout view.
2. Click any of the field text boxes.
3. Click the ARRANGE tab.
4. Click Select Layout in the Rows & Columns group.
5. Click Tabular or Stacked in the Table group.

    To remove a form layout control, do the following:

1. Switch to Design view (if you are not in Design view, you will not see the Remove Layout option).
2. Click on one of the fields that is currently part of the layout.
3. On the ARRANGE tab, click Select Layout in the Rows & Columns group.
4. Click Remove Layout in the Table group.
5. Switch to Layout view to arrange fields.

If you have removed the layout control or have a form that never had one, you can add one if you do the following:

1. Switch to Layout view or Design view (you can switch in either view).
2. Select all the controls you would like added back to the layout control, such as the field labels and text boxes. Hold down CTRL on your keyboard and click on each control, or click the FORMAT tab and in the Selection group, click Select All if you want to add everything to a layout.
3. On the ARRANGE tab, in the Table group, click Tabular or Stacked

The Rows & Columns group contains commands that enable you to insert rows and columns inside a form's layout. For example, in a form with a stacked layout, you may want to separate some fields from the rest of the fields. To do this, you could select a text box and click Insert Below. This will create a space after the selected field. This group also contains the Select Layout, Select Column, and Select Row commands. In Figure 4.14, three rows have been inserted above the Cost field.

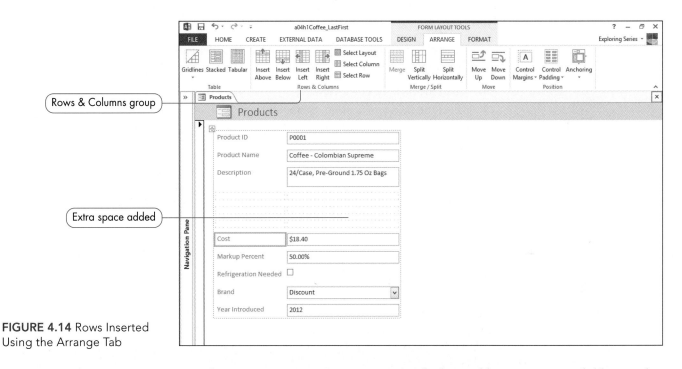

FIGURE 4.14 Rows Inserted Using the Arrange Tab

The Move group contains two commands that enable you to move a field up or down in a stacked layout. For example, if you want to move the second field in a stacked layout to the first position, select the second field's text box and label and click Move Up in the Move group. Moving fields up or down in a form may cause unexpected results; you can always use the Undo command if you need to revert back to a previous layout.

The Position group contains commands that enable you to modify the margins and the padding of controls in a form. This group also contains the Anchoring command, which enables you to change where the form's controls appear on the screen. By default, forms are anchored at the top left; however, you can change this to any of the nine options using the anchoring command.

TIP Apply a Background Image to a Form

To apply a Background Image to a form, open the form in Design view, click the Format tab, and then click Background Image in the Background group. Next, click Browse to locate the image you want to apply to the form. Once the image has been applied to the form, you can change the properties of the image so that the image is anchored and sized correctly.

Sorting Records in a Form

When a form is created using a Form tool, the sort order of the records in the form is dependent on the sort order of the record source—a table or a query. Tables are usually sorted by the primary key, whereas queries can be sorted in a variety of ways. Adding and removing sorts are shown in Figure 4.15.

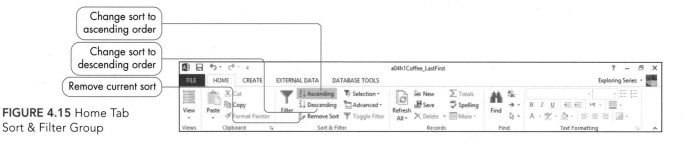

Change sort to ascending order

Change sort to descending order

Remove current sort

FIGURE 4.15 Home Tab Sort & Filter Group

Sorting by a Single Field

You can easily sort on a single field, in ascending or descending order.

To sort by a single field, do the following:

1. Open the form in Form view.
2. Select the field you want to use for sorting.
3. On the HOME tab, in the Sort & Filter group, click Ascending or Descending.

If the form is based on a query, you can instead modify the underlying query's sort order. This method enables you to create a more advanced sort order based on multiple fields. Open the query in Design view, add the sorting you want, and then save and close the query.

Remove Sorting in a Form

To remove the sort order in a form, do the following:

1. Switch to Form view.
2. On the HOME tab, in the Sort & Filter group, click Remove Sort.

> ## TIP Inconsistent Sorting Due to Spaces
>
> Including extra spaces when you enter values into fields can cause issues with sorting. To Access, the following values are not the same:
>
> Little Falls, NJ 07424
>
> Little Falls, NJ 07424
>
> Notice the extra space after the word *Little*. If you attempt to sort, these cities will end up in different places in the sort. The first Little Falls (without the extra space) would appear between Little Egg Harbor Township and Little Ferry. However, the second version would end up above Little Egg Harbor Township, because Access treats the space as a different character.
>
> Inconsistent spacing can cause inconsistent sorting. Try to remember that when performing data entry. If you inherit a database with this issue, you might consider performing a Replace, replacing two spaces with one.

1. How does a form simplify data entry (when compared to entering data into a table)? *p. 258*

2. What is the record source of a form? *p. 259*

3. What is the difference between Layout view and Design view? *p. 261*

4. What is the difference between a form with a subform and a split form? *p. 262*

5. What is a layout control? What are the pros and cons of a layout control? *p. 268*

Hands-On Exercises

1 Form Basics

It is your first day on the job at La Vida Mocha. After talking with Ryung about her data-entry needs, you decide to create several sample forms with different formats. You will show each form to Ryung and Nabil to get feedback and see if they have a preference.

Skills covered: Create Forms Using Form Tools • Use Form Views • Work with a Form Layout Control • Sort Records in a Form

STEP 1 >> CREATE FORMS USING FORM TOOLS

You will create some forms to help Ryung and Nabil with their data entry process. After discussing their needs, you created some sketches that you will implement. Refer to Figure 4.16 as you complete Step 1.

Step e: Title changed

Step c: Controls resized

Step b: Orders subform present

Customer Information

Customer ID	C0001
Customer Name	McAfee, Rand, & Karahalis
Contact	Paula Fields
E-mail Address	
HomePage	www.mrk.com
Address1	5000 Jefferson Lane
Address2	Suite 2000
City	Flatgap
State	KY
Zip Code	41219-
Phone	(555) 375-6442
Fax	(555) 375-6443
Service Start Date	1/3/2012
Credit Rating	B
Sales Rep ID	S001

Order ID	Order Da	Payment Type	Comments
O0001	1/3/2012	Cash	Will pick up order
O0006	1/6/2012	Check	
O0018	1/21/2012	Credit Card	

FIGURE 4.16 Customer Information Form After Step f

a. Open *a04h1Coffee*. Click the **FILE tab**, select **Save As**, and click **Save As**. Type **a04h1Coffee_ LastFirst** as the file name. Click **Save**.

> **TROUBLESHOOTING:** Throughout the remainder of this chapter and textbook, click Enable Content whenever you are working with student files.

> **TROUBLESHOOTING:** If you make any major mistakes in this exercise, you can close the file, repeat step a above, and then start over.

b. Click the **Customers table** in the Navigation Pane. Click the **CREATE tab** and click **Form** in the Forms group.

Access creates a new form with two record sources—Customers (with stacked layout, on top) and Orders (with datasheet layout, below). Access found a one-to-many relationship between the Customers and Orders tables. The form opens in Layout view.

c. Click the top text box containing *C0001* if it is not already selected. The text box is outlined with a shaded border. Move the mouse to the right edge of the shaded border until the mouse pointer changes to a double-headed arrow. Drag the right edge to the left until the text box is approximately half of its original size.

All the text boxes and the subform at the bottom adjust in size when you adjust the top text box. This is a characteristic of Layout view—enabling you to easily modify all controls at once.

> **TROUBLESHOOTING:** You may need to maximize the Access window or close the Navigation Pane if the right edge of the text box is not visible.

d. Ensure the labels at the left all appear without being cut off. If they are cut off, adjust the size of the labels like you did in step c.

e. Click **Save** in the Quick Access Toolbar, and then type **Customer Information** as the form name in the **Save As dialog box**. Click **OK**.

f. Click the **Customers title** at the top of the form to select it, click again, and then change the title to **Customer Information**. Press **Enter** to accept the change. Your form should now look like Figure 4.16. Close the form.

> **TROUBLESHOOTING:** If you make a mistake that you cannot easily recover from, consider deleting the form and starting over. The Form tool makes it easy to start over again.

g. Verify the Customers table is selected in the Navigation Pane. Click the **CREATE tab** and click **More Forms** in the Forms group. Select **Split Form**.

Access creates a new form with a split view, one view in stacked layout and one view laid out like a datasheet.

h. Click anywhere on the Coulter Office Supplies customer record in the bottom portion of the form (record 14). Note: You may need to scroll down to see this record.

The top portion shows all the information for this customer.

i. Click the **Customers title** at the top of the form to select it, click **Customers** again, and then change the title to **Customers - Split View**. Press **Enter** to accept the change.

j. Click **Save** on the Quick Access Toolbar and type **Customers - Split View** in the **Form Name box**. Click **OK**. Close the form.

k. Click the **Products table** in the Navigation Pane. Click the **CREATE tab**, click **More Forms** in the Forms group, and then select **Multiple Items**.

Access creates a new multiple-item form based on the Products table. The form resembles a table's Datasheet view.

l. Click the **Products title** at the top of the form to select it, click again on **Products**, and then change the title to **Products - Multiple Items**. Press **Enter** to save the title.

m. Save the form as **Products - Multiple Items** and close the form.

n. Click the **Orders table** in the Navigation Pane. Click **Form** in the Forms group on the CREATE tab.

A form with a subform showing each line of the order is created.

o. Switch to Design view. Click anywhere inside the subform and press **Delete** on your keyboard.

The subform is removed.

p. Save the form as **Order Information**. Close all open objects.

Now that you have created three forms, you will show Nabil how to use the forms to perform data entry.

a. Right-click the **Customer Information** form in the Navigation Pane and click **Open**. Advance to the sixth customer, *Lugo Computer Sales*, using the **Next Record button** on the Navigation Bar at the bottom of the form.

> **TROUBLESHOOTING:** Two Navigation bars exist, one for the main form and one for the subform. Make sure you use the bottom-most one that shows 14 records.

b. Double-click the **Customers table** in the Navigation Pane.

Two tabs now display in the main window. You will compare the table data and the form data while you make changes to both.

c. Verify the sixth record of the Customers table is *Lugo Computer Sales*, which corresponds to the sixth record in the Customer Information form. Click the tabs to switch between the table and the form.

d. Click the **Customer Information tab** and replace *Adam Sanchez*, the contact for Lugo Computer Sales, with your name. Advance to the next record to save the changes. Click the **Customers tab** to see that the contact name changed in the table as well.

The contact field and the other fields on the Customer Information form automatically change the data in the underlying table.

> **TROUBLESHOOTING:** If the change to Adam Sanchez does not display in the Customers table, check the Customer Information form to see if the pencil displays in the left margin. If it does, save the record by advancing to the next customer and recheck to see if the name has changed.

e. Close the Customer Information form and the Customers table.

f. Open the Customers – Split View form. In the bottom portion of the split form, click **Lugo Computer Sales**, the sixth record. Notice the top portion now displays the information for Lugo Computer Sales. Notice there is an error in the e-mail address—*service* is misspelled. In the top portion of the form, change the e-mail address to **service@lugocomputer.net**.

g. Click another record in the bottom pane and click back on **Lugo Computer Sales**.

The pencil disappears from the record selector box and the changes are saved to the table.

You will make some changes to the layouts based on recommendations Nabil gave you after seeing the forms in action. You will also add a missing field to the main table and add it to the form. Refer to Figure 4.17 as you complete Step 3.

Step d: Refrig?
column resized

Products - Multiple Items						
Products - Multiple Items						
Product ID	Product Name	Description	Refrig?	Brand		Year Introduced
P0001	Coffee - Colombian Supreme	24/Case, Pre-Ground 1.75 Oz Bags	☐	Discount	▼	2012
P0002	Coffee - Hazelnut	24/Case, Pre-Ground 1.75 Oz Bags	☐	Premium	▼	2012
P0003	Coffee - Mild Blend	24/Case, Pre-Ground 1.75 Oz Bags	☐	House	▼	2012
P0004	Coffee - Assorted Flavors	18/Case. Pre-Ground 1.75 Oz Bags	☐	House	▼	2012
P0005	Coffee - Decaf	24/Case, Pre-Ground 1.75 Oz Bags	☐	Discount	▼	2012
P0006	Tea Bags - Regular	75/Box, Individual Tea Bags	☐	House	▼	2012
P0007	Tea Bags - Decaf	75/Box, Individual Tea Bags	☐	House	▼	2012
P0008	Creamers - Assorted Flavors	400/Case, 8 50-count Boxes	☐	Discount	▼	2012
P0009	Creamers - Liquid	200/Case, Individual Creamers	☑	Premium	▼	2012
P0010	Sugar Packets	2000/Case	☐	House	▼	2012
P0011	Ceramic Mug	SD Company Logo	☐	House	▼	2012
P0012	Sugar Substitute	500/Case, 1-Serving Bags	☐	Discount	▼	2012
P0013	Coffee Filters	500/Case, Fits 10-12 Cup Coffee Mal	☐	House	▼	2012
P0014	Napkins	3000/Case, White	☐	House	▼	2012
P0015	Stirrers - Plastic	1000/Box	☐	Discount	▼	2012
P0016	Stirrers - Wood	1000/Box	☐	Discount	▼	2012
P0017	Spoons	500/Box, White Plastic	☐	House	▼	2012
P0018	Popcorn - Plain	36/Case, 3.75 Oz Microwave Bags	☐	House	▼	2012
P0019	Popcorn - Buttered	36/Case, 3.75 Oz Microwave Bags	☐	House	▼	2012
P0020	Soup - Chicken	50 Envelopes	☐	Premium	▼	2012
P0021	Soup - Variety Pak	50 Envelopes	☐	Premium	▼	2012
P0022	Styrofoam Cups - 10 ounce	1000/Case	☐	House	▼	2012

Record: ◄ 1 of 25 ► ► ►⊞ No Filter Search

FIGURE 4.17 Final Version of Products—Multiple Items Report

a. Switch the Customers – Split View form to Layout view. Move your mouse over the splitter bar, the border between the top and bottom portions of the window. When the pointer shape changes to a double-headed arrow, drag the **splitter bar** up until it almost touches the Sales Rep ID field. Save and close the form.

b. Open the Products – Multiple Items form in Layout view. Move the mouse over the bottom edge of cell P0001 until the pointer shape changes to a two-headed arrow. Drag the bottom edge up to reduce the height of the rows so they are as tall as they need to be to accommodate the information.

Changing the height of one row affects the height of all the rows.

c. Click anywhere on the Cost column and click **Select Column** in the Rows & Columns group on the ARRANGE tab. Press **Delete** to remove the column. Repeat the process to delete *MarkupPercent*.

d. Click the **Refrigeration Needed label** to select it. Change the label to the abbreviation **Refrig?**. Shrink the field so it is as wide as necessary. Save and close the form.

You removed fields from the Products – Multiple Items form and the other fields adjust to maintain an even distribution (after you remove the blank space).

e. Open the Customer Information form in Layout view.

f. Click **Themes** in the Themes group on the DESIGN tab. Right-click the **Slice theme** and click **Apply Theme to This Object Only**.

The font and color scheme adjust to match this theme.

> **TROUBLESHOOTING:** Recall that you can determine which theme is named Slice by pointing the mouse to a theme and waiting for a tip to display. Themes are displayed in alphabetical order.

g. Click **Shape Fill** in the Control Formatting group on the FORMAT tab. Click **Light Turquoise, Background 2**.

The background color of the CustomerID field changes to light turquoise.

> **TROUBLESHOOTING:** If you do not see a Light Turquoise, Background 2 in the first row, ensure you have selected the Slice theme.

> **TROUBLESHOOTING:** If the entire background changes to blue, undo and ensure you have selected the control containing *C0001*.

h. Select the **Customer Name field** (which should be *McAfee, Rand, & Karahalis*). Change the font size to **16**.

The customer name appears in a larger font, setting it apart from the other fields.

i. Save and close the form.

j. Right-click the **Customers table** in the Navigation Pane and click **Design View**.

You will add the HomePage field to the Customers table.

k. Click the **Address1 field** and click **Insert Rows** in the Tools group.

A new row is inserted above the Address1 field.

l. Type **HomePage** in the blank **Field Name box** and choose **Hyperlink** as the Data Type.

m. Save and close the Customers table.

n. Right-click the **Customer Information form** in the Navigation Pane and click **Layout View**.

You will add the HomePage field to the Customer Information form.

o. Click **Add Existing Fields** in the Tools group on the DESIGN tab to display the Field List pane (if necessary).

p. Click the **HomePage field**. Drag the field from the Field List pane to the form, below the E-mail Address field, until a shaded line displays between *E-mail Address* and *Address1*, and release the mouse. Close the Field List pane.

Access shows a shaded line to help you place the field in the correct location.

> **TROUBLESHOOTING:** If the placement of this field does not look correct, you can use the Undo button and try again.

q. Switch to Form view. Press **Tab** until you reach the HomePage field and type www.mrk.com into the field. Save and close the form.

r. Click the **Revenue query** in the Navigation Pane. Click **Form** in the Forms group on the CREATE tab to create a new form based on this query.

s. Display the form in Design view. Select all text box field controls (from *Last Name* down to *Revenue*) by clicking on the first field (Last Name), holding down **CTRL** on your keyboard, and clicking on each of the other controls. Click **Remove Layout** in the Table group on the ARRANGE tab. Switch to Layout view.

> **TROUBLESHOOTING:** Recall the Remove Layout option only appears in Design view, so if you do not see the option, ensure you are in Design view.

t. Resize the controls individually so they are approximately the same size as shown in Figure 4.18.

u. Click the **Price control**. Hold down **CTRL** and click the **Revenue control**, the **Price label**, and the **Revenue label**. Drag the fields to the locations shown in Figure 4.18. Switch to Form view.

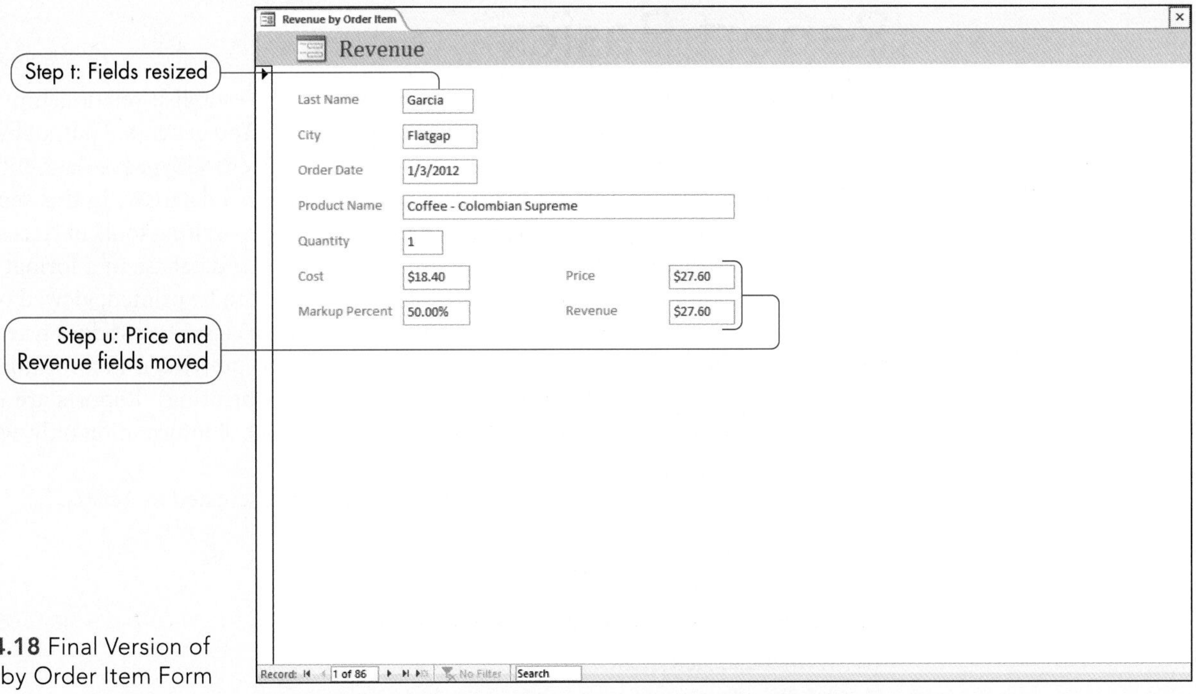

Step t: Fields resized

Step u: Price and Revenue fields moved

FIGURE 4.18 Final Version of Revenue by Order Item Form

v. Save the form as **Revenue by Order Item**. Close the form.

STEP 4 ›› USE A CONTROL LAYOUT AND SORT RECORDS IN A FORM

Ryung tested the Customer Information form and likes the way it is working. She asks you to change the sorting to make it easier to find customers with a similar customer name. She also has an old form that she hopes you can make easier to read but keep in the vertical format.

a. Open the Sales Reps form in Layout view. Notice the form is not laid out well.

b. Click **Select All** in the Selection group on the FORMAT tab.

All 14 controls are outlined.

c. Click **Tabular** in the Table group on the ARRANGE tab.

The controls are lined up horizontally.

d. Click **Stacked** in the Table group on the ARRANGE tab. Switch to Form view.

Ryung wanted the form laid out vertically. The controls are lined up vertically and are much easier to read.

e. Save and close the form.

f. Open the Customer Information form in Form view. Click **Next record** in the Navigation bar at the bottom several times to advance through the records.

Take note that the customers are in Customer ID order.

g. Click **First record** in the Navigation bar to return to customer *McAfee, Rand, & Karahalis*.

h. Click the **Customer Name field** and click **Ascending** in the Sort & Filter group on the HOME tab.

Advantage Sales displays, as they are the first customer name in alphabetical order.

i. Click **Next record** in the Navigation bar at the bottom to advance through the records.

The records are in Customer Name order.

j. Save and close the Customer Information form.

k. Keep the database open if you plan to continue with the next Hands-On Exercise. If not, close the database and exit Access.

Report Basics

By now, you know how to plan a database, create a table, establish relationships between tables, enter data into tables, and extract data using queries. You generated output by printing table and query datasheets. You also learned how to create several types of data-entry forms. These forms can also be used for inquiries about the data in a database. In this section, you will learn how to create professional reports using the report-writing tools in Access.

A *report* is a document that displays information from a database in a format that outputs meaningful information to its readers. Access reports can be printed, viewed on screen, or even saved as a file. Much like a report you might do for a class, Access does research (gets information from the tables or queries) and organizes and presents it in a meaningful way (the final report, formatted for on-screen viewing or for printing). Reports are unable to change data in your database; a report is designed for output of information only, whether to the screen, to the printer, or to a file.

The following are all examples of reports that might be created in Access:

1. A telephone directory sorted by last name
2. A customer list grouped by sales rep
3. An employee list sorted by most years of service
4. A financial statement
5. A bill or invoice
6. A bar chart showing sales over the past 12 months
7. A shipping label
8. A letter to customers reminding them about a past due payment

Although you can print information from forms, information printed may not be easily understood or economical in terms of paper use. Most of the printed documents generated by Access will come from reports. Reports can be enhanced to help the reader understand and analyze the data. For example, if you print the Datasheet view from the Customers table, you will be able to locate the key information about each customer. However, using report tools, you can group the customers by sales rep and highlight the customers who have not placed an order in six months. This is an example of converting a list of customers into an effective business tool. To increase business, the sales reps could contact their customers who have not ordered in six months and review the findings with the sales manager. A sales report could be run each month to see if the strategy has helped produce any new business.

In this section, you will create reports in Access by first identifying a record source, then sketching the report, and finally choosing a Report tool. You will learn how to modify a report by adding and deleting fields, resizing columns, and adding a color scheme. You will also learn about the report sections, the report views, and controls on reports. After having worked through forms in the earlier section on forms, you will discover that there are many similarities between forms and reports.

Creating Reports Using Report Tools

Access provides five different report tools for creating reports. The report tools are found on the Create tab, in the Reports group, as shown in Figure 4.19. Click one of these tools and Access will base the report using the table or query that is currently selected. The most common of the tools, the *Report tool*, is used to instantly create a tabular report based on the table or query currently selected. The Report Design tool is used to create a new blank report in Design view. This tool is used by advanced users who want to create a blank report with no help from Access. The Blank Report tool is used to create a new blank report so that you can insert fields and controls manually and design the report. The Report Wizard tool will ask a series of questions and help you create a report based on your answers. The Labels tool is used to create a page of labels using one of the preformatted templates provided by Access. Table 4.1 provides a summary of the five report tools and their usage.

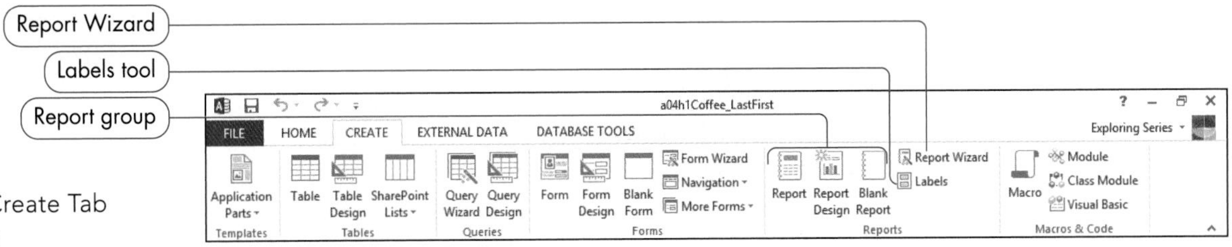

FIGURE 4.19 Create Tab Reports Group

After you create a report using one of the report tools, you can perform modifications in Layout view or Design view.

TABLE 4.1 Report Tools and Their Usage

Report Tool	Usage
Report	Create a tabular report showing all of the fields in the record source.
Report Design	Create a new blank report in Design view. Add fields and controls manually.
Blank Report	Create a new blank report in Layout view. Add fields and controls manually.
Report Wizard	Answer a series of questions and Access will design a custom report for you.
Labels	Choose a preformatted label template and create a sheet of labels.

Before you create a report in Access, you should ask these questions:

- What is the purpose of the report?
- Who will use the report?
- Which tables are needed for the report?
- What information needs to be included?
- How will the report be distributed? Will users pull the information directly from Access, or will they receive it through e-mail, fax, or the Internet?
- Will the results be converted to Word, Excel, HTML, or another format?

In the *Forms* section of this chapter, you learned that it is helpful to talk to users and sketch an Access form before you launch Access. The same holds true for creating an Access report. Users can give you solid feedback, and creating a sketch will help you determine which report tool to use to create the report.

The first step in planning your report is to identify the record source. You may use one or more tables, queries, or a combination of tables and queries as the report's record source. Sometimes, a single table contains all of the records you need for the report. Other times, you will need to incorporate several tables. When multiple tables are needed to create a report, you can add all the necessary tables into a single query and then base the report on that query. (As stated earlier, multiple tables in a query must be related, as indicated with join lines. Tables with no join lines usually indicate an incorrect record source.)

Reports can also contain graphics as well as text and numeric data. For example, you can add a company logo. After you identify the record source, you also need to specify which graphic images are needed (and the location of the images).

Use the Report Tool

STEP 1 After you sketch the report, you can decide which report tool is appropriate to produce the desired report. Access provides several tools that you can use to create a report (refer to Figure 4.20). Which one you select depends on the layout of the report, the record source, and the complexity of the report design.

The easiest way to create a report is with the Report tool. The Report tool is used to instantly create a tabular report based on the table or query currently selected. To create a report using the Report tool, do the following:

1. Select a table or query in the Navigation Pane.
2. Click the CREATE tab and click Report in the Reports group. Access creates a tabular layout report instantly. Notice, this type of report displays data horizontally across the page in a landscape view, as shown in Figure 4.20.

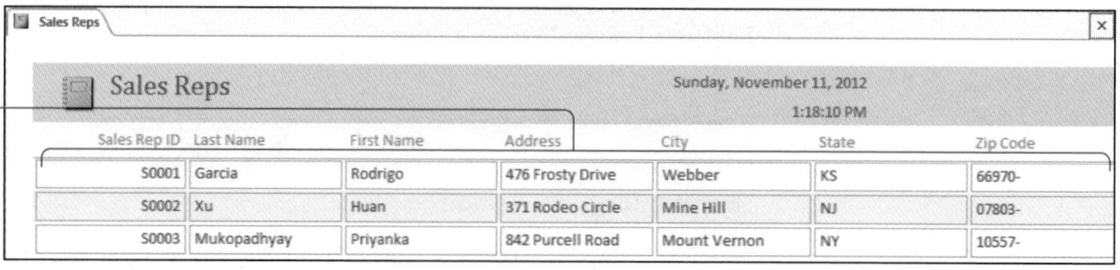

Table form allows for printing

Sales Rep ID	Last Name	First Name	Address	City	State	Zip Code
S0001	Garcia	Rodrigo	476 Frosty Drive	Webber	KS	66970-
S0002	Xu	Huan	371 Rodeo Circle	Mine Hill	NJ	07803-
S0003	Mukopadhyay	Priyanka	842 Purcell Road	Mount Vernon	NY	10557-

FIGURE 4.20 Tabular Report

If you prefer, you can display a report using a stacked layout, which displays fields in a vertical column. This type of report is less common, as it would result in longer printouts. The number of records on one page depends on the number of records in the record source. You can also force a new page at the start of each record.

Use the Report Wizard to Create a Basic Report

You can also create a professional report with the Report Wizard. The **Report Wizard** asks you questions and then uses your answers to generate a customized report. The wizard uses six dialog boxes to collect information about your report. After thinking through the structure, the layout, and the record source, you are ready to launch the Report Wizard.

1. Select the report's record source in the Navigation Pane and click Report Wizard in the Reports group on the CREATE tab.
   The wizard opens with the table or query (the record source) displayed in the first dialog box. Although you chose the record source before you started, the first dialog box enables you to select fields from additional tables or queries.

2. Choose the fields you want to include in the report. Click the Tables/Queries drop-down list to display a list of available tables or queries. As with the query wizard you used in a previous chapter, you can click > to choose a single field, >> to choose all fields, < to remove a field, and << to remove all fields from the report. See Figure 4.21. Set the desired fields and click Next.

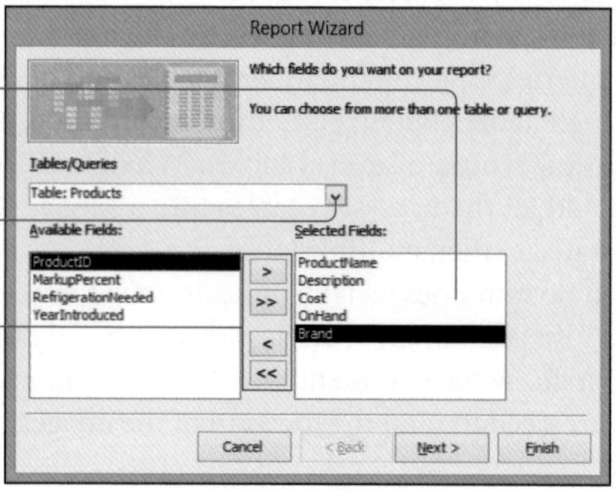

Fields in the report

Choose Tables/Queries from which to add fields

Add or remove fields

FIGURE 4.21 Selecting Fields for a Report

3. The next dialog box, shown in Figure 4.22, asks, "Do you want to add any grouping levels?" As you learned in a previous chapter, grouping lets you organize and summarize your data, based on values in a field. For a basic report, you will not select any grouping fields and instead just click Next.

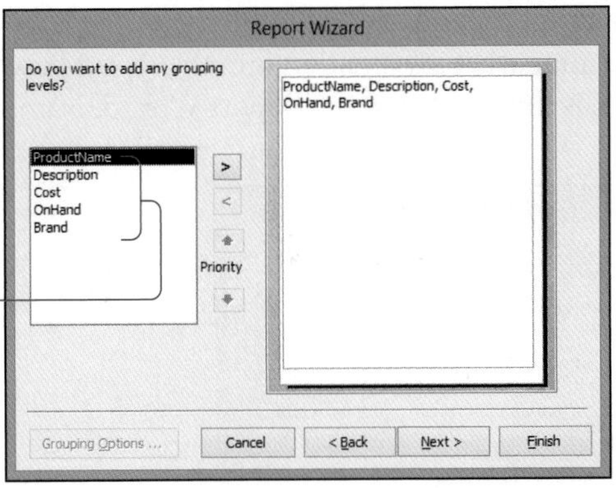

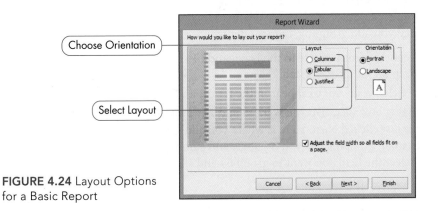

FIGURE 4.22 Grouping Options

4. The next dialog box, shown in Figure 4.23, asks "What sort order do you want for your records?" For the sort options, specify which field you want to sort by first and optionally add a second, third, and fourth sort. For each field, choose ascending order and/or descending order. Click on the word Ascending and it will toggle to Descending; clicking again will switch back to Ascending. Set the desired sort options and click Next.

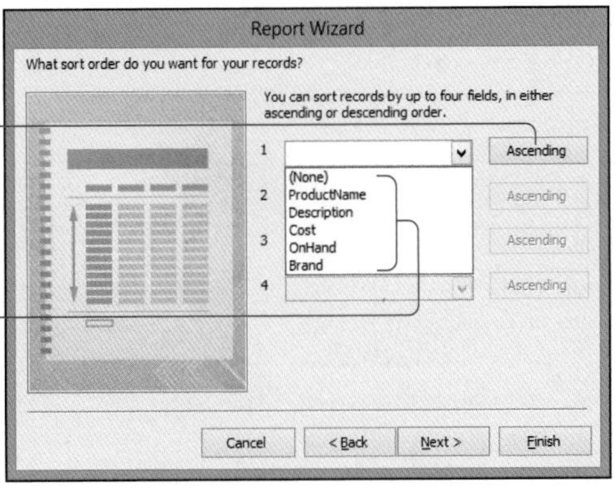

FIGURE 4.23 Sort Options for a Basic Report

5. The next dialog box will determine the report's appearance. You will be given the option to select Columnar, Tabular, or Justified as the layout.

- Columnar will display the information in a column. This leads to reports that are easier to read, but long printouts.
- Tabular will display the data in a table format. This is good for saving space, but it may be difficult to fit all fields on one printed page.
- Justified will display the information in a column as well. If you have Long Text fields, this is a good option to ensure all your data fits.

Tabular is the option you choose to fit the report on as few pages as possible. Clicking an option will give you a general preview in the preview area. You can also select the orientation for the report, either Portrait or Landscape (see Figure 4.24). Select an appropriate format for the report. Set the desired options and click Next.

FIGURE 4.24 Layout Options for a Basic Report

6. Decide on an appropriate name for the report. Type a descriptive report name so you can easily determine what information is in the report based on the title. This step, shown in Figure 4.25, is the last step in the Report Wizard. Name the report and click Finish.

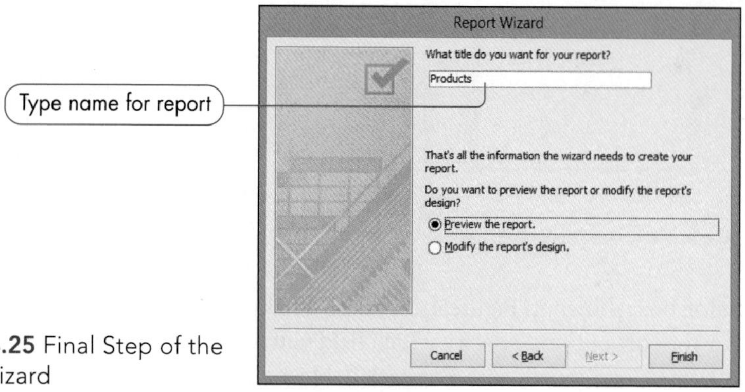

FIGURE 4.25 Final Step of the Report Wizard

Now that you have stepped through the wizard, you will get a report incorporating all the options you chose, as shown in Figure 4.26. You may need to adjust the size of fields, as some may not be fully displayed.

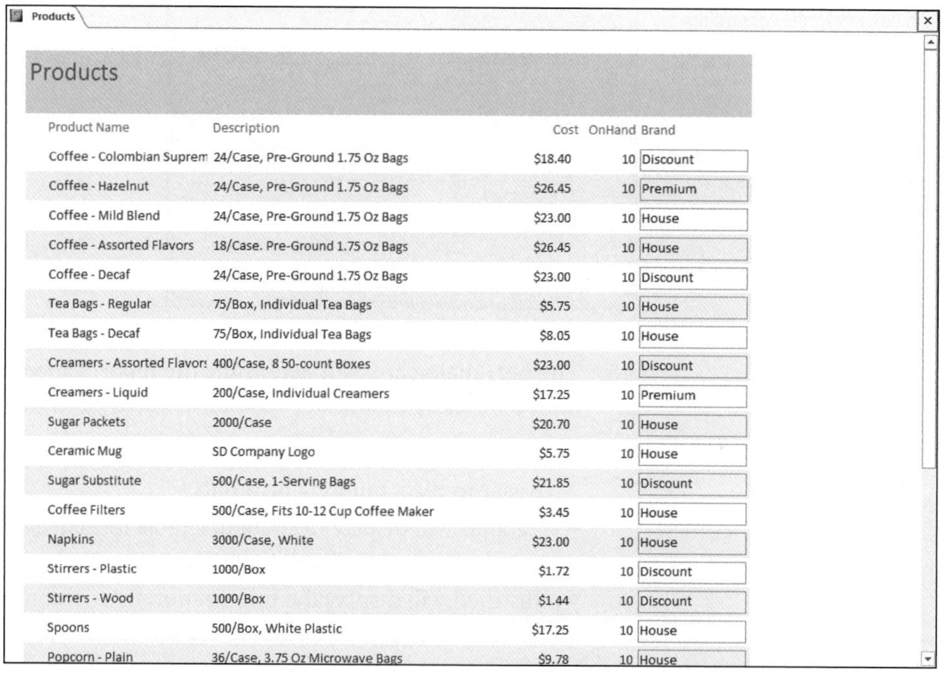
Products

Products

Product Name	Description	Cost	OnHand	Brand
Coffee - Colombian Suprem	24/Case, Pre-Ground 1.75 Oz Bags	$18.40	10	Discount
Coffee - Hazelnut	24/Case, Pre-Ground 1.75 Oz Bags	$26.45	10	Premium
Coffee - Mild Blend	24/Case, Pre-Ground 1.75 Oz Bags	$23.00	10	House
Coffee - Assorted Flavors	18/Case. Pre-Ground 1.75 Oz Bags	$26.45	10	House
Coffee - Decaf	24/Case, Pre-Ground 1.75 Oz Bags	$23.00	10	Discount
Tea Bags - Regular	75/Box, Individual Tea Bags	$5.75	10	House
Tea Bags - Decaf	75/Box, Individual Tea Bags	$8.05	10	House
Creamers - Assorted Flavor:	400/Case, 8 50-count Boxes	$23.00	10	Discount
Creamers - Liquid	200/Case, Individual Creamers	$17.25	10	Premium
Sugar Packets	2000/Case	$20.70	10	House
Ceramic Mug	SD Company Logo	$5.75	10	House
Sugar Substitute	500/Case, 1-Serving Bags	$21.85	10	Discount
Coffee Filters	500/Case, Fits 10-12 Cup Coffee Maker	$3.45	10	House
Napkins	3000/Case, White	$23.00	10	House
Stirrers - Plastic	1000/Box	$1.72	10	Discount
Stirrers - Wood	1000/Box	$1.44	10	Discount
Spoons	500/Box, White Plastic	$17.25	10	House
Popcorn - Plain	36/Case, 3.75 Oz Microwave Bags	$9.78	10	House

FIGURE 4.26 Results of Report Wizard

Use the Report Wizard with Grouping

In the previous example, we created a basic report using the Report Wizard. However, we can use grouping if we want to summarize our report by a certain field. We can also display overall totals and percentages based on a predefined format. The Report Wizard still has six dialog boxes when you add grouping, but two dialog boxes will change.

1. Select the report's record source in the Navigation Pane and click Report Wizard in the Reports group on the CREATE tab.
2. Choose the fields you want to appear in the report and click Next.
3. The next dialog box asks, "Do you want to add any grouping levels?" In the previous example, we just clicked Next. Here is where you add grouping. As we learned in a previous chapter, grouping lets you organize and summarize your data based on values in a field. Select the field you want to group by and click the > button to add the new

group. If you need a second or third grouping level, add those field names in order. The order in which you select the groups dictates the order of display in the report. Figure 4.27 shows the sort options for a grouped report. In this specific example, records are being grouped by the Brand. Once you have selected the appropriate options, click Next.

4. Because we have specified grouping, the next dialog box asks, "What sort order and summary information do you want for detail records?" Here, you can click Summary Options if you want to add aggregate functions (e.g., sum, average, minimum, and maximum) and to specify whether you want to see detail records on the report or only the aggregate results (see Figure 4.28). You can also choose to calculate percentages, so if you had one group that made up half your sales, you would see 50%. Click OK to return to the Report Wizard. The sort options are the same as before. Set the appropriate options and click Next.

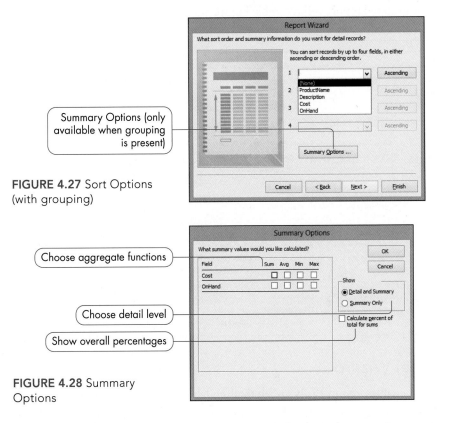

Summary Options (only available when grouping is present)

FIGURE 4.27 Sort Options (with grouping)

Choose aggregate functions

Choose detail level

Show overall percentages

FIGURE 4.28 Summary Options

5. The next dialog box, shown in Figure 4.29, will determine the report's appearance. If you have selected grouping, you will be prompted to select the layout from three options:

- Stepped Layout will display column headings at the top of the page and keep the grouping field(s) in their own row.
- Block Layout will include the grouping field(s) inline with the data, saving some space when printing. It has one set of column headings at the top of each page.
- Outline Layout will display the grouping field(s) on their own separate rows and has column headings inside each group. This leads to a longer report when printing but may help make the report easier to read.

Clicking any of these layouts will give you a general preview in the preview area. The option to choose Portrait or Landscape is still available. Click Next.

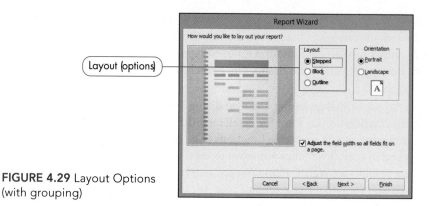

Layout (options)

FIGURE 4.29 Layout Options (with grouping)

6. Decide on an appropriate name for the report. Type a descriptive report name. Click Finish. Your grouped report will resemble Figure 4.30.

Grouping field appears as its own column

Brand	Product Name	Description	Cost	ind
Discount				
	Coffee - Colombian Suprem	24/Case, Pre-Ground 1.75 Oz Bags	$18.40	10
	Coffee - Decaf	24/Case, Pre-Ground 1.75 Oz Bags	$23.00	10
	Creamers - Assorted Flavors	400/Case, 8 50-count Boxes	$23.00	10
	Stirrers - Plastic	1000/Box	$1.72	10
	Stirrers - Wood	1000/Box	$1.44	10
	Sugar Substitute	500/Case, 1-Serving Bags	$21.85	10
House				
	Ceramic Mug	SD Company Logo	$5.75	10
	Coffee - Assorted Flavors	18/Case. Pre-Ground 1.75 Oz Bags	$26.45	10
	Coffee - Mild Blend	24/Case, Pre-Ground 1.75 Oz Bags	$23.00	10
	Coffee Filters	500/Case, Fits 10-12 Cup Coffee Maker	$3.45	10
	Milk - 1 pint	Delivered Daily	$1.15	10
	Milk - 1 quart	Delivered Daily	$2.30	10
	Napkins	3000/Case, White	$23.00	10
	Popcorn - Buttered	36/Case, 3.75 Oz Microwave Bags	$10.92	10

FIGURE 4.30 Grouped Report

Use the Label Wizard

The *Label Wizard* enables you to easily create mailing labels, name tags, and other specialized tags. A *mailing label report* is a specialized report that comes preformatted to coordinate with name-brand labels, such as Avery. Access includes most common labels built into the program. Even if you purchase a store brand from an office supply store, they will generally state the comparable Avery label number.

To use the Label Wizard, do the following:

1. Select the table or query that will serve as the record source for the report.
2. Click Labels in the Reports group on the CREATE tab.
3. Select the manufacturer, the product number, and the label type and click Next.
4. Choose the font type and size and click Next.
5. Add the fields to the label template, as shown in Figure 4.31. You will need to place the fields exactly as you wish them to appear, including adding a comma between City and State and pressing Enter after the CustomerName.
6. Add any sort fields and click Next.
7. Name the report and click Finish to generate your labels. The results are shown in Figure 4.32.

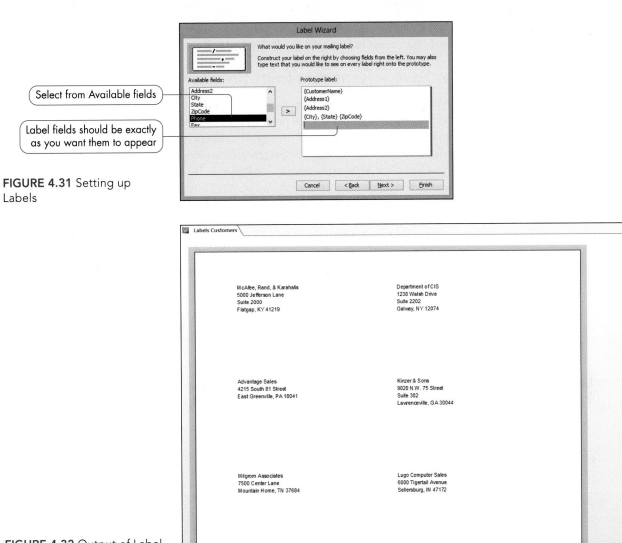

FIGURE 4.31 Setting up Labels

FIGURE 4.32 Output of Label Wizard

Using Report Views

As you work with the report tools to create and modify reports, you will find the need to frequently switch between the four report views in Access—Layout view, Print Preview, Design view, and Report view. Most of your design work will be done in Layout view, but occasionally, you will need to switch to Design view to apply a more advanced feature, such as a calculated field. Users of the report will use Print Preview or Report view. There should be no reason for a user to switch to Layout view or Design view. Modifications to the report should be done by the designated report designer. To switch between the four views, click the View arrow in the Views group and select the desired view.

View a Report in Report View

Report view enables you to view a report onscreen in a continuous page layout. Report view is similar to Form view for forms. However, because the data shown in a report cannot be changed, it is simply a way of viewing the information without having to worry about accidentally moving a control. In addition, using report view allows quick access to filtering options.

Alter a Report in Layout View

Use Layout view to alter the report design while still viewing the data. You should use Layout view to add or delete fields in the report, modify field properties, change the column widths, sort, and filter data by excluding certain records. Although Layout view appears similar to Print

Preview, you will find sufficient variations between the two views, so that you will still always need to verify the report in Print Preview to evaluate all the changes made in Layout view.

Print or Save a Report in Print Preview

STEP 2 » *Print Preview* enables you to see exactly what the report will look like when it is printed. Most users prefer to use Print Preview prior to printing the report. This enables you to intercept errors in reports before you send the report to the printer. You cannot modify the design in this view; switch to Layout view or Design view to modify the design. To switch to Print Preview, you can click View and select Print Preview. By default, Print Preview will display all the pages in the report. Figure 4.33 shows an Access report in Print Preview.

Once you are in Print Preview, you have the option to save the report to a file as well. This is a useful option if you plan on distributing some of your information electronically but do not want to distribute the entire database. On the Print Preview tab in the Data group, you will find a number of different data types. See Figure 4.33. Simply choose the type of file you wish to create, and choose the directory and file name.

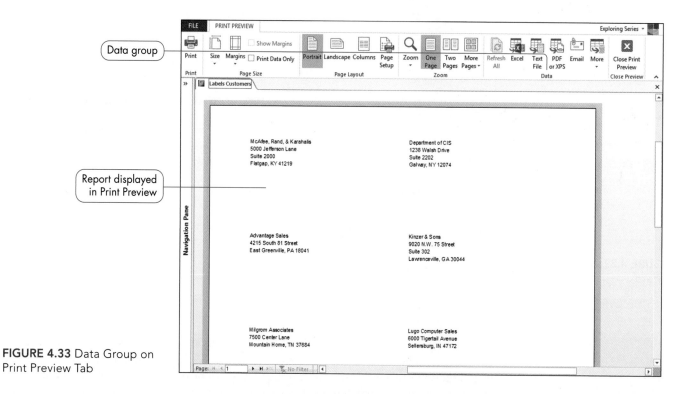

FIGURE 4.33 Data Group on Print Preview Tab

Commonly used formats include Excel, Word, or Portable Document Format (PDF). *Portable Document Format (PDF)* is a file type that was created for exchanging documents independent of software applications and operating system environment. In other words, you can e-mail files in this format to users running Mac operating system or a Linux operating system, and they can open it, even if they do not have Microsoft Office. Acrobat files often open in a program called Adobe Reader, a free tool that displays PDF files.

Because databases contain a great deal of information, Access reports may become very long, requiring many pages to print. Experienced Access users always use Print Preview prior to printing their reports. Some reports may require hundreds of pages to print. Other reports may be formatted incorrectly, and a blank page may print after each page of information. It would be better to correct this problem prior to sending it to the printer.

Modifying a Report

After a report is generated by one of the report tools, you may need to modify it. Similar to forms, the common changes to a report are add a field, remove a field, change the order of fields, change the width of a field, and modify the title. Much like a form, the Report has many options you can use to format a report. Once you are in Layout or Design view, you will have access to the report layout tools. You have four tabs available:

- Design: Use this tab to make changes to the design of the report, such as adding sorting, changing themes, and inserting additional controls.
- Arrange: Use this tab to change the layout of a report, to move fields up and down, to insert a space above or below your current position, or to insert a space to the left or the right of the current field.
- Format: Use this tab to change the font; add or remove bolding, italics, or underlining; change font size; change font color or background; adjust text alignment; or add a background image.
- Page Setup: Use this tab to change paper size, margins, page orientation, or to add columns.

Modify a Report Using the Arrange Tab

The Arrange tab displays in both Layout view and Design view. To use these commands, first open a report in Layout view or Design view and click the Format tab. Next, select a field or fields and click the appropriate command. Some key commands are highlighted in Figure 4.34.

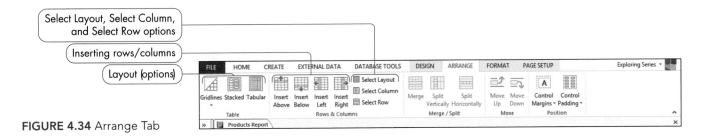

FIGURE 4.34 Arrange Tab

The Table group contains commands that enable you to add gridlines to a report's layout, to change a report's layout from stacked to tabular (and vice versa), or to remove a report's layout. The Remove Layout command is available in Design view only. For example, if a report was created with a tabular layout, you could change it to a stacked layout by doing the following:

STEP 3 >>
1. Open the report in Layout view.
2. Click the ARRANGE tab.
3. Click on any text box in the *Detail* section.
4. Click Select Layout in the Rows & Columns group.
5. Click Stacked in the Table group.

The Rows & Columns group contains commands that enable you to insert rows and columns inside a report's layout. For example, in a report with a stacked layout, you may want to separate the first three fields from the rest of the fields. To do this, you could select the third text box and click Insert Below. This will create a space after the third field. This group also contains the Select Layout, Select Column, and Select Row commands.

The Merge/Split group contains commands that enable you to merge and split the cells on a report. There are times when you may want to deviate from the basic row and column formats that the Access Report Wizards create. In this case, you can change the layout of the report using the merge cells and split cell commands. These commands do not change the actual controls, only the layout of the controls.

The Move group contains two commands that enable you to move a field up or down in a stacked layout. For example, if you want to move the second field in a stacked layout to the first position, select the second field's text box and label, and then click Move Up in the Move group. Moving fields up or down in a report may cause unexpected results; you can always use the undo command if you need to revert back to the beginning.

The Position group contains commands that enable you to modify the margins and the padding of controls in a report. This group also contains the Anchoring command, which enables you to change where the report's controls appear on the screen. By default, reports are anchored at the top left; however, you can change this to any of the nine options using the anchoring command.

Modify Report Controls using the Format Tab

The Format tab contains a series of commands that enable you change the font, display, and alignment of the controls on a report, as shown in Figure 4.35. This is useful if you need to quickly change the look of one cell. For example, you may have an important field you want to emphasize. To do so, do the following:

1. Switch to Layout view (or Design view).
2. Select the field you wish to format.
3. Click the FORMAT tab.
4. Change the format as desired. You can format the text as you would in Microsoft Word.

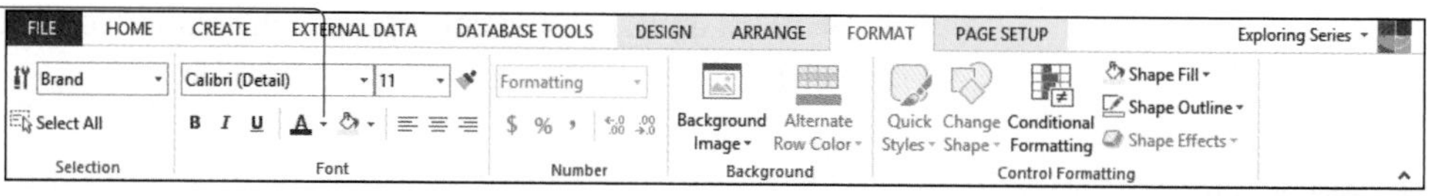

FIGURE 4.35 Format Tab

> **TIP** Apply a Background Image to a Report
>
> To apply a Background Image to a report, open the report in Layout view (or Design view), click the Format tab, and then click Background Image in the Background group. Next, click Browse to locate the image you want to apply to the report. Once the image has been applied to the report, you can change the properties of the image so that the image is anchored and sized correctly.

Add a Field to a Report

Adding a field to a report with a tabular layout is similar to adding a field to a form with a tabular layout. To add a field to a report, do the following:

1. Switch to Layout view.
2. On the DESIGN tab, in the Tools group, click Add Existing Fields to reveal the available fields in the report's record source. The Field List pane will display on the right-hand side of your screen.
3. For a single-table report, you will be presented with a list of fields. For a multiple-table report, you will first need to click the + (plus) next to the appropriate table to locate the desired field.
4. Drag the new field to a precise location on the report, using the vertical shaded line as a guide for the position of the new field, and release the mouse. The other fields will automatically adjust to make room for the new field.

The process of adding a field to a report with a stacked layout is the same as a tabular layout. The only difference is the shaded line will appear horizontally.

Delete a Field from a Report

To delete a field from the *Detail* section of a tabular report, do the following:

1. Switch to the Layout view (or Design view) of the report.
2. Click the text box of the field to be deleted. Click Select Column in the Rows & Columns group on the ARRANGE tab. Note the shaded border appears around the field and the label for the field.
3. With the shaded border visible, press Delete on your keyboard. The field disappears and the other fields fill in the gap.

Adjust Column Widths in a Report

You can adjust the width of each column in a tabular report individually so that each column is wide enough to accommodate the widest value. For example, if a report contains first name, last name, address and city, and email address, you will need to make sure the longest value in each field is completely visible. Scroll through the records to make sure this is the case.

To modify column widths in a tabular report, do the following:

1. Switch to the Layout view (or Design view) of the report.
2. Click the text box of the field you want to adjust. The field will have a shaded border around it, indicating it is selected.
3. Move the mouse to the right border of the selected field; when the mouse pointer turns to a double arrow, drag the edge to the right (to increase) or the left (to decrease) until you arrive at the desired width.

Changing Margins and Orientation

Sometimes, you may wish to print a page in Landscape or adjust the margins rather than adjusting widths. You will notice the Page Setup tab has these options. In the Page Size group, you can change the margins, and in the Page Layout group, you can choose Portrait or Landscape. See Figure 4.36 for locations of commonly used tools on this tab.

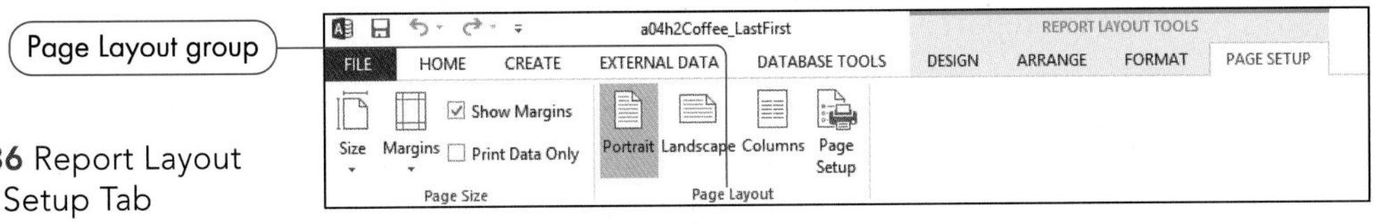

FIGURE 4.36 Report Layout Tools Page Setup Tab

Add a Theme to the Report

You can enhance the report's appearance by applying one of the themes provided by Access. To apply a theme, do the following:

1. Switch to Layout view (or Design view).
2. Click Themes in the Themes group on the DESIGN tab. Scroll through the themes until you find a theme you like; hover over one of the options to see a quick preview of the current report using the current theme. (This is easier to preview in Layout view.)
3. Right-click a theme and select *Apply Theme to This Object Only*. You can also apply the theme to all objects.

Work with a Report Layout Control

Whenever you use one of the report tools to create a new report, Access will add a layout control to help align the fields. Layout controls in reports work the same as layout controls in forms. As discussed earlier in this chapter, the layout control provides guides to help keep controls aligned horizontally and vertically and give your report a uniform appearance.

There are times when you may want to remove the layout control from a report in order to position the fields without aligning them to each other. If you want to remove the layout control from a report, do the following:

1. Switch to Design view (this is not available in Layout view).
2. Click anywhere inside the layout control you want to remove.
3. Click Select Layout in the Rows & Columns group on the ARRANGE tab.
4. In the Table group, click Remove Layout and the layout control is gone. All of the controls are still on the report, but the rectangle binding them together is gone.

You can add a layout control to a report by first selecting all the controls you want to keep together. Then, click Stacked or Tabular in the Table group and the layout control appears.

Sorting Records in a Report

When a report is created using the Report tool, the sort order of the records in the report is initially dependent on the sort order of the record source—similar to the way records are sorted in a form. The primary key of the record source usually dictates the sort order. However, a report has an additional feature for sorting. While in Layout view or Design view, click Group & Sort in the Grouping & Totals group on the Design tab. The Group, Sort, and Total pane displays at the bottom of the report. This section enables you to set the sort order for the report and override the sorting in the report's record source. Note that if you did not use the Report Wizard, this is how you would add grouping and totals to a report.

Sorting is important because sorting by a primary key may not be intuitive. For example, sorting by a field like LastName might be a better choice than a primary key so users see the records are in alphabetical order by LastName.

Change the Sorting in a Report

STEP 4 ▶ If you want to change the sorting in the report, do the following:

1. Switch to Layout view.
2. On the DESIGN tab, in the Grouping & Totals group, click Group & Sort to display the *Group, Sort, and Total* section, as shown in Figure 4.37. This will appear at the bottom of the report.

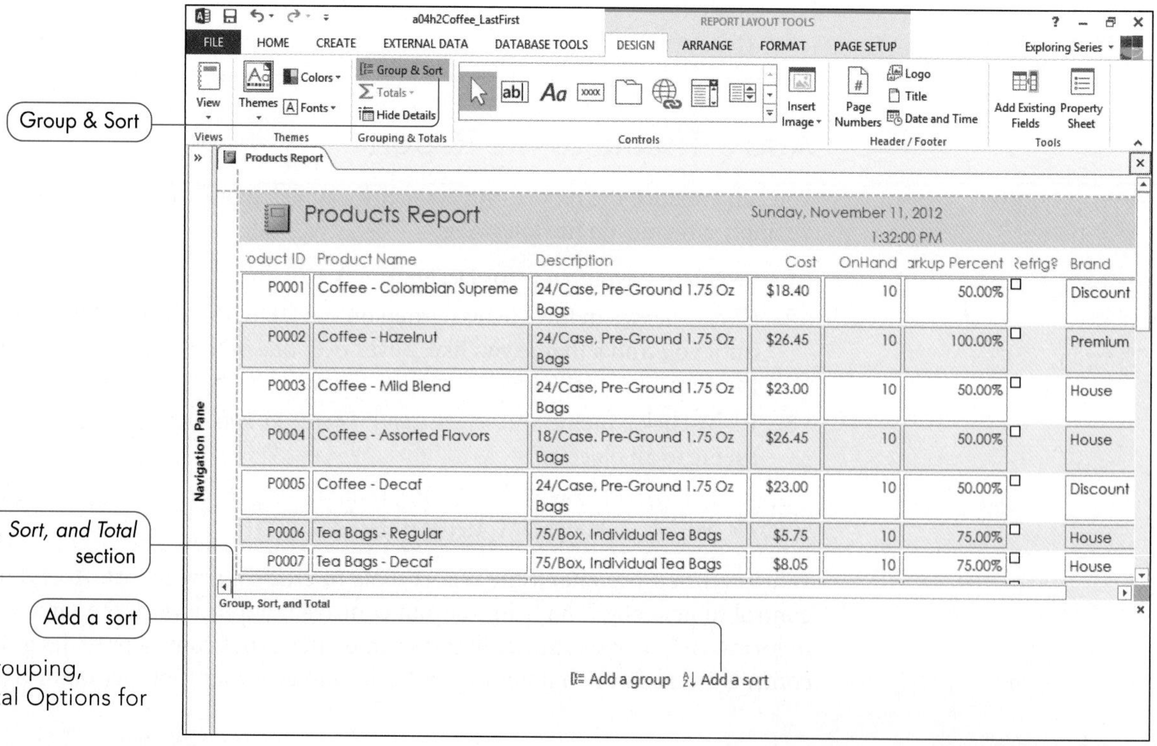

FIGURE 4.37 Grouping, Sorting, and Total Options for Reports

3. Click *Add a sort* and select the field you wish to sort by, which you can change as shown in Figure 4.38. The default sort order is ascending.

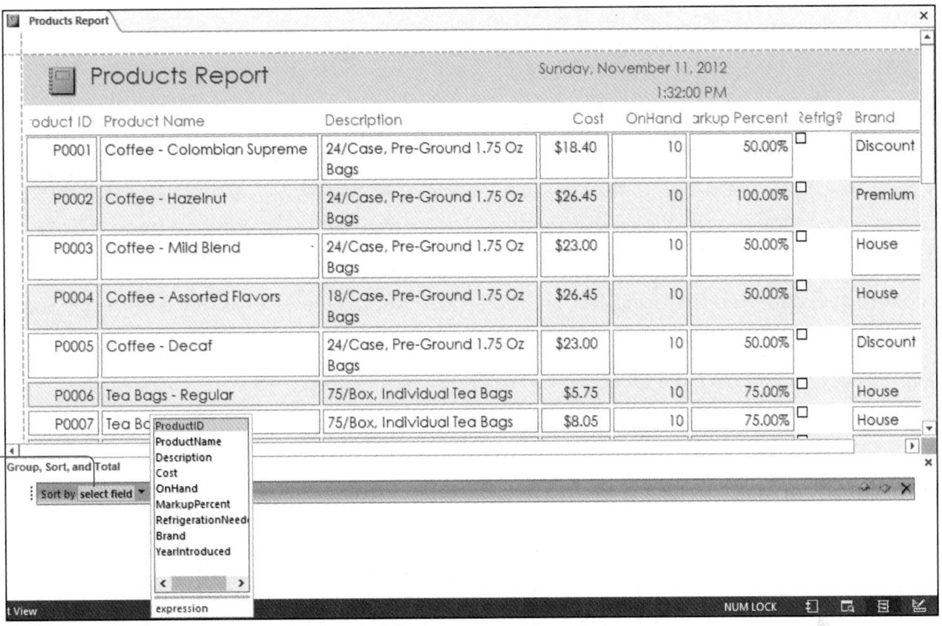

FIGURE 4.38 Adding a Sort to a Report

4. If you wish to add a second sort, click *Add a Sort* again. For example, you could sort first by Brand and then by ProductName, as shown in Figure 4.39.

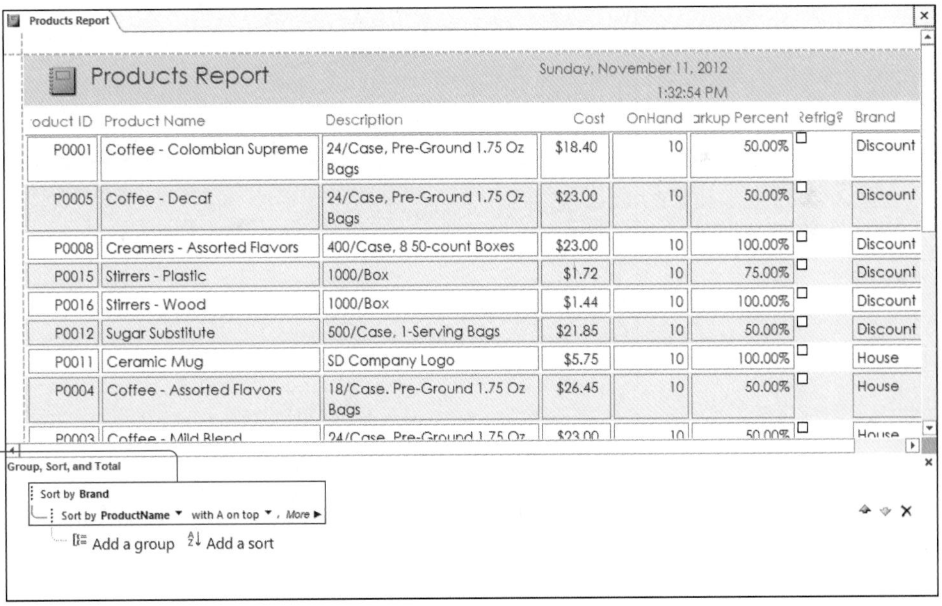

Multiple sort fields

FIGURE 4.39 Report with Multiple Sort Fields

Quick Concepts ✓

1. Compare controls in forms and controls in reports. ***p. 278***

2. What are the benefits of using the report wizard? ***p. 280***

3. What is the difference between Print Preview and Report view? ***pp. 285–286***

4. What are the benefits of a report layout control when modifying a report? ***pp. 289–290***

5. Why is sorting the records in a report important? ***p. 290***

Hands-On Exercises

MyITLab®
HOE2 Training

2 Report Basics

You create a Products report using the Access Report tool to help Ryung stay on top of the key data for her business. After Access creates the report, you modify the column widths so the entire report fits on one page (portrait or landscape, depending on the report). You also use the Report Wizard tool to create other reports for Ryung.

Skills covered: Create Reports Using Report Tools • Use Report Views • Modify a Report • Sort Records in a Report

---

STEP 1 ≫ CREATING REPORTS USING REPORT TOOLS

You use the Report tool to create an Access report to help Ryung manage her product information. This report is especially useful for determining which products she needs to order to fill upcoming orders. Refer to Figure 4.40 as you complete Step 1.

Sales By City					✕

Sales By City

City	Order Date	Price		Revenue	Product Name
Step j: Grouped by City field → Birmingham					
	1/21/2012	$32.78		$32.78	Styrofoam Cups - 12 ounce
Summary for 'City' = Birmingham (1 detail record)					
Avg			32.775		
Buckingham					
	1/23/2012	$46.00		$46.00	Creamers - Assorted Flavors
	1/23/2012	$41.40		$41.40	Sugar Packets
	1/23/2012	$32.78		$32.78	Styrofoam Cups - 12 ounce
	1/26/2012	$21.84		$43.68	Popcorn - Buttered
	1/26/2012	$10.06		$20.13	Tea Bags - Regular
	1/26/2012	$4.60		$4.60	Milk - 1 quart
Summary for 'City' = Buckingham (6 detail records)					
Step l: Average summary added → Avg			26.113		
East Greenville					
	1/5/2012	$46.00		$92.00	Creamers - Assorted Flavors
	1/5/2012	$32.78		$32.78	Sugar Substitute
	1/5/2012	$52.90		$105.80	Coffee - Hazelnut
	1/7/2012	$41.40		$82.80	Sugar Packets
	1/7/2012	$5.18		$10.35	Coffee Filters
	1/7/2012	$52.90		$158.70	Coffee - Hazelnut
	1/24/2012	$27.60		$55.20	Soup - Variety Pak

FIGURE 4.40 Sales by City Report

a. Open *a04h1Coffee_LastFirst* if you closed it at the end of Hands-On Exercise 1. Click the **FILE tab**, select **Save As**, and then click **Save As**. Type **a04h2Coffee_LastFirst** as the file name, changing *h1* to *h2*. Click **Save**.

b. Select the **Products table** in the Navigation Pane. Click the **CREATE tab** and click **Report** in the Reports group.

   Access creates a new tabular layout report based on the Products table. The report opens in Layout view ready to edit.

c. Click the **Products title** at the top of the report to select it, click again on **Products**, and then change the title to **Products Report**. Press **Enter** to accept the change.

d. Right-click the **Products report tab** and select **Print Preview**.

   The report is too wide for the page; you will exit Print Preview and change the orientation to Landscape.

e. Click **Close Print Preview**.

f. Click the **PAGE SETUP tab** and click **Landscape** in the Page Layout group.

   The report changes to Landscape orientation. Most of the columns now fit onto one page. You will make further revisions to the report later on so that it fits on one page.

g. Save the report as **Products Report**. Close the report.

h. Select the **Revenue query** in the Navigation Pane. Click the **CREATE tab** and click **Report Wizard** in the Reports group.

   The Report Wizard launches.

i. Click the **City field** and click the **>** button to add the City field to the report. Repeat the same process for the **OrderDate**, **Price**, **Revenue**, and **ProductName fields**. Click **Next**.

j. Select **City** and click the **>** button to add grouping by city. Click **Next**.

k. Select **OrderDate** for the sort order and leave the order as **Ascending**. Click **Summary Options**.

l. Click the **Avg check box** on the Price row to summarize the Price field. Click **OK**.

m. Click **Next**. Click **Next** again to accept the default layout.

n. Type **Sales by City** for the title of the report. Click **Finish**.

   The report is displayed in Print Preview mode. Some of the data values and labels cannot be seen. Next, you will adjust the controls.

o. Click **Close Print Preview**.

p. Switch to Layout view if necessary and adjust the controls so all the field values are visible as shown in Figure 4.40.

q. Display the report in Print Preview to verify your changes.

r. Save and close the report.

STEP 2 ≫ USING REPORT VIEWS

The Products report you created for La Vida Mocha looks very good, according to Ryung. However, she does not have Access at home and would like to have a copy of the report saved so she can bring it home. You will save a copy of the report for her.

a. Open the **Products Report** and switch to **Print Preview**. Click **PDF or XPS** in the Data group on the PRINT PREVIEW tab. Enter the file name **a04h2Products_LastFirst** and click **Publish**.

   Windows will open the report in your system's default PDF viewer, which may be Adobe Reader or the Windows 8 Reader app.

b. Switch back to Access, if necessary. Click **Close** when asked if you want to save the export steps.

c. Click **Close Print Preview** and close the report.

STEP 3 ≫ MODIFYING A REPORT

Ryung realized the Products table is missing a field. She would like you to add this to the table and update the report to reflect the new field. She would also like to make sure the report fits nicely onto one landscape page. She has also asked you to show her some sample color schemes.

a. Right-click the **Products table** and select **Design view**.

   You need to add the OnHand field to the Products table.

b. Click the **MarkupPercent field** and click **Insert Rows** in the Tools group on the DESIGN tab.

   A new blank row displays above the MarkupPercent field.

c. Type **OnHand** in the **Field Name box** and select **Number** as the Data Type.

d. Save the table. Click **View** to change to Datasheet view.

The new OnHand column appears empty in each row. Next, you will add sample data to the new field.

e. Fill in the number **10** for each item's OnHand field.

f. Close the Products table.

g. Right-click the **Products Report** and select **Layout view**.

h. Click **Add Existing Fields** in the Tools group on the DESIGN tab unless the Field List already appears on the right of your screen.

i. Drag the **OnHand field** from the Field List pane between the Cost and MarkupPercent fields. Close the Field List pane.

Because of the tabular layout control, Access adjusts all the columns to make room for the new OnHand field.

j. Display the report in Print Preview.

The report is still too wide for a single page.

k. Click **Close Print Preview**. Switch to Layout view if necessary.

l. Click anywhere on the **Year Introduced column**. Click the **ARRANGE tab** and click **Select Column** in the Rows & Columns group. Press **Delete** to remove the column.

The Year Introduced column is removed from the report and the other fields fill the empty space.

> **TROUBLESHOOTING:** If you cannot see the Year Introduced column, try scrolling to the right.

m. Click the **ProductID column heading** and drag the right border to the left until the Product ID heading still fits, but any extra white space is removed.

n. Click the **Refrigeration Needed column heading** and rename the column **Refrig?**. Adjust the column width of the Refrig? column so any extra white space is removed.

o. Click **Themes** in the Themes group on the DESIGN tab.

The available predefined themes display.

p. Right-click the **Organic theme** and choose **Apply Theme to This Object Only**. Display the report in Print Preview.

Access reformats the report using the Organic theme.

> **TROUBLESHOOTING:** If you cannot figure out which theme is which, you can hover the mouse over each theme and a ScreenTip will display the theme name.

q. Click **Close Print Preview**. Click the **FILE tab**, select **Save As**, select **Save Object As**, and then click **Save As**. Type **Products Organic** as the report name and click **OK**.

You saved the report with one theme. Now, you will apply a second theme to the report and save it with a different name.

r. Switch to Layout view and click **Themes** in the Themes group to apply a different theme.

s. Right-click the **Retrospect theme** and choose **Apply Theme to This Object Only**. Display the report in Print Preview.

If we do not tell Access to apply the theme to this object only, all objects will change.

t. Click **Close Print Preview**. Click the **FILE tab**, select **Save As**, select **Save Object As**, and then click **Save As**. Type **Products Retrospect** as the report name and click **OK**. Close the report.

You will be able to show Ryung two different themes.

STEP 4 ≫ SORTING RECORDS IN A REPORT

Ryung would like the Products Report report to be sorted by Product Name order (rather than ProductID order). You change the sort order and preview again to see the results.

a. Open **Products Report** in Layout view.

> **TROUBLESHOOTING:** If you cannot see the Products Report, click the Shutter Bar to maximize the Navigation Pane.

b. Click **Group & Sort** in the Grouping & Totals group on the DESIGN tab.

The *Add a group* and *Add a sort* options appear at the bottom of the report.

> **TROUBLESHOOTING:** If the options do not appear, they may have been showing. Try clicking Group & Sort again.

c. Click **Add a sort**.

A new Sort bar displays at the bottom of the report.

d. Select **Brand** from the list.

The report is now sorted by Brand in Ascending order (with Discount on top).

e. Click **Add a group**.

f. Select **Brand** from the list.

The report is now grouped by Brand.

g. Display the report in Print Preview.

h. Close Print Preview and save and close the report.

i. Close the database. Submit the database and the PDF file *a04h2Products_LastFirst* based on your instructor's directions.

Chapter Objectives Review

After reading this chapter, you have accomplished the following objectives:

1. **Create forms using form tools.**
   - A form is used to add data to or edit data in a table.
   - Access provides 14 different tools for creating forms.
   - If you use a form, you are less likely to edit the wrong record.
   - Forms can show data from multiple tables at once.
   - Forms can be customized to match a paper form.
   - Identify a record source: A record source is the table or query that supplies the records.
   - Use the Form tool: The Form tool creates a basic form.
   - Understand controls: Controls are the text boxes, buttons, boxes, and other tools you use to add, edit, and display data in a form or report.
   - Work with form views: Form view is a simplified interface used for data entry, but it allows no changes. Layout view allows users to make changes to the layout while viewing the data on the form. Design view allows you to change advanced design settings you cannot see in the Layout view.
   - Work with a subform: A subform displays data from a related table for each record in the main table.

2. **Create a split form:** A split form combines two views of the same record source—one section is displayed in a stacked layout and the other section is displayed in a tabular layout.
   - Create a multiple-item form: This form displays multiple records in a tabular layout similar to a table's Datasheet view, with more customization options.
   - Create forms using the other form tools: A Datasheet form is a replica of a table or query's Datasheet view except that it still retains some of the form properties. The Form Design tool and the Blank Form tools can be used to create a form manually. The Navigation option in the Forms group enables you to create user interface forms that have the look and feel of a Web-based form and enable users to open and close the objects of a database. The Modal Dialog Form tool can be used to create a dialog box.

3. **Use form views.**
   - Edit data in Form view: Most users will work in Form view. This allows changes to data but not to design elements.
   - Alter a form in Layout view: Layout view allows you to change the design of a form while viewing data.
   - Add a field to a form: Fields can be added to an existing form using the Field List.
   - Delete a field from a form: Fields can be removed, but you may need to select the entire control to avoid leaving empty space in the form.
   - Adjust column widths in a form: Column widths often need to be adjusted. Numeric fields may show up as #### if the value cannot be displayed in the box.
   - Use the Form Layout tools tabs: There are three Form Layout tabs that allow you to manipulate the design of a form.

   - Modify form controls using the Format tab: The Format tab allows changes to the font, including bold, italic, underlining, font size, font color, font background, and alignment.
   - Select controls: Controls can be selected manually or by using the Arrange tab.
   - Add a theme to a form: Themes can be applied to a single form or to all objects in the database.
   - Add styling to a form: Forms can have many types of styles applied. Take care to avoid too many styles on a single form, as it can distract from the form.

4. **Work with a form layout control.**
   - Modify a form using the Arrange tab: The Arrange tab appears in both Layout view and Design view and allows you to change form layout, field order, and spacing options.
   - The Table group lets you add gridlines, change from stacked to tabular layout (and vice versa), or remove a form's layout.
   - The Move group contains lets you move fields.
   - The Position group lets you modify the margins and the padding of controls in a form.

5. **Sort records in form.**
   - Default sort order is the sort order of the data source (table, query, etc.).
   - Sort by a single field: Forms can be sorted by a single field in either ascending or descending order.
   - Remove sorting in a form: Sorts can be removed from a form at any point.

6. **Create reports using report tools.**
   - A report is a document that displays information from a database in a format that outputs meaningful information to its readers.
   - Access reports can be printed, viewed on screen, or saved as files.
   - Reports cannot change data in your database.
   - Use the Report tool: Access has five report tools: The Report tool instantly creates a tabular report based on the table or query currently selected. The Report Design tool creates a new blank report in Design view. The Blank Report tool creates a new blank report so that you can insert fields and controls manually and design the report. The Report Wizard tool helps you create a report. The Labels tool creates a page of mailing labels using a template.
   - Use the Report Wizard to create a report: The Report Wizard will guide you step by step through creating a report, asking questions and generating output.
   - Use the Report Wizard with grouping: The Report Wizard options will change when you add grouping. It will also allow summary options such as creating a sum of a field for each grouping level.
   - Use the Label Wizard: The Label Wizard can produce printable labels. Access includes predefined standard formats for common labels.

7. **Use report views.**
   - View a report in Report view: Report view is ideal for viewing data onscreen. Neither data nor design can be changed.
   - Alter a report in Layout view: Layout view allows you to change the design of a report while viewing data.
   - Print or save a report in Print Preview: Print Preview shows the way the report will display when printed. It also allows you to save the report as a file in a number of formats.

8. **Modify a report.**
   - Modify a report using the Design tab: The Design tab allows you to add or change sorting, change report theme, and insert additional controls.
   - Modify a report using the Arrange tab: The Arrange tab allows you to change the report layout, move fields, and insert spaces.
   - Modify report controls using the Format tab: The Format tab allows changes to the font, including bold, italic, underlining, font size, font color, font background, and alignment.
   - Add a field to a report: Fields can be added to an existing report using the Field List.

- Delete a field from a report: Fields can be removed, but you may need to select the entire control to avoid leaving empty space in the report.
- Adjust column widths in a report: Column widths often need to be adjusted. Numeric fields may show up as #### if the value cannot be displayed in the box.
- Change margins and orientation: You can display the report in portrait or landscape format and increase or decrease margin size.
- Add a theme to the report: Themes can be applied to a single report or to all objects in the database.
- Work with a Report Layout control: The Layout control keeps the fields neatly spaced, making it harder to place fields in an exact location but keeping a standard format.

9. **Sort records in a report.**
   - Default sort order for reports is the sort order of the record source.
   - Change the sorting in a report: Sorting can be done by a single or by multiple fields.

Key Terms Matching

Match the key terms with their definitions. Write the key term letter by the appropriate numbered definition.

a. Controls
b. Design view
c. Form
d. Form tool
e. Form view
f. Label Wizard
g. Layout control
h. Layout view
i. Multiple Items form
j. Portable Document Format (PDF)

k. Print Preview
l. Record source
m. Report
n. Report tool
o. Report view
p. Report Wizard
q. Split form
r. Stacked layout
s. Tabular layout
t. Theme

1. _____ A database object that is used to add data into or edit data in a table. **p. 258**

2. _____ Used to create data entry forms for customers, employees, products, and other primary tables. **p. 258**

3. _____ The table or query that supplies the records for a form or report. **p. 259**

4. _____ Displays fields in a vertical column. **p. 260**

5. _____ Displays data horizontally. **p. 260**

6. _____ The text boxes, buttons, boxes, and other tools you use to add, edit, and display the data in a form or report. **p. 260**

7. _____ Provides guides to help keep controls aligned horizontally and vertically and give your form a uniform appearance. **p. 260**

8. _____ A simplified interface primarily used for data entry; does not allow you to make changes to the layout. **p. 260**

9. _____ Enables users to make changes to a layout while viewing the data on the form or report. **p. 261**

10. _____ Enables you to change advanced design settings you cannot see in the Layout view, such as a background image. **p. 261**

11. _____ Combines two views of the same record source—one section is displayed in a stacked layout and the other section is displayed in a tabular layout. **p. 262**

12. _____ Displays multiple records in a tabular layout similar to a table's Datasheet view, with more customization options. **p. 263**

13. _____ A defined set of colors, fonts, and graphics that can be applied to a form or report. **p. 267**

14. _____ A document that displays information from a database in a format that outputs meaningful information to its readers. **p. 278**

15. _____ Used to instantly create a tabular report based on the table or query currently selected. **p. 278**

16. _____ Asks you questions and then uses your answers to generate a customized report. **p. 280**

17. _____ Enables you to easily create mailing labels, name tags, and other specialized tags. **p. 284**

18. _____ Enables you to see what a printed report will look like in a continuous page layout. **p. 285**

19. _____ Enables you to see exactly what the report will look like when it is printed. **p. 286**

20. _____ A file type that was created for exchanging documents independent of software applications and operating system environment. **p. 286**

Multiple Choice

1. The table or query that supplies the records for a form or report is also known as the:

   (a) Control.
   (b) Record Source.
   (c) Theme.
   (d) Tabular Layout.

2. Which of the following statements is *false*?

   (a) Both forms and reports can use tabular and stacked layouts.
   (b) A stacked layout displays data in a vertical column.
   (c) A tabular layout displays data horizontally.
   (d) Stacked layouts are more common for reports because they will use less paper when printed.

3. Which of the following is *not* an example of a control?

   (a) A text box on a form
   (b) Buttons on a report
   (c) A report
   (d) A box on a report

4. The simplest interface you can use to modify control widths in a form is in:

   (a) Layout view.
   (b) Form view.
   (c) Design view.
   (d) Report view.

5. Which of the following views is the most powerful, but also the most complicated?

   (a) Design view.
   (b) Layout view.
   (c) Form view/Report view.
   (d) Print Preview.

6. Which of the following statements about reports are *false*?

   (a) Reports can be saved to a file on your computer.
   (b) Reports are primarily used to modify data.

   (c) Reports can produce output in a number of ways, including mailing labels.
   (d) Reports can be created simply using the Report tool.

7. Use the _____ to see exactly what the printed report will look like before printing.

   (a) Report tool
   (b) Report Wizard
   (c) Report view
   (d) Print Preview

8. If you have a client working on a Mac system, which of the following file formats would be the best choice to use to ensure the client can open it?

   (a) Microsoft Word
   (b) Microsoft Excel
   (c) Microsoft Access
   (d) Portable Document Format (PDF)

9. Which of the following statements is *false*?

   (a) Reports are generally used for printing, emailing, or viewing data on the screen.
   (b) Layout controls for forms and reports are the defined sets of colors, fonts, and graphics.
   (c) Forms are often used for inputting data.
   (d) Forms and reports both include controls, such as text boxes, that can be resized.

10. Which of the following statements is *false*?

    (a) You can use grouping to show a list of properties by state.
    (b) Sorting can be done on both forms and reports.
    (c) Sorting can be done in ascending or descending order.
    (d) You can either group or sort (but not both).

Practice Exercises

1 Financial Management

You are working as a customer service representative for a financial management firm. Your task is to contact a list of prospective customers and introduce yourself and the services of your company. You will create a form to help you view one customer at a time while also helping add and update the data. After creating the form, you will customize it and add sorting. You will also create a report to show you all the data on one screen, for viewing purposes. This exercise follows the same set of skills as used in Hands-On Exercises 1 and 2 in the chapter. Refer to Figure 4.41 as you complete this exercise.

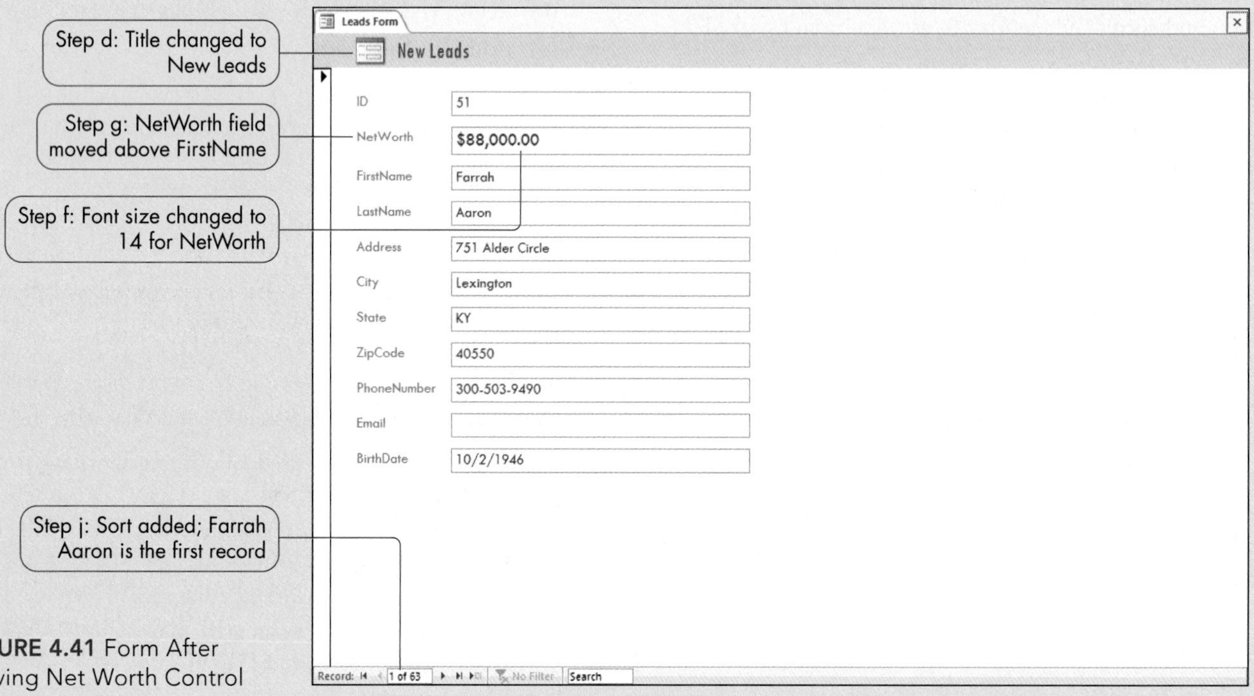

Step d: Title changed to New Leads

Step g: NetWorth field moved above FirstName

Step f: Font size changed to 14 for NetWorth

Step j: Sort added; Farrah Aaron is the first record

Leads Form	×

New Leads

ID	51
NetWorth	$88,000.00
FirstName	Farrah
LastName	Aaron
Address	751 Alder Circle
City	Lexington
State	KY
ZipCode	40550
PhoneNumber	300-503-9490
Email	
BirthDate	10/2/1946

Record: 1 of 63 ▶ ▶▶ No Filter Search

FIGURE 4.41 Form After Moving Net Worth Control

a. Start Access and open **a04p1Prospects**. Save the database as **a04p1Prospects_LastFirst**.

b. Click the **Leads table**. Click the **CREATE tab** and click **Form** in the Forms group.

   A new form based on the Leads table displays in Layout view.

c. Click the **ID text box** and drag the right border of the first field to the left to shrink the column by approximately half of its original size.

   The other columns will shrink as well.

d. Change the title of the form to **New Leads**.

e. Click **Themes** in the Themes group of the DESIGN tab. Select the **Integral theme** (first row, third column).

f. Change the font size to **14** for the NetWorth text box control.

g. Click **Select Row** in the Rows & Columns group on the ARRANGE tab. Click **Move Up** in the Move group on the ARRANGE tab until *NetWorth* appears above *First*.

> **TROUBLESHOOTING:** If both items do not move together, undo, ensure both are selected, and then follow the instructions in step g.

   NetWorth should now appear above the FirstName. See Figure 4.41.

h. Save the form as **Leads Form**. Switch to Form view.

i. Navigate to record 63. Enter your first and last names in the appropriate fields. Leave the e-mail address blank.

j. Click in the **Last field** (if necessary) and click **Ascending** in the Sort & Filter group of the HOME tab Farrah Aaron should be the first record displayed unless your last name appears before hers alphabetically.

k. Save and close the form.

l. Click the **Leads table**. Click **Report** in the Reports group on the CREATE tab.

A new report is created based on the Leads table.

m. Make fields as small as possible to remove extra white space. Do not try to fit the entire report all on one page, as you will be using this for on-screen viewing only.

n. Save the report as **Leads Report**. Close the report.

o. Exit Access. Submit the database based on your instructor's directions.

2 Comfort Insurance

The Human Resources department of the Comfort Insurance Agency has initiated its annual employee performance reviews. You will create a form for them to help organize input and a report showing employee salary increases and bonuses. The employee data, along with forms and reports, are stored in an Access database. You need to prepare a report showing employee raises and bonuses by city. This exercise follows the same set of skills as used in Hands-On Exercises 1 and 2 in this chapter. Refer to Figure 4.42 as you complete this exercise.

Step k: Location is a grouping level

Employee Compensation

Location	LastName	FirstName	HireDate	Salary	2012Increase	2012Raise	YearHired	YearsWorked
L01								
	Abrams		5/24/2012	$47,500.00	3.00%	1425	2012	0
	Anderson	Vicki	9/21/2008	$47,900.00	4.00%	1916	2008	4
	Bichette	Susan	9/10/2012	$61,500.00	4.00%	2460	2012	0
	Block	Leonard	12/13/2010	$26,200.00	3.00%	786	2010	2
	Brown	Patricia	6/12/2011	$20,100.00	5.00%	1005	2011	1
	Brumbaugh	Paige	12/25/2009	$49,300.00	3.00%	1479	2009	3
	Daniels	Phil	2/5/2011	$42,600.00	3.00%	1278	2011	1
	Davis	Martha	6/14/2010	$51,900.00	4.00%	2076	2010	2
	Drubin	Lolly	9/12/2009	$37,000.00	3.00%	1110	2009	3
	Fantis	Laurie	1/11/2011	$28,000.00	3.00%	840	2011	1
	Fleming	Karen	12/15/2009	$41,100.00	3.00%	1233	2009	3
	Gander	John	12/31/2008	$38,400.00	3.00%	1152	2008	4
	Grippando	Joan	8/30/2010	$26,100.00	3.00%	783	2010	2
	Harrison	Jenifer	10/19/2012	$44,800.00	3.00%	1344	2012	0
	Imber	Elise	1/22/2011	$63,700.00	4.00%	2548	2011	1
	Johnshon	Billy	4/28/2012	$21,800.00	5.00%	1090	2012	0
	Johnson	Debbie	6/23/2012	$39,700.00	3.00%	1191	2012	0
	Lacher	Tom	3/7/2011	$31,200.00	3.00%	936	2011	1
	Mc Key	Boo	7/29/2012	$39,600.00	3.00%	1188	2012	0
	McCammon	Johnny	6/22/2012	$43,100.00	4.00%	1724	2012	0
	Mills	Jack	11/6/2008	$44,600.00	3.00%	1338	2008	4
	Nagel	Mimi	12/29/2010	$46,200.00	3.00%	1386	2010	2
	Newman	Adam	10/12/2006	$45,000.00	4.00%	1800	2006	6
	Novicheck	Deborah	11/25/2008	$46,800.00	3.00%	1404	2008	4

FIGURE 4.42 Final Employee Compensation Report

a. Open *a04p2Insurance*. Save the database as **a04p2Insurance_LastFirst**.

b. Select the **Locations table**. Click the **CREATE tab** and click **Form** in the Forms group.

A new form based on the Locations table opens in Layout view.

c. Click the **LocationID text box** containing *L01*. Move the mouse to the right edge of the shaded border until the mouse pointer changes to a double-headed arrow. Drag the right edge to the left to reduce the size of the text box to approximately half of its original size.

The LocationID field and all the other fields should become smaller.

d. Click the subform at the bottom of the form. Press **Delete** to delete the subform.

e. Click **Themes** in the Themes group on the DESIGN tab. Right-click the **Wisp theme** (third row, first column) and select **Apply Theme to This Object Only**.

f. Save the form as **Locations**. Close the form.

g. Select the **Locations table**. Click the **CREATE tab** and click **Report** in the Reports group.

A new tabular layout report based on the Locations table opens in Layout view.

h. Click the **LocationID label** and drag the right border of the label to the left to reduce the size of the control to approximately half of its original size.

i. Repeat the sizing process with the **Zipcode label** and the **OfficePhone label**. Adjust the other columns if necessary until there are no controls on the right side of the vertical dashed line.

j. Display the report in Print Preview. Verify that the report is only one page wide. Save the report as **Locations** and close the report.

k. Select the **Employees Query**. Click the **CREATE tab** and click **Report Wizard** in the Reports group to launch the Report Wizard. Respond to the questions as follows:

- Click (>>) to add all the fields to the Selected Fields box. Click **Next**.
- Accept grouping by Location. Click **Next**.
- Select **LastName** for the first sort order and **FirstName** for the second. Click **Summary Options**.

> **TROUBLESHOOTING:** If you do not see summary options, click Back and click Summary Options at the bottom of the dialog box.

- Click **Sum** for Salary, **Avg** for 2012Increase, and **Avg** for YearsWorked. Accept all other defaults. Click **OK**. Click **Next**.
- Accept the Stepped layout. Change Orientation to **Landscape**. Click **Next**.
- Type **Employee Compensation** for the title of the report. Click **Finish**.

The report is displayed in Print Preview mode. Some of the columns are too narrow. Next, you will adjust the columns.

l. Click **Close Print Preview**. Switch to Layout view.

m. Adjust the column widths so that all the data values are showing and the report appears on one page. Some of the columns will need to be reduced, and some will need to be widened.

n. Click **Themes** in the Themes group on the DESIGN tab. Right-click the **Slice theme** and choose **Apply Theme to This Object Only**.

o. Display the report in Print Preview. Close the Navigation Pane and verify that the report is still one page wide. Compare your report to Figure 4.42. Adjust column widths to display all values.

p. Save and close the Employee Compensation report. Close the database.

q. Exit Access. Submit based on your instructor's directions.

Mid-Level Exercises

1 Hotel Chain

You are the general manager of a large hotel chain. You track revenue by categories, such as conference room rentals and weddings. You need to create a report that shows which locations are earning the most revenue in each category. You will also create a report to show you details of your three newest areas: St. Paul, St. Louis, and Seattle.

a. Open *a04m1Rewards*. Save the database as **a04m1Rewards_LastFirst**.

b. Select the **Members table** and create a Multiple Items form. Save the form as **Maintain Members**.

c. Modify the form in Layout view as follows:
   - Change the MemNumber label to **MemID** and reduce the MemNumber column width.
   - Adjust the column widths to eliminate extra white space.
   - Delete the form icon (the picture next to the title of the form) in the Form Header.

d. Change the sorting on the MemberSince control so that the members who joined most recently are displayed first.

e. Click on the **LastName field**. Change the Control Padding to **Wide**. Hint: Search **Control Padding Wide** in Access Help.

   The controls have some extra space between them.

f. Save and close the form.

g. Select the **Revenue query** and create a report using the Report Wizard. Answer the wizard prompts as follows:
   - Include all fields.
   - Add grouping by City and by ServiceName.
   - Add a Sum to the Revenue field and check the **Summary Only option**.
   - Choose **Outline Layout**.
   - Name the report **Revenue by City and Service**.

h. Scroll through all the pages to check the layout of the report while in Print Preview mode.

i. Exit Print Preview. Switch to Layout view and delete the NumInParty and PerPersonCharge controls.

j. Change the font size, font color, and/or background color of the Sum control (not the Revenue control) so the control stands out from the other controls.

k. Change the font size, font color, and/or background color of the Grand Total control (found at the end of the report) so the control stands out as well.

l. Change the sort on the report, so that it sorts by city in descending order—that is, so that the last city alphabetically (St. Paul) is displayed first.

m. Examine the data in the report to determine which city of St. Paul, St. Louis, and Seattle has the highest Sum of event revenue. You will use this information to modify a query.

n. Modify the Totals by Service query so the criteria for the City field is the city you determined had the highest sum from St. Paul, St. Louis, or Seattle. Save and close the query.

o. Create a report using the Report tool based on the Totals by Service query. Name the report **Targeted City**.

p. Close the report. Close the database.

q. Exit Access. Submit based on your instructor's directions.

2 Benefit Auction

You are helping to organize a benefit auction to raise money for families who lost their homes in a natural disaster. The information for the auction is currently stored in an Excel spreadsheet, but you have volunteered to migrate this to Access. You will create a database that will store the data from Excel in an Access database. You will create a form to manage the data-entry process. You also need to create two reports: one that lists the items collected in each category and one for labels so you can send the donors a thank-you letter after the auction.

a. Open Access and create a new database named **a04m2Auction_LastFirst**.
   A new table appears with an ID column.

b. Switch to Design view. Type **Items** in the **Save As dialog box** and click **OK**.

c. Change the ID Field Name to **ItemID**. Type **Description** in the second row and press **Tab**. Accept **Short Text** as the Data Type. Type **50** in the **Field Size property** in Field Properties.

d. Type the remainder of the fields and adjust the data types as shown:

Field Name	Data Type
DateOfDonation	Date/Time
Category	Short Text
Price	Currency
DonorName	Short Text
DonorAddress1	Short Text
DonorAddress2	Short Text

e. Open Excel. Open the **a04m2_Items** file. Examine the length of the Category, DonorName, DonorAddress1, and DonorAddress2 columns. Determine how many characters are needed for each field, and round to the nearest 5. For example, if a field needs 23 characters, you would round up to 25. You will use this to change field sizes in the table.

f. Change the field size for the Category, DonorName, DonorAddress1, and DonorAddress2 to the sizes you chose in step e. Save the table.

g. Copy and paste the rows from the Excel file into the table. Resize the columns so all data is visible. Close the table.

> **TROUBLESHOOTING:** Recall that you must click the Record Selector (pencil icon, to the left of a blank row) to paste data.

> **TROUBLESHOOTING:** Once you have pasted the data, ensure your chosen field sizes did not cause you to lose data. If so, update the field size, delete the records you pasted in, and then repeat step g.

h. Verify that the Items table is selected. Create a new form using the Form tool.

i. Change the layout of the form to a **Tabular Layout**. Resize field widths to reduce extra space. It is acceptable for field values to appear on two lines.

j. Change the title of the form to **Items for Auction**.

DISCOVER

k. Add conditional formatting so that each Price that is greater than 90 has a text color of **Green**. Use the Green color in the first row of the options.

l. Save the form as **Auction Items Form**.

m. Switch to Form view. Create a new record with the following information. Note it will automatically assign an ItemID of 27 for you.

Description	DateOfDonation	Category	Price	DonorName	DonorAddress1	DonorAddress2
iPad	12/31/2016	House	$400	Staples	500 Market St	Brick, NJ 08723

n. Add a sort to the form, so the lowest priced items appear first. Close the form.

o. Select the **Items table** in the Navigation Pane and create a report using the Report Wizard. Include all fields except the donor address fields, group by Category, include the Sum of Price as a Summary Option, accept the default layout, and then save the report **Auction Items by Category**.

p. Switch to Layout view and adjust the controls so all data is visible. Preview the report to verify the column widths are correct.

q. Sort the report so the least expensive items are shown first. Save and close the report.

r. Create mailing labels based on the Avery 5660 template. Place the donor name on the first line, address on the second, and city, state, and ZIP on the third line. Sort the labels by DonorName. Name the report **Donor Labels**. After you create the labels, display them in Print Preview mode verify everything will fit onto the label template. Close the label report.

s. Exit Access. Submit the database based on your instructor's directions.

3 | Used Cell Phones for Sale

COLLABORATION CASE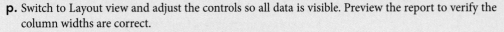

You and a few of your classmates started a new business selling used cell phones, MP3 players, and accessories. You have been using an Access database to track your inventory. You need to create several forms and reports to increase database efficiency and analysis. You have used Access forms and reports as part of your classwork, but you would like to experiment with them as they apply to you in a real-world scenario.

a. Choose one unique type of form and one unique type of report each. Based on your experience in class, you saw there were a number of different types of forms and reports that can be created. Choose one each from the following:

Forms: Form tool, Form Wizard, Multiple Items Form, Split Form

Reports: Report Tool, Report Wizard, Label Wizard

b. Open Access and open the *a04t1Phones* database individually. Save the file as **a04t1Phones_LastFirst**. Each of you will create your forms and reports in an individual database.

c. Create a form and a report based on the Inventory table, using the type of form and report you chose in step a, unless you chose Label Wizard. If you chose Label Wizard, you should create a report based on the Mailing List table, using Avery 8660 as your destination label.

d. Save the form and report as **LastFirst**, replacing Last and First with your last and first names.

e. Make the report as attractive and useful as possible. You may want to change sorting, add grouping (to reports), remove or add a layout control, change formatting options, and/or change the background color. Modify the form and report, save the changes, and exit Access.

f. Meet as a group. Open the *a04t1Phones* database and save the file as **a04t1Phones_GroupName**.

g. Import the form and report from each of your databases.

Your *a04t1Phones_GroupName* file will now have one form and one report for each student.

h. Examine the forms and reports each of you created.

i. Examine your results. Determine which forms and reports you would keep, if this were the real world. Rename the forms and reports you would keep as **Keep_LastFirst** and rename the ones you would discard as **Discard_LastFirst**. Do not delete the forms and reports you will not use.

j. Modify the forms and reports you plan to keep as a group, if necessary. Save the changes and close all forms and reports. Ensure each student has a copy of the final *a04t1Phones_GroupName* database.

k. Exit Access and submit both the *a04t1Phones_GroupName* and *a04t1Phones_LastFirst* databases based on your instructor's directions.

Beyond the Classroom

Create a Split Form

RESEARCH CASE

FROM SCRATCH

This chapter introduced you to Access forms, including the split form. It is possible to turn an existing form into a split form if you modify a few form properties. Perform an Internet search to find the steps to convert a form to a split form. First, create a new database and name the file **a04b2Split_LastFirst**. Next, import *only* the Books table and Books form from the *a04b2BooksImport* database. To import the objects, click the **External Data tab** and click **Access** in the Import & Link group. After the new objects have been imported, use the information from the Internet to convert the Books form into a split form. Make sure the datasheet is on the bottom half. Change the form so it sorts by Title in ascending order. Save the form as **Split Form Books**. Close Access. Submit the database based on your instructor's directions.

Properties by City

DISASTER RECOVERY

Munesh, a co-worker, is having difficulty with an Access report and asked you for your assistance. He was trying to fix the report and seems to have made things worse. Open the *a04b3Sales* database and save the file as **a04b3Sales_LastFirst**. In the new database, open Properties Report in Report View. Notice Munesh moved fields around and the report does not fit on one page. In addition, there is a big gap between two fields and he moved the Bed and Bath fields so they are basically on top of one another. Add all of the fields to a Tabular Layout. Add grouping by City. Sort the report by Year Built in descending order. Change the report to Landscape orientation and adjust the column widths so they all fit onto one page. Save the new report as **Properties by City**. Close Access. Submit the database based on your instructor's directions.

Performance Reviews

SOFT SKILLS CASE

Passaic County Medical Monitoring provides visiting nurse care for patients in and around Passaic County, New Jersey. They have recently moved their records into an Access database. The director of Human Resources, Farrah Hassan, brings the nurses in yearly for a performance review. Employees are rated by a survey given to patients, asking them to rate the nurses on a scale of 1 (poor) to 5 (superb). You have been asked to create a one-page summary report to show the average of each employee's ratings. You will open her *a04b4Perform* database and save it as **a04b4Perform_LastFirst**. Use the Report Wizard to create a report based on the Performance and Nurses tables, group by the nurse, and add summary options to average the results for Promptness, Attitude, Knowledge, and Gentleness. The final report should display the NurseID, NurseFirst, and NurseLast fields and the averages for each of the four columns. You will also want to format each of the columns in the final report so they show two decimal places. You calculated the results by hand for nurse 1, Lan Wang, and her averages were 3.00 for Promptness, 3.11 for Attitude, 3.67 for Knowledge, and 3.67 for Gentleness, so when you create your report, you can check that it shows the correct data. Save the report as **Overall Ratings**, close Access, and submit the database based on your instructor's directions.

Your boss asked you to prepare a schedule for each speaker for the national conference being hosted next year on your campus. She wants to mail the schedules to the speakers so that they can provide feedback on the schedule prior to its publication. You assure her that you can accomplish this task with Access.

Database File Setup

You need to copy an original database file, rename the copied file, and then open the copied database to complete this capstone exercise. After you open the copied database, you replace an existing employee's name with your name.

a. Open *a04c1_NatConf*.

b. Save the database as **a04c1NatConf_LastFirst**.

c. Open the Speakers table.

d. Find and replace *YourName* with your name. Close the table.

Create and Customize a Form

You need to create a form to add and update Speakers. Use the Form tool to create the form and modify the form as explained. You will also add a layout to an existing form.

a. Select the **Speakers table** as the record source for the form.

b. Use the Form tool to create a new stacked form.

c. Change the title to **Enter/Edit Speakers**.

d. Reduce the width of the text box controls to approximately half of their original size.

e. Delete the Sessions subform.

f. View the form and data in Form view. Sort the records by LastName in ascending order.

g. Save the form as **Edit Speakers**. Close the form.

h. Open the Room Information form in Layout view. The form does not have a Form Layout. Select all controls and apply the **Stacked Layout**.

i. Save and close the form.

Create a Report

You need to create a report based on the Speaker and Room Schedule query. You decide to use the Report Wizard to accomplish this task. You will also need to email the schedule to the presenters, so you will save the report as a PDF.

a. Select the **Speaker and Room Schedule query** as the record source for the report.

b. Activate the **Report Wizard** and use the following options as you go through the Wizard:

- Select all of the available fields for the report.
- View the data by Speakers.
- Accept LastName and FirstName as grouping levels.
- Use **Date** as the primary sort field in ascending order.
- Accept the Stepped and Portrait options.
- Save the report as **Speaker Schedule**.
- Switch to Layout view and apply the **Organic theme** to only this report.

c. Preview the report. Switch to Layout view. Adjust the column widths if necessary.

d. Switch to Print Preview and save the report as a PDF named **a04c1Speaker_LastFirst**.

e. When the PDF displays, close the program that displays it and return to Access. Exit Print Preview. Close the report.

Add an Additional Field

You realize the session times were not included in the query. You add the field to the query and then start over with the Report Wizard.

a. Open the Speaker and Room Schedule query in Design view.

b. Add the **StartingTime field** in the Sessions table to the design grid, after the Date field. Run the query.

c. Save and close the query.

d. Click the **Speaker and Room Schedule query**. Start the Report Wizard again and use the following options:

- Select all of the available fields for the report.
- View the data by Speakers.
- Use the LastName, FirstName fields as the primary grouping level.
- Use Date as the primary sort field in ascending order.
- Use StartingTime as the secondary sort field in Ascending order.
- Select the **Stepped** and **Portrait options**.
- Name the report **Speaker Schedule Revised**.
- Switch to Layout view and apply the **Facet theme** (first row, second column) to only this report.

e. Adjust the column widths in Layout view so that all the data is visible.

f. Add a space to the column heading labels as needed. For example, the column LastName should read Last Name.

g. Save and close the report. Close the database.

h. Exit Access. Submit the database and PDF based on your instructor's directions.

FROM SCRATCH

You were recently hired by your local college to help with registering all transfer students. The college's Transfer Counseling Department is a one-stop location for transfer students to come with questions. They have been working with Excel spreadsheets generated by the Information Technology department, but they are hoping to do more with an Access database. They have had a number of problems, including employees putting information in the wrong fields, putting information in the wrong format, and creating incorrect formulas. They are also hoping for more consistent ways of finding information, as well as being able to generate reports. Your tasks include importing an existing Excel worksheet as a table into your Access database; modifying the table; creating a relationship between two tables; creating queries with calculated fields, functions, and totals; creating a form for input; and creating a report.

Set Up the Database File and Import an Excel Worksheet

To start, you have been provided with a database the Information Technology department created. The database has one table and one form. You will be importing an Excel spreadsheet into a table and creating a primary key.

a. Start Access. Open *a00c1College* and save the database as **a00c1College_LastFirst**.

b. Import the *a00c1Transfer* Excel workbook into a table named **Transfer Schools**. While importing the data, choose **StudentID** as the primary key field. Ensure *StudentID* has a data type of Short Text.

Modify a Table

Now that you have imported the data from the spreadsheet, you will modify the field properties in the Transfer Schools table and demonstrate sorting.

a. Set the StudentID field size to **10**.

b. Remove the @ symbol from the StudentID format property.

c. Change the AdmittingSchool field size to **75**.

d. Change the RegistrationFee and TuitionDue fields to have **0** decimal places.

e. Switch to Datasheet View. Resize all columns so all data are displayed.

f. Sort the Transfer Schools table on the CreditsTransferred field in ascending order.

g. Save and close the table.

Create Relationships

Now that the table is imported and modified, you will create a relationship between the two tables.

a. Add the Transfer Schools and Transfer Students tables to the Relationships window.

b. Create a one-to-one relationship between the StudentID field in the Transfer Students (primary) table and the StudentID field in the Transfer Schools (related) table. Enforce referential integrity between the two tables.

c. Save the changes and close the Relationships window.

Modify Data in a Form

You will demonstrate changing information in a form.

a. Open the Transfer Students Data Entry form.

b. Change the major for *Cornelius Kavanaugh* to **Elementary Education**. Close the form.

Create a Query

Rey Rivera, a counselor in the center, would like your assistance in helping him find certain information. You will create a query for him and demonstrate how he can change information.

a. Create a new query using Design view. This query will access fields from both the Transfer Schools and Transfer Students tables. From the Transfer Students table, add the FirstName, LastName, Major, Class, and GPA fields. From the Transfer Schools table, add the AdmissionDate, TuitionDue, CreditsEarned, and CreditsTransferred fields.

b. Save the query as **Transfer Credits**.

c. Set the criteria in the AdmissionDate field to **8/1/2015**. Run the query (144 records will display).

d. Enter the TuitionDue for Diana Sullivan as **$1500** and the GPA for Audrey Owen as **3.51**.

e. Save the query.

Create Calculated Fields

Now that you have created the query, you will create a second query for Rey that will calculate the number of credits students lost upon transfer, the tuition payments for which they will be responsible (assuming three payments per semester), and the payment due date.

a. Switch to Design view of the Transfer Credits query. Save the query as **Transfer Credit Calculations**.

b. Remove the criteria from the AdmissionDate field.

c. Create a calculated field in the first empty field cell of the query named **LostCredits** that subtracts CreditsTransferred from CreditsEarned.

d. Create another calculated field named **TuitionPayments** that determines tuition paid in three installments. Using the Pmt function, replace the rate argument with **0.025/3**, the num_periods argument with **3**, and the present_value argument with the student's tuition payment. Use **0** for the future_value and type arguments. Ensure the payment appears as a positive number.

e. Format the TuitionPayments calculated field as **Currency**.

f. Create another calculated field named **DueDate** after the TuitionPayments field. To calculate the due date, add **30** to their AdmissionDate. Run the query and verify that the three calculated fields have valid data.

g. Add a total row to the query. Average the GPA column and sum the LostCredits column. Save and close the query.

Create a Totals Query

Cala Hajjar, the director of the center, needs to summarize information about the transfer students for the 2015–2016 academic year to present to the College's Board of Trustees. You will create a totals query for her to summarize the number of transfer students, average number of credits earned and transferred, and total tuition earned by transfer institution.

a. Create a new query in Design view. Add the Transfer Schools table.

b. Add the AdmittingSchool, StudentID, CreditsEarned, CreditsTransferred, and TuitionDue fields.

c. Sort the query by AdmittingSchool in ascending order.

d. Show the Total row. Group by AdmittingSchool and show the count of StudentID, the average CreditsEarned, the average of CreditsTransferred, and the sum of TuitionDue.

e. Format both average fields as **Standard**.

f. Change the caption for the StudentID field to **NumStudents**, the caption for the CreditsEarned average to **AvgCreditsEarned**, the caption for the CreditsTransferred average to **AvgCredits Transferred**, and the caption for SumOfTuitionDue to **TotalTuition**.

g. Run the query. Resize columns so all data are shown.

h. Save the query as **Transfer Summary**.

i. Close the query.

Create a Form

Hideo Sasaki, the department's administrative assistant, will handle data entry. He has asked you to simplify the way he inputs information into the new table. You will create a form based on the new Transfer Schools table.

a. Create a Split Form using the Transfer Schools table as the source.

b. Change the height of the AdmittingSchool field to reduce extra space.

c. Remove the layout. Shrink each field so it is only as large as it needs to be.

d. Click on record 123455 in the bottom half of the split form. Make sure all fields are still visible. If not, adjust the controls so all values are visible.

e. Move the CreditsTransferred field so it is to the right of the CreditsEarned field on the same row.

f. Change the format of the TuitionDue field so the font size is **18** and the font color is **Red** (last row, second column in the *Standard Colors* section).

g. Change the fill color of the StudentID field to be **Yellow** (last row, fourth column in the *Standard Colors* section).

h. Save the form as **Transfer Schools Form**. Save and close the form.

Create a Report

Cala Hajjar, the director of the center, saw the query you created for Rey. She is hoping you can create a more print-friendly version for her to distribute to the Board of Trustees. You will create a report based on the Transfer Credits Calculations query.

a. Create a report using the Report Wizard. Add the Class, FirstName, LastName, Major, GPA, and LostCredits fields from the Transfer Credit Calculations query. Do not add any grouping or sorting. Ensure the report is in Landscape orientation.

b. Save the report as **Transfer Students Report** and view the report in Layout view.

Format a Report

Now that you have included the fields Cala has asked for, you will work to format the report to make the information more obvious.

a. Apply the **Wisp theme** (third row, first column) to this object only.

b. Group the report by the Class field. Sort the records within each group by LastName then by FirstName, both in ascending order.

c. Change the font size of the Class field to **16**.

d. Adjust the text boxes so the values are completely visible.

e. Switch to Print Preview mode and verify the report is only one page wide (note: it may be a number of pages long).

f. Export the results as a PDF document using the file name **a00c1Transfer_LastFirst**.

g. Save and close the report.

Close and Submit Database

a. Compact and repair the database.

b. Create a backup of the database. Accept the default name for the backup.

c. Close all database objects and exit Access.

d. Submit the database, backup, and PDF based on your instructor's directions.

Glossary

Access (Office Fundamentals) Relational database management software that enables you to record and link data, query databases, and create forms and reports. (Access) A database management system included in the Microsoft Office 2013 Professional suite.

Aggregate function Performs calculations on an entire column of data and returns a single value. Includes functions such as Sum, Avg, and Count.

AND logical operator Returns only records that meet all criteria.

Argument Any data needed to produce output for a function.

Ascending A sort that lists text data in alphabetical order or a numeric list in lowest to highest order.

AutoNumber A number data type that is generated by Access and is incremented each time a record is added.

Back Up Database An Access utility that creates a duplicate copy of the database.

Backstage view A component of Office 2013 that provides a concise collection of commands related to common file activities and provides information on an open file.

Backup A copy of a file or folder on another drive.

Calculated field Produces a value from an expression or function that references one or more existing fields.

CamelCase notation Uses no spaces in multiword field names but uses uppercase letters to distinguish the first letter of each new word.

CAPTCHA A scrambled code used with online forms to prevent mass sign-ups. It helps to ensure that an actual person is requesting the account.

Caption property Used to create a more readable label that appears in the top row in Datasheet view and in forms and reports.

Cascade Delete Related Records An option that directs Access to automatically delete all records in related tables that match the primary key that is deleted from a primary table.

Cascade Update Related Fields An option that directs Access to automatically update all foreign key values in a related table when the primary key value table is modified in a primary table.

Charms A toolbar for Windows 8 made up of five icons (Search, Share, Start, Devices, and Settings) that enables you to search for files and applications, share information with others within an application that is running, return to the Start screen, control devices that are connected to your computer, or modify various settings depending on which application is running when accessing the Setting icon.

Clip art An electronic illustration that can be inserted into an Office project.

Clipboard An Office feature that temporarily holds selections that have been cut or copied and allows you to paste the selections.

Cloud storage A technology used to store files and to work with programs that are stored in a central location on the Internet.

Command A button or area within a group that you click to perform tasks.

Compact and Repair An Access utility that reduces the size of the database and can repair a corrupt database.

Comparison operator An operator used to evaluate the relationship between two quantities.

Constant A value that does not change.

Contextual tab A Ribbon tab that displays when an object, such as a picture or table, is selected. A contextual tab contains groups and commands specific to the selected object.

Controls The text boxes, buttons, boxes, and other tools you use to add, edit, and display the data in a form or report.

Copy To duplicate an item from the original location and place the copy in the Office Clipboard.

Criteria row A row in the Query Design view that determines which records will be selected.

Criterion A number, text phrase, or an expression used to select records.

Custom Web app A database that can be built, used, and shared with others through the use of a host server (e.g., SharePoint or Office 365).

Cut To remove an item from the original location and place it in the Office Clipboard.

Data redundancy The unnecessary storing of duplicate data in two or more tables.

Data type Determines the type of data that can be entered and the operations that can be performed on that data.

Database A collection of data organized as meaningful information that can be accessed, managed, stored, queried, sorted, and reported.

Database management system (DBMS) A software system that provides the tools needed to create, maintain, and use a database.

Datasheet view A view that enables you to add, edit, and delete the records of a table.

Date arithmetic The process of adding or subtracting one date from another, or adding or subtracting a constant from a date.

Default Office settings that remain in effect unless you specify otherwise.

Delimiter A special character that surrounds the criterion's value.

Descending A sort that lists text data in reverse alphabetical order or a numeric list in highest to lowest order.

Design view A view that enables you to create tables, add and delete fields, and modify field properties; or to change advanced design settings not seen in Layout view, such as a background image.

Dialog box A window that displays when a program requires interaction with you, such as inputting information, before completing a procedure. This window typically provides access to more precise, but less frequently used, commands.

Dialog Box Launcher An icon in a Ribbon group that you can click to open a related dialog box. It is not found in all groups.

Enforce referential integrity A relationship option that ensures that data cannot be entered into a related table unless it first exists in a primary table.

Enhanced ScreenTip A feature that provides a brief summary of a command when you point to the command button.

Excel A software application used to organize records, financial transactions, and business information in the form of worksheets.

Expression A formula used to calculate new fields from the values in existing fields.

Expression Builder An Access tool that helps you create more complicated expressions.

Field The smallest data element in a table, such as first name, last name, address, or phone number.

Field property A characteristic of a field that determines how a field looks and behaves.

Field row A row in the Query Design view that displays the field name.

Field selector The column heading of a datasheet used to select a column.

File Electronic data such as documents, databases, slide shows, worksheets, digital photographs, music, videos, and Web pages.

File Explorer A component of the Windows operating system that can be used to create and manage folders.

Filter Displays a subset of records based on a specified criterion.

Filter by Form A filtering method that displays records based on multiple criteria.

Filter by Selection A filtering method that displays only records that match selected criteria.

Find An Office feature that locates a word or phrase that you indicate in a document.

Folder A directory into which you place data files in order to organize them for easier retrieval.

Font A combination of typeface and type style.

Foreign key A field in one table that is also a primary key of another table.

Form A database object that is used to add, edit, or delete table data.

Form tool Used to create data entry forms for customers, employees, products, and other primary tables.

Form view A simplified interface primarily used for data entry. Does not allow you to make changes to the layout.

Format Painter A command that copies the formatting of text from one location to another.

Function A predefined computation that simplifies creating a complex calculation and produces a result based on inputs known as arguments.

Gallery A set of selections that displays when you click a More button, or in some cases when you click a command, in a Ribbon group.

Group A subset of a tab that organizes similar tasks together; to combine two or more objects.

Grouping Allows you to summarize your data by the values of a field.

Homegroup A Windows 8 feature that enables you to share resources on a home network.

Indexed property Setting that enables quick sorting in primary key order and quick retrieval based on the primary key.

Join line A line used to create a relationship between two tables using a common field.

Key Tip The letter or number for the associated keyboard shortcut that displays over features on the Ribbon or Quick Access Toolbar.

Label Wizard Enables you to easily create mailing labels, name tags, and other specialized tags.

Landscape An orientation for a displayed page or worksheet that is wider than it is tall.

Layout control Provides guides to help keep controls aligned horizontally and vertically and give your form a uniform appearance.

Library A collection of files from different locations that is displayed as a single unit.

Live Preview An Office feature that provides a preview of the results of a selection when you point to an option in a list or gallery. Using Live Preview, you can experiment with settings before making a final choice.

Macro A stored series of commands that carry out an action.

Mailing label report A specialized report that comes preformatted to coordinate with name-brand labels.

Margin The area of blank space that displays to the left, right, top, and bottom of a document or worksheet.

Microsoft Office A productivity software suite including four primary software components, each one specializing in a particular type of output.

Mini toolbar The feature that provides access to common formatting commands, displayed when text is selected.

Module An object that is written using Visual Basic for Applications (VBA) and adds functionality to a database.

Multiple Items form Displays multiple records in a tabular layout similar to a table's Datasheet view, with more customization options such as the ability to add graphical elements, buttons, and other controls.

Multitable query Contains two or more tables. It enables you to take advantage of the relationships that have been set in your database.

Navigation bar Bar located at the bottom of a table, query, or form that is used to move through records.

Navigation Pane (Office Fundamentals) A section of the File Explorer interface that provides ready access to computer resources, folders, files, and networked peripherals. (Access) An interface element that organizes and lists database objects.

Normalization The practice of good database design involving grouping data into the correct tables.

NOT logical operator Returns all records except the specified criteria.

Null The term Access uses to describe a blank field.

Number data type A data type that can store only numerical data.

Object A main component that is created and used to make a database function.

One-to-many relationship A relationship established when the primary key value in the primary table can match many of the foreign key values in the related table.

Operating system Software that directs computer activities such as checking all components, managing system resources, and communicating with application software.

OR logical operator Returns records meeting any of the specified criteria.

Order of operations (order of precedence) Determines the sequence by which operations are calculated in an expression.

Paste To place a cut or copied item in another location.

Picture A graphic file that is retrieved from storage media or the Internet and placed in an Office project.

Pmt function A predefined formula in Access that calculates the periodic loan payment.

Portable Document Format (PDF) A file type that was created for exchanging documents independent of software applications and operating system environment.

Portrait An orientation for a displayed page or worksheet that is taller than it is wide.

PowerPoint A software application used to create dynamic presentations to inform groups and persuade audiences.

Primary key The field (or combination of fields) that uniquely identifies each record in a table.

Print Preview Enables you to see exactly what the report will look like when it is printed.

Property sheet Enables you to change settings such as number format, number of decimal places, and caption, among many others.

Query Enables you to ask questions about the data stored in a database and then provides the answers to the questions by providing subsets or summaries of data.

Query Design view Enables you to create queries; the Design view is divided into two parts—the top portion displays the tables and the bottom portion (known as the *query design grid*) displays the fields and the criteria.

Query sort order Determines the order of records in the query's Datasheet view.

Quick Access Toolbar A component of Office 2013, located at the top-left corner of the Office window, that provides handy access to commonly executed tasks such as saving a file and undoing recent actions.

Record A group of related fields representing one entity, such as data for one person, place, event, or concept.

Record selector A small box at the beginning of a row used to select a record.

Record source The table or query that supplies the records for a form or report.

Referential integrity Rules in a database that are used to preserve relationships between tables when records are changed.

Related tables Tables that are joined in a relationship using a common field.

Relational database management system (RDBMS) A database management system that uses the relational model to manage groups of data (tables) and rules (relationships) between tables.

Relationship A connection between two tables using a common field.

Replace An Office feature that finds text and replaces it with a word or phrase that you indicate.

Report An object that contains professional-looking formatted information from underlying tables or queries.

Report tool Used to instantly create a tabular report based on the table or query currently selected.

Report view Enables you to see what a printed report will look like in a continuous page layout.

Report Wizard Asks you questions and uses your answers to generate a customized report.

Ribbon The long bar of tabs, groups, and commands located just beneath the Title bar.

Run command Used to produce query results (the red exclamation point).

Select query A type of query that displays only the records that match criteria entered in Query Design view.

Short text data type A text field that can store up to 255 characters but has a default field size of 50 characters.

Shortcut menu Provides choices related to the selection or area at which you right-click.

Show row A row in the Query Design view that controls whether the field will be displayed in the query results.

Simply Query Wizard Provides dialog boxes to guide you through the query design process.

SkyDrive An application used to store, access, and share files and folders.

SmartArt A diagram that presents information visually to effectively communicate a message.

Snip The output of using the Snipping Tool.

Snipping Tool A Windows 8 accessory program that provides users the ability to capture an image of all (or part of) their computer's screen.

Sort The process of listing records or text in a specific sequence, such as alphabetically by last name.

Sort row A row in the Query Design view that enables you to sort in ascending or descending order.

Split form Combines two views of the same record source—one section is displayed in a stacked layout, and the other section is displayed in a tabular layout.

Splitter bar Divides a form into two halves.

Stacked layout Displays fields in a vertical column.

Start screen The display that you see after you turn on your computer and respond to any username and password prompts.

Status bar A horizontal bar found at the bottom of the program window that contains information relative to the open file.

Subfolder A folder that is housed within another folder.

Syntax The rules that dictate the structure and components required to perform the necessary calculations in an equation or to evaluate expressions.

Tab A component of the Ribbon that is designed to appear much like a tab on a file folder, with the active tab highlighted, that is used to organize groups by function.

Table   An object used to store and organize data in a series of records (rows) with each record made up of a number of fields (columns) and is the foundation of every database.

Table row   A row in Query Design view that displays the data source.

Tabular layout   Displays data horizontally.

Template   A predesigned file that incorporates formatting elements, such as theme and layouts, and may include content that can be modified.

Theme   A collection of design choices that includes colors, fonts, and special effects used to give a consistent look to a document, workbook, database form or report, or presentation.

Tile   A colorful block on the Start screen that when clicked will launch a program, file, folder, or other Windows 8 app.

Title bar   A component of Microsoft Office that identifies the current file name and the application in which you are working and includes control buttons that enable you to minimize, maximize, restore down, or close the application window.

Toggle   The action of switching from one setting to another. Several Home tab tasks, such as Bold and Italic, are actually toggle commands.

Total row   A table row that displays below the last row of records in an Excel table, or in Datasheet view of a table or query, and displays summary or aggregate statistics, such as a sum or an average.

User interface   The screen display through which you communicate with the software.

Validation rule   Prevents invalid data from being entered into a field.

View   The way a file appears onscreen.

Wildcard   A special character that can represent one or more characters in the criterion of a query.

Windows 8   A Microsoft operating system released in 2012 that can operate on touch-screen devices as well as laptops and desktops because it has been designed to accept multiple methods of input.

Windows 8 app   An application specifically designed to run in the Start screen interface of Windows 8 that is either already installed and ready to use or can be downloaded from the Windows Store.

Word   A word processing software application used to produce all sorts of documents, including memos, newsletters, forms, tables, and brochures.

Zoom slider   A horizontal bar on the far right side of the status bar that enables you to increase or decrease the size of file contents onscreen.

Index